Speculation in Commodity Contracts and Options

Speculation in Commodity Contracts and Options

L. Dee Belveal

Second Edition

DOW JONES-IRWIN
Homewood, Illinois 60430

Market Information
and Trade Data
courtesy of
Chicago Board of Trade
and
Chicago Mercantile Exchange

This publication is designed to provide accurate and
authoritative information in regard to the subject matter
covered. It is sold with the understanding that the
publisher is not engaged in rendering legal, accounting, or
other professional service. If legal advice or other expert
assistance is required, the services of a competent
professional person should be sought.

*From a Declaration of Principles jointly adopted by a Committee
of the American Bar Association and a Committee of Publishers.*

ISBN 0-07094-672-2

Library of Congress Catalog Card No. 85–70802

Printed in the United States of America

1 2 3 4 5 6 7 8 9 0 K 2 1 0 9 8 7 6 5

Dedication

*To my emissaries
    to the future—
Scott and Barbara,
Todd and Shannon,
Jennifer and Benée*

By the author of—

Charting Commodity Market Price Behavior

Commodity Solicitor's Examination

Commodity Trading Manual

Preface

This book has been in research, preparation, and refinement for almost 40 years.

It began with a first venture into the unknown waters of commodity speculation in February 1946, which involved one contract of eggs. Surprisingly, this first trade produced nearly $300 in profit; and the three positions which followed it were also "winners." Flushed with four straight victories, the speculative road to riches seemed both short and straight!

Trade number five, involving two carloads of potatoes, wiped out all the accrued profits and took an additional $281 along with it. Making a quick million in the market suddenly seemed fraught with at least as many problems as opportunities—but the opportunities still looked too good to pass up.

It was at this point that the "paper trading" system which is explained in this book was developed. It provided a means of gaining experience in the market, but without paying the high prices charged for instruction in the real arena. Fourteen months later, I returned to my broker's office and sold 5,000 bushels of wheat "short." From March 1948, until the present day, commodity speculation has continued to be both a topic of engaging intellectual interest—and a highly profitable economic pursuit.

In half a lifetime of almost constant exposure to it, I have, at one time or another, made all of the mistakes possible in speculation. Each one of them has carried its own price tag, so the information between these covers has all been "bought and paid for."

Speculation in commodities is an intriguing business, but it is also a vital economic function. We will never fully understand how important the commodity speculator is unless, through short-sighted legislation, free markets are destroyed in favor of price-making by electronic computer—or imposed by self-annointed experts.

The existence of free markets as price-discovery mechanisms, and as "control valves" in the distribution supply lines importantly depends on maintaining sufficient public speculative interest to accommodate the huge and growing commerce involved in provisioning our worldwide population. The task grows ever larger, and the supply of speculative capital must grow with it. If the need is to be met, the ranks of speculators must be swelled by newcomers who have the courage and the resources to take a hand in the Herculean job. But they should not be invited into the market without being afforded a chance to begin with some reasonable opportunity for success. There are enough hazards always present in professional speculation without multiplying the inherent risks by ignorance of elemental market procedures and basic trading strategy.

A heartfelt word of appreciation is due the hundreds of traders, hedgers, brokers, and market technicians who have, over the years, had a hand in my trading education. In an era when the only way to learn about commodity trading was by word of mouth and by doing it, most of the "old pros" were surprisingly willing to share their hard-bought information with a young competitor. Although they had neither the time nor the patience to reduce their wisdom to printed form, they served as your author's unpaid professors, both in the pits and out of them; and they still do.

The suggestion which first kindled the idea of developing this work came out of a discussion with Paul F. McGuire, who prior to becoming a full-time speculator, distinguished himself in financial administration both in the United States and abroad. A great many of the ideas contained herein are his, gleaned from a long succession of conversations which have been spread over an acquaintanceship of many years.

A complete list of individuals who have had some part in shaping the ideas and framing the contents of this book would read like a roster of the Chicago Board of Trade. In the course of a long-standing business relationship with this organization, the world's largest agricultural commodity exchange, I have enjoyed the priceless opportunity of ready access to such market authorities as Robert L. Martin, Alfred H. Gruetzmacher, Bernard P. Carey, Joseph J. Kane, C. W. Schultz Jr., Robert Liebenow, Warren W. Lebeck, and innumerable other floor traders, brokers and exchange officials. Untold hours have been spent with these busy people, ferreting out information and answers which, in my considered opinion, add up to the best perspective and the highest degree of expertise on the subject to be found anywhere.

Additional assistance has also been freely given by people connected with commodity activities in several of the nation's outstanding brokerage firms. Indeed, it would have been impossible to complete this project without such help from those who conduct the mechanics of trade.

A special word of thanks is due to Roger W. Gray, distinguished Stanford professor and one of America's most knowledgable contemporary market authorities. Extensive and protracted exposure to his theoretical competence and practical understanding of market function added immeasurably to this final result.

The original manuscript was first read and criticized by William J. Mallers, himself a professional speculator and emeritus chairman of the board of the Chicago Board of Trade.

Having thus acknowledged the major sources of assistance, it must now be stated that there has always been some greater or lesser disagreements with the contents of this volume. Unanimity is not to be found among traders; and the more expert they are, the more sharply defined are the gulfs which separate the individual opinions on moot points. This should not be surprising, since the concept of a free market is necessarily based upon differences of opinion.

It has been my continuing objective to stay as close to consensus as possible, where consensus will strengthen the hand of the public speculator. Where persuasions differ too broadly to permit identification of any useful middle ground, conservatism has been—and is—the guideline. It's hard to imagine a situation in which caution can do the public speculator any lasting damage; and lack of caution can certainly destroy his speculative future.

Little space has been devoted in these pages to the huge winnings and equally monumental losses of the "big time operators." That fortunes are made and lost in the commodity market needs no underscoring, particularly when we see that total contract values that trade in agricultural categories alone exceed a *trillion* dollars per year! But our attention has been focused directly on the interests of the *novice* to the marketplace. Our objective is to keep him or her out of the clutch of disaster until he or she can acquire some experience and develop a settled trading technique. With sufficient capital resources to justify it, traders need no urging to undertake ever larger involvements in the business.

Neither this nor any book can guarantee success. Like a good road map, all it can do is show directions, point out major obstacles and draw attention to principal points of interest. The user is still going to have to keep his eyes open for hazards which may lurk around any turn.

Finally, whatever compliments this treatise elicits must be shared with a great many highly skilled and most gracious mentors. Its shortcomings must all be laid at the door of the author. Hopefully, this will prove to be another step along the road to better understanding and greater usefulness of the institutions which provide a dependable and increasingly efficient mechanism for collecting, standardizing, and distributing the world's commodity wealth.

The repetitions which occur textually, it should be noted, are journalistically regrettable but editorially intentional. In the interest of making the volume optimally useful as a continuing reference source, each major section has been presented in as close to self-sufficient context as space and reader patience permits.

Thus, collateral points of demonstration, rules, and key trading procedures are often set forth in more than one location. It is hoped that in so doing, the particular information sought will be findable with a minimum of reliance on cross-referencing and maximum economies of time to the reader.

L. Dee Belveal

Contents

Schedule of Exhibits

1

Introduction

The title of this volume is *Speculation* but the subject is profit.

Protracted and inconclusive debate continues to surround the topic of speculation, as it has since time immemorial. There are otherwise astute individuals who claim to see no difference between speculation and gambling, damning both with equal vigor. It is to be hoped that these blind critics may find at least some small measure of enlightenment in the following pages. Speculation and gambling are two completely different kinds of activity. The distinction, moreover, doesn't depend on the intention of the participant so much as it does on the classification of risk involved in each.

The confusion doesn't end in trying to clarify *speculation* versus *gambling,* either.

Self-styled authorities that range from the late billionaire, J. Paul Getty, to politicians—and from university professors to members of the television and print media "fourth estate"—are constantly confusing the issue with their misuse of economic labels, delivered in the most stentorian tones. In so doing, each of these individuals may reveal something about his or her own money-management inclinations; while deluding their audiences—and perhaps even themselves—about the real nature of the activities under scrutiny. With speculation on organized exchanges now soaring to multiples of the totals reflected in equity investment categories, perhaps it's time to draw some clear lines of distinction among the three economic uses to which surplus money can be committed.

Investment as defined by economic purists involves the placement of money in a property from which one intends to receive *earnings*.

Speculation is the acquisition of property or "rights" without the hope of earnings in the form of dividends, interest, rent, etc., but with hopes for profit pinned exclusively to an expectation of *price change*.

The distinction is clear and should be easily understood. It is often muddled, however, by the proponents of investment, who credit investment with being more noble than speculation. Then they forge far beyond the ridiculous and unfounded moral distinction, in blanketly ascribing investor interests to virtually all buyers and sellers of common stocks. While true investors are present in substantial numbers among the stockholder class, there is another large, active, albeit diminishing, group of participants in the securities markets with influence—and holdings—far too large to be ignored. They are clearly stock speculators, by the economic definition set forth earlier.

A great deal of corporate equities listed on the major exchanges and sold over-the-counter are in strong hands including, but not limited to, the founding families of the companies involved, investment trusts, insurance companies, banks, and the treasuries of the corporations that issued them in the first place. The balance of the shares outstanding in most securities classifications tend to change hands at an impressive velocity, and properly so.

A buyer of stock which is selling at 30 or 40 times earnings must view his earnings of 3 percent or less as cheap "rent" for use of his money, unless he can see added returns coming from changes in price. Obviously, IBM, which at this writing is selling at $120 per share, and pays a $4.40 dividend on earnings of $8.00, has little "investment" attraction. Its buyers must be speculatively inclined, or they would buy higher-return government bonds. Were it not for a speculative interest, many of the most popular securities wouldn't find buyers at all—or they would be exceedingly rare. Most profit-minded individuals would prefer insured savings accounts or alternative money-use opportunities which guarantee superior long-range earnings return.

In actuality, buyers of high price/earning-ratio equities have both an investor and a speculator interest. They welcome the dividend (if any) *and* fervently hope for a price increase, price being the value measurement of their assets at any given time. Securities market participants who are interested in fixed-price investments obviously represent a small minority among investors of all classes, as evidenced by the meager public participation in 10- or 20-year bonds compared with common stocks.

In short, it is patent absurdity to accept the view that buyer interest doesn't go beyond dividends or other promised investment return. To the extent that an investor hopes for price appreciation (and who doesn't) he must stand identified, even in the definition of Mr. Getty, et al., as a speculator.

Economic activity, however, rests on much firmer foundations than subtle definitions of terminology. The problems are real. The possessor of money resources faces a constant dilemma:

1. Use his capital creatively and make it grow, or
2. Bury his capital in inactivity and watch it deteriorate in value.

History is replete with instances where inflation, devaluation, confiscation, and every intermediate kind of fiscal prodigality has sharply altered the value of money. Whether it be the pound sterling, yen, franc, mark, dollar, lira, kopek, kronen, or peso, currency stands as only a *relatively* reliable long-term substitute for physical goods and services. Whatever its other virtues, that money deteriorates over time is too obvious to require documentation at this point. No one of voting age could be ignorant of the fact.

Local currency is theoretically convertible into the totality of things offered in the immediate economy. Hopefully, it is also acceptable in international commerce, at a fair rate of exchange, for an infinite variety of the world's tangible and intangible resources. Contemporary economics suggests that, since the supply of money and the supply of goods and services should maintain a measure of parity with each other (if monetary stability is to exist), ownership of corporate stock (which represents productive physical assets) should provide a useful hedge against inflationary pressures. Unfortunately, however, the axiom too often falls short of needs when put in practice, because the money/goods ratio is not constant.

The last decade in the United States has seen the purchasing power of the dollar impaired to the extent of some 45 percent by inflation measurement standards used by the Bureau of Labor Statistics. While some of the corporate stocks listed on the New York and American Exchanges have increased more than this, there are at least as many which have done infinitely worse. So the constant dilemma of the hard-pressed investor is how to get *out* of deteriorating money, and *into* appreciating capital assets. The most obvious means for doing this has always been by purchasing shares in one or more of the 4,000 or 5,000 publicly owned—"listed"—firms whose equities are freely traded.

Whether the individual investor actually finds the protection against inflation he seeks depends directly on the caliber of judgment he brings to bear in choosing between literally thousands of uneasy alternatives.

In any case, even as the most orthodox investor comes to grips with the ever-present spectre of inflation and makes his decisions as to the most advantageous use for his free capital resources, he is speculating on the shape of things to come. His speculation concerns earnings, growth, inflation itself, and the relative attractiveness of the broad range of choices which beckon. Speculation, to repeat for emphasis, is inescapable.

Everything which has been said about investing in securities can be said with equal validity about entrepreneurship. The individual who has a million dollars to put to work may do so by purchasing shares in a going concern—or he may use his money to establish a new business. The course he chooses will likely be determined by his profit expectations from the capital being committed. Thousands of newly established firms are victims of bankruptcy every year in the United States. Regardless of what occasions their demise, it can be said that each of them represents an unsuccessful speculation. The funds involved in these failures would have brought better results in other use situations.

However, speculation in new business enterprise is a vital and indispensable element in any dynamic business system. Some new business ventures succeed and become profitable. A few of them grow into impressive institutions. Most of them fail. Yet, without the speculative spirit in an economy, stagnation is the certain result. Doing business *always* involves the assumption of risks.

So, speculation is a word endlessly abused and misunderstood. Regrettably, some of the greatest confusion is evidenced by people whose backgrounds and experience should enable them to reflect better insight into the matter. *Speculate* evolves from two Greek roots which mean literally to *foresee* and to *foretell* the future. There is another consideration also. Speculation concerns risks which exist in the nature of things.

Unlike a *gamble,* which is a risk situation contrived for purposes of entertainment or a hoped-for gain based on predicting the outcome, a speculation is coming to grips with a natural hazard. In the words of an 18th century poet, it is "an open threat, held in the hand of God."

A house may burn; a person may die; a crop may be destroyed; prices may rise or fall; the value of money may increase or deteriorate. Each of these possibilities carries the seeds of disaster to those whose interests they affect. Some of these events may be assisted or precipitated by human action, but none of them is totally preventable by purely human means. As a consequence, the results of each of these events must be contemplated in the future plans of prudent individuals. Risk avoidance is a constant exercise for most of us.

In some situations, the institution of insurance offers a means of indemnification against the economic penalties that may arise from the speculative hazard being considered. In other situations, the individual can only exercise caution and hope for the best. In still other risk situations, the possible outcome can be subjected to economic measurement; a dollar value can be assigned to the results of misfortune—should it occur—and the risk exposure passed on to someone else for a fixed monetary consideration—or for a flexible opportunity to profit. Such a voluntary risk bearer is accurately identified as a professional speculator, which brings us to the most useful definition of the personality being examined in these pages.

In the interest of a clear perspective, one further thought must be kept in mind in appraising professional risk bearing. It is the fact that everyone feels himself quite able to cope with all of the good fortune that might come his way. The risks offered to professional speculators are, at least in the minds of those who seek to pass them on, of such magnitude and likelihood that it is worthwhile to pay something—a risk premium—for escaping or lessening their impact. Consequently, the speculator must always choose between hazardous alternatives.

There is only one way for him to upgrade his average safety factor: through selection of only the brighter opportunities; which are opportunities unseen or shunned by the sellers or shifters of risks, usually referred to as *hedgers*. If a situation promises profit, it would make no sense to hedge it and surrender the profit. Therefore, the risk offerings made to professional speculators regularly entail clear-cut negative implications or, at best, are too problematical to permit reliable analysis by those who seek speculative protection.

Speculation is invariably present in the holding of property over time. A speculator is one who assumes property ownership risks over time in the hope of realizing a profit from his accuracy in forecasting events to come. The function is real and valuable.

As implied earlier, an individual can meet the definition without being conscious of the fact that he is speculating. Thousands of farmers, for example, grow grain and hold their harvest in storage buildings, pending its sale and removal to a flour mill or a country elevator. Many, if not most, of these producers would passively or actively resent being termed speculators. They prefer being called owners of grain. The fact still remains that the prices of farm products are constantly fluctuating; and each change in the market price of wheat alters the value of wheat stocks held on farms and elsewhere. The farmer who holds unhedged wheat is certain to benefit or suffer—from higher prices or lower prices in the market—when the time arrives at which he elects to sell it. This is because price does fluctuate.

From this brief statement, it should be apparent that every independent farmer must be a speculator. He has no choice! He must speculate to prepare a field, plant a crop and hold a product inventory for sale or use. Unless temperature and moisture relationships are benign, his labor and seed are wasted; his speculation that a crop could be raised in a given growing season may be unsuccessful. Conversely, nature may cooperate and help him produce a bumper yield, in which event his basic speculative risk has paid off.

With the crop raised, the producer is now interested in selling it and realizing cash-in-hand payment for his time, effort, investment, and *risk* in bringing it to harvest. Whoever elects to buy a large inventory of relatively perishable merchandise—especially during a period of great seasonal oversupply—has placed himself in a position of considerable risk. Obviously, he will not "buy the risk" unless he feels that demand for the product will, over a period of time, take it off his hands at a profit. Moreover, he must be confident that he can protect the merchandise from physical deterioration and other loss for the period he owns it.

The greatest area of speculative risk, and one to which no easy answer exists, is in the matter of price itself. If supplies prove to be excessive or if demand fails to come up to expectations, the owner of a given commodity may do an optimum job with his maintenance and protection tasks and still suffer great loss through inventory devaluation. The price hazard is inherent in ownership and cannot be removed.

Risk in changing values is the eternal concomitant of property ownership over a period of time.

To a greater or lesser extent, everyone who owns anything which is for sale—or could at any point in the future be offered for sale—is likewise speculating on future events. Some risks are hidden, while others are clear, and are undertaken with full knowledge of the hazards present; but with the hope that the feared contingency will not occur and that a risk margin can be earned based on accurate analysis and sagacity in predicting future events.

It has been said that people buy life insurance because they know they must die. The speculation always present is in whether each of us will die sooner, or later. Insurance companies undertake contracts which indemnify the heirs and estates of the deceased. In so doing, insurance companies stand preeminent among speculative institutions. Their risk margin is statistically determined from actuarial tables which reflect the years of life remaining on the average to people of good health at various ages (and policy-cancellation experience prior to death). So long as the mortality and policy cancellation averages are maintained, the insurance underwriters make an average profit. Should widespread epidemics or proliferation of accidents occur to invalidate the actuarial tables, the insurance companies concerned will lose money. If the opposite happens—an increase in average life span—the insurance companies' speculation will prove to be commensurately more profitable, for obvious reasons: They will make bigger returns from premiums.

Two thoughts should be kept constantly in mind in evaluating both the methods and the morality of speculation. First, the speculative risk is ever-present; it cannot be avoided; it can often be evaluated; it can, in certain situations, be economically shifted from one risk bearer to another. Second, the objective of professional speculation is that of seeking profit. There is—there can be—no other economic justification for voluntary speculation.

Profit seeking, whether through investment, entrepreneurship or speculation, is a thoroughly acceptable, even laudable, activity in an economic society; so long as the general tenets of legality, honesty, ethical responsibility, and fair play are observed. To question the social propriety or economic rectitude of speculation in commodities is as absurd as an argument against the production of them. The latter inescapably gives rise to the former. Production and ownership both involve speculation, usually conducted by specialists in the given area of risk. Producers and subsequent owners of commodities presumably understand their hazards and weigh them against the opportunities for profit. From such an appraisal, each accepts or rejects a given proposition.

Economic quarrels which center on moral considerations can always be expected to contribute more heat than light to the topic being examined. This is true since economics is not a moral field; it is functional, like mechanics.

Speculation deserves to be understood, but needs no special pleading. It exists as an ever-present element of human existence. If formalized speculation as practiced on stock and commodity exchanges and in the money markets did not exist, it would have to be invented for the valuable contribution it makes to the continuity and stability of a broad range of financial and productive activities. Future events lose a great deal of their terror when discounted by professionals who have the courage, the information, and the financial wherewithal to assume the risks of the unknown and protect those who are unwilling or unable to speculate on possibilities of events they fear.

Professional speculation must be viewed as the greatest single moderating influence available for apprehension and extremes of viewpoint. It brings a leveling influence between the present known situation and the future unknown possibility. It softens the blow of disaster when and if it does strike. It strikes a balance between the best that can be reasonably hoped for and the worst that can possibly happen, and reflects the composite result in price, or "premium," level.

Speculation brings a tempering influence into the marketplace. It is an activity which demands a cool head, a clear eye, and adequate financial resources to underpin a fundamental equanimity. Without these things, a speculator will not succeed in gaining the profits he seeks. Without profits he will soon be rendered incapable of further speculation because he will lose out to more capable operators in the field.

The speculator who does succeed can expect excellent rewards. His prowess will be documented by financial gains which, in turn, permit him to take an ever larger role in the business activity of his choice.

In summation, to the extent that a speculator knowingly assumes hazards that he could avoid, he shows himself to be a person of courage, financial ability and possessing a commendable confidence in his own powers of evaluation. Add also, a large measure of faith in the future. To the extent that he succeeds, he stands as living proof that the worst—which is always expected by some—rarely if ever turns out quite that bad.

The voice of the professional speculator is the voice of balance and reason under stress. He or she shuns the rosy-hued optimism of the Micawbers as unrealistic. But most importantly, the speculator is the crucial buffer between the doomcriers and the rest of us.

Without the professional speculator, negative possibilities would turn into black certainties, and the places now occupied by professional speculators would quickly be filled by professional crepe hangers.

Courtesy of the CME

Exhibit 1–1

   With the second tower to be completed soon, the Chicago Mercantile Exchange Center is the largest futures trading facility in the world. In addition to perishable commodities, its 2,600 members also trade in international currencies, financial instruments, and options.

2

Evolution of Trade

Before delving into the operational complexities of modern commodity trading, a brief review of trade evolution should be helpful in terms of overall perspective.

It is certain that man has been a trader since his earliest appearance on earth. Individual existence must have always depended on some measure of mutual cooperation, however rudimentary. It still does. Trade is the most basic and at the same time, the most vital communal activity imaginable.

Authorities seem agreed that earliest exchange of goods between individuals was probably accomplished by simple expropriation or theft. In the prehistoric jungle, devoid as it was of social amenities, the simplest, most expedient method of obtaining either a stone ax or a Stone Age bride was to steal the item in question. Since "survival of the fittest" means survival of the strongest or the wiliest, it also seems logical to suppose that where mere theft would not suffice to accomplish the transference of property, violence was a natural adjunct. When it became necessary to crack the owner over the head before taking his possessions, our early ancestors probably had little hesitancy in adopting such strong-arm tactics.

As the social climate in the Neanderthal jungle became somewhat better ordered, relationships between individuals and tribes improved. Alliances were formed between family groups which carried the three-fold benefit of strengthening their collective efforts in hunting food, better protecting themselves, and improving their harsh conditions of existence. As mutuality of endeavor developed, so did the social relationship we know as friendship. Gift giving came into being to serve the distributive requirement between friends, just as theft persisted as the transfer device between enemies.

Direct Exchange

Barter or direct exchange gradually evolved as a useful means of "impersonal" commerce between those who were neither close friends nor active antagonists. From earliest recorded history until about the 12th century, barter remained as the essential method of commerce over most of the world. While it is true that much of the trading involved foodstuffs in exchange for gold or silver, the precious metals involved represented intrinsic rather than monetary values. The use of coins of designated values in buying and selling seems to have originated in the Orient or the Middle East, somewhere around 800 to 700 B.C. However, it remained for the Caesars to "internationalize" coinage by spreading it throughout the continent of Europe.

Money Appears

The Roman legions carried money which bore Caesar's likeness and, in the best tradition of invading conquerors, they forced the acceptance of Roman coins upon their reluctant victims. As time went by, however, it was learned that Roman specie could be trusted as a reliable medium of exchange. The coins themselves were struck from gold and were, therefore, not as susceptible to counterfeiting as other local money devices. While the Roman soldiers initially forced the introduction of their currency in trade, they hastened its popular adoption by also accepting it back as a measurement of stable values. Use of Roman coinage grew apace and, as it did, the basic tool of modern commerce stood identified: Money is both a surrogate and a storage system for values over time.

Money thus became an acceptable interim substitute for goods and services. It functioned as payment for a limitless range of both tangibles and intangibles, as well as providing a versatile measurement of values which had never before existed within the more restrictive system of barter. Money made it both more efficient and simpler to conduct trade.

Spot Markets

The earliest form of money/goods transaction involved what we recognize as a "spot" sale. The seller presented his goods to the buyer, a price was negotiated, and the exchange of money for the merchandise took place "on the spot." Both payment and physical transfer were immediate. A great deal of trade is still accomplished in this same fashion.

Farmer's Markets and other "cash and carry" enterprises are spot markets in the truest sense of the word.

Efficient as spot markets were compared to earlier trading methods, problems still existed which clamored for solution. Supply and demand imbalance in the spot situation was a major inconvenience then, as it is even now.

Whether the spot merchant is dealing in field-fresh strawberries or used automobiles, his constant challenge is to match market demands with equivalent supplies. Should he overestimate the demand for his goods, it goes without saying, he will have excess unsold inventory on hand at the end of the market period. This is especially a problem when it concerns perishables. However, all products are at least theoretically perishable since owning, protecting, and maintaining inventory entails costs, to whatever extent applicable. Every inventory, whether it "spoils" or not, suffers somewhat from devaluation as it ages on the shelf.

The spot marketer also stands to lose if he underestimates market demands. In this case he will offer his wares at a lower price than that which his customers would be willing to pay, with the result that his profits are needlessly reduced. The ideal situation, of course, (from the standpoint of seller profits) is to offer the precise amount of merchandise which the market will buy, at price levels which will generate the largest available net profit. Few spot marketers have either the ability— or the opportunity—to assess buyer response with sufficient accuracy as to make pinpointing such a return possible.

The situation ordinarily is one in which demand exceeds supply and the seller realizes less than he could have from his inventory, or supply exceeds demand and the seller loses through inventory depreciation, spoilage, or otherwise.

Trade Fairs

The hazards of spot marketing are likely to be less in a large market than in the small, remote one. This was as true in Renaissance Europe as it is in contemporary America. The fact played a vital part in what must be viewed as the most important commercial innovation of the 11th and 12th centuries: It was known as the trade fair. At more or less regular intervals, itinerant merchants would congregate in designated locations to display their wares and conduct business with the populace.

Pursuing a marketing program of this kind called for transporting a great deal of valuable merchandise long distances over rough and dangerous terrain. Bandits made a lucrative specialty of waylaying these merchant travelers, stealing their possessions and murdering them if the situation seemed to suggest it. Even if the bands of marauders were successfully avoided, ruling princes and territorial chieftains charged the merchants exorbitant fees for permission to travel through the country and conduct their trade. It is from this practice that the term *robber baron* first came into being.

In spite of the handicaps, however, the merchants prospered and so did their customers. Spices, fabrics, jewels, unguents, and a broad array of hard goods were made available in the hinterlands only through the existence of the institution known as trade fairs. One of the largest of the fairs took place periodically, from the 12th century on, in the Champagne district of France. It should be noted that the Champagne Fair attracted hundreds of merchants, thousands of customers, and transacted an impressive volume of business, even by modern standards.

The more enlightened rulers finally came to recognize that commercial activity deserved to be encouraged rather than opposed through harrassment, excessive taxation, or both. Therefore, it developed that some of the medieval rulers actively undertook to attract trade fairs into their principalities. Merchants were issued valuable "Letters of Franchise" which authorized the holder to transact business and guaranteed the safety of his person and possessions "Under the King's Writ."

Time Element Enters Commerce

No longer fair game for looters and murderers, encouraged by the reigning personage and met by eager buyers, the itinerant merchants became more numerous, and the volume of business they transacted grew apace. It was in this stage of development that a time dimension was first introduced into buying and selling. Precious metals and jewels were important elements of trade on the part of the fair merchants. Transporting such valuable, highly salable merchandise entailed risks that most owners preferred to avoid. As a result, a practice grew up whereby the only such goods actually presented at the fair were samples. Buyers made their selection from the samples, then placed and paid for their orders. In return, the buyer received a "fair letter," which was actually a delivery order drawn against the merchant's warehouse and which entitled the holder to exchange the document for the designated quantity and quality of merchandise. The fair letter was, in fact, an early version of the item known in contemporary commerce as a "bill of exchange."

Once business could be conducted on the basis of deferred performance, it must be granted that a high order of trust had already entered the marketplace. It was said of many such early merchants that their word was "as good as the gold."

Concern for the morality of the marketplace also asserted itself in this period. Whereas *caveat emptor*—buyer beware—had been the rule in earlier times, merchants now organized among themselves and laid down broad rules of fair dealing which were calculated to prevent the unprincipled cheating of unsuspecting customers. Merchants who violated the rules of trade were summarily tried before the Merchants' Court and, if found guilty, were heavily punished. In some instances, the judgment went so far as to forever forbid the crooked merchant from doing business at future fairs. Such a banishment amounted to depriving an individual of his livelihood. But harshness paid dividends and accomplished two major results; a vastly improved ethical atmosphere in commerce, and a previously unheard of measure of confidence among public customers. Then, as now, without mutual trust between buyer and seller, trade could hardly be conducted at all.

Evolution of Credit

A *sellers' market* is one in which demands exceed supply and the possessor of goods held for sale is clearly in the position of authority. It is only in quite recent times that some nations have developed productive capacities to equal or at times exceed their national demand. As a consequence, sellers' markets through history have, more often than not, prevailed.

The institution of credit is obviously an invention of the sellers rather than buyers. So long as a merchant can dispose of his inventory on a cash basis, this is certainly the way he would prefer to do it. However, conditions prevail for greater or lesser periods of time, in which there are more goods offered for immediate sale than there are immediate market demand and immediate ability to pay. It is in situations of this sort that credit performs its most important function—and always has.

To use grain for purposes of demonstration once more, the prime owner of this foodstuff at the conclusion of harvest is the farmer himself. His supplies vastly exceed his own requirements, and aggregate supplies may actually exceed a year's consumption requirements within the region where it is produced. The producers or "first owners" of commodities must have learned a long time ago that there were two alternatives available by which to dispose of excess crops: to accept exceedingly low prices—or no prices; or to sell them under payment and/or delivery terms which permit users to anticipate future needs and buy or "contract" for larger than normal quantities, in advance of immediate requirements. Extension of credit makes deferred performance part of a transaction, and functions as a quasi alternative to seller storage.

Credit had become an important element of continental commerce by the early 1500s. A French writer commenting on social decadence during that period remarked that "the populace staggers tenuously between its current needs and its current indebtedness; present abilities are limited by old commitments, still undischarged. Present earnings are insufficient to meet accrued obligations and—day by day—keep body and soul together. Universal ruin is inescapable." Credit excesses, it appears, are no modern-day developments. But, even though often subject to abuse, credit is indispensable in trade.

Earlier societies engaged in all manner of activities calculated to improve consumer credit risks. Defaulting debtors were, in ancient Oriental societies, tortured or executed. By medieval times, the penalty for failing to meet just obligations had been generally reduced to public whippings, a period on public display in pillory, or a term in debtors' prison, until the debt was paid off by the prisoner or his sympathetic relatives. It remained for the United States to constitutionally forbid imprisonment for mere inability to pay one's debts.

In addition to the familiar kind of consumer credit extended by a seller to his buyer, there is another form which amounts to supplier credit, extended to the seller on the part of the buyer. In this situation, the purchaser of a given commodity commits himself to accept delivery of a specified amount of merchandise, at an established price, at some point in the future. Thus, he gives his supplier time in which to perform. Examples of this are to be found in examining trading practices in the jewelry trade during the 15th and 16th centuries. Fabricators of jewelry during that era were major artists and the principal consumers of precious metals and gems.

The flow of gold followed a somewhat direct channel from the mine, through the smelter, to the manufacturing jeweler. It was not unusual for such a fabricator of rings and brooches to set up a firm arrangement with his supply source for delivery of a designated amount of precious metal at specified intervals of time. It was customary for the raw material supplier to require prepayment of a portion of the total cost of the commitment as a "binder" on the deal. The practice is still encountered in contemporary business.

Cash-Forward Contracts

A flour miller, for example, may contract for a specified amount of wheat to be delivered during the first 10 days of each month of the year. The contract price may be one firm price, or it may be flexible, depending on other considerations; particularly "going prices" in the cash market at the time each unit delivery of the total contract is made. A purchase arrangement of this kind in the grain market is called a *to-arrive* or *cash-forward* contract. The terms both denote that it is cash or physical grain, which has been purchased, and its delivery is scheduled forward—at a later date. The arrangement involves credit extension to the seller: He has been given time in which to meet his delivery obligation.

Deferring performance often serves the interests of both the seller and the buyer. In the first instance, the seller is assured of a total volume of business, as represented in the aggregate order. By scheduling delivery segments at intervals, the seller is able to also schedule purchases, thereby saving the investment costs and inconvenience of owning and storing the commodity in his own facilities over the full period of time covered in the contract.

From the buyer's standpoint, the benefits are equally real. Assume his milling capacity to be 1 million bushels of wheat per month. By scheduling arrival of this quantity of wheat at 30-day intervals, he can be sure of uninterrupted production without ever needing to hold much more than this amount of grain in store. A cash-forward, or deferred delivery commitment involves bilateral obligations, or credit, between seller and buyer. The seller owes wheat and delivery; the buyer owes delivery acceptance and money. Default on the part of either will seriously penalize the other. Unless the miller can depend on his constant supply of grain, his production schedule cannot be maintained. Interruptions can be very costly. By the same token, unless the supplier can be assured of his buyer's dependability in accepting each delivery and paying for it, he may be placed in the position of owning substantial amounts of grain for which he has no other buyers.

It was precisely this kind of consideration which led to the development of futures markets, the largest of which came into being in Chicago during the first half of the 19th century.

Development of the Chicago Grain Market

Authorities are unable to agree on the year in which grain was first traded on a deferred arrival basis in the city of Chicago. The practice, however, was well established as early as 1840. The mechanics of trade were really quite simple. A farmer would harvest his crop and load it on wagons or a river barge enroute to the Midwest's grain capital. This done, the farmer would then take the fastest transportation available, in order to arrive in Chicago well ahead of his shipment.

Grain brokers, merchants, and processors congregated in Haine's Feed Store on the bank of the Chicago River. Here, for several hours each day, they negotiated with producers for grain stocks which flour milling and other activities required. The farmer with a harvest on the way offered his grain for sale "to-arrive" a few days or a few weeks later.

When the transaction was made, it involved a firm price. However, it was entirely possible that in the period pending arrival of the shipment, market prices could increase greatly, in which case it would be to the financial advantage of the seller to default on his end of the previous contract and sell the grain to someone else at the higher price; or the reverse could occur. Prices might fall to a level where the buyer no longer wanted to accept the expensive grain, preferring to default and obtain his needs at the now more attractive price level. Both buyers and sellers sought protection against default on the part of their opposite numbers.

Margin Deposits to Bind Performance

It was this consideration which gave rise to the practice of posting "margin" on grain trades. With a transaction completed, buyer and seller each deposited a mutually acceptable amount of cash with a disinterested but dependable third party. In the event of default on the part of either, the margin deposit was paid over to the other to reimburse him for the inconvenience and direct financial loss occasioned by the other party's nonperformance.

Margin deposit was never viewed as a down payment. It stood, rather, as a performance bond, binding the seller to deliver the specified merchandise, and binding the buyer to acceptance of the delivery and payment in full. Margin is no longer held by disinterested third parties, and is no longer negotiable between buyers and sellers on organized exchanges. However, margin still constitutes an essential element in futures trading and affords the same stability in transactions presently as it did more than 100 years ago.

Speculation Appears

Trading in to-arrives entailed no immediate need for storage, since some of the deferred shipments were not scheduled for arrival for 30, 60, or 90 days. Still, a substantial risk was present, growing out of the possibilities of price change. Grain processors were primarily interested in obtaining their raw materials at stable prices, which would enable them to turn out their finished products uninterruptedly and at competitive price levels. A flour miller who bought wheat at $1.00 per bushel and saw the price go to $1.25 per bushel before the commodity reached his hands had made an impressive speculative profit. However, the opposite could also occur, resulting in a monumental loss. The risks from price fluctuation, however, were inescapable. The hazard had to be borne by the owner of grain, or passed on to someone who was willing to speculate on price in the hope of making a profit from his position.

Professional grain speculation thus grew out of the situation which naturally existed in a market which was vastly oversupplied with product during the post-harvest season and was, more often than not, confronted by real or relative scarcity throughout much of the balance of the year.

Early speculation took two forms. The "long" speculators would buy to-arrive offerings of the farmers, hoping that in the interim, between their purchases and the arrival of the physical merchandise, prices would increase and offer them an opportunity to sell out at a profit. Other speculators sold to-arrive grain "short," for 30, 60, or 90 day delivery, in the hope that during the interval, prices would fall, enabling them to obtain the cash grain required for their delivery commitment at a lesser price than their selling price. If this happened, they stood to make a profit.

Neither the long nor the short speculators claimed ownership of physical grain at the time they bought or sold it. They, and the grain trade generally, understood that in speculating, these individuals were merely assuming the risks of price fluctuation over a specified period of time, in the hope of profiting from subsequent price changes. Grain speculators were a welcome and most important element in grain trading, since the price risks present 50 or 100 years ago were staggering in comparison to current grain price behavior.

Feast and Famine

Wheat at harvest time often sold as low as 15 cents per bushel. Barge loads of wheat and corn clogged the Chicago River, waiting for buyers at almost any price. Exposure to weather resulted in extensive damage to the merchandise. It was not unusual in peak harvest years for millions of bushels of grain to spoil at dockside and later be towed into Lake Michigan and dumped. Terminal storage facilities in those early days were woefully inadequate to needs, and transportation methods were unequal to the task of spreading the crop throughout the major markets and getting it all under cover against winter weather.

Spring and summer often presented an almost opposite situation. Wheat which sold in October for 15 cents per bushel might, in July, bring 10 or 20 times that much, and with little to be found. Buyers, sellers, and consumers were all penalized by the gross inefficiencies of pricing, storage, and distribution. Price fluctuations were fierce, but even the highest prices could not recreate grain which had been lost or wasted six months before. It was truly a "feast or famine" as the Chicago grain market struggled valiantly to even out supply and demand and meet the ever larger food demands of a burgeoning national population.

It was against this background of alternating shortage and over-supply, high prices and low prices, that grain speculation came into being in the United States. One effect of speculation has been to reasonably ration available supplies and put a premium on storage of surplus during times of plenty. Speculation is not an economic contrivance. It is a practical outgrowth of risks inherent in highly unpredictable businesses. It has brought a leveling influence into the marketplace and has stood as perhaps the most effective countermeasure available for excesses which otherwise always develop in the face of unuseable surplus or inadequate supplies.

Speculation is often explained as a form of future "price insurance." The parallel is not well drawn, even though it has some usefulness in making the activity more understandable to newcomers to the field. The institution of speculation is a practice in evaluating risks and "discounting" present facts into future possibilities. Changing price level is a contingency which invites speculative evaluation—and seeks speculative protection. Futures markets accomplish both.

Professional speculation is a somewhat recent innovation, inasmuch as it is considered to have originated in Japan only a few hundred years ago. It has been raised to its highest level in the United States. It is at least noteworthy that the same nation which reflects the majority of all speculation conducted in the world, also enjoys the highest standard of living the world has ever seen. It may be too much to infer that one thing grows directly out of the other. Still, there is every reason to think that speculation makes a far more significant contribution to both productive and distributive efficiencies than even its strongest supporters suspect.

3

The Business of Speculative Risk Bearing

Life for everyone is a series of exposures to various orders of risk, chief among which is the matter of survival itself. Success or failure in meeting the problems of existence depends mainly on how well an individual and a society are able to forecast the future and make prudent plans for capitalizing on opportunities and tempering or escaping the impacts of various threats. Fortunately, the human race seems to be somewhat equally divided between optimists and pessimists or, to use the terminology of the marketplace, "bulls" and "bears." Thus, public opinion concerning the future always represents a composite of positive and negative attitudes.

Among the essential considerations in preparing to cope with the future is the matter of ensuring an adequate supply of the things required to sustain and protect life. These may be, for purposes of simplification, covered in the all-inclusive term of *vital commodities*. Foodstuffs properly head the list in order of importance, since all must eat or die. Following closely, however, are a long list of things man cannot eat, but which he requires in order to fabricate tools, construct housing, produce clothing, and maintain a system of commerce. As a result, vital commodities denote such things as grain, meat, and fiber. Commodities also include metals, ranging from aluminum to zinc, including gold and silver; since these are the stuff upon which international monetary systems are largely based, or against which currencies are measured— regardless of whether a given country happens to be on the gold standard. Since the *world* respects gold, politicians have no other choice!

Economy of Scarcity

All commodities usually share a common economic condition: relative scarcity. It is their scarcity which renders them valuable. Supplies, it seems, are rarely if ever adequate to fill all existing demands, even though distinct oversupply of a usually scarce commodity may occasionally exist for a relatively short period of time. The most recent examples of this have been seen in the United States, where agricultural production for the past 40 years has tended to outstrip domestic demand, and has prompted the accumulation of government stockpiles to handle surplus, along with acreage restrictions calculated to suppress excessive output.

Scarcity Is Usually Regional

Even in the face of such surpluses as have existed in the United States in recent years, however, a large portion of the earth's population has existed with malnutrition as a constant companion. Thus it must be said that the situation of oversupply existed only regionally (in the North American continent) and existed only because distribution methods and ability to buy were insufficient to accomplish the economic leveling-out process.

Like individuals, few nations of the world have an ability to buy that equals their propensity to consume. Moreover, transport methods are not universally available to efficiently accomplish the task of physical distribution. If these two considerations were met, instead of approximately one third of the earth's population existing on the bleak edge of real hunger, all would theoretically subsist in a condition of mere undernourishment. This, because world food supplies are not now, and probably never have been, fully adequate to meet *all* of the nutritional needs of all of the people, everywhere.

Assigning responsibility for this apparent impasse is basically simple. Virtually all foodstuffs are raised under some seasonal limitations. While wheat, the most widely grown cereal crop on earth, is being harvested somewhere on the face of the globe every month of the year, the wheat harvest in North America takes place mainly during July and August. It is harvested in Australia during November and December. Each regional harvest takes place in the span of a few weeks, while consumption of the crop is necessarily spread over 12 months. There is a period of time immediately following harvest when available local food supplies vastly exceed any current need for them, even in such chronic food short localities as India's interior. Whether foodstuffs are available during periods between harvests depends on several factors, not the least of which is the ability and willingness of individuals to invest in, store, and protect excess supplies in anticipation of needs in periods of relative shortage between crops.

Man has been described as a "planning animal." The compliment, to some limited extent, is deserved. In certain areas, however, human planning performance is less than impressive. Prodigality in a time of plenty is a common human failing. Some of the world's major catastrophes have been confidently predicted and could have been largely avoided, or their impact vastly reduced by countermeasures. Yet, precautionary steps are not always taken in the face of impending crisis, and the lapses stand as black marks against individuals, nations and the world as a whole.

Faced with a present problem, reason often succumbs to unreasoning fear, and a situation which could be solved with intelligence and deliberation is multiplied by fright into totally unmanageable proportions.

Pessimists versus Optimists

It is in a situation of this kind that the dyed-in-the-wool pessimist seriously contemplates and loudly forecasts "the end of the world." Optimistic voices may occasionally be heard, but the criers of doom usually occupy center stage until overwhelming evidence appears to rebut their prediction of the worst.

In the area of food supplies, the pessimist operates on both ends of the topic. During periods of oversupply, he insists that available commodities will never be consumed, hence, are relatively worthless. If his counsel is accepted, the result is seen in low prices, food waste, and the profligate utilization of high quality commodities in low priority activities; for example, the feeding of wheat to farm animals when the total supply is actually inadequate for all human needs.

In the opposite frame of reference, when serious scarcities do exist in food supplies, the pessimist compounds the problem with his opinion that starvation is inescapable. As such a position gains adherents, the actual shortage which exists can only be worsened, since the spectre of hunger is the stoutest possible argument in favor of food hoarding; and hoarding has probably starved as many as famine has. The best prescription in either situation is a measure of equanimity and a more balanced perspective.

Experience should remind us that future events will probably not equal the worst that can be feared nor the best that can be hoped for. Something between these two extremes usually represents a manageable situation which may require effort and sagacity to cope with; but given some industrious and intelligent attention, will likely prove to be somehow surmountable.

The counterbalancing influence for the pessimist is, of course, the optimist. His vision of things to come accentuates the positive factors and discounts some or all of the negative considerations. The optimist never seems to lose his abiding faith that, in the words of Mr. Micawber, "something will turn up." His unsinkable confidence at times eclipses good judgment, since he errs in one direction as much as the pessimist errs in the other.

These are the thrusts which comprise the essential inputs in any free market. The opposing economic camps wage a constant struggle to make their divergent viewpoints prevail. One may gain clear ascendancy over the other for a period of time but, if so, the tide is usually not long in turning. More often than not, market psychology is a quite closely balanced composite of bearish and bullish attitudes. "Bears" live with an ever-present feeling that prices are too high and will fall. They are always more or less ready sellers. The "bulls" invariably feel that prices are too low and will rise. They are usually ready buyers.

Cash/Futures Prices

The interplay between these forces which represent the "attitudes" of supply and demand, strikes an equilibrium which the market translates as a price/value level for the given moment and, through the institution of futures trading, projects its economic "shadow" for days, weeks and months to come. The nearest price is, of course, the cash price. The cash price may be taken as reflecting *things as they are* since, assuming a free and informed market, it is the one price above which the marginal buyer would not buy, and below which the marginal seller would not sell. We can largely ignore any time dimension in a cash price.

The futures price must be viewed in a somewhat different light, since it represents a moving, progressive refinement in values over the life of the contract involved. It must be remembered that although a futures contract in commodities calls for ultimate delivery of merchandise, or offset, delivery day may be days, weeks, or months away. As long as time still remains in which to resolve issues which bear on the matter of price, market attitudes will continue to change and futures prices will change also.

Once a cash price is determined, and money and the physical commodity change hands, reselling the "cash" is certain to involve some measure of inconvenience: elevation, loading, grading, etc.

In futures markets, conversely, although each transaction is firm and conditions of the transaction are irrevocable within the requirements of the contract involved, buying and selling entails no physical handling. A speculator need never hold a pound of the cash item. There is a further difference between a cash transaction and a trade in futures. The buyer of a physical commodity invariably undertakes certain costs of storage, insurance, and so forth, along with possession of the inventory. There are substantial attendant costs in connection with the buying or selling of cash merchandise which cannot be escaped or ignored.

This is not true in a futures contract, since the physical commodity is not involved, and will not be until delivery date. Costs which relate to storage and protection of the product are only theoretically involved in the futures pricing consideration. As will be seen later, the supply/demand situation will govern the amount of carrying charges, if any, we might find in the price of the merchandise represented in a commodity futures contract.

Where do Prices Come from?

Every student of commodity marketing quickly comes to grips with the question of price leadership in the marketplace. There are those who believe that cash prices enjoy ascendency over futures prices, in terms of establishing composite values. Their argument is ordinarily based on a contention that cash prices are the only *real* prices, inasmuch as they relate to *real* merchandise. In pursuing this thesis, devotees of cash price leadership insist the market deals first with the present, and then projects future values—in the form of futures prices—based on expectations of improvement or deterioration from the present state of things. Reasonable as such a case might appear on the surface, it falls under close examination.

To begin with, futures prices *precede* cash prices by a considerable period of time. Trading in wheat futures for delivery in May, 1985, began in May, 1984. The price at which trading in this contract commenced represented the market's composite judgment of the available supplies likely to be on hand a year later, as compared with projected demand on the scheduled delivery date. Development of this "price idea" had to take into consideration such things as harvest expectations, projected usage, possible export requirements, and a host of lesser factors. As each day in the life of such a contract passes, new information comes to light which bears on all of these things. Each new bit of information refines and sharpens the traders' individual opinions—which all help make up the market's perspective about the price of wheat in May. The price constantly fluctuates—it rises in response to larger than average consumption indications, or smaller than expected production. It falls in response to opposite influences. But, by the time delivery day on the contract arrives, the price of May wheat futures and cash wheat of contract grade will stand at practically the same level, since they are now interchangeable.

In view of the greater period of time over which futures prices are being examined and adjusted by commercial interests, speculators, and traders of all sorts, their ultimate consensus—as represented in the maturity price—must logically be viewed as more carefully developed; hence more substantive than the cash price. There is an additional and most important factor: The volume of trading in a given cash commodity represents but a small fraction of the trading volume in the same commodity's futures contracts. Since trading volume must reasonably be viewed as a direct reflection of supply/demand forces, there is little choice but to accept the futures prices as being a more reliable measurement of price equilibrium than cash trading activity; if for no other reason than that futures volume is so very much larger.

There is still a further point in support of the case that futures prices take the lead in determining cash prices, rather than vice versa. Unexpected dislocations in supply and demand can and do bring sharp, short-duration price swings in the cash market. Immediate shortage of wheat must be immediately faced by the flour miller, since his survival as a processor depends on obtaining raw materials. Paying an exorbitantly high price for cash wheat over a short period of time is infinitely preferable to interruption of his production schedule. Part of the inflated wheat price can perhaps be passed on to end product users, but even if the miller is forced to absorb all of these added costs, he would still rather do so than close down his mill. In short, commercial processors must maintain reasonable continuity of operation. In order to do this, they have no choice except to do business in the market; and at whatever price levels the market reflects.

The reverse is equally true when supplies vastly outstrip demand. At harvest time, for example, sellers of the cash commodity may be confronted by distressingly low prices, and for reasons which are perfectly obvious. Supply and demand balance out *over time,* but cash prices involve no time dimension; hence, offer no opportunity for the immediate situation to be tempered and discounted in the light of mitigating probabilities. The individual who must sell "cash" today must accept today's cash bid, whatever it is.

The fluctuations which occur in futures prices may also be dramatic in both extent and suddenness. They are, for the most part, however, predicated on more fundamental alterations of market conditions. A shipping strike which halts the flow of foodstuffs could be expected to exert a profound influence on cash prices in affected localities. The same strike would have a far lesser influence, if any at all, on the prices of a futures contract several months away from maturity.

All of the evidence, taken at face value, offers an eloquent argument that futures prices are usually in a position of relative leadership over cash prices.

Futures prices are refined and adjusted over a longer period of time and represent broader supply/demand forces than do cash prices. Except for technical market aberrations which will be dealt with in another place, futures prices are more deliberately determined and, therefore, deserve to be considered as more "rationally" determined. Clearly, they are less influenced by short-term problems of over or undersupply than are prices for cash commodities.

Both Cash and Futures Are Real

Finally, the contention of some that cash prices should enjoy preeminence in total pricing function because they refer to *actual* commodities, is specious at best. Both cash prices and futures prices relate to actual commodities; the only difference being that in one instance the merchandise is for immediate delivery and, in the other, delivery may be scheduled a year or more after transaction. The fact that a futures trade may be offset by an equal and opposite transaction at any time prior to maturity does not alter the situation either, except to importantly mitigate the effect of market apprehension which can grow out of supply/demand dislocation in short-term situations.

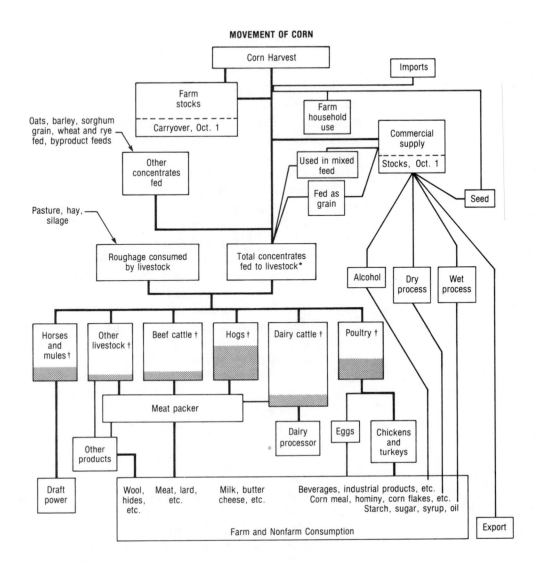

MOVEMENT OF CORN

*Grains and byproduct feeds fed as such or in commercially-prepared feeds.
†The entire box measures the total feed fed; the shaded areas the amount of corn fed.

U.S. Department of Agriculture.

Exhibit 3–1

Most commodities pass through a great many hands in the chain which begins with production and ends with consumption.

The commodities speculator will quickly learn that the relationships between cash and futures prices offer an important indication of near-term supply/demand balance. This aspect must be given careful consideration in any trading decision, but the trader should never forget that cash prices are far more susceptible to short-term influences than are futures prices. If a choice must be made between the two as concerns market condition and directional trend, futures prices are almost invariably the ones to be trusted.

This brings us to the kernel of our topic: A speculator in commodities is a dealer in *pricing risks*. He will hardly ever be a receiver of, or a deliverer of, the physical commodity. His concern with the facts which surround the cash product in the market is related to the continuing exercise in price forecasting, rather than any direct involvement with, or in, the cash commodity or the cash market.

The successful futures speculator will be a close observer of changing balances between supply and demand in "actuals," because this is part of the total equation which will determine prices at a later date. In the same manner, a speculator must also keep his appraisal up-to-date with regard to market psychology. If the bulls have recently taken heavy losses in the form of a substantial price drop, they may be somewhat slow in coming back for another try—at least until the opportunity looks most inviting. In the meantime, the bears may have it all their way. Or vice versa.

The speculator will keep a current notion about the level of export activity, weather patterns, and transportation tie-ups which may be pending; along with interest rates and government farm policy practices and attitudes. Not all of these things will merit equal weight in making market judgments, but they all deserve some weight.

Speculative profits must be viewed as a risk premium which the trader earns for undertaking the hazards of property ownership for a period of time. Such profits are only earned on the basis of right judgments, and losses are the opposite side of profit.

Not only does it *pay* to be right—it *costs* to be wrong—in any business decision! And speculation is a business. As a measurable fact, speculation is the biggest and most universal economic involvement on earth. It could not be otherwise. This because speculation defines the confrontation between humanity's struggle for survival and security on one hand, and fickle nature on the other. The quality of life and affluence we enjoy depends directly on the quality of speculative decisions we make—individually and collectively.

4

The Nature and Function of a Futures Contract

In order to understand the characteristics which make a futures contract different from any other form of merchantable holding, one must begin by getting rid of any stylized notions about similarities with other commercial documents.

A futures contract is thoroughly unique. While it is an actual contract binding both seller and buyer to specific performance obligations, a futures contract has rarely existed in printed form. The terms of a futures contract are contained in the rules and regulations of the exchange upon which it is traded. The bilateral commitments which it imposes are specific and completely enforceable, and have been declared so by the United States Supreme Court. However, it is unlikely that a speculator could obtain a copy of his futures contract even if he wanted to, and there is no reason to even try.

A futures transaction does not transfer ownership or constructive physical possession of anything. Execution of a futures trade only involves *firm commitments* on the part of the buyer and seller to mutually carry out their respective responsibilities, in a designated manner and within an established time table, set forth as conditions of their transaction.

1. A futures contract firmly binds the seller to deliver a fixed amount of a certain grade or grades of a designated commodity, within a given geographical area, during a specified time period.
2. A futures contract firmly binds a buyer to accept delivery of the commodity and, upon delivery, to pay for it in full in cash.

3. A futures contract affords both the buyer and the seller a continuing opportunity to avoid the making or taking of delivery, through execution of an equal and opposite transaction in the same commodity and futures month. Once having *offset* by an equal and opposite transaction, the buyer and/or seller have fully discharged preexisting contract obligations and have no remaining responsibilities under it, either directly or collaterally.

No Limit to Futures Trade Volume

Newcomers to commodity trading often make the mistake of thinking there is some actual or theoretical relationship between the volume of trading in futures and the amounts of the physical commodity in existence, and which the futures contracts represent. This is absolutely incorrect. There is, for example, no limit—either theoretically or practically—to the number of futures contracts in soybeans which might be bought and sold in the course of a crop year.

The actual soybean harvest in the United States in 1983 was less than two billion bushels. Volume of trading in soybean futures in Chicago alone during that 12-month period totalled nearly 60 billion bushels—30 times production! The statement appears to be a paradox, so let's examine the considerations that validate the strange-sounding fact.

Everyone understands that automobile manufacturers currently produce some 7 or 8 million automobiles per year. However, total car sales in a 7-million car year may easily reach 30 million. This will happen because the automobile manufacturer first sells his car to a distributor, who resells the car to a retailer, who finally sells the car to the end user. Each new automobile in this example is involved in three separate transactions as it passes through the distributive chain from producer to retail customer. Then, don't forget used car sales. The same succession of reselling also exists in grain, metals, oil, and practically every other commodity in existence.

In tracing the movement of grain from farmers' fields to the consumer's dining table, we know that it passes through many hands—and in various forms—as it moves from producer, to wholesaler, to processor and product manufacturer, distributor, retailer, and ultimately to the customer. A bushel of oats may be bought and sold a dozen times before it finally is taken out of existence through consumption. To the extent that successive owners of this bushel of oats engage in *hedging,* its equivalent in oats futures will be both bought and sold each time the commodity changes hands. The farmer may hedge his crop by selling a quantity of oats futures equal to part or all of his anticipated harvest, several months before he plants the grain. The commodity merchant who buys the farmer's grain may simultaneously hedge his purchase of the cash product through a short sale of equivalent oats futures. When the grain merchant later resells the cash oats to a processor, he will lift his hedge by buying back the short oats futures he had previously sold. And so on, each step of the way.

Hedgers Have a Choice

When a hedger sells commodity futures, he may or may not intend to deliver the cash product in settlement of his contract at maturity. It really makes no difference what his delivery intentions are. The fact is that he can and will either offset by buying back futures, or he may elect to deliver the cash product. The course of action he chooses will depend on which best serves his operational and profit objectives.

Speculators Must Offset

The same thing may not be said, as concerns the speculator. When he buys or sells commodity futures, he does so purely as a means of assuming the positive or negative price risks of commodity ownership. He owns none of the product and he wants none. He rarely, if ever, has the slightest intention of either taking delivery or obtaining the physical commodity in order to deliver it against an open short position. Of course the opportunity always exists for him to do so if events urge it. Still, for the most part, the number of contracts, long or short, which a speculator has open should be viewed as nothing more than a measurement of the ownership or risk he has taken on. His profits or losses will be computed on the basis of cents per bushel, per pound, per hundredweight, or per ton. But the speculator's position will almost invariably be offset prior to the date when trading ceases and delivery becomes mandatory.

To repeat for emphasis, speculative trading takes place in search of profit. The speculator *does not* want to *own* cash grain, minerals, or metals; he *does* want the opportunities for profit which are inherent in *changing prices*. His assumption of ownership risk is stated in terms of designated quantities of commodities, but doing so is only a communications convenience. The only thing the speculator really seeks is *risk,* as a means to profit.

Supply and Demand Governs

Newcomers to speculation are often puzzled by the question of what would happen if the wheat futures sold, for example, exceeded all available wheat supplies. How could the outstanding obligations possibly be met? The answer is that they could *not* be met if all of the longs in such a situation stayed long and insisted on delivery. Obviously a product which does not exist cannot be delivered. But the odds against this happening are overwhelming.

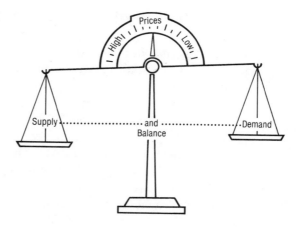

Exhibit 4–1

Price measures the balance between supply and demand.

To understand the reasoning behind this statement, we must remember that the balance between supply and demand in traded commodities usually maintains a close equilibrium. Market prices on commodities are established in trading, at levels which generally reflect supply/demand balance. Relative scarcity represents the normal state of things. When demand outstrips supply, prices rise, and the higher prices serve to ration the available product into areas of greatest usefulness. For example, when wheat is selling for $2 per bushel (and stocks are excessive) a great deal of cheap wheat will be fed to poultry and livestock. When wheat is selling for $5 per bushel, consumption of the expensive grain will be almost totally limited to conversion into food products for human consumption.

Price Rations Use

Thus it may be stated that so long as prices can fluctuate, relative price levels will ration whatever supplies exist into channels of use which justify their effective price. When prices are high, low-end, less valuable usage will dry up, and substitute stuffs obtainable at lower prices tend to take over the function either temporarily or permanently.

It is for these reasons that it is so vitally important that free markets exist and are able to establish commodity prices. Whenever the price on a given product is dictated by government edict or otherwise, the rationing influence of price fluctuation is frustrated and consumption proceeds without respect to the realities of supply/demand relationships. Dire results are to be expected.

Futures May Pass through Many Hands

Now let's give our attention to the matter of futures trading, for the purpose of developing an understanding of how supply and demand in futures contracts also tends to be self-balancing throughout the life of a given contract. To begin with, there must be a seller for every buyer of a future; wheat futures, like cash wheat, can only be bought from a *seller*.

Consider a contract in July wheat, which opens for trading in July of the year preceding harvest. On the first day of trading, we will imagine that only two traders are interested in transacting business in the maturity. Trader A offers to sell one contract—5,000 bushels, at $2.50 per bushel. Trader B considers the price attractive, and he buys the contract. The transaction is noted on their trading cards and the price is posted "on the board." Time passes, but no further trades are made. As the end of the session approaches, Trader A decides that he does not want to carry the short position overnight; so he offers to buy back one contract of July wheat (hopefully at a profit) and he bids for "five July at $2.49" per bushel. His bid attracts no sellers. He progressively raises his bid to $2.49¼, later to $2.49¾. He offers $2.50 per bushel, which is precisely what he sold the contract for earlier, but he still finds no seller. At last he raises his bid to $2.50¼ and Trader B, who previously purchased the contract at $2.50, accepts Trader A's offer. The offsetting trade is made.

Now, let's recap these events. When the first transaction was made, the *opening price* was established at $2.50 per bushel on July wheat. With the first trade execution, *open-interest* in the contract amounted to 5,000 bushels, since open-interest reflects *one side* of all positions held. As the session wore on, bids on July maturity ranged from $2.49 per bushel up to $2.50 per bushel, but no transaction took place at these levels. Finally, a second transaction was executed at $2.50¼, and was consummated between the same two parties involved in the first execution. Having made the second trade, both Traders A and B have *offset*, since their second transaction was *equal and opposite* to their first transaction: A initially sold 5,000 bushels of July wheat and later bought back the same amount in the same contract. B first bought 5,000 bushels and later sold 5,000 bushels in the July contract. *Volume* on this unlikely day's trading amounts to 10,000 bushels, which is the aggregate amount of futures which changed hands in the course of the session. The *trading range* was from a *low* of $2.50 per bushel to a *high* of $2.50¼ per bushel. Open-interest at the close of the day is zero, since all positions were offset by the closing bell.

Now let's involve a somewhat larger group of traders in the situation and consider the next day's trading in the same contract.

When the second session opens, Pit Broker X holds an order which was placed by a grain producer to sell 10,000 bushels (two contracts) of July wheat at $2.50¼ (which was the previous day's closing price). When the offering is called, Trader A buys it. As the session runs on,

Trader A subsequently sells the 10,000 bushels to Trader B, who in turn sells it to C, after which it is in turn bought and sold by Traders D, E, F, and G. Trader G is interested in "accumulating" a larger position in the contract, in line with his conviction that the price is low and will go higher. He therefore keeps the 10,000 bushels of July wheat and devotes his attention to buying more of the same.

Time passes—some 11 months pass—and the July contract now approaches maturity. The First-Notice-Day on this contract falls in the last week of June preceding the delivery month. Trader G still holds the two contracts "long" which he purchased nearly a year before. The grain producer is still "short" the 10,000 bushels he sold a year earlier.

Oldest Net Long Usually Gets Delivery

The seller's crop has now been harvested and he wishes to make delivery. In order to do this, he has executed a Notice of Intention to Deliver and passed it to the clearinghouse, which, in turn, passes it to Trader G, who is the oldest "net long" in the contract. Trader G is a speculator. He has held the position in order to profit from price improvement. He does not, however, wish to take delivery of the physical commodity. When he receives the delivery notice, he immediately sells 10,000 bushels of July wheat futures in the pit. His buyer is Broker P, who represents a commercial processor. Having made the futures sale, Trader G has offset his position, and he "re-tenders" the delivery notice by returning it to the clearinghouse along with the name of the buyer.

When the wheat is delivered, it will go directly to processor P. The interim holders of the contract (Traders A-B-C-D-E-F-G) are not concerned in any way. The futures passed through their hands, but they subsequently offset by an equal and opposite transaction; hence, they are out of the contract and have been out of it since the moment of their earlier offsetting trades. The producer will make his delivery to processor P (through a regular warehouse) and receive a certified check for the total value of the shipment. The buyer's check is transmitted through the clearinghouse and on to the seller. The diagram (Exhibit 4–2) should further clarify the various steps in this chain of events.

Volume and Open-Interest

As outlined above, this 10,000 bushels of July wheat changed hands eight times during the trading life of the contract. It accounted for 80,000 bushels of trading volume and 10,000 bushels of "open-interest" throughout the life of the contract, since someone held the position at all times. It was cleared for the last time and disappeared from open-interest at the point at which delivery was finally made.

All trading in futures contracts proceeds along these same lines. Trading rules and regulations vary, depending on the commodity involved and delivery requirements surrounding it. Each exchange reflects some slight variations in the particulars. In all futures contracts,

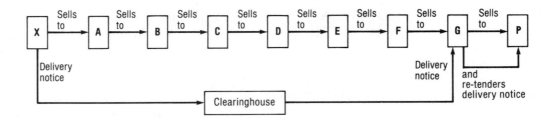

Exhibit 4–2

A single commodity contract may pass through many hands during its trading life, but only the deliverer and the receiver are involved in the transfer of cash merchandise.

however, for every buyer there must be a seller and, unless previously offset by an equal and opposite transaction, a short must make delivery and a long must accept delivery and make full payment for the merchandise.

Who Buys—Who Sells

The seller of a commodity contract has no way of knowing—and no interest in knowing—whether his offering is bought by a speculator, a commercial processor, or an exporter. He is only interested in two things: First, the price which he receives and second, that he will have someone to accept delivery, *if he chooses to make delivery,* upon maturity. During the trading interim, the contract position which came into being with the first transaction between X and A, may change hands dozens or hundreds of times. Regardless of intervening events, however, the seller is always protected against default on the part of his initial buyer and all subsequent buyers who replace the first one through progressive transactions.

The same may be said for the purchaser. His interests are always ensured. He can be confident that if he holds the contract to maturity, he will receive delivery. In the meantime, he can obtain his profits in cash whenever he offsets; from the original seller, or some other seller who has replaced him on the short side of the trade. Protection for both the buyer and the seller is accomplished through the device of *margin,* which will now be examined in considerable detail.

Commodity Margin

It was pointed out earlier in this text that margin is not a down payment on commodities represented in a futures contract but, rather, stands as a performance bond to indemnify both the buyer and the seller against possible default on the part of the interest on the opposite side of the position. In the early days of to-arrive trading, the amount of margin required on a given transaction was flexible and mutually determined by the parties involved. Depending on the financial reputations of the buyer and seller, margin required on an individual transaction might have ranged from 2 percent or 3 percent of the total value represented in the trade, to perhaps as much as 15 percent or 20 percent.

Now, as then, margin is equally required from both buyer and seller since, if prices fall in the interim between execution of the trade and offset or delivery date, the purchaser or "long" loses; therefore, the seller or "short" requires protection from possible default on the part of the buyer. In the opposite frame of reference, if prices rise between the time of sale and the offset or delivery date, the seller or short loses; as a consequence the long seeks, and is entitled to protection against possible default on the part of his short seller.

In early days of commodity trading, margin deposits put up by the long and short in a given trade were turned over to a mutually acceptable third party, to be retained until the transaction was subsequently completed through delivery of the merchandise on the part of the seller and payment in full on the part of the buyer. In modern commodity futures markets, *minimum* margin amounts are firmly established in the rules and regulations of the market, and margin deposits are held by the clearinghouse organization which usually functions as a closely related but structurally separate organizational entity. The role of the clearinghouse will be discussed more broadly later. For now, it is sufficient to say that the clearing organization serves as interlocutor between all buyers and all sellers in futures contract trading. Once a transaction is made in the pits, it is turned over to the clearinghouse which, in recording the trade, puts itself, by substitution, in the position of seller to all buyers—and buyer to all sellers.

Minimum Margin Is Fixed

The minimum margin required from the principals in a futures transaction is set forth in the rules and regulations of the exchange, but individual brokerage houses may require greater margin amounts from their customers if they wish. Ordinarily, margin levels represent something like 5 percent to 8 percent of the value of the commodities in trade. However, the margin minimums established by the particular exchange depend largely on the volatility expectations in each commodity category. If a daily trading range of 20 cents in a given commodity is commonplace, the margin required will understandably be greater than this amount. Unless this is so, normal price fluctuations would be triggering margin calls constantly and thus threaten the economic stability of the entire activity.

As a further safeguard of an orderly market, commission houses often require their customers to post margin amounts that greatly exceed the minimums established by the exchanges. Today's Board of

Trade (BOT) requirements for margin on a corn contract, for example, are $600 *initial* and $400 *maintenance*. A major brokerage firm is presently requiring $1,000 initial, and $700 maintenance to margin that trade. A commission house is free to establish any margin levels it wishes, so long as they are not less than exchange minimums.

In soybeans, at this writing, the BOT minimum margin is $1,750 initial and $1,250 maintenance, per 5,000 bushel contract. This is to say that, after a trade is accomplished, the price on the contract may fluctuate in a range of 20 cents per bushel (10 cents per bushel to the disadvantage of the long or short) without requiring either of them to post additional margin money. However, should the soybean contract concerned fall 10¼ cents per bushel, the holder of the long side of the contract would immediately be required to post sufficient additional money to bring his margin back up to the initial margin level of 35 cents per bushel. If he fails to answer the call for additional margin, the broker may liquidate part or all of the position to keep the holding within established margin requirements.

Critics of commodity futures trading often base their criticism on the fact that buyers and sellers of contracts post a relatively small amount of cash. It is a recurrent contention of market critics that commodity traders have unrealistically small "investments" in futures positions and, as a consequence, the financial foundation of the trade is shaky. A commodity position is *never* an investment!

As a matter of fact, margin requirements in futures trading are properly based primarily on the consideration of historic price *fluctuation*. Commodity price is at best a secondary factor. Buyers and sellers of futures are dealing in fluctuative risks. They are not dealing in physical commodities. The cash commodities will not be involved in the trade until contract maturity makes delivery necessary. In the meantime, each contract may be bought and sold many times, with each holder of an open position responsible only for indemnifying his opposite number to the extent of the price change which occurred while he held the position.

For example, when corn is selling for $1.40 per bushel, there is an excellent possibility that the price may rise to $1.45 per bushel or fall to $1.35 per bushel. There is a smaller possibility that price will increase to $1.50 or fall to $1.30. The probabilities are heavily weighted against the chance that corn prices might increase to $1.60 per bushel or fall to $1.20.

Margin performs its full function when it is sufficient to cover the "risk end" of price. It would be absurd to require a commodity trader to post 50 percent margin on a position in corn. Doing so would be tantamount to saying that corn currently selling at $1.40 per bushel could be reasonably expected to suddenly increase to $2.10 per bushel, or suddenly fall to 70 cents per bushel. While such an eventuality could perhaps conceivably occur, such a huge price swing would certainly take place over a substantial period of time, during which disadvantaged traders could close out their losing positions by offset (sales or

Chicago Board of Trade Cuts Margin Rules for 6 Contracts

CHICAGO—The Chicago Board of Trade said it lowered margin requirements for six major futures contracts because of a decline in price volatility.

Margin is the minimum amount of money a trader must deposit to begin trading.

Effective tomorrow, the exchange reduced soybean futures margins to $1,500 a contract from $1,750. Margins for soybean meal were cut to $700 a contract from $750. In corn, margins were reduced to $500 from $600, the exchange said.

For contracts in Treasury bonds, Treasury notes and Government National Mortgage Association certificates, margin requirements were cut to $2,000 from $2,500.

purchases) to other parties who were willing to undertake the risks of ownership at the new price levels. Even if a few hardy souls did not close out their positions in disappointment or despair as prices moved so far against them, additional maintenance margin would be required in order that they would constantly have a minimum deposit against their positions.

The foregoing should not be taken to mean that price moves in commodities are always of small scope or gentle occurrence. Cataclysmic events which may arrive in the form of unforeseen weather developments, a crop forecast which contains a big surprise for the trade, an outbreak of war, or events of similar impact, can reflect themselves in sudden and sharply precipitous price changes. When this happens, speculators may find themselves in a situation which involves great losses or great profits. But if so, it must be acknowledged that human illness, fire, flood, or theft can be even greater catastrophes; all of which must be occasionally faced up to as an inescapable hazard of being alive and/ or undertaking ownership of property which is susceptible to devaluation, damage, or loss.

At least the individual who speculates in commodity futures can draw quite reliable conclusions about the probable range of price fluctuation on his contract from readily available historical data. He can be certain that the price of his contract will not be doubled or halved in value, except as the result of an almost incredible event; and even then the change in value will almost certainly be spread over a considerable period of time. Due to the constant world market which exists for commodities, they are always in demand at some price; and such time as there is will offer an opportunity for the speculator to cut his losses by closing out his position and transferring the risk to other hands.

How Much Margin Is Needed

In view of the foregoing, we can categorically state that margin is adequate whenever it is sufficient to cover the *probable price-change* risks present, for whatever minimum period of time is involved in "getting out." The clearinghouse has the prerogative of calling on its members for additional margin at any time, and requiring that the new funds be deposited within one hour. Since a variation margin call will be initiated by the clearinghouse whenever the maintenance margin level is impaired, it goes without saying that considerable latitude still remains under the call level for further price fluctuation, without endangering the financial interests of the other party. If the call for additional margin is not met in the prescribed time, the broker and/or clearinghouse has blanket authority to liquidate part or all of the position, freeing remaining margin funds to a point of adequacy in covering whatever portion of the member's position still remains open.

As a practical matter, it deserves to be noted that there is no recorded instance of a buyer or seller failing to receive his full settlement—either through delivery of the commodity or equivalent cash values—on any cleared position on the nation's oldest and largest exchange, the Chicago Board of Trade. When it is considered that more than 136 million contracts were traded on U.S. exchanges in 1983 without a single failure to settle, it seems clear that both margin structures and clearinghouses are performing commendably.

It would be hard to overestimate the importance of the clearinghouse, in substituting itself as "the other party" in all transactions. The clearinghouse, upon accepting each trade at the close of each session, stands as the seller to all buyers and as the buyer to all sellers. The individual seller is actually responsible to the clearinghouse, rather than to the party who bought his contract. Likewise, the buyer can look to the clearinghouse for either delivery of the commodity or payment of profits accrued while the position is held.

Money/Credit Balance

The commodity market is somewhat like our total national economy in one respect: Aggregate obligations outstanding on the part of longs and shorts in commodity trading constantly exceed margin funds on deposit, by some 15 or 20 times over. The same thing can be said of the American business system. Obligations to pay, as represented in accounts receivable held by department stores, services stations, mortgage companies, and employees of operating firms, greatly exceed the total amount of money in circulation at any given time. There is, however, little restrictive relationship between obligations outstanding in the form of total debt, and total money in circulation. So long as the money supply is sufficient to permit buyers and sellers to transact business uninterruptedly, the *quality* of any debt depends directly on the reliability of the person who owes it, and only incidentally on the fact that on the day it falls due there must be sufficient gold, silver, paper money, or acceptable substitute in existence to pay off the obligation.

Commodity trading merely creates a specialized form of debt which, on the part of the seller, involves a commitment to deliver the commodities, or offset the open position by an equal and opposite transaction. The case of the buyer is precisely the opposite: He must accept delivery of the commodity and pay for it in full or—prior to deliver date—offset his long position by sale of an equal amount of the same futures.

Margin from each party to a trade must be adequate to insure that both will carry out their commitments. With performance ensured, there is no conceivable justification for asking more. History provides the most inarguable evidence that margin levels have been and are sufficient. One hundred thirty-five years of consistent settlement on the world's largest agricultural commodity exchange, without a single dollar's loss being sustained as a result of default, is the clearest proof that the commodity market is a sound and reliable institution. Moreover, it shows that traders themselves can be expected to fully perform on their obligations undertaken in the marketplace.

5

Leverage Theory in Speculation

Profits can be considered the primary objective in all economic activity, although certain projects are undertaken by individuals, organizations, and governments without a specific dollar profit goal in mind. Effort is almost always expected to result in accomplishment of something which, from a standpoint of worth appraisal, should be at least theoretically reducible to stated values. Values, in turn, are usually translatable into monetary terms. Put another way, economic activities, in order to maintain analytical coherence, must be viewed as producing economic results: *positive results,* identified as a *profit*—and *negative results,* as a *loss.*

Any situation in which a dollar is able to undertake more than a dollar's worth of economic work is properly identified as a *leverage* situation. Leverage is a primary measurement of the earning potential of money in a given situation. Thus, leverage is a major speculative factor. As we shall see, it constitutes one of the prime considerations which encourages speculative risk bearing on the part of those who have the financial ability and the personal sagacity to undertake such a function in the marketplace.

At current margins, a buyer of securities (on margin) is only required to produce 50 percent of his purchase price in cash. Fifty dollars will thereby obtain "constructive possession" of $100 worth of stock. The $50 deficit which remains constitutes a form of specialized credit extended by the broker to his customer. The $50 provided by the customer can be considered a *down payment* on the stock purchase, with the balance remaining outstanding over whatever period of time suits the mutual interest of the broker and the customer. Most stock purchases and sales are handled on margin, and involve broker loans.

Stock, it should be noted, changes hands when it is bought on margin. Along with the physical asset, entitlement to dividends, etc., also passes to the new owner.

In commodities, margin also figures importantly; but as stated earlier, rather than constituting a down payment, commodity margin is a performance bond. Unlike trading in stock, a commodity futures transaction does not result in the transfer of any physical property. All that is exchanged between buyer and seller are mutually binding bilateral commitments to do certain things in the future. The sole purpose of commodity margin is to *indemnify* each party to the trade against possible default on the part of the other.

Leverage in Commodities Versus Securities

Margin in commodities, therefore, is more properly viewed as a contract binder or performance bond, rather than down payment, as is the case in securities. With commodity margins usually set below 10 percent of the value of the trading unit involved, leverage on the commodity situation is ordinarily about 90 percent, compared to 50 percent on stocks.

To demonstrate, consider a speculator who is considering two propositions:

1. Buy 5,000 shares of ABC common stock at $3.00 per share; value of the block of stock is $15,000. Margin money required (50 percent of the price) $7,500. The balance ($7,500) is covered by a broker's loan at the current short-term interest rate.
2. Buy a futures contract (5,000 bushels) of soybeans at $6.00 per bushel: contract value, $30,000. Initial margin deposit is 35 cents per bushel ($1,750). No broker's loan is required.

The ABC stock pays no dividend; hence any financial return from the stock, as with the soybeans, can only result from an increase in the prices of the two holdings. Both constitute speculations on market value. One important difference exists, however, in the relative leverage available in each situation.

A 10 percent increase in the price of the stock would be worth 30 cents per share, or $1,500. However, a 10 percent increase in the price of the soybeans represents a 175 percent return on the commodity margin, since the speculator was only required to post $1,750 (about 6 percent) to bind the trade. (Margin requirements are subject to change as often as the exchange sees fit to do so.)

Here, in a nutshell, is one of the most practical and compelling reasons why commodity speculators are willing and able to assume the risks of ownership through the holding of commodity futures contracts—either long or short. There are few other financial situations in which a dollar can enjoy such leverage.

As a result, profits on risk capital can be most impressive and, by the same token, so also can losses. With $15,000 to work with, for example, a speculator can obtain some 5,000 shares of the ABC stock used in the example above. In so doing, he will have gained the opportunity to profit from increases in the price of the holding, and he will have to absorb the disadvantages which will come from a price decrease. The same $15,000 used to margin commodity trading will enable the speculator to hold eight contracts (40,000 bushels) of $6.00 soybeans and profit or lose in accordance with the commodity's price fluctuations.

Financial leverage, to repeat, is of unparalleled importance in obtaining maximum return on risk funds, wherever they may be put to work in the business area. Everyone who uses credit in any form is recognizing the benefits of leverage, since their credit purchases—insofar as they result in acquisitions in excess of immediate capital on hand—are all obtained via the leverage route.

The Risk Area Concept

Arguments against speculation in commodities usually seek foundation in the fact that speculators ordinarily put up only a small proportion of the full price of the product represented in the contract. While the point is valid, it has little relationship to the real topic at issue. Earnest money, down payment, or binder in a credit purchase, performs the function of protecting the seller from subsequent default on the part of his buyer. Down payment on equipment, for example, is usually calculated to cover initial depreciation and bridge the gap from "new" to "used" in the event the item must be repossessed on default and resold. So long as the amount of the down payment is adequate to cover this eventuality (and repossession costs), the interests of the seller should be secure.

In buying or selling commodities, the extent of risk involved is not the full price of the commodity, but only the latitudes within which prices may be expected to fluctuate. This, because it may be assumed that wheat, for example, will always have buyers somewhere, at some price level. The only question which remains to be answered—and upon which the amount of margin required must therefore be predicated—is how far prices are likely to move up or down, to the disadvantage of the seller or buyer. As previously pointed out, commodity margins ordinarily represent approximately 10 percent or less from each party to a contract. Past experience is the best evidence that 20 percent of *total price* is quite adequate in view of the scope of risk involved in medium-term price change.

Consider a situation in which on February 1, Speculator A sells 5,000 bushels of July wheat futures to Speculator B at a price of $2.75 per bushel. Cash wheat of contract grade, at the time of the futures transaction, is selling at $2.65 per bushel with the 10 cents differential in price between immediate and July delivery representing partial payment for carrying charges on the grain for some five months.

Since the seller does not own an inventory of wheat when he sells the futures, he clearly expects he will be able to obtain the physical commodity (or equivalent futures) at a lower price than his selling price, sometime during the period between his sale and the delivery date. However, should events in the interim indicate otherwise (should prices move to his disadvantage) he has the constant prerogative of clearing his obligation by buying back an equal amount of the futures that he previously sold. In so doing, he will have offset his short position and taken himself out of the market. His loss will be measurable in the differential between the price at which he sold the futures short and the higher price at which he bought the futures back.

From the point of view of the buyer, his commitment binds him to accept delivery of the physical goods on delivery day and pay for it, or prior thereto to sell an equal amount of wheat futures, offsetting his long position and taking himself out of the market. Should the price of wheat fall after the speculative long has purchased it, the latter alternative is very likely the course of action he will follow. As a speculator, his interest is not in obtaining the physical commodity. He only bought wheat futures in the hope of profiting on price appreciation during his period of ownership.

In the given situation, we have Speculator A who has sold short in the belief that prices will fall, enabling him to buy the commodity or its equivalent at a lower price in the future and thereby realize a profit. On the other side of the transaction, we have Speculator B, who considered the selling price a bargain and so he purchased the futures expecting that prices would rise, permitting him to sell out later and realize a profit.

In appraising buyer and seller risks, it is necessary to first consider the *worst* things that can happen to the interests of each, and later to consider the *probable* limits of disaster that might operate in the given situation. Clearly, the worst thing that could happen to the short seller would be for the prices to *rise* from the selling price of $2.75 per bushel to, let us say, $4.00 per bushel, which would represent an historic high price for contract grade wheat. In such a case, the short stands to lose $1.25 per bushel on his contract. Conversely, the speculative buyer would be equally disadvantaged if March wheat immediately fell to $1.50 per bushel, costing him $1.25 from his earlier purchase price.

Prices Are Limited by Practicalities

While it cannot be said with certainty that such events are impossible, they are most unlikely for several reasons, the most important of which is that regional and world supply/demand equilibrium stands as a virtual bar to such dramatic price changes, except over an extended period of time. While it is conceivable that March wheat could, in a given situation, command a price of $4.00 per bushel or more, several months would likely be involved in reaching such a lofty plateau from a price of $2.75. Each trading session in the period would offer the short an opportunity to close out his position, take his loss, and protect the balance of his speculative capital.

The reverse is equally true—the value of a bushel of wheat in the market could conceivably deteriorate from $2.75 down to $1.50 per bushel. However, a protracted period of time would certainly be required for such a move, and the long who was suffering from the development would have a succession of opportunities to close out his position through offset and thereby shift the risk to someone else at the lower price level.

Daily Price Fluctuation Limits

There is a further protective device for the speculator in commodities which is contained in the trading rules of most exchanges. Prices are only permitted to move a designated interval away from the closing price on the previous day's session. In wheat for example, as this is written, a 20 cent advance or decline from the previous day's close is the maximum allowable fluctuation on the Chicago Board of Trade. If March wheat closes at $2.75 today, it can go no higher than $2.95 tomorrow, and no lower than $2.55. In addition to installing an important safeguard against excessively wide price swings, fluctuation limits serve a further purpose. Rising prices in Chicago attract supplies from outlying areas and with the increase in wheat inventories (attracted by the high prices) fears of shortage are allayed and prices are moderated.

This is not to say that commodity prices hold within narrow ranges. They do not. The 1985 March wheat contract, for example, stood at $3.65 per bushel on May 14, 1984. On May 25, this contract posted an intrasession high of $4.04 per bushel, which represents an increase of 39 cents on a bushel of wheat—but nine trading sessions were required to accomplish the move. The largest single day increase came on May 18, and amounted to 11½ cents. By dividing the total move of 39 cents by the nine-day trading period, the daily average comes out to about 4 cents per bushel. Certainly this is enough to make problems for the disadvantaged shorts, but taken in overall perspective it can hardly be considered a disastrous amount.

Under rules in effect at this writing, both buyers and sellers of wheat futures are required to post minimum margin deposits with their respective brokers of 12 cents per bushel. They must *maintain* a margin of 8 cents per bushel in the contract throughout the period the position remains open. Should prices move against a trading position sufficiently to bring the trading margin below the required maintenance level, it will be remembered, the broker must call for more margin; and unless it is provided, the broker is authorized to liquidate part or all of the impaired position by either purchase or sale.

Thus it will be seen that, barring the most cataclysmic events, a trader's margin is always substantially more than the likely daily trading range on his position. Also, buyers and sellers are always present in the pits, thereby permitting quick offset of an impaired position, usually in a matter of seconds. The possibilities of contract default on the part of the buyer or seller are most unlikely, even if it can't be deemed impossible.

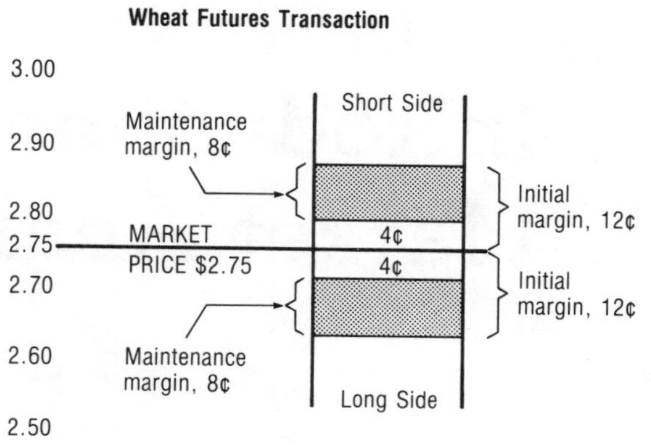

Wheat Futures Transaction

Exhibit 5-1

In posting equivalent margins on a given futures position, both buyer and seller have indemnified the other against default. Commodity margins cover the risk end of prices.

6

Introduction to Market Analysis

It should be noted at the outset that statistical projection affords a method of determining where you are likely to be going, by reexamining where you have been. The greatest weakness in most market analysis concepts is in placing too much reliance on events that are past, and failing to properly appraise new factors which will help shape the future.

Certainly there are cyclical patterns in commodity price behavior, as elsewhere, which repeat themselves with sufficient regularity as to make them valuable as possible projective clues. However, cyclical or seasonal price behavior, when it does develop according to form, does so because fundamental forces of supply and demand, and related market influences, have materialized once more. The speculator must always remember that price levels, like temperature, are merely a measurement of forces operating in the marketplace. Prices, like temperature, rise in response to one set of circumstances and fall in the face of opposite forces.

Although market participants regularly speak of "forecasting price," a more accurate designation would be "forecasting conditions which result in price." To the extent that an individual succeeds in forecasting price, credit must be given to his more or less accurate appraisal of the forces exerting themselves in the market. Price *per se* is not susceptible to direct analysis. Price only takes on objective quality in the light of the market inputs which give rise to it.

In order to examine a price, the trader must always look behind it. He must seek out the positive factors which can be expected to maintain

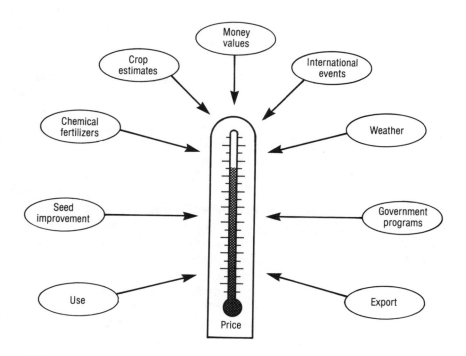

Exhibit 6–1

Price influences include a broad range of natural and human events, some of which are quickly discounted while others may persist.

---

or raise the price; and array against these the negative forces which can be expected to maintain the price or lower it. Prices, like physical bodies, have an inertial factor: in motion, they tend to keep moving; at rest, they tend to stay at rest. The balance is ordinarily a delicate one.

Speculation as Economic Warfare

Market analysis calls for great care in dealing with a long list of pricing components, and requires appraisal of three distinctly different levels of interrelated concern. Speculation can be viewed as a form of economic warfare. In the prosecution of a war, the overall perspective is the so-called "big picture." This level of military decision-making is designated as being the "grand-strategy" function. In actuality it concerns the setting of "policy," to which all subordinate activities are answerable.

The second level of decision making in warfare involves medium-range "field strategy," and permits wide latitudes for exercising initiative; providing doing so does not exceed overall policy restrictions which must govern everything.

At the third level, warfare necessarily requires short-range "tactics"—maneuvering to exploit short-term opportunity—or avoid short-term loss. Tactical decisions are made in the face of small advantages or small threats, and are often calculated to gain only limited objectives. In total, however, proper tactics are vital to the meeting of both strategic and overall policy goals.

To demonstrate the simile in speculation, the policy level relates to the overall market situation in the particular commodity of interest. There are few generalizations that can be applied at any time to several commodities. Strong markets and high prices may prevail in wheat and copper, accompanied by weak markets and low prices on corn and cocoa. Each commodity leads a life of its own. Each must be examined separately. The speculative policy which a trader adopts concerning a selected commodity should be founded on a firm opinion concerning the long-term expectations for the chosen merchandise. This is only the beginning.

It is conceivable that the long-term outlook for a commodity might be overwhelmingly *bullish,* but with the medium-term and short-range prospects being either *bearish, bullish,* or *neutral.*

Take beef, for example: Red meat consumption has increased at a greater than proportional ratio to U.S. population expansion for the last 25 years. This, due to the fact that average beef consumption per person is variable and elastic: a more prosperous America will consume more beef per capita than a less prosperous one. Thus it can be said that if disposable income continues to increase and population also continues to increase, the increase in beef consumption will be a function of these combined factors, pointing to unusually strong demand in good times and less than arithmetic reductions in demand, even in periods of economic slowdown.

In the medium-range consideration, however, beef production and breeder stock may stand at levels which substantially exceed consumption capacity at a given price level. If so, lower prices may be predictable for one, two, or three years into the future. The time period will depend on how long it takes for surplus productive capacity to be brought back into economic correlation with market demand. The medium-range prospects, therefore, could be for *lower prices;* notwithstanding the fact that the long-range trend clearly calls for *higher prices.*

We come now to short-term considerations, and this is the frame of reference within which most commodity trading takes place. Consider a beef situation involving futures contracts for delivery in January, with a position decision to be made the preceding September. It is well known that beef cattle are at less than top form during the winter months. Moreover, the various activities involved in preparing stock for market—penning them, shipping them, and delivering them—present difficulties during the winter which are mitigated or nonexistent during milder weather. As a result, stock raisers tend to reduce their beef shipments during the dead of winter.

With lighter offerings expected in January, the speculator might decide that higher prices would prevail at that particular contract maturity. If so, he might buy January live cattle futures in anticipation of a price rise prompted by smaller offerings some four months hence.

To recapitulate, we have developed a hypothesis in which the long-range cattle projection shows *higher* prices to come based on total population increase and larger per capita consumption. The medium-range data points to *lower* prices based on beef inventories having temporarily outstripped demand at a given price level. The short-term condition is one in which *higher* prices may be expected to develop from reduced offerings in a specific period on the part of beef producers, in turn prompted by a most transitory consideration—weather.

To recast this situation in the language of economic warfare:

1. Our speculative *policy* on cattle is to expect higher prices on the basis of supply/demand fundamentals (i.e., more people, with more money to spend for the meat products of their choice).
2. Our speculative *strategy* recognizes that the lower prices we are seeing is a result of a temporarily oversupplied market (i.e., increased market offerings and a burdensome "inventory" still remaining in the hands of the cattle industry).
3. Our speculative *tactics* anticipate higher beef values in response to the weather-market (i.e., cattle producers and feedlot operators curtail their marketing activities in the winter months).

Similar evaluations must be made in any commodity category before a speculator can hope to make the *right decision* at the *right time*. Prices rarely move in an orderly fashion from one level to another level over extended time intervals. Changes in supply/demand equilibrium—and erroneous decisions on the part of composite trader judgment—have the effect of "overbuying" or "overselling" whatever implications are present. The result is seen in a price graph which, although perhaps reflecting a clear trend upward, downward, or sideways, regularly contains a great many sharp reversals of direction.

Speculative Interval Is Fixed

Futures contracts usually have a trading life of about one year. There is no way the fixed speculative interval on a given contract can be extended. Trading in December grain futures begins in December and terminates in December of the following year. A trader may buy or sell any time on or after the first trading day, but he must deliver in the month of maturity, or offset before. His calculation of profit or loss only relates to price change during the interval he holds his position. The time consideration in a futures can be shortened through offset at any time. It can never be extended. (Contract "life" varies widely among commodity categories.)

This knowledge occasionally prompts otherwise astute individuals to the thought that they can ignore all except relatively short-term considerations. Provided a trader is able to critically develop valid opinions about events which will affect market equilibrium within the life of a given contract, it is fair to say that this is all of the information he will require. The problem is rarely this simple, however. Short-term considerations are closely bound up with the medium-range situation,

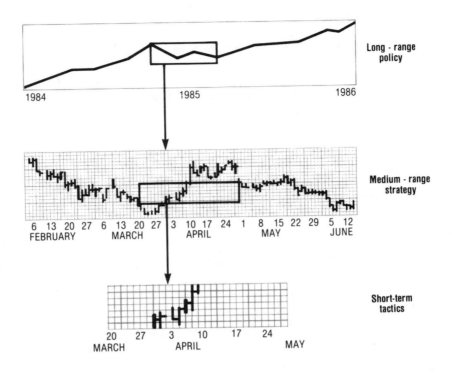

Exhibit 6–2

and this in turn can almost never be viewed sensibly except in the light of a longer-range perspective.

How Much Must You Know?

There is no reliable substitute for doing one's homework on the commodities in which he intends to be active. The more a speculator knows about soybeans, for example, the better the quality of his speculative decisions in soybean futures should be. Nor can the trader's information be limited to price behavior and product usage. He should understand something of the nature of the soybean plant, including its growth season, geographical distribution of the crop, optimum growing temperatures and moisture requirements, climatic extremes which will impede crop development, per acre yields, and production costs. He should also know the end uses to which the products—soybean oil and soybean meal—are put. He should also have some understanding of the other crops (cotton seeds, olives, groundnuts, etc.) that can compete directly with soybeans, as substitute sources of fat and protein for both humans and animals.

The price impact of an unusually small soybean crop will be importantly mitigated if, in the same year, groundnuts, sunflowers, olives, or cotton seeds prove to be in superabundant supply. Soybean oil often represents up to one half of the processed bean in terms of relative value. However, oil is also extracted from all of the aforementioned crops, and can serve as a substitute for soybean oil in the broad spectrum of human usage. If high prices prevail on soybean oil and lower prices prevail on alternative oils, users will buy the lower priced supplies insofar as they are acceptable for their purposes. Consequently the speculator, if he takes a long position in soybean oil purely on the basis of a threatened small bean crop, may have his profit plans upset by outside developments. Substitute crops always deserve consideration in pricing forecasts, but an inexperienced speculator often overlooks these vital factors in favor of giving all of his attention to figures on the single crop in which he intends to establish a position.

International Relationships

Similar risks should be understood in the medium-range also, especially as they grow out of the activities of governments, and exert profound influences on world trade conditions. The marked reduction of trade tariffs and embargoes, which has been a continuing pattern for the past 30 years, has freed up world commerce appreciably, but the situation still falls far short of being an unimpeded world market. The international trade situation merits close and continuing examination.

Wednesday, January 16, 1985

GRAINS AND SOYBEANS: Corn futures prices rose, following new signs of brisk export demand. Wheat and soybean futures also rose. Corn exports for the week ended January 10 totaled 65.1 million bushels, one of the highest weekly export figures on record, analysts said. Despite sluggish foreign demand for other U.S. grains, corn exports have remained strong, largely because of big Soviet purchases. Also, a drought in South Africa, one of the three major corn exporters, may be prompting more importers to turn to the U.S. Wheat also rose, after figures released yesterday showed that wheat supplies suitable for delivery against futures contracts are small. Wheat supplies are ample. But many farmers, frustrated by current prices, have removed their grain from market channels by putting it into government reserve programs instead, holding it off the market until prices rise.

In spite of the fact that most of the corn raised in the U.S. is consumed on the producing farms, as animal feeds, international trade is crucial to maintaining good prices in the domestic market.

This report also points up the role of government loan and price support programs as devices for aiding producers in withholding their supplies from the market. Excessive farmer-holding can result in huge government storage stocks overhanging the market and depressing prices for months or years at a time.

Relationships between nations tend to be stable over appreciable periods of time. Our enemies usually succeed in staying in our bad graces; our friends tend to retain our good will, barring cataclysmic events. Small disagreements between nations usually result in small reprisals, chief among which is reduction in trade. Since the balance between supply and demand is so fine, a difference of two or three percentage points in exports can create havoc in the marketplace. A relatively small adjustment in international trade activity can dislocate supply/demand balance enough to sharply distort price focus in our own domestic market. Moreover, when such steps are taken on the part of governments, reversals in position ordinarily require several months or several years for the point at issue to be forgotten or adjusted through ponderous and slow-moving diplomacy.

Trade balances and competitive situations between nations do change, and each change alters the market equation somewhat. The astute trader must constantly keep an eye on government policy and practice as it bears on international trading. Failure to do so can make him victim of some terrible surprises.

Federal Involvement in Markets

Government machinations must be reckoned with in domestic areas as well. In some countries commodities like coffee, cocoa, crude oil, silver, and gold are produced under strict government regulations and enter the market at statutory prices. Other commodities, including grains, cotton, potatoes, etc., are subject to acreage limitations and covered by loan programs which are calculated to exert controlling influences on total production. Loan rates on regulated commodities are usually adjusted each year. Each adjustment prompts a careful reappraisal in the marketplace in the light of what the new loan, or the new acreage allotments, can be expected to bring in the form of altered output. There is perhaps no more important medium-range influence on the prices of all major commodities than federal policy concerning the production and marketing of them.

Price history in the United States firmly supports the case that government loan rates provide a most effective "floor" under market prices. On the other end of the scale, stockpiles of regulated commodities held by government agencies exert a strong "ceiling" price influence. This latter effect grows out of the fact that sales from government commodity stockpiles are often authorized by law when market prices exceed government accumulation prices by a designated amount or an established percentage. Additionally, the government may sell stockpile commodities in the marketplace at any time when, in the judgment of the appropriate federal agency, they have stocks which are in danger of going out of saleable condition for any reason.

Past events are the clearest indication that decisions to hold or sell stocks held by the Commodity Credit Corporation are often made for the *specific purpose of influencing prices,* either up or down. Such a program, of course, can do either. In the first instance, the government acquires commodities and removes them from the market, which has the effect of raising prices. In the second instance, government reintroduces products into the market and thus forces prices downward.

While the thought of "administered farm prices" is anathema to most people, especially farmers—and is vociferously denied by the bureaucrats who do it—the end result accomplished via the regulated commodity route amounts to about the same thing: As long as our government remains an active participant in pricing, storing, and selling of commodities, the speculator has no choice except to try to read Washington's mind with regard to future plans. He must constantly weigh market decisions in light of federal price policies and degree of market interference discernible on the part of the government.

Scholars have developed innumerable theories, axioms, and more or less stylized explanations for price behavior. While it may be said that the main forces which constitute the price/value equation are quite well understood as separate entities, the interaction of these forces—which results in price—still presents an enigma of the first order. There is no substitute for extensive training in economics and statistics for the individual who hopes to become a professional market analyst. Price elasticity, price-value theory, marginal-return concepts and Thorstein Veblen's doctrine of conspicuous consumption all figure in the problem, along with ideas propounded by Adam Smith, Malthus, Keynes, Holbrook Working, Milton Friedman and many others.

Expert Speculators Need Not Be Experts

Familiarity with the full range of economic dogma is not necessary for successful speculation, however. On the contrary it appears, embarrassingly enough, that the best economists are perhaps the worst speculators. The reason may lie in the fact that it is possible to have so much information about peripheral influences that a clear-cut decision cannot be made. In the short-term scheme of things, there is no opportunity to carefully appraise all the facts and conditions which bear on the issue, even if one were technically competent to do so.

Reduced to its simplistic essentials, a commodity market approximates a giant computer which accepts only two kinds of inputs: positive and negative. The positive input is a *buy order,* the negative input, a *sell order.* So long as positive and negative influences are equal, prices neither rise nor fall; they remain stable. When positive inputs exceed negative inputs, prices rise. In the reverse situation, they decline.

We may totally disregard the reasons which underlie orders to buy or sell a given commodity at a given time. Only the order itself has the slightest pertinence to the matter of price equilibrium. Some critics of the free market seize on this fact as proof that the establishment of prices through unfettered bids and offers results in random price determination. The usual supportive argument hinges on the *quality* of trade decisions. Let's examine the case.

Quality of Trading Decisions

An order to buy 100,000 bushels of corn, when placed by a processor, is probably prompted by operating requirements. A corn processor must have corn in order to stay in business. Hence, his buying decision is founded on a practical requirement.

On the other side of the trade, we may find a speculator who is selling 100,000 bushels of corn short purely out of a profit motive, and for no other reason except that he thinks prices are due to fall. In this example, the practical decision of a corn processor to buy is matched in the marketplace by the speculative decision of a trader to sell. It is the price case of those who argue along this line that the decision of the commercial processor deserves greater weight than the action of the speculator, because the processor's activity has a firmer foundation in reality.

Interesting though the hypothesis appears to be, the market is not equipped to deal with secondary considerations. One party elected to buy and one party elected to sell. One decision may be wise, the other foolish. The market does not qualitatively evaluate either motive or wisdom. It measures supply and demand pressures as represented in orders to acquire or dispose of specific property. The resulting balance is then translated into a price. The more desirable or necessary a commodity, and the greater its relative shortage, the higher the price it will bring from those who have none and want some, or who have some and want more. Overabundance is measured in lower prices: The larger the surplus of a traded commodity one has, the lower the price he will accept for the first unit of the surplus. As his excess dwindles, his urge to unload diminishes and the price at which he is willing to sell correspondingly tends to increase.

These are the basic considerations present in price fluctuations, and while they may be set forth in far more extensive and more professional language, for our present purpose the foregoing will suffice. The more critical the buyer's need, the higher price he should be willing to pay. The more urgently a seller wants to dispose of an overabundance of property, the lower the price he will likely accept. The market accepts orders to sell and to buy, weighs them against each other at a given time, and strikes a composite balance which is the "current quotation." Note that current quotation is not necessarily the same as "valid price."

Valid Price Theory

In order to be theoretically valid, a price must be one below which the seller would not sell, and above which the buyer would not buy. Commodity trading involves open-outcry which is, in effect, an auction. The market accepts "market orders" which authorize a broker to buy or sell at whatever price then prevails. It goes without saying that sellers who enter market orders occasionally get higher prices than they expect.

Buyers, it follows, occasionally acquire merchandise at prices lower than they expect to pay. Hence, "pit prices" in a commodity market cannot always be subjectively defended on the basis of their theoretical validity, but there is no gainsaying the fact that all buyers want to buy, and all sellers want to sell.

To some extent, both buyers and sellers may elect to accept the judgement of the market in establishing the price level at which their wishes are realized. From a practical point of view, composite market judgment as to relative values must be generally viewed as far more dependable than individual opinion on the part of any single trader.

7

Analyzing the
Long-Term
Market Situation

Developing a long-range opinion about a commodity calls for close appraisal of many fundamental factors which have direct or indirect influence on the adequacy of supplies. Long-term analysis of a selected commodity situation always seeks to discover which of the three following conditions prevails:

1. Demand is tending to outstrip supply (and prices will therefore go *higher*).
2. Demand and supply are in close balance (and prices may be expected to *fluctuate* in reasonably close ranges).
3. Supply is tending to outgrow demand (and *lower prices* can be expected to result).

Only three possibilities exist concerning price behavior—they will *increase, fluctuate* in a range, or *decrease.*

In the absence of statutory restrictions which may be imposed through price regulation or other governmental edict, prices will always fluctuate. The range of price movement may be wide or narrow, but some degree of change is a certainty.

For the purpose of demonstrating long-range commodity analysis techniques, we will confine our attention to wheat. The selection is made for several excellent reasons. First of all, this major grain crop is produced in some quantity over most of the world. While the quality of the crop varies from region to region, and the types of wheat grown in various localities represent a wide range of species, almost full interchangeability exists. Soft wheat is preferred for some uses, and hard wheat preferred for others; but if one type is not available another type can, to some degree of effectiveness, suffice. In addition to being almost universally produced, wheat is consumed throughout the world. Some civilizations rely more heavily on wheat than on any other cereal grain, others put rice in the first order of importance. But man is, to some extent, a wheat eater—regardless of where you find him.

World Market for Wheat

World trade in wheat is greater than in any other comparable foodstuff. Annual yields vary significantly from year to year in given localities, but world production of wheat presents a quite consistent picture over-all. Since 1950, total production has increased by 75 percent, due largely to improved fertilizers, better seed and more efficient machinery.

Nearly half of the world's wheat production comes from only three countries: Russia—22 percent; United States—15 percent; China—12 percent. India, Canada, France, Australia, and Argentina complete the roster of major wheat producing countries. India, Russia, and China, in spite of being large producers of the grain, still must import extensively to meet their total requirements. In recent years the United States and Canada have provided about two thirds of all world wheat exports.

Like other agricultural crops, optimal harvests depend on ideal temperature and moisture conditions along with proper crop management including fertilizers, pest controls, and harvest methods. The Western world has developed a superior technology of wheat raising, but without the cooperation of nature, disappointing yields still occasionally occur. Thus it is that in any given year, relatively larger crops may be produced in so-called backward nations, and these may be accompanied by subnormal crops in the more advanced nations. When this happens, a reduction in the volume of international wheat trading naturally occurs. In the first instance, the wheat deficit areas are better supplied by their own improved yield and therefore require less outside shipments. At the same time, the wheat surplus areas, due to a disappointing harvest, have less of the grain to offer in the world market.

World Prices

There is a further and most important consideration in the international trade analysis: A world wheat price is negotiated at intervals as situations require. The parties to the International Wheat Agreement include, but are not limited to, the United States, Canada, the Common Market nations, Great Britain, Russia, Japan, Australia, New Zealand, some of the South American countries, and several African governments. Discussions between these wheat-surplus and wheat-deficit nations give rise to a world price which is in practical effect, a "pegged price" for trading between the governments involved. At this writing, the hard red winter wheat price is about $3.30 per bushel in so-called hard currency. Other grades are priced from this base. When U.S. market prices exceed this world price, in order for domestic wheat to move abroad, the federal government must subsidize the export activity to the extent of whatever differential may be present. With the world price at $3.30 per bushel and the U.S. market price at $3.50 per bushel, for example, sale of wheat in the export market would involve a 20 cent federal subsidy to the selling interest in order to put the foreign transaction on a par with domestic sales.

The reasoning behind export subsidies of this kind deserves to be at least generally understood. Treaty relationships with friendly nations often involve firm or implied commitments to augment their food supplies. In order to make grain move overseas, the seller must be able to realize at least as much for the product in export as he would in domestic trade. The only way this can be done is for the government to absorb a certain portion of the cost of the grain and charge it up to foreign aid, international assistance, Food for Peace, etc. To the extent that exports are subsidized, the process is one of maintaining an artificial world price on the commodity in question.

In evaluating the overall world wheat situation, it is important to be aware of the world wheat price and its relationship to probable effective free market prices, in the United States and Canada particularly. Should domestic prices exceed the world price by too large a differential, the U.S. government might be reticent to absorb the heavy subsidy involved in moving large quantities of wheat into foreign channels. As pointed out previously, if export activity is curtailed appreciably as a result of price disparities or otherwise, the excess supplies which accrue can have great influence on free-market prices and can contribute to accumulation of surplus grain inventories that may take years to work off.

U.S. Farmers Plant 9 Percent Fewer Acres for Winter Wheat

By Albert R. Karr
Staff Reporter of The Wall Street Journal

WASHINGTON—Farmers planted 57.6 million acres of winter wheat for next year's harvest, 9 percent less than last year's seeding of 63.4 million acres and the lowest in six years, the Agriculture Department said.

The decline was sharper than analysts had predicted; they had estimated that the wheat planting would drop 6.7 percent or less from last year. Planting was lowered by wet weather in the Corn Belt and Mississippi Delta, and apparently by increased participation in the government's crop-reduction program, according to analysts in and out of the department.

Winter wheat accounts for about 75 percent of all U.S. wheat production. It is planted in the fall for harvest the following spring and summer.

Separately, the department estimated the December 1 inventory of the nation's hogs and pigs was 54 million head, 5 percent less than the total

December 1, 1983. Breeding stock held back from slaughter fell to 6.9 million, 6 percent less than a year ago. The decline from a year earlier was somewhat steeper than that reported as of September 1, indicating that farmers are continuing to reduce their hog herds, instead of starting to rebuild them as livestock analysts had expected.

Farmers had an inventory of hogs scheduled for market of 47.1 million head December 1, or 4 percent less than a year ago, the department said. The 1984 crop of pigs was 86.5 million head, 7 percent below 1983. And 5.9 million sows farrowed during the period of June through November, down 5 percent from a year earlier.

In Chicago, analysts said the report is likely to boost hog futures because it showed a smaller breeding herd than analysts and traders had anticipated.

The 57.6 million acres of winter wheat planted this fall was the lowest total since 51.8 million acres were planted for the 1979 harvest, the Agriculture Department said. But the 1985 winter-wheat crop isn't likely to fall as much from 1984 as the 9 percent drop in seedings from a year ago, grain analysts suggested. They said that wheat per-acre yields will probably resume year-to-year gains, after easing slightly this year from their 1983 highs.

Production of all types of wheat in 1984 was estimated by the department at 2.6 billion bushels, up 7 percent from 1983.

A department analyst estimated that about two thirds of the 5.8 million-acre decline in winter-wheat plantings this fall was attributable to more growers deciding to sign up for cutbacks.

Farmers must idle at least 20 percent of their wheatland to qualify for federal wheat price supports. Under legislation enacted by Congress last spring, they can also get cash payments for idling an additional 10 percent of the acreage for the 1985 harvest. And under a decision by Agriculture Secretary John Block, wheat growers get half of those cash acreage "diversion" payments and 50 percent of the price-support "deficiency" payments in advance—soon after they sign up for the 1985 program.

Price-deficiency payments are made to make up the difference between crop market prices and usually higher "target" prices set by law. The wheat target price for 1985 is $4.38 a bushel, and the market price for the crop year ending next May 31 could settle as low as $3.35 a bushel, down from the preceding year's average of $3.54, the department predicted.

In Chicago, grain analysts called the report a "bullish surprise," noting that the government's estimate of plantings was significantly below even the lowest trade estimate. They predicted that wheat futures on the Chicago Board of Trade and the Kansas City Board of Trade will open several cents a bushel higher today, with contracts for delivery after March registering the largest gains.

Late yesterday, the Agriculture Department said private grain merchants had reported that China canceled purchases of 108,200 metric tons of wheat. That will probably lead to selling of wheat contracts for near-term delivery, limiting the price gains in those contracts, analysts said.

Each year offers a new problem in balancing supplies with demand. It's a dynamic equation, with farmers, processors, exporters, and importers constantly revising their activities in light of altering balances. Price is the readout in the unending efforts to ration and distribute the world's commodity wealth.

From a purely domestic point of view, there is another area of function which can exert great influence on price viability. The United

States, through the Department of Agriculture, carries out a spate of programs related to acreage control, price supports, and commodity stockpiling, which exert important restrictions on the matter of supply. Through the so-called land bank program, agricultural acreage is taken out, or brought into production in light of projected needs for the affected crops. Price supports are extended through the vehicle of crop loans which insure the participating producer of a minimum price for his output. Excess supplies which find no higher bids than "the loan" in the free market are accumulated by the Commodity Credit Corporation (CCC), and held in storage against future needs.

Attitudes vary as to what constitutes an adequate stockpile of wheat in the United States, but 600 million bushels represents some kind of a useful consensus. When stockpiles exceed this amount, their existence may constitute a costly burden from the standpoint of both lending outlays and physical storage requirements. When stocks are less than this, the possibility exists that a disappointing harvest could face the nation with some real shortages in this vital food supply.

The impact on prices is clear: When excessive stocks are in CCC control, the possibility always exists that the administrators may release large quantities into the market and peremptorily drive prices down. When stockpiles are inadequate, the reverse effect is seen in rapidly rising prices and persistent fears as to the adequacy of supplies to historic needs. It can be noted that, as long as a loan rate is in force and a stockpile of wheat exists, the former tends to represent a floor under which prices are not likely to fall by very much. Stockpiles impose a ceiling of sorts, since the holdings can be used to depress prices, should they exceed the government opinion of what constitutes reasonable levels.

Finally, it must be remembered that orderly pricing presumes an orderly flow of supplies. Any constriction in the distributive chain can produce temporary or protracted shortage in the first instance; and this condition will often be followed by a temporary or continuing surplus when the immobilized stocks finally begin to reach the market in volume.

Farmer Holding

Recent years have reflected a phenomenon that deserves particular attention. Whereas the historic pattern has been for the grain producers to raise their crop, harvest it, and sell it almost immediately, we have seen noteable departures from this pattern in the past 20 years in particular.

In both 1965 and 1966, and subsequently, postharvest periods have often been marked by major holding actions on the part of farmers.

Instead of selling their wheat in the weeks immediately following harvest, a considerable proportion of wheat growers have placed their crop in storage—on the farm or elsewhere—and held out for higher prices which they confidently expected would result from meager offerings. Subsequent events may validate their judgment. Producers who hold their inventories may obtain better prices later on. With an occasional success to encourage them, it must be expected that farmer holding will continue to occur from time to time. Hence, the speculator must understand its price effect.

While the first effect of a farmer holding movement may likely result in *higher* prices, if their holding persists too long, the second effect may be *lower* prices.

The reason should be apparent. If wheat is held out of trade channels for a few months following harvest, export and other trade activities will be significantly reduced as a direct reflection of the contrived shortage—and proportionately higher prices on the commodity. When stocks are finally released by the holders, time may not remain—and the market situation may not permit—total recoupment of business which was lost during the preceding period. Optimal consumption of any commodity usually requires more or less *consistent flow*. If the material involved is unavailable for any reason over a period of time, substitutes must be found and, once found, will have irretrievably displaced a certain amount of the demand for the preferred product. People only eat fixed amounts, at designated intervals. Yesterday's meals were all eaten *yesterday!*

In a free market, price is expected to ration available supplies into areas of demand which represent the highest relative priorities; most urgent uses being filled first (at the higher prices) and less vital needs being filled later (at lower prices). Holding a commodity out of the market is a far different thing than offering the commodity at a higher price. When availability of a commodity is largely or totally denied to potential users of it, higher prices may be expected to result, but the quantity of trading to which the higher prices apply is reduced. Consumption or disappearance of the withheld product will inescapably be *reduced in total amount,* as well as within the period during which the contrived shortage or absence of the item persists. Thus, while buyers may be willing to pay a large premium for the product in the short term, substitute merchandise and alternative sources for it will predictably over the long term effect a correction through market displacement.

The willingness and ability of primary producers to hold commodity stocks out of the market has already been noted in connection with wheat. Opinions vary as to whether such a practice has a composite long-term effect of raising or lowering average prices for the products involved. Actually, results may be expected to vary from year to year, depending on other considerations. Withholding of wheat on the part of American producers might prove effective from the farmer's point of view if supplies in other parts of the world were only adequate, or less.

If other wheat producing nations, notably Canada and Russia, have succeeded in raising bumper crops, however, the wheat deficit nations would probably exercise the buyer's prerogative of finding alternative sources—and lower prices—for the product they require. U.S. wheat producers would, in this situation, perhaps get a somewhat higher price for the portion of their output which they succeed in selling in domestic channels, but a sizeable proportion of the total crop would not be locally salable, since we must rely on exports as an important factor in crop disappearance, year in and year out.

Thus, while receiving higher prices on the portion of the crop which found domestic purchasers, this initial benefit could be more than offset by inability to move the *entire* crop, bringing a lower *total* return for the aggregate harvest.

International Competition

A dramatic demonstration of the ongoing conflict in the world market for foodstuffs is shaping up in the first month of 1985. In spite of government programs designed to curtail wheat production, American farmers still raised 2.6 billion bushels of it in 1984, which was 7 percent ahead of the previous year. This proved to be an excessive amount, insofar as it kept market prices at levels that the farmers found unattractive. The first effect of farmer dissatisfaction with price in any given year is a reduction in that particular crop in the following year. Thus we see that 9 percent fewer acres will be planted to wheat in 1985 than in 1984. In the meantime, however, there are other problems.

Cargill Set to Import Wheat; Some Believe Move Is Political Ploy

BY WENDY L. WALL
Staff Reporter of The Wall Street Journal

CHICAGO—In an apparent attempt to pressure U.S. lawmakers into changing farm policy, Cargill Inc., the world's largest grain merchant, is preparing to ship to the U.S. the first Argentine wheat ever imported into this country.

The move by the Minneapolis-based company has raised the ire of farm groups in the U.S. It is seen by many as a political step designed to pressure farm-state congressmen, who may oppose proposed reductions in farm-price supports that traders say curb U.S. grain exports.

The strong U.S. dollar, global recession, and fierce competition from other exporting nations, particularly Argentina, have led to a four-year decline in U.S. grain-export volume. Farm-policy critics also contend that U.S. price supports enable other producing nations to undercut U.S. prices easily.

"Cargill may be trying to make a point," said Steve Nutt, grain analyst in Chicago for Cargill Investor Services Inc., a unit of the grain merchant. "The idea of importing Argentine wheat into the bread-basket of the world tells you there's some economic problem here," added Mr. Nutt, who wasn't speaking for Cargill.

The company said it has purchased 25,000 metric tons of Argentine wheat, which it intends to ship this week for sale to U.S. millers in coastal regions. The wheat competes with the hard red winter wheat grown by U.S. farmers.

Cargill said world market conditions make the transaction profitable despite shipping fees, export taxes and import duties. Trade sources said Argentine wheat is selling for roughly $112 a ton, compared with about $150 a ton for U.S. wheat at Gulf locations.

However, a company spokesman said, "The real significance of this event is less that wheat is being imported, but that it's economically feasible to do so."

Analysts and trade sources speculated that Cargill's prime motivation is political. In the current debate over 1985 farm legislation, Cargill has argued that existing policies keep U.S. wheat prices artificially high, and the company has been pushing for a bill like that favored by the Reagan administration.

The plan currently being considered by the administration would sharply reduce crop loans. However, it is expected to meet substantial opposition from some congressmen and groups concerned about the already severe financial plight of many farmers.

Cargill's import decision is "a dangerous precedent," said Howard Tice, executive director of the Kansas Association of Wheatgrowers. "They're using imported wheat to compete against American farmers in America."

However, Margie Williams, director of government affairs for the North American Wheatgrowers Association, added that the move supports the organization's contention that the strong dollar is one of the biggest problems plaguing U.S. farmers.

The U.S. idea of the "right" price for wheat, as given force and effect in federal loan programs, stockpiling activities, etc., is at great variance with the prices found in the rest of the world. Not only do our competitors turn out wheat for less per bushel, but the relative strength of the American dollar in comparison to other currencies imposes further economic hurdles in the path of much-needed export activities.

The threat by Cargill to import Argentine wheat into the United States was later put aside in the interests of farm and public relations, but the decision not to go through with it was social, rather than economic. Argentine wheat is at this writing available at about $3.30 per bushel to anyone who wants to buy it. The U.S. target price for wheat in 1984 was $4.45 per bushel, and the Commodity Credit Corporation would not release its stored stocks into the market until the farmers were receiving $4.65 for the hard red winter type. Translating this into the international market situation, in order for our wheat to compete with the same product grown in Argentina (or in other localities), an export subsidy on the order of $1.10 per bushel must be picked up through one of our various foreign aid programs, and charged back to the American taxpayer. Unless our excess wheat is exported, under present farm policy it is put under government loan, at $4.00 per bushel, and the farmer is paid another 26½ cents per bushel to store it. All of this might make for good politics, but it is atrocious economics.

Wheat is an "international" product. In order for us to continue to be a major world supplier of the grain, our output must be able to flow competitively into the channels of global trade. Failing this, we will have no choice in the long run but to curtail production to meet our own domestic needs—and some modest excess for international charity and trading with allies who are willing to overlook the price disparities.

One thing is absolutely certain: The United States cannot continue, through politically oriented farm programs of various kinds, to turn out vast surpluses of overpriced wheat and other farm products—and then use federal subsidies to make this excess salable in the world market.

Perhaps Cargill will not import Argentine wheat into the United States *this* year or next. But if the price disparity continues, the time will come when foreign wheat will come our way—just as foreign cars, cameras, and steel have. There is a practical point where even as affluent a nation as ours must cease trying to outlaw market reality via contrived controls and monetary support for uneconomic activities.

Nations May Contrive Shortages

Producers are not the only interests who may engage in withholding actions. Nations are often involved in attempts to contrive scarcities in commodities which represent important segments of their export trade. Central and South American coffee offers an excellent case in point. In an attempt to maintain attractive producer prices on this popular beverage, Colombia, Honduras, Nicaragua, Brazil, and other western hemisphere coffee producing countries have created what amounts to an international cartel in the commodity. Through negotiative process they assign annual export quotas to each national participant in the group, establish minimum prices in world commerce, and impose other trading requirements. The same practices mark world trade in sugar, cocoa, cotton, spices, and crude oil.

Domestically, similar activities take place in connection with so-called market orders. In citrus fruits, as a case in point, market orders are developed cooperatively by the U.S. Department of Agriculture and the citrus producers. An individual farmer may put his crop "under the order" or not, as he sees fit. If he accepts the market order conditions, however, he can expect to receive a certain minimum price for a fixed proportion of his crop. Prices, of course, may still range widely, depending on current and projected supplies and demand for the product. However, if harvest yield is expected to exceed demand, the market order may require deliberate destruction of part of the fruit prior to picking. This is sometimes designated "frost drop."

Planned Crop Destruction

If the market order calls for a 15 percent frost-drop on oranges, then the orange growers who put their production under the program must go into their groves and shake an estimated 15 percent of the fruit off of the trees. Failure to do so is a violation of the market order, and such noncompliance deprives the orange grower of his guaranteed market price. He will, in effect, be left at the mercy of the free market. Depending on the price situation, he may either prosper or suffer from his refusal to conform.

Production controls are established by governments over a wide range of commodities. Since price is a function of supply and demand in a free market economy, and since both political and private manipulations affect price, the speculator must always make his appraisals in the light of whatever restrictions may be placed on output at the source. The results are the same, whether occasioned by actions in concert on the part of the producers, or through the device of government edict.

The more volatile the overall situation is, the more difficult it may be to develop firm appraisals, and the greater the risk inherent in speculation in commodities which are actually or potentially susceptible to federal manipulation. It should be added that governments have a long, but not particularly brilliant record in their efforts to "manage" economic forces.

To sum up, whether a trader is attempting to develop a long-term opinion about the situation in grain, metals, or fiber, his first equation will probably have to be worldwide in scope. "No man is an island," and there are few places where Donne's statement is as valid as it is in commodity marketing.

Improvement in transport technology and ever increasing recognition of the interdependence of nations in feeding their populations have brought almost incredible increases in the volume of world trade. There is no reason to expect that the trend will not continue, escalating at an even faster pace in the future.

Politics and World Trade

Ideological alignments tend to segregate buyers and sellers to some degree. The United States, as a case in point, does not, at this writing, trade with Cuba nor with Libya. However, our allies do. It is by no means inconceivable that American agricultural products exported to Great Britain could, in some subsequent transaction, be physically included in food shipments which Britain or China makes to our avowed enemies. We could, therefore, be a supplier of commodities to these Communist nations through the trade activities of a middleman.

General opinion seems to view trade in foodstuffs and other nonmilitary commodities as meriting a different set of ground rules than business in steel, copper, uranium, and related items, which constitute the raw stuff of armaments. A long-term viewpoint must contemplate a steady, perhaps slow, but inexorable move toward free trading around this globe. The accomplishment may take a decade, a generation, or a century for total accomplishment. Once it arrives, however, speculation in commodities will be a much simpler thing, if for no other reason than the fact that price differentials will then theoretically grow directly and exclusively out of locational differences and the realities of original production costs, handling, and transportation between points.

As it now stands, a good deal of speculator time must be devoted to the frustrating and well-nigh impossible task of trying to read administrative minds and translate obscure and transitory official attitudes into pragmatic price inputs. In spite of the level of sophistication to which economics has come, the state of the art will probably always fall short of being able to fully meet this kind of challenge.

8

Analyzing the Medium-Range Market Situation

For purposes of this discussion, we will view the medium-range time segment as being one year or less. The reasons for doing so appear compelling. First and foremost, agricultural crops—which underpin much of the total speculation in futures contracts—are produced seasonally, within a 12-month period wherever they appear. Mining activities have greater overall continuity, but even here established practices in doing business, preparing tax reports, and scheduling market activities, suggest the use of a 12-month calendar for speculative appraisals.

Certain crops reflect longer periods of time from beginning to end, but these can most effectively be dealt with as exceptions to the rule. Beef offers a case in point. The production cycle in the "red meat" commodity extends over a period of some three years; this being the approximate time required to bring a calf to breeding maturity and produce an offspring for slaughter. As a consequence, fluctuations in breeder-stock populations tend to separate themselves statistically over something like a 36-month time span. Biological considerations impose the minimum limitation, although collateral activities on the part of stock raisers may lengthen the intervals between the peaks and valleys in the graph.

This second level of consideration in speculation has been identified previously as "strategy." It has also been pointed out that while this level of strategic, or medium-range appraisal, may be consistent—or in diametric conflict—with long-term projections, strategy must be cast in a frame of reference which gives proper consideration to the long-term trend of things. Failure to do so will put the entire speculative program in needless jeopardy. The reasons for this will become apparent as the topic is developed.

History Provides a Base

Comprehensive evaluation of a commodity market situation must begin somewhere. There seems to be no better foundation for developing a trading hypothesis than to take available figures from the past as the best available evidence of how things have been. With this data in hand, current information can be arrayed against the historic pattern, and a future projection developed.

For the purpose of this discussion, soybeans have been selected for the following reasons: First, the crop is in a distinctly upward long-term trend, with respect to both production volume and consumption usage. In spite of this, the medium-range—year by year—soybean situation offers a complex and highly interesting study in balancing the changing forces of supply and demand. Soybeans are not extensively cultivated throughout the world. However, there are several substitute crops which are grown in quantity over broad areas of the earth, and which provide other sources for cooking oil and protein materials such as those obtained from soybeans.

In terms of our domestic situation, processing capacity has by no means kept pace with crop production. U.S. producers harvested a crop of about 600 million bushels of soybeans in 1962. However, only 472 million bushels of soybeans were crushed in American factories in 1962. With a soybean crop of 2 billion bushels in 1984, U.S. "crush" capacity is estimated at about half that. Clearly, we have no choice but to export a huge and growing proportion of the crop.

Soybean exports are growing at a phenomenal pace. In 1954, 60.6 million bushels of soybeans were exported. In 1964—10 years later— the export total had reached 205.9 million. In 1983 the figure was up to three times that. In terms of percentages, about 17 percent of the 1954 crop went to foreign buyers; in 1964, exporters took more than 26 percent of our total crop of 769.2 million bushels.

In 1983, we exported over three fourths of our soybeans to foreign customers. Viewed in this light, the tremendous importance of foreign trade in commodities becomes apparent. In appraising each crop year, the speculator must not only carefully weigh domestic demands for the products and available storage and/or crushing capacity, but he must also develop a useful opinion as to probable outmovement to foreign shores. Unless both channels of usage maintain their past levels of performance and continue to grow proportionately to the increase in harvest yields, oversupply and depressed prices could be a suddenly developing result.

Crop Report Price Impact

As the first edition of this book was being written, indications were that the 1967 soybean harvest would amount to about 1 billion bushels.

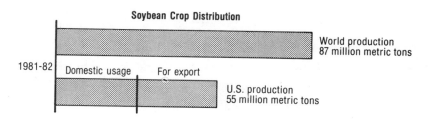

Soybean Crop Distribution

1981-82

World production
87 million metric tons

Domestic usage   For export

U.S. production
55 million metric tons

Exhibit 8–1

The U.S. raises almost two thirds of the world's soybeans, with more than half of the crop exported in 1983. Relative prices exert important influence on crop size, since the same land that produces soybeans can also raise corn and cotton.

In 1966, the harvest had come to some 930 million bushels. The 1966 figure represented about 84 million bushels more than 1965 crop, and furthermore reflected approximately 69 million bushels increase over the USDA estimate made on March 1, 1966. (According to official USDA figures, 36 million acres of land were expected to be planted to soybeans for harvest as beans in 1966. Applying an average yield of 24 bushels per acre, the figure of 864 million bushels arose.)

The initial impact of this projection was to send new crop soybean futures well over $3.00 per bushel, since the trade doubted seriously that the crop estimate would be adequate to meet historic needs. As the year progressed, dry weather added further pressure to already unusually high prices. The market clearly turned into an overbought situation. Then, in the September 1, 1966, crop report, the USDA revised its previous estimate upward by about 100 million bushels. The effect on prices was devastating. From a close of $3.27 on November soybean futures which was posted September 9, 1966, prices dropped 20 cents in the next two sessions and drifted on down to an intraday low of $2.87½ on October 11.

This price behavior is cited to demonstrate the fine balance which exists between supply and demand in a crop which demonstrates close historical equilibrium. Speculators who held short positions in anticipation of a dramatically increased harvest profited handsomely. Those who stayed long, expecting the more modest previous crop forecast to be confirmed in the September estimate, suffered monumental losses.

After release of the USDA estimate, the market seethed with protests that the figure was unrealistically high; but valid or not, prices moved in response to the new projection—and profits or losses depend exclusively on price movements. All information which affects prices is not, and need not be, valid. A rapid-breaking and totally unfounded rumor can register its presence in the marketplace and occasion broad swings in prices, until it is ultimately laid to rest by more substantial facts. In the meantime, however, the price movements are exceedingly real, whether or not the thing which occasions the move is subjectively true. Also, the less "news" there is in the market at any given point, the more responsive it is likely to be to anything which appears to alter supply/demand perspective.

Considerations of the sort noted above have their primary impact in the short-range, or tactical scheme of things. However, they have a medium-range impact insofar as they help establish the overall market tone of a given commodity, as being "bearish" or "bullish."

War and Peace

International relationships are another most important consideration in the medium-range price situation. The United States has deliberately or unwittingly taken the position of being the food warehouse for much of the world. Involvement in "cold war" and armed conflict has, for the past 40 years, involved us in furnishing vast amounts of commodities to friendly nations who align themselves with our policy positions. Cessation of hostilities has almost invariably brought peace arrangements which include feeding our erstwhile enemies. As a consequence it might be generally said that international tensions are bullish, with respect to food commodities; armed conflict even more so. Peace, regrettably enough, must be broadly viewed as bringing lower commodity prices in the first instance, and somewhat higher prices later on, as food exportation to the vanquished enemy gets underway.

Commodity Glamour Girls

Glamour is a word well understood in connection with movie stars and stocks, but it is less frequently heard in connection with commodities; still, there are glamour commodities. It is difficult to identify the forces which bring a particular commodity to the wide attention of the public, but once this has happened, the "fan club" demonstrates amazing loyalty. Wheat, cocoa, and pork bellies are currently enjoying widespread public interest and speculative participation. Corn shows some indications of dropping out of the group. Medium-term trading considerations must give careful attention to the amount of public interest in the commodity category. There are several characteristics which can be expected to arise from broad public speculation, which grow directly out of the fact that most of these public buyers and sellers have little continuing market interest, or market information, and are only occasional speculators.

The Public Will Be Long

Of all the behaviorisms which can be ascribed to the public, its tendency to be long rather than short is the most pronounced. The novice speculator always seems to prefer buying something to selling it. It may be that optimism about rising prices is a universal trait (or—in view of inflationary history—resignation to a recurrent fact). Whatever the underlying cause, large public interest in a commodity contract will usually show the public to be long—and the commercial hedgers and professional speculators to be short.

It is also demonstrable truth that the public is wrong in their market judgment *most* of the time. This is evidenced by the fact that about three fourths of all occasional speculators lose money rather than make it. Losing money grows out of occupying the wrong position, or improperly managing the position; both arise from bad decisions. However, setting forth the *average* public speculator experience does not automatically guarantee that the public will *always* be wrong—nor wrong in a given situation.

In the soybean developments outlined earlier, the public was overwhelmingly short. They held the *right* position. Soybean prices advanced sharply in the session preceding release of the government's increased harvest figure. A great many public traders were "stopped out" of the market by the sudden price increase, which turned into a classical "short squeeze." However, those who had the funds and the courage to hold their short positions were richly rewarded when the crop figure was finally learned.

Weather Makes Price

Of all of the tactical considerations in speculation, weather is perhaps one of the most important. In connection with growing crops, obtaining even an average harvest directly depends on the right combination of temperature and moisture, along with relative freedom from insects and plant diseases, which can strike suddenly and with devastating results.

Each crop has its own climatic requirements and, generally speaking, the areas in which the crop is produced reflect the environmental conditions necessary to good production. It must be constantly borne in mind, however, that the weather characteristics in any given locality are usually stated in terms of statistical composites or averages. Averages, in turn, grow out of *all* pertinent data including extremes; and extremes ruin crops.

Too much moisture will delay planting, since farm equipment cannot be operated in wet fields; nor can harvesting be undertaken unless the ground is firm enough to support reaping machines. Likewise, excessively dry conditions make planting a crop futile since, unless moisture is adequate to produce germination, nothing will grow.

Plant characteristics vary widely, with respect to moisture and temperature conditions required during the growth period. Winter wheat, for example, produces maximum yields when the seed grain is planted in soil containing 15 to 18 percent moisture. Once the seed is germinated and "stooled", lesser amounts of moisture will induce adequate growth so long as soil moisture does not drop below 9 percent. Once the crop has made its full structural growth, two or three weeks of temperatures in the 80° to 100° F. range aids in firming the kernels and maturing the crop. It is also helpful if the relative humidities which accompany such temperatures are below 50 percent, since this will reduce the moisture content in the maturing grain, and improve its grade characteristics. Excessively high temperatures will, of course, dehydrate the young, growing wheat plants and "burn up" the crop. Constant rain will retard wheat growth and support heavy infestations of weeds in the fields. Hail can knock a wheat stand down, making it impossible to harvest with conventional equipment. Abnormally high humidity accompanied by lower than average temperatures encourages infestations of wheat rust and other forms of disease.

Soybeans present quite a different picture as concerns crop hazards. It is said that if you are going to destroy a soybean crop, you must do it in August. Once soybean plants are established, they will survive wide extremes of unfavorable temperature and moisture, and still produce quite a good yield—provided the weather challenge is not too serious during the month of August. It is at this point in the growth cycle (in the Midwest) that soybeans are setting on blooms which will determine the number of pods per plant. If temperatures are high and moisture is inadequate, the bloom is correspondingly light and yields are reduced proportionately. Since soybeans are a "photoperiodic" plant with blossom development geared closely to a designated period in the life cycle, there is no second chance. Unless the crop can set its blossoms in or around the August period, the subsequent harvest is doomed.

Similar restrictions exist to greater or lesser degrees for each of the agricultural commodities. It can be said that freezing weather or unrelieved drought will destroy any growing crop, but the recuperative powers of plants vary widely. While a given situation may result in irretrievable damage to one, the same condition may only delay the harvest for another. A serious speculator needs to have a fine understanding of the climatic vulnerability of the commodity in which he is trading. Without this information, he will more than likely render faulty judgments in appraising the probable effect of weather aberrations on the harvest potential of the crop. Here again, the speculative results can be disastrous.

Expect an Annual Weather Market

A phenomenon of most agricultural commodity trading, during the spring and summer in particular, is what the business terms a *weather market*. The designation is both accurate and useful. There is a saying in trade circles that "most crops are usually lost two or three times before they are harvested." The statement merely underscores the fact that while a crop is growing, each change in weather outlook will be immediately reflected in price changes in the market, in terms of its possible impact on yield. Weather market price fluctuations tend to be greatly magnified beyond the actual, measurable impact of transitory temperature/moisture changes on crop production.

A 30-day forecast on the part of the U.S. Weather Bureau which calls for below-average moisture during the month of July may immediately be reflected in an increase of 5 cents or 8 cents per bushel in the price of corn. Each appreciable rain storm within the month (which—according to the official forecast—is expected to be dry) will probably occasion a greater or lesser downward fluctuation in the price. Weather markets can be treacherous trading situations because of the suddenness with which summer storms occur, and the outsized impact which such a development may exert on prices.

1965 offered a classic demonstration of weather market behavior. June had generally been a dry month and the 30 day forecast for July offered little hope for improvement. Agricultural commodity prices had responded to this situation, which seemed to indicate serious reductions in harvest expectations. On the day before the 4th of July weekend, both corn and soybean prices were sharply higher as longs established positions in what they considered to be drought-damaged crops. The holiday weekend had hardly begun when totally unforeseen weather changes took place and parched farmland was drenched with what the newspapers referred to as "a billion dollar rain storm." At the opening of the first session following the three day holiday, soybean prices opened down 4 cents per bushel and corn opened down 2½ cents per bushel. Speculators who anticipated the billon dollar rain storm realized great profits. But the traders who accepted the Weather Bureau's 30-day outlook as the last word paid dearly for their unfounded confidence.

Of all of the commodity categories, frozen orange juice concentrate (FOJC) is perhaps the most weather sensitive. Florida, which produces most of the oranges-for-juice crop, is not the land of uninterrupted sunshine that its Chambers of Commerce claim it to be. It is a rare winter season that doesn't bring frost scares or actual freezing over most of that state. Every time this happens, pictures of ice-coated oranges appear in the newspapers and on television—accompanied by lamentations from the growers that some, most, or *all* of the crop is ruined.

When the frost or freeze scare hits the market, prices on FOJC take off in response to the headlines. Limit-up-prices may devastate the trapped short-holders for days at a time, as trade ceases and fear of the impending crop loss is "discounted" into market attitudes. Brokers press customers for additional margin money, while the "squeezed" shorts pray for deliverance.

Then, gradually, some elements of reason and perspective emerge. The agricultural experts offer some balanced estimates of the frost damages inflicted. Test results on fruit from the cold areas reassure the trade that all is not as grim as earlier accounts had indicated. Trade attitude begins to change.

The *longs* who have profited tremendously from the weather scare begin accommodating the fleeing *shorts,* and cashing their own paper profits in so doing. The *shorts* succeed in buying back the contracts they must have—and the market turns quiet as prices drift lower.

The frost scare is over.

The event will appear on the charts as an aberrational run-up in the life of the contracts involved; followed by a subsequent fall to—or near—the earlier price-idea-range for the commodity.

All of this assumes that the weather scare was *over-bought*—and they usually are! An axiom in the market is, "Whatever the traders do, they overdo!" Weather markets are the finest example of this behavior.

Absence of a Freeze Depresses Contracts for Orange Juice

By Kathleen A. Hughes
Staff Reporter of The Wall Street Journal

Orange juice futures prices plunged after a weekend freeze that was expected in the Florida citrus belt failed to occur.

Forecasts late last week of possible sub-freezing temperatures in Florida on Sunday or today sparked a speculative rally last week. But when temperatures remained at safe levels, traders "came in and sold out. The rally was totally in anticipation of a freeze," said Tom Griffo, an analyst at Thomson McKinnon Securities Inc. in New York.

David Taylor, a meteorologist at Weather Services Corp. in Bedford, Mass., said he now sees little chance of a freeze in the region through Thursday morning. To cause a damaging freeze, temperatures would have to drop down to the mid-20s, he noted.

Orange juice futures for January delivery fell 2.1 cents a pound to $1.554 yesterday, as the freeze fears dissipated. Two strong rallies have boosted orange juice futures in the past year—the first in response to a killing freeze around Christmas 1983, and the second on fears that citrus canker would damage groves—and prices remain about 25 percent above the levels before the 1983 freeze.

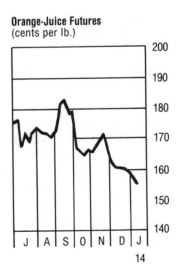

Orange-Juice Futures
(cents per lb.)

14

But current prices have fallen about 15 percent from 1984's highs last September, when speculative fervor over the incurable citrus canker disease peaked. Despite widespread fears that discovery of the canker in mature fruit-bearing groves would force the destruction of the crop, the disease still hasn't been detected in any commercial orange groves.

Heavy Brazilian imports of concentrate and a larger-than-expected 1984 U.S. government crop estimate have since helped depress prices. Three damaging Florida freezes in the past five years have encouraged the sharp increase in Brazilian imports. A sizable Brazilian crop this year is also a factor.

"There's plenty of juice around," said Mr. Griffo at Thomson McKinnon. "And there's no sign that the influx of juice into the U.S. is slowing down."

Also, the size of the Florida crop has fallen on average in recent years, dropping to current levels of an estimated 119 million boxes from 206.7 million boxes in the 1979–1980 crop year. Meanwhile, imports of juice into Florida have risen more than sixfold to 101.2 million gallons last year from 16.5 million gallons of frozen concentrate in the 1979–80 crop year. Brazil is the largest exporter of juice to the U.S., and most juice is imported through Florida.

"Brazil has had the perfect climate and soil to grow oranges. And now they have the perfect market, since our crop has declined steadily. Without a freeze (in Florida futures) prices are going lower," said Mr. Griffo.

Weather can be a two-edged sword. In this situation the trade overbought the contracts, expecting a freeze. When it didn't arrive, they oversold the same contracts. The result offered great opportunities to buy dips and sell bulges in the distorted market.

Suffice it to say that price changes which are occasioned by weather tend to be sudden in their development and wider than the facts justify; weather improvements trigger unrealistic price decreases and bad weather occasions equally excessive price increases. The fact is that, while the vagaries of weather do exert very real influences on harvest expectations, the impact of weather on trader psychology is infinitely greater than it is on the crops themselves. The successful speculator must learn to position himself in such a way as to anticipate events like the one just described. They are to be *expected* in most growing crops. When they do occur, the astute trader will take them in stride and maintain a measure of equanimity over all. When he considers that the market has "overbought" bad weather or "oversold" good weather, he "sells the bulge" or "buys the dip" in expectation that when a balanced appraisal returns he will profit by having resisted overreacting to short-term and limited news.

In summation, it must be said once more that medium-range trading strategy, to be effective, depends on keeping long-term considerations in background perspective, and dealing with more immediate probabilities as the first order of business. Long-range and medium-range conditions may not coincide. Whether they do or not, successful speculation requires that the trader keep in step with the *existing* market.

Courtesy of the CME

Exhibit 8–2

Pit trading has been called the fastest business in the world. In a busy market, a few hundred floor brokers and pit traders often transact $25 to $50 million worth of business per minute.

The International Monetary Market is one of the busiest futures trade locations in the world.

Sometimes this may call for trading against the longer trend. But short-term events do not *change* trends, they often *extend* trends. "Trading against the trend" can be profitable, but it must be recognized as dangerous; and precautions must be taken which will permit quick escape from a too-hazardous exposure. Trading against the trend is always a short-term tactic, rather than medium-term strategy.

We are now ready to give out attention to short-range considerations.

9

Short-Term
Trading Tactics

This subject should ideally begin with a firm definition of what constitutes *short-term* in commodity trading. Unfortunately, finding a usable definition is not as easy as noting the need for it.

The period of time involved in short-term trading depends greatly on individual perspective. It is not likely to be more than a week; it will often encompass only a session or two; and in fast moving, highly volatile market situations, 10 minutes might cover a particular price move from beginning to end.

The minimum period one can effectively deal with in short-term trading activities is largely governed by the amount of time and concentration an individual trader is able to devote to the market. Public traders rarely have any continuing awareness of intrasession price behavior. Each evening they check their newspaper to see where prices opened and closed, what the highs and lows for the session have been, what the trading volume was, etc. On the basis of this brief data, they then decide whether to maintain their present market position, buy, or sell.

There are other public traders who maintain sufficiently close broker relationships as to be able to get prices a few times during each session, and appraise their daily activities in light of market behavior at reasonably regular intervals. Still other short-term market participants have immediate and constant access to prices through "ticker" equipment which reports each price change as soon as it occurs.

It is difficult to select any single group of market participants as enjoying a distinct trading advantage. The "tape trader," unless he exerts great self control, can be stampeded into unwise decisions by exceedingly brief price aberrations which quickly fade and which, in the final analysis, have little if any significance with respect to trends in the near- or medium-range of things. It must, at the same time, be acknowledged that the individual who limits his market contact to checking opening prices, and intraday highs and lows is in a position of considerable risk unless he establishes continuing safeguards in the form of "resting orders."

Once a commodity position is taken, its holder is at the constant mercy of market prices. Minute by minute throughout the trading session, price quotations on the contract involved publicly declare its value and measure profits and losses. Whether the going market price evolves from solid information or the flimsiest kind of gossip, the quoted price is still the only effective price.

Someone once asked J. P. Morgan, "What will the market do?" The fabulously successful old speculator with the bulbous, purple nose had a short reply: "The market will fluctuate." No one has ever materially improved on Mr. Morgan's prognosis. Prices endlessly fluctuate—the only question to be resolved is whether they will fluctuate narrowly or broadly and whether they will fluctuate in an upward, downward, or a sideways trend—but fluctuate they will.

Three areas of consideration deserve analysis in attempting to evaluate price movements. They are, in no particular order of importance:

1. Fundamental changes in balance between supply and demand forces.
2. Technical market conditions (which relate to overbought or oversold imbalance).
3. New information (which may be hard fact or groundless rumor).

Only Two Market Inputs

The fundamental elements in a market are only two: demand, as measured by buying orders; and supply, as measured by selling orders. There are those who hold that all selling orders do not represent supply, and all buying orders do not represent demand, since speculators are selling and buying with no intention of ultimately making or accepting delivery. The point, even if true, is not pertinent. As already noted, a selling order from a speculator is given the same weight in the market's pricing function as a selling order from a producer or a commercial handler who has and wants to dispose of a warehouse full of the commodity in question. Likewise, a buying order placed by a speculator who has never taken delivery of any commodity, and never intends to do so carries the same weight in the market as a buying order from a flour miller who needs the physical product desperately.

The market has no way of differentiating between the motives of buyers or sellers. Indeed, from a purely economic point of view, there is no difference. Both the speculator and the processor buy and sell commodities futures as necessary steps in their search for profit. Whether profit shall accrue from milling delivered wheat and selling flour, or from holding a wheat futures contract and selling it later at a higher price, makes no particular difference. A search for profit (or avoidance of loss) prompts both interests to take their respective actions.

It is imperative that in considering the economic function and the operational methods of commodity markets, the examiner keep his viewpoint completely clear as concerns these basic inputs: The positive element in the market is the order to buy. It makes no difference who originates a buy order, or what his motives or justification may be. The buy order is definitively positive because the very act of buying reflects a new demand element which was not communicated in the market until the order arrived. Once known, a buy order urges prices upward.

The negative force in the market is the order to sell. Again, we need spend no time trying to qualitatively differentiate between the several classes of sellers. An order to sell represents new supply availability which was not in the market until the order arrived. Once entered, a sell order urges prices downward.

Don't Forget the Fundamentals—Even in the Short-Term

The market *fundamentalist* is usually a long-term trader who tends to limit his viewpoint to the adequacy of known or projected supplies in light of known or projected demand. To vastly oversimplify the situation, the fundamentalist would consider that a finite market which had historically consumed a fixed amount of wheat—say 600 million bushels a year—would be adequately supplied by a crop which promised to be in the volume of 600 million bushels. He would, furthermore, take historic supply and demand and, from this, strike a balance at the historic price.

Now, assuming that demand remained constant, but supplies decreased by 5 percent, the fundamentalist would translate the imbalance into a higher price. How much higher would depend on "price elasticity"

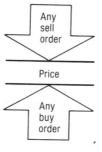

Exhibit 9–1

in the commodity category and other related economic considerations. If demand remains constant and supply increases 5 percent over the historic level, the fundamentalist would translate this imbalance into lower prices. His appraisal would hinge importantly on marginal demand for the 5 percent surplus.

The commodities in which organized trading takes place have been produced and consumed over long periods of time. While historical data leaves much to be desired, production and consumption statistics for the last 20 years or so are surprisingly good in most respects. The student of the topic can readily avail himself of information which will permit drawing some sound and well-documented conclusions about the fundamental factors surrounding each of the traded commodities. Historical market behavior is less than a sterling criterion for future events, but it does provide an indispensable foundation for creating the base for a projection of things to come. Certainly the speculator who undertakes to make decisions without an awareness of fundamentals is engaging in a most hazardous practice.

Changes in fundamentals can have long-range implications. For example, when the changes involve such things as increased planting intentions on the part of producers, a lifting or easing of a government imposed production restriction, a new use for the commodity in question, etc. Changes in the fundamental market balance, as previously noted, may also relate to medium-range considerations. A transportation strike, for example, while not altering the actual physical supply of a commodity, can temporarily limit its availability in localities of use or consumption. Natural or man-made events such as earthquakes or border hostilities may, likewise, impede the flow of a commodity until the situation returns to something approaching normal.

Fundamental Balances Can Make Short-Term Prices

Changes in the fundamental balance between supply and demand may also be seen in the short-range of things. Unexpectedly excessive arrivals from outlying points of supply may exceed storage capacities for the product in a terminal market location. The reverse may also occur; inadequate arrivals may result from supplier holding or interference by the weather or other natural considerations, giving rise to sudden shortage. The possibilities are almost without limit and each event will create a price reaction which reflects the market's appraisal of the seriousness of the matter and the period of time over which it is likely to persist. Generally, it can be said that small problems result in small short-lived price fluctuations; large problems bring greater longer-lasting price swings.

It is most important that the speculator always look at price behavior in terms of attempting to define its underlying reason. A well-tried axiom is: "Never trust a price move you don't understand." Until some explanation for the market's reappraisal of price is developed, the speculator has no way of knowing whether he agrees or disagrees with the consideration which is sparking the market's fluctuation. Establishing a position in a "blind" situation may prove profitable but, if so, the result must be attributed to good fortune rather than good judgment.

Technical Imbalances Can Make Short-Term Prices

"Technical" market conditions often occasion short-term price moves, with no change of consequence in fundamentals. Understanding the technical vulnerability and technical strength in a market can sometimes provide the key to quick and impressive profits. In attempting to analyze this facet of price behavior, it is well to begin with the thought that there are two kinds of market participants, both of which are to some extent continually involved in buying and selling futures contracts. For lack of better labels, we may call them weak hands and strong hands. The distinction refers to their respective capital and other resources, rather than to the commercial motives or lack of them—which may be represented.

Weak Hands and Strong Hands

The public speculator tends to be a weak market participant for several reasons. First of all, he reflects an unfortunate tendency to overtrade, with the result that when prices move against him even moderately, he may have no choice except to liquidate his position. The public speculator is also likely to be a poor student of the commodity in which he is trading. His information, as often as not, consists of rumor, hunch, and market tips from others, who are probably no better informed than himself. Lacking solid confidence in the reasons which prompted him to establish a commodity position to begin with, at the first sign of a problem he may peremptorily liquidate his holdings as the only way to find protection against threatening and unforeseen developments. A further reason the public speculator tends to constitute weak hands in the market is his unending search for a quick million. He is a *plunger*.

Patience a Virtue

Commodity speculation, like other forms of economic activity, requires information, perspective, and above all, great patience. The public speculator who has had a few successes in the market wants to be constantly committed. To do so is to court certain disaster. The wise speculator only takes a position when he has strong reason to believe that "the trade is wrong" and will subsequently revise its price opinion. As long as prices are at levels which appear reasonable in the face of known facts, then it follows that there is no reason for prices to change appreciably. Taking a position in a commodity ties up money. Until prices do move in the speculator's favor, he will merely succeed in inactivating a portion of his risk capital on the flimsy hope that something beneficial, but totally unforeseen, will happen. Such a course of action is, at best, folly. It will certainly lead to eventual failure.

The strong hands in the market are strong for good reason. First, they represent well-financed professional speculators, along with commercial interests who use the market for hedging purposes. With adequate resources to underpin their judgment and absorb some reasonable paper losses while they wait for their expectations to be realized, they are much harder to shake loose from a good position. They have the financial ability and the speculative professionalism to take a loss and forget about it when events refute their earlier appraisal. But as long as their first judgment continues to appear valid, they will not be driven into liquidating a position for small or transitory reasons.

The strong hands in the marketplace are, for the most part, careful students of the topic. They have made it their business to acquire broad knowledge of each commodity in which they interest themselves; including its production, processing methods, trade channels, and vulnerability to substitution by other materials. Finally, these strong hands are invariably pursuing an established speculative policy which includes firm profit expectations and maximum limitations on total commitments—and acceptable losses—at any given time. They do not mind occasionally being out of the market, having learned that the opportunities they seek are not always present. However, when an attractive situation presents itself they have both the capital and the courage to exploit it fully. In speaking of *technical* market conditions, we are referring in large measure to the behavior of strong and weak hands in establishing and managing commodity positions; and how they perform in the face of adversity. This, in turn, is greatly influenced by the respective objectives and expectations of the two major classifications of market users.

Price Is Secondary to a Hedger

It was previously pointed out that the strong hands in the marketplace include well financed professional speculators and *commercial interests*. The latter group is made up of merchants, processors, transporters, etc., who conduct business in the commodity involved. These interests use the market for the purpose of hedging and, as will be seen in the section devoted to this topic, are less concerned with "flat price" movement than they are with the relationship between prices in the different delivery months, different geographical locations, and between similar products. As a consequence, the commercials view price movement in a substantially different light than does the individual whose hopes for profit are exclusively pinned to a flat price change in his favor.

The professional speculator, while often at the mercy of flat price movement in his search for profits, tends to establish a position with a well-developed frame of reference as concerns his profit expectations on the one hand, and the paper loss he is willing to accept in the interim, while waiting for his objective to be realized.

Weak Hands Make Bad Matters Worse

Public speculators usually operate without the advantages of a firm opinion concerning either profit goal or loss limit, and are further handicapped by a scarcity of solid information upon which to govern trade decisions. When they run for cover, the retreat is seldom an orderly one.

For example, in a market situation in which the public overwhelmingly occupies the long side, downward price movement which results in losses on the part of the weak hands may set off a rash of selling orders as the public speculators scramble to escape from their losing positions. The added selling volume, of course, merely adds downward pressure on the prices, accelerating and worsening the situation. The farther prices move downward, the more desperate the weak-handed longs become. The price slide may not be halted until all of these weak holders are driven out of the market.

The same thing, in the opposite frame of reference, may occur when a large public interest is present on the short side of a contract. An increase in price represents losses to the shorts. Without either adequate financing to weather the storm or sufficient information to enable them to see a temporary price fluctuation for what it is, the public shorts, in their rush to offset their impaired positions, may send prices sharply higher on the crest of a flood of orders to buy back and offset their previously established short positions.

It is precisely this kind of market phenomenon which regularly grows out of alternative situations that are usually described as "overbought" or "oversold" market conditions.

Overbought / Oversold

Let us consider an overbought market in which there is a substantial long public interest. Obviously the longs want prices to move higher. Some rapidly developing piece of news may have bearish implications. Prices fluctuate downward slightly in response to the new information and, in doing so, they touch off resting "stop-loss" orders, or precipitate defensive selling on the part of public longs who are keeping a close eye on the market. In the face of this increasing "bear" pressure, prices continue to move lower; much lower in fact, than the news which set off the initial fluctuation would conceivably call for.

The result is that what could have ordinarily—and should have logically—been a minor downward adjustment, is turned into a substantial price slide due to the general selling chain reaction which the bearish news only started.

When this happens, the overbought condition may quickly turn into an oversold situation. Now we have the exact opposite frame of reference. The predictable tendency on the part of weak hands in the marketplace to abandon commodity positions quickly and in concert, tends to overemphasize price fluctuations; price rises are carried higher than the facts indicate they should go, and price drops fall farther than reasonable appraisal of the news actually justifies.

Trading Bulges and Dips

Since this tendency to overbuy good news and oversell bad news is so pronounced, it offers an excellent opportunity for seasoned and more sagacious traders to capitalize on the price extremes which are thus produced. A well-recognized trading technique among professionals consists of selling "price bulges" and buying "price dips." This merely presupposes that a price move downward in a contract with a large public interest will probably be driven further than it should go. Once the selloff has run its course, the alert speculator can often turn a quick profit by taking a long position near the bottom of the dip and riding it back up to the point or range of reestablished market equilibrium.

In the opposite situation, once a price bulge has taken place as a result of "squeezing" public shorts, the more discerning speculator can profit by going short at the crest of the bulge and riding the position back down into the price balance range.

Commodity markets vary widely, but it is perfectly safe to say that the larger the public participation in any given market, the more susceptible it is to wide fluctuations precipitated by stop-loss orders triggered by news, rumor, or mere suspicion. Commodity exchanges all have rules prohibiting the spreading of rumors and yet, human nature

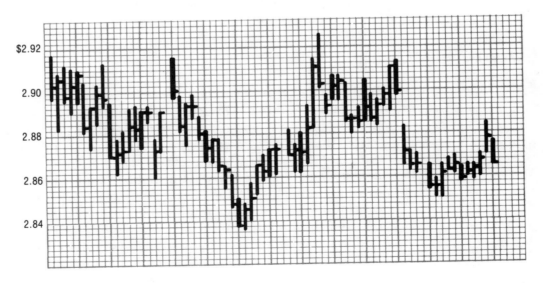

Exhibit 9–2

being what it is, rumors endlessly float across the trading floors. Some of these tales later prove to be reliable. Many of them prove to be largely or completely false. But each new piece of information, whether valid or not, will probably be given credence by a few traders. If the story catches on it can, like a small rock tumbling from the top of a snow covered mountain, precipitate first a slide and then an avalanche. In the short-term scheme of things, sharply breaking news or gossip must be accorded an important place among all of the things which can affect prices.

The position trader must be constantly on guard against being stampeded into unwise action which grows out of this sort of transitory consideration. The public trader is rarely in any position to capitalize on these small price movements. Therefore, he has little choice except to steel himself against the urge to make longer-range judgments on the basis of exceedingly short-term considerations.

To sum up, analyzing a commodity market calls for three levels of evaluation:

1. Long-range or big picture *policy*.
2. Medium-range trading *strategy*.
3. Short-term *tactics*.

The answers developed in connection with each of these time segments may not coincide at any particular point. However, unless all three intervals of concern are brought into focus, the speculator runs the risk of being misled in pursuit of his overall objective. It takes perspective and steady nerves to keep from giving a short-term price development weight out of all proportion to its true value.

The experience of millions of traders is the best possible evidence that it is easier to establish a position than it is to close one out. This is all the more reason that the trader should have confidence in his reasons for placing an order to buy or sell any commodity; and that he have a loss limit firmly in mind, or formally entered with his broker, along with a solid profit expectation, before establishing any position.

Speculation is not an exercise in lucky guesses. It is an activity which depends on knowledge, courage, and financial ability. Only by keeping this operational trinity constantly before him can a speculator enter the market with reasonable hope of profit from his activities here.

10

How Hedgers Use the Market

In order for the speculator to be able to render reliable judgments about market behavior, he must be at least generally aware of the interests and methods of his competition. Among the several classifications of buyers and sellers, one of the most important groups can be broadly identified as *hedging interests*. By and large, hedgers are commercial firms who deal directly in the various commodities. In grain, for example, hedgers include farmers who produce the crops, merchants who buy and then resell the cash grain, processors who convert the commodities from their natural form into various products, and wholesalers who put the finished products into their ultimate channels of consumption and use.

In order to explain hedging, it seems best to begin with the chronological events in a normal cash or spot sale. A grain merchant might buy 5,000 bushels of oats from a farmer and immediately resell it to a breakfast food manufacturer. Provided both the purchase "at wholesale" and the sale "at retail" could be made at about the same time, there would be slight, if any, risk to the merchant on the basis of price change on the commodity during the short interval between his acquisition and resale of the merchandise.

We might even consider a situation in which a grain merchant consummates the (short) cash sale to the breakfast food manufacturer first and then later makes the purchase of the grain required to fill his sales commitment. In either event, the grain merchant's profit will be the difference between his buying and his selling price. (For purposes of this example, we have ignored handling and transportation costs.)

Trade Sequence Doesn't Affect Profit or Loss

It is important to keep in mind that trading *profit always and only accrues from selling at a price greater than the cost of acquisition*. It makes no difference whether the purchase comes first followed by the sale; or the sale is made first followed by the purchase. The chronology of events can be ignored. A profit arises from selling something for more than you pay for it. A loss results from selling something for less than you pay for it.

Returning now to our example of the grain merchant who acquires oats from the farmer and resells them to a manufacturer, it was noted that if both ends of this transaction could be accomplished without delay, there would be little opportunity for price changes to alter the profit position of the middleman. Now let us add a longer time dimension to the hypothetical case.

Time Involves Risk

Let us assume that the grain merchant has purchased oats from the producing farmer in early October and must put them in storage because he has no immediate sale for the product. Let us furthermore assume that at the time of his purchase from the farmer, the market price of oats in the country is $1.70 per bushel. With the product now on hand, the owner of the grain must recognize that the price of oats will certainly fluctuate. He has purchased the commodity at $1.70 per bushel. If the market price increases beyond this level, he will profit in terms of an increase in inventory value. If the price falls from this level, he will sustain a loss on the value of his inventory. Certainly a profit is always welcome, but the opportunities for a loss should be avoided, if at all possible. Hedging provides a means for *reducing negative risks* while still leaving an *opportunity for a trading profit* on stored commodities.

The Perfect Hedge

Fundamentally, a hedge is a protective device. A simple example is that of the individual who makes a $5.00 bet on runner A in a two-man race a week in advance of the contest. At the time he places his wager, he is confident that his man will win. Two days before the event, however, track star A pulls a muscle, which changes the situation completely. The bettor is, at this point, virtually certain that his man will lose. However, he has already wagered that A will be victorious. He cannot nullify the original bet, but he can hedge his risk exposure. A "perfect" hedge can be placed by taking an *equal and opposite position*. He now

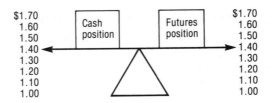

Exhibit 10–1

Theoretically "perfect" profit protection. Extremely rare!

places a second $5.00 wager that A will *not win* the upcoming race. (A and B may run a tie, and the hedge is still perfect.)

Having bet *with* runner A in the first instance and *against* him in the second instance, he can watch the contest with complete equanimity, knowing that whichever way the event turns out, he will win one $5.00 wager and lose the other. Profit and loss will offset exactly. He has a perfect hedge against loss, which he obtained at the price of surrendering any opportunity to gain.

Commodity Hedges Are Seldom Perfect

Commodity hedging is not this precise, for reasons which will be explored in detail later. However, although commodity hedges are something less than perfect, they still provide a means of removing or minimizing possibilities for loss, while also offering opportunities for extra hedging profit.

Reduced to its simplest terms, commodity futures markets permit a hedger to make *substitute purchases* and *substitute sales* which offer some measure of profit protection until such time as *actual* customer transactions in cash merchandise can be consummated.

Consider once more the grain merchant who buys 5,000 bushels of oats at $1.70 per bushel. On the October date when he purchases the commodity, July oats futures are selling on the Chicago Board of Trade at $1.79 per bushel. On the surface this would appear to present a clear opportunity for 9 cents profit, but this is not the case. The merchant purchased the oats "in the country." In order to get the $1.79 price, the product must be moved into the Chicago market, which involves transportation costs and handling fees. Also, the oats must be stored until July, some eight months away. It is therefore seen that, while the grain dealer has purchased oats at "9 cents under July," if he is to realize the $1.79 price the market promises him at the later date, he must first defray loading and transportation costs and carrying charges for the period involved.

Still, the fact remains that by *selling* the July oats *futures* against his *purchase* of the *cash* commodity, the market will offer a form of profit insurance during the period of time he holds the inventory, whether or not he elects to hold the oats until the following July and ultimately deliver it against a short futures position.

We might assume that the grain merchant would prefer buying from the farmer and immediately contracting its sale to a customer at an established markup and at a designated point in the future. However, purchase and sale of cash commodities cannot always be simultaneously arranged. In order to stay in business, the merchant must own and store a grain inventory. Although willing to hold huge stocks, commercial firms are usually reluctant to speculate on price behavior—and for excellent reason! With a million bushels of grain in storage, a price drop of 1 cent per bushel means a $10,000 loss in product inventory value. In order to avoid this possibility, large holders of commodity stocks usually accumulate their supplies from producing sources and immediately hedge it by sale of an equivalent amount of commodity futures. The sales of futures contracts (against purchases of cash grain for physical inventory) are nothing more than *substitutes* for the sales of physical goods which will be made later.

After purchasing grain from the farmer and selling an equivalent amount of futures contracts, the grain merchant will later transact sales with customers for the cash product. As rapidly as cash sales are consummated, the short hedges in the futures market will be bought back—offset—since there is no longer any purpose for maintaining the futures position. The hedge in futures has performed its function for the period of time the inventory needed profit protection.

Prices Move in Concert

Hedging is an effective means of minimizing risk exposure, because of the tendency of futures prices and cash prices to maintain *more or less stable relationships*. For purposes of demonstration, we shall consider three levels of values.

Consider contract oats in the Chicago cash market as selling for $1.75 per bushel on September 1. The carrying charge on oats, which is comprised of insurance, storage costs, and interest on money represented in stock, will be put at 2½ cents per bushel per month. Consequently, if the spot price is $1.75, the same grade of commodity in the same location might be expected to reflect a price of $1.82 on the futures contract which calls for delivery three months hence. The 7½ cent differential would be comprised of the carrying charges for the period of time involved: 2½ cents per month multiplied by three months. The futures contract for delivery six months later will usually reflect a larger carrying charge, based on the longer storage time involved. This element in price relationship may be viewed as a *time differential*. There is also a differential based on geographic location.

Location Differences Affect Prices

The major grain market is in Chicago and prices in the Chicago market are predicated on location (or delivery) of the commodities within the market complex. "Out of position" products are worth proportionately less, since they must be moved to the market city in order to command the market price. If cash oats in Chicago is quoted at $1.75 per bushel, we might expect to see cash oats in Peoria, Illinois, quoted at $1.70, since freight rates indicate that it will cost about 5 cents per bushel to load and move oats by rail over the 200 miles or so involved. Oats in Lincoln, Nebraska, would be worth proportionately less because freight costs would be greater. Oats in Wichita, Kansas, could be worth even less than the same product in Omaha, because of the greater distance it would have to be hauled before it would be "in position" for delivery in the pricing market.

The price surface chart in Exhibit 16–1 (p. 202), although necessarily useful only as a rough gauge of locational price differences, will indicate the magnitude of transportation considerations in establishing values on grains in key production and market locations. These relationships are constantly changing, also.

Discovery of price, as has been noted previously, takes place in the market in which the commodity is traded. Although central market prices and country prices differ, both with respect to geographical location and the period of time which the merchandise must be held pending delivery date, cash prices, futures prices, and country prices, all tend to move up and down together. As we will subsequently see, the differentials between these price levels may narrow or widen, depending on considerations of current local shortage or oversupply. But— with occasional exceptions—they *do move in concert*. An increase in the central market price will usually bring an increase of about the same magnitude in all of the other commodity's categories, both locationally and timewise.

Futures Price Is the Cash Price Reference

Offers to buy or sell traded commodities are usually quoted in terms of a designated premium or discount "on" or "off" the nearby futures contract. Thus, if the nearby (December) oats futures contract is selling at $1.75 per bushel in Chicago, the Peoria offering for oats might be "3 cents off December," and the Wichita bid might be "6½ cents off December." In certain situations, the country bid might be a premium over the nearby futures market price; but, in any event, the nearest futures price quotation is the usual basing point for cash bids. An increase of 2 cents a bushel in the futures price will therefore bring an immediate 2 cent increase in the country bid, inasmuch as offers are not communicated in terms of established prices, but rather of price relationship "on" or "off" the futures.

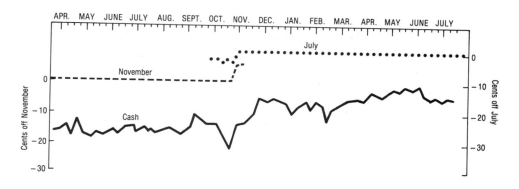

Exhibit 10–2

A normal market pays a premium for delivery at a later date.

To return now to the interest and the market activities of the hedger, let us again direct our attention to the basic purpose for which the commercial dealer in physical commodities uses the futures markets. We have stated previously that a hedge is an *equal and opposite* position in futures to the position held in the cash commodity. If a hedger is long—owns—cash coffee, he will be short coffee futures. Conversely, if the coffee merchant has contracted to deliver the cash product at some point in the future at a fixed price, his position is one of being short the cash commodity, and his risk will be hedged by holding a long position in futures contracts. In trade terminology, a short hedge consists of selling futures contracts; a long hedge involves buying futures contracts.

An unfortunate tendency exists on the part of most economic writers to demonstrate hedging with examples of perfect price correlation, where the market value of the cash product raises a prescribed amount and the price on its futures climbs in perfect step with it. Thus, the hedger who holds a cash inventory gains (or loses) a designated amount on his inventory and recaptures precisely the same amount on the value of his hedging position.

Ideal though this perfect hedge may appear to be, price behavior is seldom so closely attuned between the two markets. A hedge in actual practice is rarely perfect. (It seldom results in a zero net outcome on the combined cash and futures situation.) In the world of reality, hedges, imperfect as they are, can be used to reduce risks; and in some cases, a well placed hedge can produce an impressive additional profit.

It deserves to be emphasized that the additional hedging profit opportunity is an important, if not the principal, reason that commercial interests engage in hedging. A badly placed hedge may, on the other hand, actually *increase* risk exposure. It can be assumed that the highly skilled professionals who conduct this type of operation for their firms, earnestly attempt to place profitable hedges. They studiously avoid those situations which promise little, if any, mitigation of risk exposure and offer only limited opportunities for enhanced return from their combined cash/futures operations.

From a practical point of view, the speculator must recognize that the commercial hedger, more often than not, represents his principal competition for profits in the market. This, because when a commercial firm places a hedge, the public speculator is usually on the other side of the transaction, as either buyer or seller. If the hedger is to profit from his hedge, it follows that he must do so at the expense of other parties in the market. If the speculator profits, it must come from a commensurate loss sustained by the other parties who hold the opposite positions.

Hedgers Select the Risks They Pass to the Market

It has been said before, but it cannot be overemphasized—hedgers seek more than mere profit insurance from their market operations. While a great many firms pursue a consistent policy of hedging, it must be understood that hedging is not an automatic procedure. Unless a given cash position presents substantial elements of risk from price change, a hedge may not be placed at all. Or, in another situation, where the futures market shows an attractive opportunity for trading profits, so-called anticipatory hedging may take place which, until the related cash transactions are consummated, represents speculation in futures.

It is not unusual for a commercial interest to describe his position as being "90 percent hedged" or "110 percent hedged." This merely indicates that people who deal in cash commodities also render subjective judgments about the good risks which they are willing to bear themselves and the bad risks which they prefer to pass along to the market. Hedging, as practiced in the commercial trade, is a highly selective kind of thing. This knowledge should serve to underscore the importance of the speculator also carefully selecting the risks he is willing to undertake; using equal, or—if possible—even greater caution than the hedger does. This, since the risks which hedgers and other traders offer to the market must *always* be viewed with some degree of suspicion.

The speculator must make his choices between propositions which, in the appraisal of other traders or commercial hedging interests, are too negative, or fraught with too much uncertainty to permit their being carried directly. If this were not so, they would probably not be hedged in the first place.

Basis in Hedging Activities

The key consideration in commercial hedging is the price relationship between cash commodities and the nearby futures price. This price differential is ordinarily spoken of as the *basis*. As pointed out earlier, futures prices in a normal market are higher than current cash prices by part or all of the costs of carrying the merchandise from the present date to the projected date of delivery. Bear in mind that this is nothing more than statement of the average condition. Depending on relative scarcity or oversupply, the basis may vary substantially. In understanding the differential between cash prices and the nearby futures prices, or the differential between the nearby futures price and prices on more deferred contracts, it is well to begin with a closer look at what carrying charges entail.

First and foremost is the matter of storage itself. Each commodity has its own storage requirements which are translatable into a *storage cost,* and which must be absorbed by someone. The second element in carrying charges is *insurance* on the commodity in question. Depending on its susceptibility to spoilage or other deterioration in quality or quantity over time, and further depending on the kind of warehouse or other storage facility in which it is being held, insurance rates can differ widely. The third cost of carrying a commodity is *interest* on money, since if the commodity exists, someone owns it; and so long as it is in storage status, it represents invested capital to the extent of its full market value. An interest charge for use of money tied up must be theoretically accepted, whether interest is actually paid to a bank or other financial institution, or not.

Carrying charges, therefore, are made up of three separate items; storage costs, insurance, and interest. In a market situation where supply and demand are in reasonable equilibrium, the market will reflect a carrying charge premium on products being held for later delivery. In a situation where an immediate scarcity exists, however, carrying charges on deferred contracts will narrow, disappear, or actually reflect an *inversion,* which may be viewed as a negative carrying charge.

Inversion—Negative Carrying Charge

For example, in a situation where wheat is in relatively short supply and good demand, the immediate crisis in this foodstuff would bring high prices in the cash market as well as into the nearby futures. The

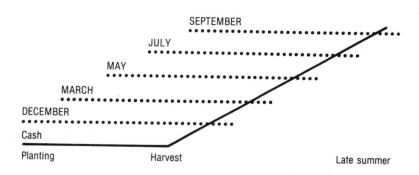

Exhibit 10—3

market gives priority attention to the immediate situation and tends to "discount the future." Therefore, in the situation outlined, we might find cash wheat selling at $4.00 per bushel, with the nearby futures at about the same level. The more deferred futures—six months or more off—may be selling at several cents per bushel less than either the cash price or the nearby futures contract.

In practical effect, the market is saying to the holder of wheat, "Your merchandise is needed *now*. Present it in the market, and we will pay you a premium for it. If you continue to hold it, we will not only refuse to pay you for your carrying costs, but you will likely realize an even lower price for the merchandise itself."

In a period of serious scarcity, current and nearby prices always rise more precipitously than deferred prices. It is in such a situation that steep *inversions*—negative carrying charges—are invariably encountered.

In the face of excessive supplies, the absolute opposite situation exists. Immediately following harvest, for example, the market is usually vastly oversupplied with grain. The postharvest glut nearly always produces low prices for the cash and nearby deliveries, with relatively higher prices offered in the more distant contracts. Here, the message of the market is, "We have more grain now than we can presently use. If you insist on selling your wheat now, you must accept a low price for it. However, if you will hold the product for a few months, we will pay you a carrying charge and may pay a higher price for the commodity itself."

In periods of oversupply, distant contracts usually reflect the greatest premiums. The phenomenon arises directly out of the fact that the

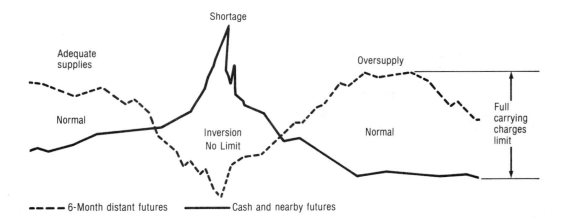

Exhibit 10–4

In an adequately supplied market, deferred futures will reflect some carrying charge over cash and nearby prices. Shortage puts a premium on the present, and discounts the future. Oversupply may produce a differential between cash and futures prices which is equal to full carrying charges for the period involved. The premium on deferred futures will never exceed full carrying charges, although inversions may reflect any extent of discount.

market is attempting to discourage increases in the already excessive physical stocks on hand in the market. By offering premiums for later deliveries, it encourages holding stocks back until consumption has a chance to catch up with supplies.

In view of the foregoing, it should not be surprising to learn that the basis (which may refer to the price differential between cash and any named futures), fluctuates significantly throughout the year. Immediately following harvest, the basis tends to be at its widest point, reflecting high costs of insufficient storage. The result is produced by an excess of commodities seeking a home. In order to find storage, owners of cash commodities must be willing to pay a high price for it (or accept lower prices for their merchandise).

In periods of current scarcity, the basis reaches its smallest differential, since this condition produces an excess of available storage space and a shortage of commodities to occupy it. The price that storage, like other services, can command in an oversupplied market is reduced; it may be nil. Or, if the situation is sufficiently extreme, the carrying charge may go below zero, producing a price inversion defined earlier as a negative carrying charge.

Buy Discounts—Sell Premiums

Excessive supplies of cash commodities in the market produce *discounts* on cash commodities usually accomplished by the appearance of *premiums* on futures. A shortage of cash supplies tends to put premiums on cash and the nearby futures prices, accomplished by appearance of discounts on more distant maturities. Hedgers and experienced speculators—if they can do so—prefer buying discounts and selling premiums. Therefore, it is logical to discover that at the end of a harvest season, commercial interests are usually large buyers of the discounted cash grain and equally large sellers of the premium priced futures. The price differential is the basis for their hedging.

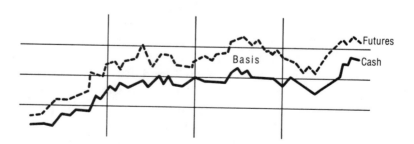

Exhibit 10—5

Even in normal markets, the price differential between cash and futures fluctuates widely, offering opportunities for profitable hedging and attracting a great deal of speculative spreading between multiple futures contracts.

As the season wears on, and the stock of cash commodities is reduced through distribution and consumption, commercial hedgers gradually become net buyers of futures. They must do so. As they transact cash business out of their inventories, they lift their previously placed short hedges by buying them back in the market. With the previously existing oversupply problem reduced or nonexistent, the hedger may not be able to actually buy discounts in offsetting previous short premium sales in futures, but any narrowing of the basis can bring a good profit, as we shall see.

> Rule: Theoretical price relationships limit the amount a deferred futures contract can exceed a nearby, to the amount reflected in carrying charges on the commodity.

This is to say that if carrying charges on a given commodity amount to 3 cents per month per bushel, the July premium over May will not exceed 9 cents (three months × 3 cents per month). As a practical matter, it will probably never reach the full carrying charge. As it approaches the point, commercial interests will sell the distant, almost-full-carrying-charge month, and buy back their hedges in the nearby—discounted—month, thereby assuring themselves a better return on their storage space and inventory investment.

In moving their short hedges out, their buying activities will tend to raise the lower priced nearby contract, while their selling activities will lower the higher priced distant contract. The same consideration will also prompt speculators to simultaneously buy the discount and sell the premium, thereby taking a *spreading* position. As a result, the price differential between the two will be narrowed to something less than full carrying charges.

Similar evaluations can be made of price dislocations which may exist between markets. If the price of Minneapolis wheat goes out of line either negatively or positively with respect to Chicago prices, speculators will buy in the relatively underpriced market, and sell in the higher priced market. Their activities will reestablish something approaching a reasonable pricing equilibrium between the two, in light of transportation costs, etc.

Although the carrying charge theory limits the amount by which the price on a deferred futures may exceed a nearer futures to the carrying costs involved on the commodity, there is *no* theoretical limit to the amount of inversion between futures prices.

As the first edition of this volume was being written, expiring November soybeans futures in the Chicago market were trading at $3.06 per bushel. January soybeans were trading at $2.98. Thus, an 8 cent per bushel premium was being offered for contract grade soybeans for immediate delivery. In that situation the owner of soybeans not only failed to receive a carrying charge by holding onto his inventory for two months; he was promised 8 cents per bushel *less* for them two months hence, on the basis of then-current prices!

Of course, further price changes over the next 60 days could alter the January quotation significantly. However, a serious shortage of soybeans had produced a steep price inversion. The market was saying, "Your soybeans are needed far more urgently now than they will be two months from now when new crop supplies should be adequate. If you sell them today, we will pay you more for them than we will in January. If you hold them, you stand to lose both your costs of carrying them to the later date, as well as sustaining an appreciable reduction in their intrinsic value."

It is important that the speculator clearly understand the various factors which can create price inversions like the one set forth above. In the given soybean situation, there were ample stocks of the product in existence. However, the farmers, following harvest, elected to hold their beans rather than sell them. This concerted holding action on the part of producers created a shortage which could only be corrected by offering sufficiently higher prices to lure farm stocks out of their "first hands."

The market is not concerned with the reason behind the shortage. It can only reflect the fact that demand for this product substantially exceeds offerings. Until such time as supply/demand forces resume a measure of balance, prices can confidently be expected to hold at this level or work higher. Should the holders of soybeans suddenly decide to bring their stocks to market, oversupply could quickly replace the current scarcity, forcing prices down, and reestablishing a carrying charge on more distant futures months.

As pointed out earlier, excessive holding on the part of producers or any other group of interests, or a bottleneck of any kind in the distributive chain, may be reflected in price increases in the first instance, and in substantially lower prices later on. As concerns agricultural crops particularly, consumption must necessarily be spread somewhat evenly over the crop year. If owners or events hold the product out of the market too long, the result can create a situation in which existing supplies cannot be physically consumed in the time remaining before the next crop. If such a condition develops, it could be expected to result in depressed prices on the hoarded, hence excessive stocks.

In summation, it can be said that price relationships between nearby and more distant futures contracts are a measurement of shortage or oversupply. A normal market will reflect *some* premium for carrying an inventory. If supplies are excessive, the carrying charge may be a large one, covering most or all of the costs involved.

In a situation of undersupply, the carrying charge on the deferred futures will be reduced, may disappear entirely, or may come to an *inversion*. To repeat for emphasis, there is no limit to the extent of price inversion which may develop, depending on the market's appraisal of the crisis which exists.

The private speculator should always bear in mind that commercial hedgers try to *buy discounts* and *sell premiums*. Whether establishing flat-price speculative positions or *spreading,* when a speculator departs from this practice, he should have strong reasons for doing so. Whenever he can be in the position of also buying discounts and selling premiums, he can usually count on hedging activity to assist in moving prices in his favor.

11

Launching a Program in Commodity Speculation

There are few, if any, beginning flight students who would undertake to "solo" without first getting a good deal of ground training and "dual" instruction. It would be an equally rare individual who would go into a world series without pregame preparation. Yet, strangely enough, the speculative plains are literally strewn with the bleached bones of courageous, inexperienced speculators who felt it completely unnecessary to develop their techniques and pretest their abilities in the market through study and practice. Most of these speculative casualties enter the market with little more than a notion that "there is money to be made in commodities." They leave the market convinced that money can be both *made* and *lost* in commodities. Their own experience is grim documentation of the second fact.

A highly qualified agricultural economist who combines academic distinction with a firsthand knowledge of the commodity markets, is authority for the statement that most public speculators suffer two financial debacles before they leave the market for good. Perhaps it does take two disappointing experiences to convince the average newcomer to commodity speculation that he has neither the finances nor the nervous system to withstand its demands. Perhaps it takes three such catastrophes, or only one. The number of failures required to accomplish the result is not so important as the fact that a high proportion of speculative failures could be turned into successes by some common sense preparation in advance of actual entry into the market. Commodity speculation should be learned without risking money on one's untried judgment.

Most people are less than satisfied with their first efforts in any demanding field. It should not surprise anyone to learn that unskilled speculators are prone to lose a lot more money than they make in the beginning stages of their speculative careers. There is hardly a successful professional speculator alive who will not admit that his first speculative undertakings produced highly disappointing results. With experience comes ability, however, and provided one has the intelligence, tenacity, finances, and strong nerves required to take the speculator's role in the marketplace, rich rewards await him.

There is no such thing as having a natural talent for agricultural commodity speculation. While the field is far less complex—and therefore safer—than speculation in stocks, real estate, or international currencies, it is, nevertheless, a most demanding business. Those who seriously apply themselves to it have a good chance for success. Those who approach it haphazardly, as a financial fling, will certainly lose their money sooner or later—and they deserve to lose it.

Picking Your Commodity

The first step in embarking on a speculative program is to equip yourself for efficient function. Ships of the U.S. fleet, combat pilots, and performing artists make innumerable "dry runs" or rehearsals to sharpen judgment and develop reflexes necessary to insure efficient operation when faced with the "real thing." This is precisely the way commodity speculation should be approached. Several months of practice, is minimal preparation before a beginning speculator should hazard his first dollar in the market.

The first question which requires answering involves selection of a single commodity in which to concentrate initial attention. Whether the choice be coffee, corn, pork bellies, or silver, an almost limitless amount of information is available from both private and official sources. Let's assume that a domestic agricultural crop is selected for a beginning. The homework should follow a more or less firm outline:

1. Using the facilities of a good library, familiarize yourself with all of the pertinent information you can find about the crop itself; its geographic distribution, growing season, historical production and use patterns, federal support and acreage control program, if any, and other commodities which compete directly or indirectly with it in the marketplace.
2. Accumulate a background of price and trading information on the futures contracts, including historical highs and lows, seasonal price behavior, open-interest, hedging activity, crop disappearance, and trading volume. The pertinent exchange or any good brokerage office will be glad to furnish this kind of material to you.

By seeking out such information and digesting it, the serious student of the subject will, in a surprisingly short period, have acquired well-above-average knowledge about the commodity. With his interest thus concentrated, he will discover that the daily newspaper, business press, weekly news magazines, and trade publications, constantly add to his fund of knowledge about the crop and enhance his feel for the commodity and its market.

3. As soon as the commodity is selected, the speculator-in-training should begin immediately to follow daily price quotations on the exchange or exchanges where it is traded. Note particularly the price behavior of the selected commodity, as compared with the market in general. Attempt to develop an understanding of why the *general market* might be up, and prices on the *selected commodity* unchanged or lower; or why the selected commodity might outperform all other agricultural commodities on a given day or week. Do not abandon interest in finding the answer to a question of this kind just because the event has passed. Market analysts are always experts in hindsight. They can invariably explain why a particular price adjustment occurred—24 hours later. The successful speculator must learn to *project* a given piece of news in terms of probable impact on prices. The function of the speculator is to forecast changes in value in the future. If he can do this, he has no other worries. Learning to do it takes both knowledge and practice.

4. While a professional charting service can be an important aid and a great time-saver for the individual who is unable to maintain his own price behavior data, at the outset subscribe to only a weekly or monthly service and mark your own daily price data. A daily newspaper, pencil, and ruler are all that is required.

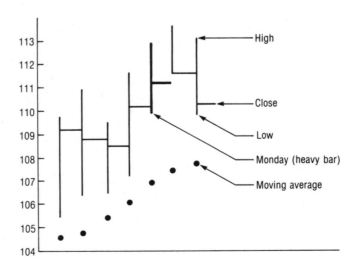

Exhibit 11–1

After each day's trading range is known, enter the high, low, and closing price on the contracts in which you are interested. In addition to maintaining this simple bar chart on price ranges and closes, plot a 10 or 20-day moving price average as well. Moving price is arrived at by taking all daily *settlements* prices for the period involved, adding them together and dividing by the number of days in the control interval. Each day thereafter, the *oldest* settlement price is dropped, the *latest* settlement price is added, and the total figure is redivided by the number of days being used. The result is plotted as a dot on the chart. A moving average will help you identify short-term aberrations, and think in terms of trend.

Charts and Chart Traders

Chart devotees are by no means agreed as to the best charting method. Nor, for that matter, do they concur as to the theoretical validity or practical usefulness of charts as price projection devices. This much can be said for the charts, however, and with no fear of contradiction:

There are sufficient traders in the market whose activities are influenced to some degree by chart patterns, that the individual trader—whether or not he is willing to pin his success exclusively to the chart concept—can ill afford to ignore the chart traders. Those who follow charts exclusively, or to some extent, are legion! They can move a market.

The mere exercise of maintaining a chart on daily prices and moving averages will force the newcomer to speculation to think critically about trading ranges and general movement of price levels—higher, sideways, or lower. While the beginning student of speculation is developing his

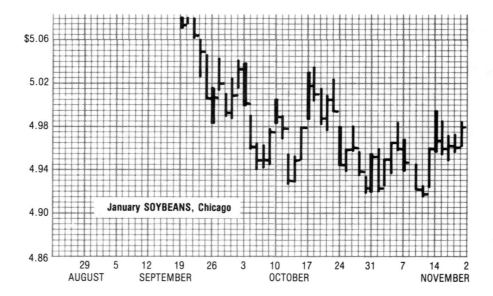

Exhibit 11–2

own powers of analysis, chart patterns will materially assist him in developing a firm notion about new position points, and profit expectations and loss limits in any particular position he might take.

In Exhibit 11–2, for example, a long position established at $4.96 in January soybeans has an obvious stop-loss point. If prices should break through the 4.91½ level, it would represent an important downside penetration and would probably trigger heavy selling on the part of people who put important store in chart trading techniques. The stop-loss order should, therefore, be placed no lower than $4.91 to protect against such a possibility.

If the trader chooses to establish a short position at $4.96 per bushel in January soybeans, the chart again clarifies the point at which his stop-loss should be placed. If the price moves above $4.99½, it would constitute a new interim breakout on the topside, with the next higher objective at about $5.04.

The stop-loss on such a short position, therefore, should be at the point at which the initial upside penetration is sufficiently obvious to prompt concerted buying on the part of chart traders.

Statistical price projection techniques and chart analysis has been dealt with in great detail in a companion volume entitled *Charting Commodity Market Price Behavior*. In combination, these two books constitute a no-risk means for learning about commodity markets and how to trade in them without putting up money until some expertise has been acquired and demonstrated.

Price-Only Chart Traders

For this work, suffice it to say that whether one agrees with the theory of price forecasting solely on the basis of past price behavior—and your author most emphatically does not—there are enough market participants who do place some degree of store in this notion as to constitute a significant force in the market. While it may be argued most effectively that their reasons are not valid, the fact that chartists do tend to trade in concert produces price behaviorisms which attest to their collective "muscle" in the marketplace. *One need not unequivocally endorse any particular chartist doctrine in order to recognize it as a force in price determination.*

Experimental Trading

5. As soon as the beginning speculator has developed some reasonable background information on his chosen commodity field and has prepared his basic charts on the selected contracts in the commodity, he is ready to begin experimental trading. Exhibit 11–3 shows a trading card which the author employs regularly, and which will serve the beginning speculator as effectively as the practicing professional.

```
┌─────────────────────────────────────────────────────────────────┐
│ LONG                          COMMODITY ORDER                     │
│ SHORT                                                             │
│ OFFSET—NEW                    Date _____│
│                                                                   │
│ Order No. _____      Time of Day _____ : _____ │
│                                                                   │
│ Brokerage House _____│
│                                                                   │
│ Solicitor Rep. _____│
│                                                                   │
│ BUY   SELL    Amount _____ Contract _____│
│                                                                   │
│               Price _____ Limits _____ │
│                                                                   │
│               Stop-Loss _____ Profit Obj. _____  │
│                                                                   │
│ Time-Limit  DAY    OPEN    OTHER _____  │
│                                                                   │
│ Disposition  EXECUTED    CANCELLED    EXPIRED                     │
│                                                                   │
│ Confirmed by _____ Date _____ Time _____ : _____ │
│                                                                   │
│ Remarks _____ │
└─────────────────────────────────────────────────────────────────┘
```

Exhibit 11–3

Permission for the purchaser of this book to duplicate this form is granted.

Using a letter shop or a copying machine, get a supply of these order forms. Number each one of the forms in advance to make sure that in days to come every practice trade is recorded.

There is an overwhelming human tendency for us to remember successes and forget failures. Speculation requires that profits be added and losses be subtracted with equal diligence. Unless this is meticulously done, the student of speculation will have no reliable scorecard against which to check his progress in outperforming the general market.

6. In addition to the trading cards, a sheet like the one shown in Exhibit 11–4 should also be prepared. Column 2 is for the entry of practice positions taken. Column 5 carries the margin deposit which would be required. Column 6 reflects the profit objective at the time the position is taken. Column 7 reflects the stop-loss level where—should prices move against you—the position will be automatically closed out by offset. Column 11 is for the gross profit or loss on each individual trade. Column 12 carries the brokerage commission which must always be deducted from profits, or added to losses. Column 13 will show net profit or loss on each trade.

Position								Offset										
Date	Long (Short) Price	Amount	Contract Code	Margin	Profit Objective	Stop-Loss	Date	Buy (Sell) Price	Amount	Gross Profit (Loss)	Broker-age Commis-sion	Net Profit (Loss)	Total Position Profit (Loss)	Risk Capital Balance			Margin Calls

Exhibit 11–4

Permission for the purchaser of this book to duplicate this form is granted.

Date	Position Long (Short) Price	Amount	Contract	Margin	Profit Objective	Stop-Loss	Offset Date	Buy (Sell) Price	Amount	Gross Profit (Loss)	Broker-age Commis-sion	Net Profit (Loss)	Total Position Result	Risk Capital Balance	
														2	500|00
6/23	132½	10	CZ	$800	140	130⅝	7/12	(142)	10	$950					
28	136¼	10	CZ	800	140	133⅝	7/12	(142)	10	575					
7/5	139½	10	CZ	800	147	135½	7/12	(142)	10	250	$132	$1,643	$1,643	1	643ᵒᵒ
														4	143ᵒᵒ
8/16	(151⅛)	10	CZ	$800	145	153¼	8/22	153¼	10	($212⁵⁰)	$44ᵒᵒ	($256⁵⁰)	($256⁵⁰)		(256⁵⁰)
														3	886⁵⁰
9/1	(146¾)	10	CZ	$800	140	147⅜									

Exhibit 11–5

Each trade should be entered as soon as it is executed, and the data completed after it has been offset.

By documenting each position taken on a trading card and arraying the salient points of the trade on the recap sheet, the beginner in speculation will have an immediate check on his open positions, and a running recap of consolidated gains or losses to date. It is also urged that the losses be entered on the recap sheet in red, for added emphasis; and—hopefully—to prompt careful reexamination of the factors which lured you into an unsuccessful speculative position in the first place.

Practice Trading at a Realistic Level

A key consideration in this program is to begin your theoretical trading with a *fixed number of dollars* in the hypothetical margin account. The practice trading figure should be governed by the level at which the novice intends to conduct his *real* trading activity, later.

It makes no sense for a training program in speculation to be set up with the fictional million dollars, when one's later entry into the real market will be made with a bankroll of a few thousand. For maximum benefits from practice trading, it should be conducted within the same practical limitations that will apply to the real thing. Unless this is done, the exercise is little more than an intriguing game. Amusing though such an engagement might be, it won't have much direct connection with reality. More importantly, it won't contribute much to the search for speculative profits, which is the exclusive purpose of the project.

Establish your hypothetical margin account at the same amount you may expect to ultimately deposit with your broker. *Don't overextend yourself.* It often pays to settle for modest victories, in return for having to face only small defeats. *Patience, courage,* and *conservatism* are the three keys to successful speculation.

In any event, an initial market position should never tie up more than 50 percent of margin funds. For example, the highest minimum margin requirement of any of the grains is that of soybeans which, at this writing, is 35 cents per bushel. The initial margin on one contract (5,000 bushels) of soybeans is therefore $1,750. In order to prudently undertake such a program, the practicing speculator should have a minimum of $3,500 of margin funds available. Moreover, until the soybean position is closed out and margin funds committed to it are freed, no further *initial* speculative positions should be taken, although a winning position may later be added to. This is a most important reason to always keep part of your speculative capital in reserve.

The thinking behind this method of risk-capital management is exceedingly basic: The overwhelming majority of speculative failures grow directly out of overtrading. Newcomers to the field fail to realize that the only survival insurance a speculator can have is additional cash resources to draw on. As will be demonstrated later, the commodity trader *need not be right even half of the time* in order to make a profit from his speculative endeavors. If 4 out of 10 positions are right, your survival as a speculator can be confidently predicted; if 6 out of 10 positions taken prove profitable, the profits should be impressive, indeed.

The reason this is true is that throughout his speculative career and in every trading situation, without exception, the successful speculator rigidly adheres to rules which maximize profit opportunities and minimize loss exposures. In the language of the marketplace, he cuts losses short and lets profits run.

As a result, the average profit on all profitable positions will be appreciably larger than the average loss taken on all losing positions. Proven techniques for "pyramiding" can have the effect of multiplying returns from profitable positions. This multiplying factor never operates in the loss realm, because additions are never made to a losing position—regardless of the circumstances!

So, now, the beginning speculator is set:

1. He has selected his commodity area and informed himself about it.
2. He has obtained basic charts which graphically show short- and medium-range price movement patterns.
3. He has prepared numbered trading cards which will document every hypothetical position he takes and, later, assist in analyzing the components of success or failure in each trade.
4. He has a trading recap sheet which constantly shows consolidated profits or losses to date, while red and black entries offer a realistic basis for evaluating his batting average as trading skills, market information, and speculative judgment improve.

With this preliminary research done and the simple trading tools at hand, the beginner is ready to begin speculating "on paper."

The effectiveness of this method of study depends entirely on the consistency of the individual in maintaining complete records on the hypothetical operations. Each position should be most carefully appraised before it is taken. At the time it is taken, it must be entered on a numbered trading card, so that it cannot be later forgotten, regardless of its outcome. The reason should be abundantly clear: Once real trading has commenced, every position involves a firm order placed with the broker, and commitment of margin funds to secure it. *Profits* and *losses* are the only two words that mean anything in the real world of speculation, because money is going to be made or money will be lost on every trade.

The beginner who fails to apply the same hardheaded yardstick to his exploratory activities as the market will impose on him later is needlessly depriving himself of information and experience which will have to be gained somehow. The only pertinent question is whether the learning process will be carried out without jeopardizing funds, or whether speculative lessons will have to be learned later, in the expensive "school of hard knocks."

12

Selecting Your Risks

For purposes of this discussion we will assume that the novice to speculation has selected soybeans as the commodity area in which he intends to concentrate attention. Soybeans have been, and continue to be, an exceedingly popular area for public speculation. There are several reasons for this, chief among which is the fact that soybean production in the United States is an expanding activity but one which does not yet appear to have succeeded in catching up with total world demand for the product. In view of the continuing relative shortage, higher prices appear to be in prospect as the general trend—subject, of course, to the constant reminder that prices fluctuate in the short-term, regardless of what their longer-range trend may be.

Soybeans offer a good speculative exercise for the serious student for still another reason: There is essentially no use for soybeans in their natural state. The worth of the soybean depends on prices commanded by its two products: soybean meal and oil. Both meal and oil futures are also traded, thus providing the bean speculator with two additional and important points of reference. *Soybean prices* can be evaluated as being too low, too high, or about right, as measured in product values. The relationship between prices on beans versus meal and oil will be explored in considerable detail later on. For now, we will restrict our attention exclusively to soybean futures, with a view to selecting a particular contract for trade.

Six Contracts from Which to Choose

Six or more different soybean maturities are open for trade at any given time. As this is being prepared, the Chicago Board of Trade has contracts in soybeans open for delivery in November, January, March, May, July, August and September; along with "new crop" contracts in November 1985, and January 1986. Some comment regarding this trading calendar may be in order. (Soybeans are also traded on the MidAmerica Commodity Exchange, in 1,000-bushel contracts.)

The crop year begins in October and runs through the following September. The first "new crop" contract therefore is November, followed by another contract maturity at two month intervals, until July. The August contract was added to the market schedule to assist cleanup of "old crop" beans and preparation for storage and marketing of the new harvest.

In some years, depending on the weather patterns, a substantial amount of new crop beans may reach the market in September. Consequently, the September contract has some quandaries in it that are not encountered in other months. If the harvest is late, September supplies may be scanty. If the harvest is early, September may turn out to be a new crop month. As a result of this variable, the September maturity tends to be one of the most volatile in the entire soybean futures calendar.

To set the stage for the basic trading problem, we will use current conditions as they actually exist. The bean market closed yesterday (October 12, 1984) as follows:

Cash market price—$6.26 per bushel.

The Wall Street Journal reported the futures contracts as follows:

						Lifetime		Open
	Open	*High*	*Low*	*Settle*	*Change*	*High*	*Low*	*Interest*
Soybeans (CBT) 5,000 bu.; cents per bu.								
Nov.	622	627	619 1/2	625	+12	772 1/4	568 1/2	32,323
Jan85	633	637	630	635 3/4	+11 3/4	779	580 1/2	13,818
Mar	648 1/2	651 1/2	644	649 1/4	+ 9 1/4	790 1/2	593 1/2	6,741
May	661	663 1/2	656 1/2	661 1/4	+11	797	601	3,327
July	663	668 1/2	661 1/2	667 1/4	+12 1/2	799	607	6,084
Aug	664	668	663	667	+12 1/2	756	610 1/2	688
Sept	652	657 1/2	652	657 1/2	+14	667	605	238
Nov	648 1/2	657	648	655 1/4	+12 3/4	660	602	1,503
Jan86	668 1/2	668 1/2	668 1/2	668 1/2	+13 1/2	668 1/2	643	5

Est vol n.a.; vol Thur 26,665; open int 64,727, +1,216.

In analyzing the significance of the price differentials between these contracts, it must be remembered that if the value of the product is fixed and carrying charges are constant, price relationships between commodity months should ascend in a uniform stair-step fashion. Lack of uniformity reflects varying degrees of supply/demand imbalance, as appraised by the market and discounted in its assignment of price values.

For example, assuming that $6.26 per bushel represents the "right" cash price for soybeans on this date and further assuming carrying charges of 4 cents per bushel per month, we could expect to see the several bean contracts reflecting prices as follows:

October 12 — $6.26 per bushel (Chicago) (cash price)
November — $6.30 per bushel
January — $6.38 per bushel
March — $6.46 per bushel
May — $6.54 per bushel
July — $6.62 per bushel
August — $6.66 per bushel
September — $6.70 per bushel
November — $6.78 per bushel (new crop)
January '86 — $6.86 per bushel (new crop)

These figures are based on acceptance of $6.26 per bushel as the *right price* for contract quality soybeans in Chicago's *cash* market on October 12. The same product scheduled for delivery one month hence should theoretically carry a price tag of $6.30, with the added 4 cents representing storage costs, insurance, and interest over the period involved. The same quality product scheduled for delivery 90 days later will have incurred 12 cents in carrying charges over the three month interval, and so on.

Instead of finding this orderly state of affairs, however, we see that the currently-quoted *cash* price for contract grade beans stands at $6.26 per bushel, while the nearby November contract stands at $6.25; a penny-per-bushel premium for immediate delivery. Or, stated another way, the November maturity is showing a 1 cent *negative carrying charge* off the cash price.

Now let's look further into our soybean situation. Except for the inversion between cash beans and the nearby November, we see a normal market persisting through the July maturity. A *normal* market is one that reflects carrying-charge premiums between nearer and more distant deliveries. The premiums need not equal anything approaching full carrying costs—and usually will not—but if *any* premium exists on a deferred delivery, the trade labels it *normal*.

August, we note, stands ¼ cent under July, with September 9½ cents under August, and November at 11¾ under the August delivery. Why should this be? Let's think it through:

The August contract represents a cleanup of the current year's crop that may still be languishing in expensive storage. If the harvest (1984 crop) has proved to be a large one, there may be a lot of storage beans coming into the market in August 1985. If so, the sellers of those old stocks may have to accept somewhat lower prices for them, in order to clear their storage facilities and get ready for the new-crop harvest, represented in the November delivery.

Thus we may hypothesize that the trade is keeping the price on August a bit under July, because of uncertainty about the amount of old crop beans that might then remain to be processed. The steep discount on September is evidence that the traders know that if weather and temperatures are benign, a lot of *new crop* beans can hit the market well before their scheduled November debut. Should this happen *along with* a large carry-over inventory from the 1984 old crop stores, the resulting glut could devastate prices until the oversupply is handled.

The November contract, which is the designated new crop appearance, is only slightly under (1¼ cents below) the September. Does this indicate that good long-range weather forecasts suggest an early soybean harvest in 1985? Or does it merely reflect failure of the trade to bring these two contracts into a proper basis relationship? These are questions for speculators to speculate about!

Now consider the January 1986 quotation. It carries more than 13 cents premium over the November. Granted, there are only 5 contracts open in this most distant listing; as compared with 1,503 contracts open in the November. Again, it must be asked, is this just a reflection of poor market "tone?" Or is it someone's speculative notion that the 1985–86 winter will be sufficiently severe as to seriously interfere with deliveries of the product to the crushers. When this happens, prices climb dramatically in recognition of the fact as the processors bid up for short offerings, in an effort to keep their mills busy. Again, it's a speculative puzzle that each trader can evaluate and deal with as he sees fit.

When a trader sees a price out of line on the high side, he sells it. If the price appears unrealistically low, he buys it. If the differential between deliveries offers an attractive carrying-charge premium, the "spreading" speculator buys the nearby and sells the deferred in anticipation of a narrowing between the two. If immediate shortage runs nearby prices to steep *inversions,* the astute speculator will be looking for a place to sell the nearby premiums and buy the deferred discounts, and profit from a return to normal relationships when the shortage problem is solved.

We shall now begin sharpening the analytical tools that enable a trader to settle on the right decision, at the right time.

In evaluating the trading opportunity in soybeans, the first decision is that of selecting the best contract for trade, in light of the personal desires and trading pattern of the speculator.

In a *normal market,* often referred to as a *carrying-charge market,* we will expect to find cash prices slightly under nearby futures contracts, with more distant contracts reflecting carrying charges in the form of somewhat higher values. Any time this pattern is reversed, it is a reflection of some degree of immediate—and perhaps urgent—scarcity.

Whenever prices on the deferred futures show discounts rather than premiums over the nearby contracts, it is spoken of as an inversion, indicating that the normal price relationships are inverted—upside down.

In the situation being examined, the current shortage of cash beans is a result of light offerings on the part of farmers, country elevators, and commercial grain dealers who own and/or control disposition of the physical inventories. There is no shortage of soybeans in the interior. Quite the contrary.

With the end of the crop year, the trade had developed an idea about how many old-crop beans remained to be used up or exported. The consensus settled around 115 to 130 million bushels. However, when the USDA "Stocks In All Positions Report" came out in September, it surprised the trade with an estimate of 175 million bushels of soybeans still overhanging the market from the 1983 crop year. The effect of this larger-than-expected figure was seen in a 45 cent break in the November contract over the next three sessions.

The large amount of remaining old-crop stocks was, by itself, a major blow to the bulls—but there was more to come. The USDA "Crop Production Report" issued on the 12th of September estimated the 1984 domestic soybean harvest at 2,027,000,000 bushels! Taken together, the remaining beans in store and the new crop production estimate was too much for the hard-pressed bulls to handle. All prices on soybeans broke dramatically, with the nearby November contract going from $6.33 on September 12, to an intrasession low of $5.69 per bushel on September 21.

This price action was triggered by information that seemed to promise copious supplies of soybeans, both currently and during the projected crop year. In spite of this, cash beans were in relatively short supply—as witness the one cent premium processors were forced to pay in order to lure inventories out of "first hands" and the commercial pipeline. Thus we see that there is more than mere *quantity* considerations present in the supply/demand equation. If the owners of a commodity refuse to release it at a given price level, they may—for some period of time—distort prices upward to their temporary advantage.

The market has a consistent record of dealing with "first things first." Present shortage is the high priority problem. The market always seeks to solve it by offering a higher price. The 1 cent premium for cash will lure some soybeans out of storage and into the channels of distribution. At the same time, *carrying charges* on more deferred deliveries indicates that the market feels that as time goes by, soybean supplies will be released in sufficient quantities, and that overall, total supply will be adequate.

The price pattern is a clear example of the market discounting the future. It may be that in months to come, the present holding might persist. If this happens, the price on cash and March soybeans may very well move up to a par with the current quote on January, or may even go higher if the relative shortage becomes more acute. At this point, however, the market "doesn't think" this will happen. *Normal* (carrying-charge) premiums on deferred contracts are clear proof of the statement.

The overriding considerations in trading soybeans in the situation being examined are these:

1. Ample stocks of the product are available in the "country," but they have been held out of the market by producers as a means of obtaining higher prices.

2. Present stocks in processor hands are less than they would like them to be, because farmers have not sold their in-store stocks as freely as they might have.

3. Crushing percentages to date are running somewhat behind the same period a year ago, as are exports. Unless the commodity "comes out" it can't be consumed.

4. The composite projection must be that bean supplies in 1985 will be even larger than they were in 1983–84. Unless disappearance rates can be accelerated, oversupply problems await in months to come.

Two distinct possibilities exist for the soybean trader:

1. If he believes the holding movement on the part of farmers will continue beyond the first of the coming year, then the January (and perhaps March) contracts should appear inviting from the *long* side. Moreover, if the farmer holding movement is expected to continue through the first quarter of 1985, then both May and July should offer attractive *short* sales.

The reason is, quite simply, that 1984 beans which do not come to market in the year of their harvest must certainly come to market *prior to the 1985 harvest*. By withholding beans for several months and influencing prices upward, the producers will have obtained their high prices in the interim at the cost of disrupting orderly patterns of consumption through processing and export.

It is logical to assume that *concerted farm holding* will have to be followed by *concerted farm selling*. At some point in early spring or summer, 1985, unseasonally heavy arrivals—and resulting oversupply—will drive prices down, probably creating a bear market situation in soybeans for the last four or five months of the old-crop year.

2. The second possibility is that current premiums on nearby months will be eased by larger soybean arrivals immediately after January 1, 1985. It may be that current farmer holding grows out of a desire on their part to merely defer income on the 1984 crop until the new year, in order to avoid proportionately higher taxes on it. If this case proves to be correct, then the speculator might expect an easing of prices in the January maturity; and relatively lower prices in more deferred contracts as well, as the impact of heavier releases is felt in the market.

The only thing which can sustain premium on cash or the nearby months is shortage. At whatever point the shortage is broken, carrying charges may be expected to reappear on all later deliveries.

Trading Nearby versus Deferred

In choosing a futures month in which to trade, it is imperative that the speculator remember that in the face of increasing shortage, prices on the near delivery will move higher and faster than on the more deferred maturities. In a situation of increasing oversupply, prices on nearby delivery will move lower and faster than on the later months. Generally speaking, trading in the nearby month calls for closer attention to price behavior, for the reasons stated earlier. Trading in a more deferred contract, while still requiring careful attention, does not call for the day-by-day or hour-by-hour surveillance that the maturing contract does.

Entering the Order

With the foregoing information as a basis for judgment, let us now assume that on October 1, the speculator decides to buy 10,000 bushels of May soybeans—market—"on the opening."

He fills out the hypothetical market order on a card, to be transacted "on the opening," October 1. The following evening, the newspaper shows that the opening gave a price of 622½ per bushel (a slightly lower opening than the previous day's close).

In addition to marking execution and price on the trading card, he also enters the transaction on his recap sheet. Checking Exhibit 12–2, we note that the first profit objective on the position is $6.40½ which is just over the intraday highs established on September 23, and 27. The rationale for this decision is that if price succeeds in bettering the two recent intraday highs, there might be enough chart followers to keep pushing it higher, perhaps with a view to filling the gap left on September 13.

```
 ┌─────────────────────────────────────────────────────────┐
 │ (LONG)         C O M M O D I T Y   O R D E R            │
 │  SHORT                                                   │
 │  OFFSET (NEW)    Date  10-1-84                           │
 │  Order No.  1    Time of Day        :                   │
 │  Brokerage House  Practice Trade                        │
 │  Solicitor Rep. _____                │
 │ (BUY) SELL, Amount  10   Contract  SK-May Beans         │
 │         Price 622½   Limits _____              │
 │         Stop Loss 618½   Profit Obj. 6.40½              │
 │  Time-Limit (DAY) OPEN  OTHER _____             │
 │  Disposition (EXECUTED) CANCELLED  EXPIRED              │
 │  Confirmed  Press   Date 10-1  Time Opening            │
 │  Remarks:  Opening price                                │
 └─────────────────────────────────────────────────────────┘
```

Exhibit 12–1

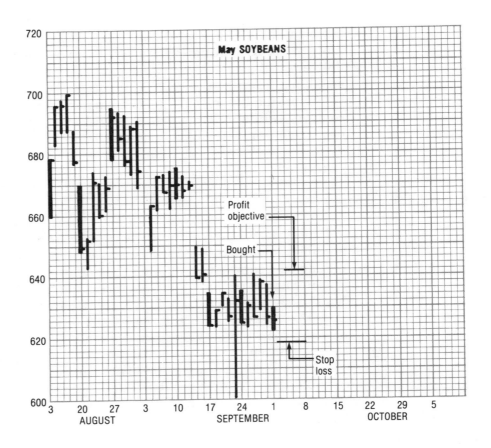

Exhibit 12–2

However, should price fail to penetrate the $6.40 level and fall below $6.20, it would be indicative of sufficient weakness to perhaps carry on down to a new life-of-contract low—under $6.00. Inasmuch as the $6.00 low was established by impaired longs fleeing in the face of an 80 cent break that covered about four weeks, we can be sure that a lot of nervous bulls have been chased out of the contract. A move higher, therefore, is a logical expectation. In any case, the market is better technically situated to accept a move up than it is to follow further price deterioration so soon on the heels of a major break.

We have to be prepared for the price to test the $6.20 level, however. Recognizing this, the stop-loss order on this position is put at $6.18½, allowing a 1½ cent leeway, before the stop is hit. This should be sufficient latitude to minimize the possibility of getting *stopped-out* of the position by some fairly routine fluctuation.

Thus situated, we can now analyze the position in its essentials: profit and loss.

If events move in our favor, and the price does indeed rise, we will be waiting and *expecting* it to reach $6.40 and above; which will produce an 18 cent *profit*. Should the opposite occur and prices fall, we stand to *lose* 4 cents before the stop-loss order is activated and the position is offset. The initial profit expectation on this position, therefore, is more than four times the amount of impairment to be accepted before closing it out.

A word about the placement of stops: It is *never advisable* to place a stop-loss at the *even dollar, even dime, or even cent*. These levels represent "hurdles" in price movement. It is not uncommon for prices to move precisely to the even-money mark and then reverse directions. Experienced traders keep their stop-losses away from even money in all commodities which are traded in eighths or quarters of the cent; ⅝ to ½ above or below the even cent is a much safer stop point.

The initial position is now established. It has been documented on a trading card and entered on the recap sheet. The initial profit objective is identified and the stop-loss order is established. The speculator knows that his potential loss is limited to about 4 cents which, on 10,000 bushels, will amount to $400. His initial profit objective calls for a gain of $1,850. Now all that's required is patience.

Unless new information comes to light which urges abandoning the position entirely, there is nothing to be done now except wait for one eventuality or the other to develop. If the reasoning was sound at the outset, higher prices can be expected eventually; in the meantime, prices will fluctuate.

Patience Is a Virtue

As long as they move within the designated range, the speculator is still right and he must patiently wait for events to unfold. If he is wrong, he will know it when the price on his contract breaks $6.18½ on the downside and triggers his stop-loss. One thing is certain, however; the speculator will never know whether he is right or wrong until the market tells him.

Inexperienced traders suffer as much from impatience as from any other malady. This reflects itself in overeagerness to take positions without sound reasons for doing so, and to later abandon positions because the hoped-for developments do not immediately occur. So long as a position is not "hurting," there is probably no reason to close it out. One of two things will certainly happen if given time to do so: it will produce a profit or a loss!

No Trade Is Free

On the other hand, a position closed out prematurely carries a sure penalty in the form of brokerage commission. We will assume in this example that establishment of a position involving 10,000 bushels of soybeans will cost $160; with $80 the fee for each contract, to get the "in" and "out" sides of the transaction executed. Commission is the same, regardless of whether the position involved stays open for 10 minutes or 10 months. Viewed in this light, the public speculator should recognize that most of the first penny he makes on any grain contract is earmarked for the broker. It is only after this initial profit has been chalked up and deducted that the trader is adding to his own capital. All the more reason that good positions should be left alone and given an oportunity to produce their full return.

Don't Temporize with a Loser

If patience is a virtue in connection with letting profits run, short temper is even more so in connection with positions which reach loss limits. As previously pointed out, no position should be established without first having a firm expectation of the profit objective, and an inflexible limit on the loss you are willing to take before closing it out.

There is no better way to determine profit objectives and loss limits than by use of a bar chart. Other methods exist, which involve sophisticated application of price/value theory and equilibrium forces. Generally speaking, though, such an approach is too complex for all except highly trained practitioners of agricultural economics and statistics. Such a trading system is usually far too time-consuming to permit its

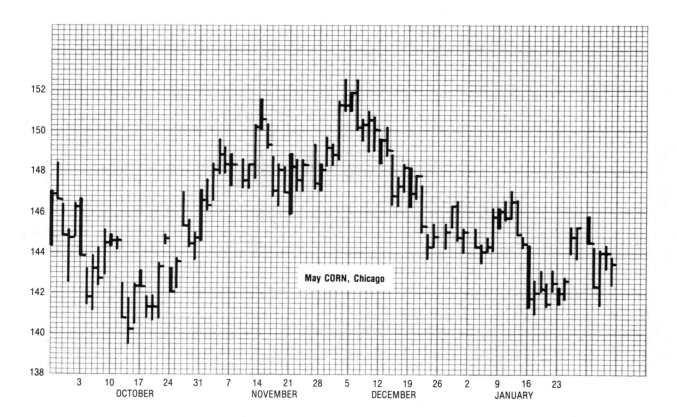

May CORN, Chicago

Exhibit 12–3

regular application to trading problems, even if you can do the math involved.

Charts are admittedly less than perfect trading tools, but their strengths more than offset their weaknesses. With experience in their use, a speculator will find that relatively simple charts meet his need for a quick picture of price behavior, as well as providing strong clues as to the probable behavior of a large group of competitors in the market. To repeat for emphasis, charts are not infallible. Neither is any other system of trading, except the axiom of cutting losses short and letting profits run. If this is done, the net outcome will produce *profits*. If the practice is not rigidly pursued, the result will be *losses*. All of the charts, statistics, and fundamental data in Christendom will not take the place of strict application of the basic speculative rule.

Watched Pots Never Boil

Once a commodity position has been taken, it is imperative that the trader steel himself to practice a high order of self-restraint. Prices which seemed to move most dramatically before you were in the contract now appear to have gone to sleep. The price on your contract may trade inside the range between your initial profit objective and your stop-loss for days at a time. In another situation, prices may immediately move against you and flirt maddeningly with your stop-loss level; or they may move to within a fraction of your first profit objective and then back away.

Impatience is the hallmark of an inexperienced trader. With a small profit on paper, his inclination more often than not, is to close out the position and take the profit. When price on his contract fails to move decisively in either direction, the impulse is to close out the position and find another which promises more action. It is only when prices

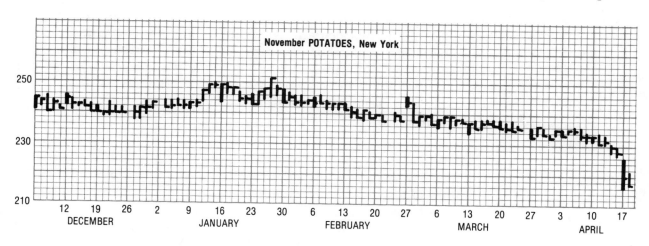

Exhibit 12–4

move against him that the newcomer to speculation usually demonstrates real firmness. It has been said that all it takes is a drop in prices to make a long-term "investor" out of a short-term "speculator." Strangely enough, it's true. The beginning speculator regularly shows steadier nerves in the face of adversity than he does when confronted by success.

Once situated in a position which makes no really definitive move in either direction, it pays to "sit steady in the boat." Until something happens to demand a new decision and justify a specific action with respect to the position, *do nothing*. The speculative program for the trade was laid out *before* the position was ever undertaken; barring new information which invalidates the previous concept—or price movement which triggers the stop-loss or reaches the first profit objective—there is nothing to be done except wait.

Don't Move Stops Away

A losing position, however, should never present a quandary. If the price reaches the stop-loss level, let the stop-loss take you out of it. It's hard to envision a speculator ever making a mistake by such action. Moving a stop-loss higher or lower to avoid being closed out is, in the overwhelming majority of cases, a serious mistake.

Adding to a losing position on the basis that in so doing you have "averaged" your buying price downward, or "averaged" your selling price upward, is also invariably a mistake, in spite of the fact that one may occasionally profit from such an atrocious trading practice. It's known as *cannon-balling*—and it will break you!

Never Add to a Loser

A speculative position is always taken in the search for profit. Only the market can tell the speculator whether his judgment is right or wrong. Until price movement has given the speculator a profit in his initial trading position, enlarging the position simply increases risk exposure and imposes heavier demands on the available risk capital. *More money will never improve a bad trade!*

To sum up, then:

1. When prices move against you, do nothing; or close out part or all of the position in accordance with your stop-losses.
2. As long as the price on your position "waits," the trader must wait also.
3. When price moves in your favor and develops a paper profit, a decision must be made concerning enlargement of the position or closeout to convert the paper profit into a cash profit.

Fledgling speculators tend to understand the first half of the trading admonition, "cut losses short and let profits run," but they have great difficulty in putting the second part of the rule into application.

Persistence in Price Movement

Prices, like weather, demonstrate a well recognized persistence factor. This is to say that when prices are moving higher, their tendency is to continue in an upward trend. When prices are moving lower, they tend to maintain their downward path. When prices are moving in a sideways channel, they tend to stay in a recognizable trading range, with neither decisive upward or downward movement.

The laws of momentum seem to apply to price behavior, as they do to physical bodies at rest or in motion. Prices moving in a given direction will maintain their direction until diverted or reversed by a new and stronger force. Prices at rest tend to stay at rest until "shoved" by some new consideration.

Beware of Trying to Pick Reversal Points

Countless speculative careers have been brought to an untimely halt by efforts to "pick tops and bottoms." This is to say that when prices are moving downward, the brave but misguided speculator may, at some particular point, decide that prices have dropped far enough. He takes a long position in the face of a clear-cut downtrend. All too often, prices continue to move lower, to the dismay and the financial damage of the trader who thought he had seen the bottom of the move.

There is no measurement which can be effectively applied to the market and which will subjectively prove that a given price is right or wrong. The *right price* for anything is that price which represents the composite market level at which *buyers will buy it* and *sellers will sell it*. Influences from the supply and demand sectors will alter prices upward or downward, and occasionally such a change in market value appraisal will be highly predictable. But the market is the only authority on price. The trader who undertakes to argue with the market had better base his case firmly on all available facts. This warning should be especially heeded as concerns speculative positions which are producing profits.

In the long-soybean position previously discussed, the trader has bought the May contract at $6.22½ per bushel, in anticipation of an 18 cent profit on the upside. When price moves to $6.40, for example, the trader might feel a strong urge to offset and take his profit. If he succumbs to the urge, he ignores the rule of "letting profits run." In moving up, the market has confirmed the trader's forecast of higher prices. It has rewarded the bulls, and it has penalized all of the short-holders. If price goes through the previously repeated interim high and continues up to $6.40½, the move may very well trigger increased offset buying

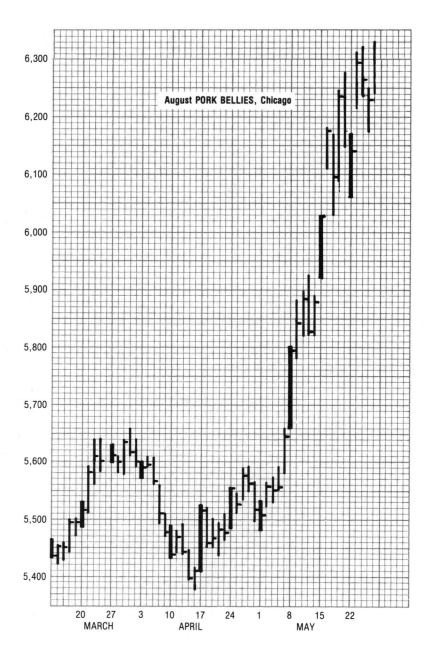

Exhibit 12–5

May 1 demonstrates a trap that caught a lot of short-selling bears.

by short-holders who previously placed their stop-loss orders around this point on the chart. Their added buying can be expected to send the price higher still, further increasing the speculative longs' profit and increasing the pressure on all of the impaired shorts. Should the price

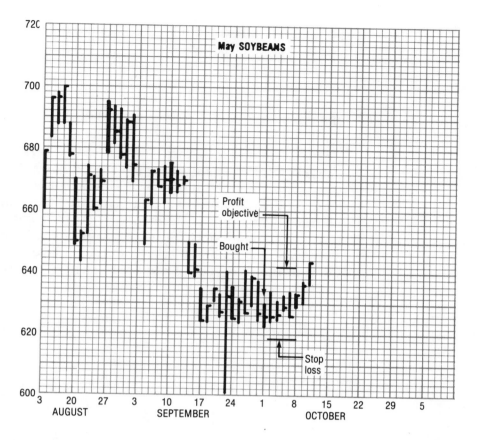

Exhibit 12–6

---

on May beans reach this important interim chart point ($6.40½) two courses of action are available to the speculative long, and only two:

1. *Hold the position* as it is and wait for the higher price that may materialize from sheer upward momentum and short-covering.
2. *Add to the position* by buying an additional quantity of soybean futures, which will enhance returns on any further price appreciation. This additional buying will also add its element of upside pressure, aiding the longs' quest for higher prices.

Pyramiding Increases Leverage

There is a further argument in favor of enlarging a profitable position: Whereas sale of the first 10,000 bushels called for posting margin in the amount of $3,500 out of the trader's risk capital, the second sale of 10,000 bushels (at $6.40½), while requiring another $3,500 in margin, will not reduce remaining speculative risk funds proportionately, because $1,800 of the new margin requirement is available from the paper profit already accrued on the position. Hence, the speculator is in the position of "trading on profits" and from a vastly improved leverage situation, as concerns his own risk dollars.

Picking Initial Risks

There is no single criterion which will separate a speculation which should be taken from one which should not be taken. This, in spite of the "voice from the tomb," and similar successes that one may occasionally hear about in which a given trader "*always* buys May corn in November and sells it the last week in January—and *always* makes a profit." The market is full of such ready-made timetables. As a rule, they have some basis in price trends on a given contract at a particular point in the crop year. If accepted at all, such formulas should only be

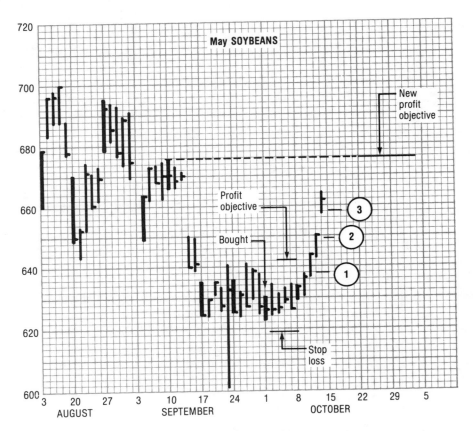

Exhibit 12–7

By staying with the May beans—or adding to the position at $6.40—subsequent sessions carry the price 40¢ higher in orderly steps. At each daily level the trader can move his stop-loss order up a penny or so under the "even dime," and keep on chalking up profits. An aggressive trader would add another story to his pyramid at each 10 cents up; at the same time he raised his stops to levels marked 1, 2, and 3.

viewed as suggestions based on historic price patterns. If infallibility could be ascribed to any such trading timetable, speculation would cease to involve risk; traders would need only to adhere to the rule to make a fortune. You can be sure that *everyone* would soon know the rule.

Initial risk selection is the most demanding part of speculation. Once a position is established, a given chain of events may call for its being closed out when losses reach allowable limits. Or, in the opposite frame of reference, a contrary series of events will suggest that the position be held, added to, or closed out to protect the profits it has produced. But there is no established formula for picking a risk which a reasonably conservative speculator should undertake, although there are a few guides to the matter which can be helpful.

In order to properly understand risk evaluation, we first need to recognize that the future always holds three major classifications of events to come:

1. Under the first heading must be placed all of those possibilities which, although confidently expected, *are not susceptible to any rational analysis,* such as guessing the color of the next automobile which will turn a particular corner. A proposition of this kind is *random*—it is devoid of statistical continuity or a cause-effect relationship which can be evaluated or preexamined. As such, it is unpredictable and, if one attempts to guess such an event, he is trying to make a selective forecast in an area which must be statistically viewed as chaos.

2. At the extreme other end of the scale, we have the *solidly predictable* event. Although it may be absolutely dark at midnight, we can predict sunrise a few hours away and precisely estimate the time at which it will occur; the solar cycle is stable, recurrent, and known. We are dealing with certainty.

3. Somewhere between absolute chaos and complete predictability, we have an area for qualitative evaluation which can be called *risk;* and which might be viewed as comprised of some elements

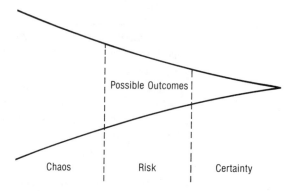

Exhibit 12–8

of *predictability* and other elements of *unpredictability*. Qualitatively, greater risk relates to a reduction in certainty and an increase in chaos.

Speculation centers itself on values as measured by price. While we may not be able to firmly fix the right price on corn as of this moment, it should not be hard to gain agreement with the notion that deliverable grade corn in the present market would command a price within a range of 30 cents above or below $3.50 per bushel. Accepting this, $3.20 per bushel may be viewed as something like the lower margin of price movement probability; $3.80 per bushel is identified as the upper limit of probable price value in the current state of things which affect the selected commodity. The price range spelled out stands as a *qualification of the degree of risk* involved in buying or selling corn at $3.50 per bushel.

As an extreme demonstration of the above hypothesis, consider a seller who wishes to dispose of commodity X, the character and usefulness of which is unknown, both to his market and to himself. Being unfamiliar with the nature of X commodity, there is no theoretical limit to its maximum value; and its lowest possible price is only found at zero—since worthlessness in the market sense represents the bottom of the value scale.

Dealing in commodity X involves dealing in randomness, an exercise in attempting to forecast in an area of total unpredictability.

Now let us consider trade in a commodity like copper, which, under a wartime emergency, is rationed and governed by price control. So long as these strictures are imposed, there can only be one effective price, except at the hazard of breaking the law. The price on the commodity must remain at the *administered price*.

Now let us consider these three market situations in the light of a speculator's interest and function:

1. Trading in commodity X is not a speculation; it is a *gamble,* since no criteria exists by which price/value judgment can be developed. Any outcome of a trade in commodity X would be based purely on chance, not speculation.
2. Trading in a commodity in which price is fixed by law and in which fluctuation is not permitted offers no opportunity for profit. Speculation is always directed to predicting price change in a search for profit or an effort to minimize loss. Hence, there is no speculative opportunity here.
3. Trading in corn which has a price value in range from $3.20 to $3.80 per bushel offers a 60 cent per bushel *speculative opportunity,* within which a speculator can be rewarded for being right in his price analysis, or penalized for his error in price judgment. *This is the essence of speculation.*

Of the three situations outlined, neither commodity X nor the fixed price commodity offers the slightest attraction to the speculator. Trading in either of these classifications of merchandise would represent

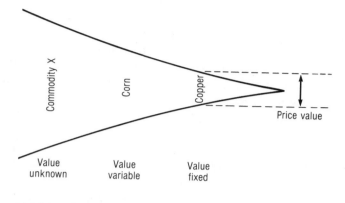

Exhibit 12-9

something other than speculation, in the first instance by reason of *no opportunity to make an appraisal of value;* and in the second, by reason of *no opportunity to make a profit.* It is only in trading situations where prices can move, and intelligent appraisals can be made, that speculation is feasible.

Components of Risk

We have displayed a hypothesis above that helps us quantify relative risk in a traded commodity by offering some rational guidance concerning the probable amplitude of price fluctuation, *above* or *below* whatever *equilibrium value* exists at any moment in time. Now we will undertake to separate and identify the kinds of considerations that in combination comprise the total risk element that is measured in price changes.

The first category of risk in commodity pricing is the larger one; and shall be identified as *systematic risk.* This labeling includes macro-inputs that exert important influence on the fundamental supply/demand situation for the commodity as a whole. As concerns wheat, for example, the *systematic* risks include such things as:

Farmer planting intentions.

Weather, diseases, and insects.

World production.

Exports.

War and peace.

Government policies and programs.

Obviously our nation's farmers must plant the crop if we are to have it. However, unless moisture and temperature are conducive to growth, and diseases and insects are controlled, there will be no harvest. Wheat is grown and consumed worldwide, so the demand that exists for our wheat in the international market will be importantly influenced by the quantities of wheat produced in Canada, Australia, Russia, China, and by other world competitors. During the five-year period from 1975 to 1980, almost 60 percent of our total wheat production was exported.

International strife tends to accelerate "disappearance" of wheat and other cereal grains. Some authorities attribute this increased usage to wasteful practices in overdistribution and excessive stockpiling, but it makes no difference what occasions it. In terms of economic effect, the sinking of a ship loaded with grain has the same impact on supply/demand balance as if the cargo was made into bread and eaten.

The category of *systematic* risks that often proves to be the most difficult to assess involves government activities that are intended to support farm prices, or reduce consumer prices, or bestow commercial favors on our international trading partners: An export subsidy will encourage export activities. An embargo halts exports. A high farm support price encourages increased production. A land bank program takes acreage out of production.

Each of these actions carry important implications for the commodity concerned. The difficulty a trader may have in appraising these risks is often multiplied by the peremptory, if not capricious, fashion in which our federal functionaries announce, alter, lift, or reimpose these programs.

To sum up, the *systematic risks* in a commodity category may be defined as those contingencies that grow out of *natural influences, producer decisions, and governmental interference* with the free market mechanism. In sum, they impact basic supply and demand, and are usually considered in connection with the fundamentals of the commodity.

Contract-Specific Risks

The second classification of risk in commodity pricing may be best described by the label, *contract-specific risks*. Now we have entered the realm of technical analysis. Contract-specific risks are micro-inputs that are of smaller magnitude and shorter periods of influence, than the systematics.

Contract-specific risks include such considerations as:

Overbought/oversold situations.

Commercial hedgers posture and buy/sell activities.

Time remaining to contract maturity.

Government report schedule.

Basis change.

Weather apprehensions.

Deliverable stocks on hand.

These are all considerations of the sort that impel the traders to "do something—even if it's wrong!"—and it often *is* wrong. But the actions precipitated by each of the risks listed above are written out in lower or higher prices that may, through hindsight, stand out as clear distortions below or above the *equilibrium value* that reflects the market's composite judgment of the right price. A price dip or bulge may last a few minutes or a few sessions, but while it lasts it is the *effective price,* and all of the fundamental evidence in the world won't change it until the traders buy and sell it back into line.

It's difficult to assign any continuing relative weights to systematic risk, as compared to contract-specific risk. At a given moment in the life of a futures contract, the single most important consideration influencing price direction might be a continuing drought across the southwestern plains. A month later the wheat pit might explode in recognition of a big increase in deliverable stocks in Chicago.

Whatever the composition of the total perceived risk, and whether it seems subject to evaluation or not, there is no gainsaying the fact that someone has to be willing to *sell* it before someone else can *buy* it. Each transaction requires a long and a short. Without this basic dichotomy in attitude, trading would necessarily halt.

The commodity market offers a full range of risks from which a speculator may pick and choose those which appeal to him. Obviously, a *long* position should be established in a contract in which price behavior and fundamental market considerations lead one to believe that downside hazards are minimal; or at least somewhat less than the probability of upside movement. A *short* position should be established in a contract in which the reverse is true: Where the current price level appears to be higher than the facts justify, and where the prospects for downside movement outweigh the probability of further price escalation.

Speculation is concerned with risk assumption. The successful speculator will never forget that all of the propositions offered to him represent risks that others are *unwilling* or *unable* to carry. This knowledge in itself should keep him eternally on guard. Although risk is his "stock in trade," a prudent commodity speculator will give every potential position benefit of the closest scrutiny. Unless he can find a risk he likes, he will keep to the sidelines and bide his time.

The speculator can also be comforted by the knowledge that if he is right only half of the time—but manages the "losers" and "winners" properly—he is certain to emerge with average profits that are larger than average losses. Success in speculation requires nothing more than this.

Success in speculation makes for beautiful bank statements!

Exhibit 12–10

Short, sharp-breaking countertrends may interrupt a clear march to higher or lower price ground. Technical imbalance is invariably the cause. Such an event, in the face of a well-established trend, must always be viewed with suspicion until time and persistence validates it.

13

Use of Charts in Trading Decisions

There is no end to the strange and wonderful devices which have, from time to time, been seized upon by frustrated traders who seek a foolproof key to market price behavior. Theories which have been seriously advanced run the gamut from measuring lunar attraction, as evidenced in high and low tides, to correlation of price levels with the relative elevation of women's hemlines. Even the spirit world is consulted regularly by some who incline to put more faith in seances than in scholarly research.

A spate of trading schedules circulate through the market, each with its own band of devotees. The most famous of these is the so-called voice from the tomb. The story is told that an old and highly successful speculator lay on his deathbed. As he neared the end, he called his family to him and told them that they would find their most valuable inheritance in a strongbox which contained his personal papers.

The old tycoon went to his reward and, understandably, the heirs went to the strongbox—expecting to find some kind of king's ransom in it. Instead of gold or jewels, they discovered a scrap of paper on which the old trader had written:

Voice from the Tomb

Buy Wheat	Sell Wheat
February 22d	January 10th
July 1st	May 10th
November 28th	September 10th

Buy Corn	Sell Corn
March 1st	
June 25th	May 20th
	August 10th

Exhibit 13–1

The story fails to include any enlightenment concerning the outcome. We don't know whether the heirs were able to turn the instructions into additional millions or not. We do know, however, that there are a lot of present-day traders who still consider these dates to be highly significant, as key points of reference in wheat and corn futures prices. An examination of historical price behavior in the two commodities will suffice to shake one's confidence in blind application of the advice conveyed by the voice from the tomb—but it does conform to seasonal price behavior in both wheat and corn often enough to deserve consideration.

Perhaps the most valuable instruction the voice gives to speculators is not even related to price levels. It will be seen that *both commodities* are traded alternately long and short. If a trader can learn to be as comfortable in one position as the other, he will be well along the road to real professionalism in his market activities.

Charts Can Help Decision Making

The best capsulized appraisal of chart usefulness your author has ever heard came from a physician, who mixes some serious commodity speculation with his primary engagements as a chest surgeon. "Whether I'm trying to make a diagnosis of a patient or a market," he once said, "a good chart goes a long way toward settling my attention on the things that are probably important." The parallel between medical charts and commodity charts is not as farfetched as might appear at first glance. The three basic indicators of human health are temperature, pulse, and respiration. In the market, three indicators are also present for those who take time to consult them. They are *price level, trading volume,* and *open-interest.* In combination, they offer some critical insights to current market condition, and permit the trader to draw some highly useful conclusions about possible future developments.

Like so many aspects of market activity, it is futile to try to evaluate these measurements subjectively. *Price level* means nothing, unless it

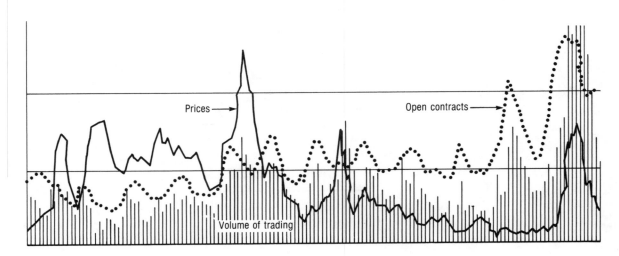

Exhibit 13—2

is viewed as part of the continuum which measures supply/demand balance over time. *Trading volume* tells us nothing, until it is considered in light of the events which prompt it. *Open-interest* clarifies nothing until it is arrayed against the background of time sequence and trader motivation.

However, when we put these three market dimensions together, they provide some of the best clues we can find for both present conditions and future probabilities:

Price/Volume/Open-Interest Signals

When open-interest goes up, as:	prices go up—new buying is present; bulls are in command
	prices go down—new selling is present; bears are in command
When open-interest goes down, as:	prices go up—shorts are offsetting, indicating technical weakness
	prices go down—longs are offsetting, indicating technical strength
When trading volume goes up, and:	prices go up—increased buying pressure; either shorts offsetting, or new demand, or both
	prices go down—increased selling pressure; either longs liquidating, or new offerings, or both
When trading volume goes down, and:	prices go up—reduced buying pressure; downside reaction likely
	prices go down—reduced selling pressure; upside reaction likely

Exhibit 13—3

Behavior of prices, along with open interest and trading volume can usually be taken as good indicators of both *direction* and *dependability* of a particular price move. When all three market factors are in agreement, there is usually little room for argument about price prognosis.

When: Prices go up, along with Increase in open-interest Increase in trading volume }	Extremely bullish—may signal the beginning of a major price move upward
When: Prices go down, along with Increase in open-interest Increase in trading volume }	Extremely bearish—may signal the beginning of a major price move downward

Exhibit 13—4

In order to better understand the relative significance of the market trinity, each should be looked at in terms of the reflection it offers of trade attitude and behavior.

Price Level

Price change, whether up or down, can *never* be trusted by itself. New buying pressure can send prices higher, certainly, and this kind of development calls for constructive appraisal. But "squeezed" shorts can also send prices higher and, once they have succeeded in buying back their untenable positions, lower prices can nearly always be expected.

The opposite is also true. New short-selling pressure can send prices lower in a hurry, but not nearly as fast as concerted liquidation on the part of disenchanted longs who have all decided to get out at about the same time. Once the wave of long-liquidation has run its course, higher prices are a near certainty.

Open-Interest

Open-interest changes are only slightly less of an enigma when standing alone. This figure only indicates the willingness of all classifications of market participants to hold positions in a given contract or commodity. An *increase* in long interest on the part of strong handed commercial interests and professional speculators must usually be taken as constructive for prices; but if the rise in long holdings is largely attributable to the weak hands of the public, the opposite interpretation must be at least considered.

COMMODITY INDEXES

	Close	Net Chg.	Yr. Ago
Dow Jones Futures	124.39	− 0.30	139.08
Dow Jones Spot	120.69	− 0.33	136.05
Reuter United Kingdom	1965.9	+ 12.3	1971.6

FUTURES OPTIONS

Monday, Jan 14, 1985

T-BONDS (CBT)—$100,000; points and 64ths of 100%.

Strike Price	Calls—Last Mar	Jun	Sep	Puts—Last Mar	Jun	Sep
64	6–32	5–60	....	0		
66	4–34	4–23	4–24	0		
68	2–48	3–01	3–17	0		
70	1–18	1–61	2–24	0		
72	0–30	1–11	1–42	1		
74	0–09	0–43	1–07	3		

Est. vol. 28,000, Fri vol. 19,234 calls, 1
Open interest Fri; 129,997 calls, 104,90:

GOLD (CMX)—100 troy ounces; dollars

Strike Price	Calls—Last Apr	Jun	Aug	Ap
280	29.00	....	....	2
290	22.30	28.00	....	4
300	14.80	21.00	25.50	7
320	4.00	9.00	14.50	16
340	.90	4.30	8.00	33
360	.40	2.00	4.30	52

Est. vol. 8,000, Fri vol. 3,036 calls, 5,20
Open Interest Fri; 39,795 calls, 25,805 p

SILVER (CMX)—5,000 troy ounces; cer

Strike Price	Calls—Last Mar	May	Jly	M
500	108.0	120.0	127.0	.
550	63.0	78.0	89.0	.
600	26.0	44.0	59.0	2
650	8.5	23.0	36.5	5
700	2.3	12.5	22.5	9
750	1.0	7.0	13.5	14

Est. vol. 1,800, Fri vol. 1,015 calls, 993
Open interest Fri; 21,785 calls, 12,145 p

NYSE COMPOSITE INDEX (NYFE)—$

Strike Price	Calls—Settle Mar	Jun	Sep	M
96	4.85	7.05	9.00	
98	3.40	5.70	7.60	1
100	2.25	4.45	6.35	1
102	1.45	3.40	5.20	3
104	.85	2.55	4.25	4
106	.45	1.90	3.40	6

Est. vol. 373, Fri vol. 142 calls, 112 puts
Open Interest Fri; 1,954 calls, 2,030 put

S&P 500 STOCK INDEX (CME)—$500

Strike Price	Calls—Settle Mar	June	Sept	M
165	9.30	....	....	1
170	5.65	....	....	2
175	3.05	6.65	9.70	4
180	1.65	4.45	....	.
185	0.75	3.05	....	.
190	0.35	....	....	.

Est. Vol. 4,299; Fri vol. 1,837 calls; 35
Open Interest Fri; 11,609 calls; 11,045

SUGAR—WORLD (CSCE)—112,000 lbs

Strike Price	Calls—Settle Mar	Jly	Oct	M	0.
3.00	1.60	2.52	....	0.03	0.
4.00	0.61	1.50	2.00	0.14	0.
5.00	0.11	0.80	1.40	0.48	0.
6.00	0.03	0.40	0.69	1.45	1.
7.00	0.02	0.29	0.40	2.45	2.10
8.00	0.01	0.14	0.30	3.45	3.10

Est. vol. 24; Fri vol. 66 calls; 4 puts
Open Interest Fri; 4,781 calls; 367 puts

W. GERMAN MARK (CME)—125,000 marks, cents per mark

Strike Price	Calls—Settle Mar	Jun	Puts—Settle Mar	Jun
30	....	2.04	0.13	0.42
31	0.81	1.40	0.40	0.75
32	0.36	0.90	0.94	1.22
33	0.17	0.57	1.72	1.88
34	0.06	0.35	2.59	....
35	0.03	0.21	3.58	....

Est. vol. 5,024, Fri. vol. 2,009 calls, 1,281 puts
Open Interest Fri.; 26,959 calls, 14,574 puts

SOYBEANS (CBT)—5,000 bu.; cents per bu.

Strike Price	Calls—Settle Mar	May	Jly	Puts—Settle Mar	May	Jly
550	....	....	....	1	4	....
575	19	35	46	5⅛	9½	11½
600	6⅜	20½	32½	16½	32½	22
625	1½	10¾	21½	37	21½	33
650	¼	5½	13⅜	61	13⅜	48
675	⅛	2¾	8¼	86	8¼	....

Est. vol. 2,100 Fri. vol. 1,429 calls, 791 puts
Open Interest Fri.; 12,670 calls, 4,537 puts

CATTLE—LIVE (CME) 40,000 lbs.; cents per lb.

Strike Price	Calls—Settle Feb	Apr	Jun	Puts—Settle Feb	Apr	Jun
62	3.12	....	....	0.05	0.22	0.45
64	1.37	3.35	....	0.30	0.40	0.75
66	0.35	1.90	2.40	1.27	0.92	1.25
68	0.05	0.97	1.50	2.95	1.92	2.25
70	0.02	0.45	0.90	4.92	3.50	....
72	....	0.20	0.47	....	5.25	5.15

Est. vol. 542, Fri. vol. 191 calls, 340 puts
Open Interest Fri.; 5,006 calls, 3,569 puts

Other Futures Options

Final or settlement prices of selected contracts Volume and open interest are totals in all contract months.

Cotton (CTN) 50,000 lbs.; cents per lb.

Strike	Mar-C	Jly-C	Dec-C	Mar-P	Jly-P	Dec-P
67	0.45	2.30	2.40	0.85	1.00	1.53

Est. vol. 75, Fri. vol. 221, Op. Int. 2,982.

Wheat (KC) 5,000 bu.; cents per bu.

Strike	Mar-C	May-C	Jly-C	Mar-P	May-P	Jly-P
350	6½	5	5	2½	....	19

Est. vol. 9. Fri. vol. 22. Op. Int. 681.

Wheat (MPLS) 5,000 bu.; cents per bu.

Strike	Mar-C	May-C	Jly-C	Mar-P	May-P	Jly-P
360	5	....	12½	2¾	5¾	....

Est. vol. 0. Fri. vol. 20. Op. Int. 323.

Wheat (MCE) 5,000 bu.; cents per bu.

Strike	Mar-C	May-C	Jly-C	Mar-P	May-P	Jly-P
350	.	5¼	5⅜	3¼	4⅜	13⅛	....

Est. vol. 25. Fr. vol. 32. Op. Int. 1,110.

Trade volume and open-interest is compiled daily by each exchange clearinghouse, then reported to CFTC and the press. A few good newspapers print the complete price, volume, open-interest data on a contract-by-contract basis. A serious trader should have a chart service and a newspaper that does this. Consolidated numbers are meaningless in technical analyses. They may, in fact, be *dangerously* misleading. Compare the quality of information provided in this chart, with that in 13–8 and 13–10, which covers the same time interval. Availability of volume and open-interest data clearly identifies the trade's minimum price-idea around $1.18 to $1.20, and signals the bull-move the week of May 23 and the first week of June. The August break from $1.50 was also presaged in open-interest shrinkage as the top was neared (shown in Exhibit 13–12).

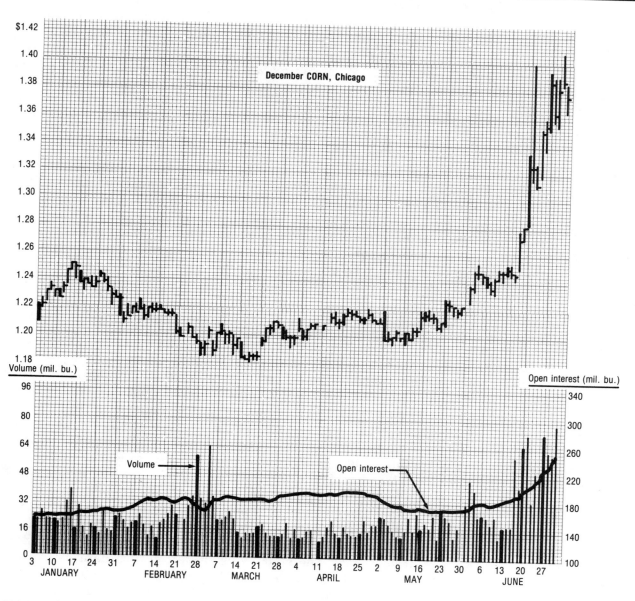

Exhibit 13–5

A *decrease* in open-interest may be either a cause for rejoicing or alarm, depending on who is leaving and why. If strong hands are withdrawing from their market positions, the side they are abandoning is probably in for trouble. But if the departing holders are weak hands, the cause of the strong hands may be actually improved after the temporary setback.

Trading Volume

Trading volume can be no less difficult to analyze objectively, unless appraised with respect to the stimulus which prompts it. Volume often explodes in the face of burgeoning demand from those who see a new price level developing, and scramble to get aboard for the move. The same thing can happen to volume when large numbers of longs or shorts are caught in a price move that triggers concerted stop-loss selling.

Trading volume can dry up as a result of either *insufficient interest* in the contract to sustain market activity, or as a result of sheer *unwillingness* of present and potential position holders to do business at the given price level.

Whether appraising prospects for an already existing position or weighing the wisdom of establishing a new position, price level, trading volume, and open-interest are always fundamental elements in the equation. It should be hastily added that there are traders who succeed without using these indexes to market condition. There are also some race car drivers who ply their trade without crash helmets, but the practice shouldn't be encouraged. Anything that can reduce risk exposure deserves to be considered.

How Reliable Are Charts?

The question cannot be answered without narrowing it down a bit further. The usual bar chart which most traders employ is nothing more than a means of creating a picture with statistical data. In terms of efficiency, as a communications tool, a chart is vastly preferable to columns of figures. A glance may be sufficient to gain a useful impression of trading range, general trend, and notable exceptions to either. To this extent, a chart is the best means available for reminding oneself of what the market response was to a given set of circumstances in the past. The major fallacy in chart trading procedure lies in placing too much confidence in the past, as a guide to the future.

Charting techniques can be usefully employed as a projective method, but in order to do so, the chart must reflect future data estimates. Usually, bar chartists do not do this. They consider only that which has passed, and, by looking backward, they attempt to determine where things are going. If we operated automobiles and airplanes in the same fashion, population control would never be a problem.

Suffice it to say that, from this writer's experience, charts are an indispensable trading tool—even though they are only slightly better than random determination as a method of long- and medium-range price forecasting. Their accuracy, quite naturally, improves in direct proportion to the number of people using them in given areas of endeavor; and as their accuracy *improves,* profitability *decreases.* This is to say that if everyone traded December corn futures from a chart, and meticulously followed the same buy and sell signals, everyone would be right about the direction of prices on the contract. Unanimity of action would insure the result. The only aberrations would be predicated on time differences in executing trades, since everyone would always have to be in agreement about price direction. But, by being endlessly in agreement (and therefore always right), no one could be wrong. Unless someone is wrong, there is no theoretical loss possible; and without a loss, there can't possibly be a profit.

Under the above hypothesis, trade would not necessarily cease. It just wouldn't amount to much. When prices were headed down, everybody would want to sell, but there would be no buyers; and vice versa. Fortunately, such a possibility is quite remote. Difference of opinion is the essence of trade. For each buyer there must be a seller and, at some price level, there always is.

Charts Offer Clues to the Past

The foregoing statements should not be taken as a blanket indictment of charts in trading—nor a diatribe against the intelligence of those who use them. The tools for success in speculation are sufficiently scarce and inexact as to urge a trader to use *anything* that helps him render better judgments. A less than perfect tool is far better than no tool at all. Charts fall into this category.

A companion volume, *Charting Commodity Market Price Behavior,* is strongly recommended for the serious trader—beginner or professional—who wants to upgrade his profit performance in selecting and managing commodity positions. In it, the reader will find a wealth of explanations and demonstrations of how charts reflecting price, volume, and open-interest can be used to analyze market strength and weakness, and to probe the psychology of the traders at any given time. By knowing what the traders are doing, forecasting the course of near-term prices is infinitely simplified.

Examination of any commodity price bar chart will disclose several areas of useful trading information. The tracings document past actions of all the traders—not just chart followers—in the contract, as they pursued their composite price idea. Each daily bar covers the trading range for one session; and the close is marked by a crossbar. Thus, one quite simple structure visually presents daily high, daily low, and closing price. In combination, the individual bars offer a graphic picture of price development, movement, and congestive pressures at various levels.

Cash Prices

Friday, July 7,1
(Quotations as of 3 p.m. Ce
FOODS

	Fri
Flour, hard winter NY cwt	$6.
Coffee, Santos 4s NY lb	
Cocoa, Accra NY lb	
Sugar, Refined NY lb	
Sugar, Raw NY lb	
Butter, Fresh A–92 sc NY lb	
Eggs, Lge-mix Ext, Chgo., doz.	
Broilers, 3 lb & under DelMV lb	
Hogs, Chicago top cwt	24.
Steers, Chicago choice cwt	27.
Pepper, black NY lb	

GRAINS AND FEED

Wheat, No. 2 ord hard KC bu	1
Corn, No. 2 yel Chicago bu.	1
Oats, No. 1 wh. heavy, Chgo., bu	
Rye, No. 2 Minneapolis bu.	1
Barley, malting NY bu	1
Soybeans, No. 1 yel Chicago bu	2
Flaxseed, Minneapolis bu	3
Bran, Buffalo ton	43
Linseed Meal, Minneapolis ton	74
Cottonseed Meal, Memphis ton	75
Soybean Meal, Decatur, Ill. ton	78

FATS AND OILS

Cottonseed Oil, crd Miss Vly. lb	
Corn Oil, crude Chicago lb.	
Soybean Oil, crd Decatur, Ill. lb	
Peanut Oil, crd Southeast lb	
Coconut Oil, crd Pac Cst lb	
Copra, Pacific Coast ton	177
Lard, Chicago lb	
Tallow, bleachable, NY lb	
Linseed Oil, raw NY lb	

TEXTILES AND FIB

Cotton, one in. mid Memphis lb	
Print Cloth, 64 × 60 38½ in. NY yd	
Print Cloth, 80 × 80 39 in. NY yd	
Sheetings, 56 × 60 40 in. NY yd	
Burlap, 10 oz. 40 in. NY yd	
Wool, fine staple terr. Bstn, lb	1.
Wool tops, NY lb	1.
Rayon, Satin Acetate NY yd	

METALS

Steel Scrap, 1 hvy melt Chgo, ton	29.
Copper, Conn Valley lb	
Copper Scrap, No. 2 wire NY lb	
Lead, NY lb	
Zinc, East St. Louis lb	
Tin, NY lb	
Aluminum, ingot, NY lb	
Quicksilver, NY 76 lb flask	485.
Silver, (H&H) NY oz.	1.

MISCELLANEOUS

Rubber, smoked sheets NY lb	
Hides, light native cows Chgo lb.	

Gasoline, 92 Oct. Mid-cont. gal	.12¾	.12¾	.12½
Fuel Oil, No. 2 Mid-cont gal	.09¼	.09¼	.08¾

a-Asked, b-Bid, n-Nominal, x-Corrected.

Dow-Jones Commodity Indexes 1924-26=100
Spot
Futures
APR. MAY JUN. JUL.

COMMODITY INDEXES

Dow-Jones Futures, Friday 131.59. off 0.36; last year, 141.07.

Dow-Jones Spot—135.80, up 0.08; last year, 150.90.

Reuters' United Kingdom—429.2, off 3.5; last year, 463.9. (1931 equals 100.)

FUTURES PRICES

Lower—Cocoa, copper, soybean meal, frozen pork bellies, Winnipeg rye and flaxseed.

Irregular—Soybeans, soybean oil, potatoes, platinum, eggs, cotton, live hogs, Chicago and Kansas City wheat, Chicago corn, oats and rye.

Higher—Silver, frozen orange juice concentrate, hides, wool, sugar, coffee, cattle and Minneapolis wheat.

By comparing cash prices, futures prices, and the overall commodity index, a good notion of market "tone" can be had.

Do Prices Agree?

By arraying open-interest data and trading volume in chronological sequence with prices, the experienced trader will be able to better identify the speculative opportunities he seeks. He will also become increasingly expert in spotting those situations that can only be labeled "traps." The majority of all bad trades are the result of putting too much confidence in a single aspect of market behavior, usually price. The prudent speculator will always look for confirmation of price reliability in technical and fundamental considerations. Unless it can be found, he will view the move as being suspect and perhaps of no more than short-term significance.

For example, when a strong case exists for higher wheat prices, most wheat contracts in the given crop year should reflect it to some degree. Nearby prices can be expected to reflect the situation to a greater extent than more deferred maturities, since the market discounts the future. But if a real shortage is developing, the condition is not likely to be restricted to a single contract, except at the extreme end of the crop year. When excessive supplies are on hand, either in private hands or held by the government, it usually takes an extended period of time to work off the surplus through increased domestic consumption, or export, or both. The revised price attitudes may or may not carry through into new crop contracts, depending on whether the projected harvest is calculated to aggravate, relieve, or merely prolong the situation.

Based on this thinking, a trader will not put much confidence in a bulge or a dip in a given maturity which generates no corresponding activity in other contracts in the same crop year. Moreover, even if the price move does apply generally, he will still check open-interest figures—as reported by the individual exchange and CFTC—to see whether it is probably a result of people "getting in" or "getting out" of the situation. He will take a hard look at trading volume, to see how willing the market participants are to go along with the change and continue to buy and sell at the new price level.

The experienced speculator soon learns that every substantial price change offers a major trading opportunity, but before either buying or selling, he has to answer the crucial question of whether or not the move can be trusted. Short-term price action alone is not sufficient evidence upon which to make the judgment.

Picking New Position Spots

Examination of any commodity price chart will show that the path of existence for values on any traded futures is truly a series of ups and downs. Ignoring smaller interim fluctuations which occur constantly, there are distinct levels which clearly stand as the top and bottom limits within which traders will—during a period of time—trade in the product. To use the December 1966 corn futures for demonstration, $1.25

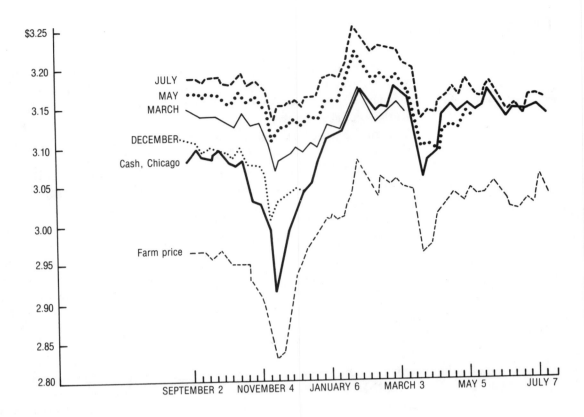

Exhibit 13—6

While it can be said that cash and futures prices always tend to move in concert, this should not be taken to mean that they maintain stable price differentials. As the above chart shows, the country basis keeps in much closer step with market *cash* prices, than futures prices maintain with each other.

The two major price dips in these corn prices reflect heavy marketings immediately following harvest, and another period of heavy selling shortly after the first of the year. Most years do reflect a winter selloff in corn; hence, the phenomenon is an important factor in the commodity's seasonal price pattern.

and $1.18 per bushel represented the full trading spectrum for nearly six months of the contract life. Volume and open-interest remained at unimpressive levels, and the narrow daily ranges contained little to attract widespread speculative interest.

Then suddenly, on June 16, a weather scare triggered an upsurge which took the contract over $1.53 in 90 days. Untold thousands of traders who wanted no corn at $1.20 were eager buyers 25 cents higher. Short sellers who had shunned the weak market offered billions of bushels as prices soared. The market's price idea on December corn as seen in data following was revised upward and widened to a maximum of $1.33. Toward the end of contract life, the range narrowed progressively, and it went "off the board" at $1.41.

By trading this contract on the basis of about a 4 cent maximum daily range, accepting the market's "word" as a reliable guide to trend

Exhibit 13–7

Your author would have liked to use a more current recapitulation of trading activity than the one set forth. However, the increasing voracity and demonstrable zeal on the part of our Internal Revenue Service fills commodity traders—indeed, taxpayers of every stripe—with an understandable reticence to "tell the devil too much." In any case, this recap of day-to-day speculative activity is as valid as ever. Its object lessons for the market student are as applicable today as they were when they were taking place.

at all times, and conservatively pyramiding profitable positions, one trader's records show what can be done in such a situation. The details are shown in Exhibits 13–8 through 13–17. It should be noted that the prices reflected in the recapitulation are the levels at which the orders were placed. Actual executions varied slightly from order levels, depending on the type of order involved and market conditions. Also worth mentioning, the quantities reflected here are not the actual trading volumes of the speculator whose records we are examining. On October 26, for instance, he was short more than 400,000 bushels. Total December contract trade activity produced a net profit to the trader, after broker commissions, in excess of $41,000.

At the risk of undertaking to argue with success, there are a few points which deserve to be made with respect to the trading program which is reflected here. Ordinarily, the first few days of contract life after the futures opens is a high risk proposition. Until open-interest in the contract builds up to some reasonable total, price may be susceptible to undue influence by what amounts to extremely small buying or selling pressures.

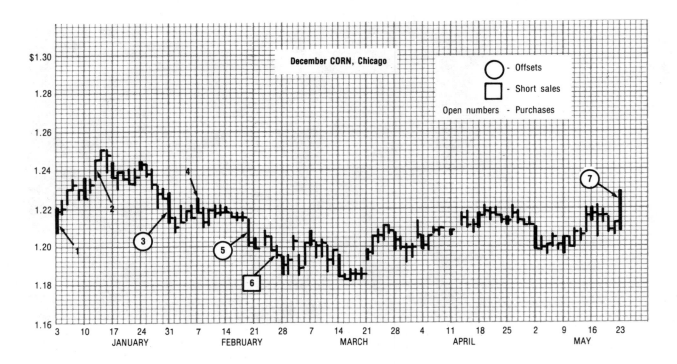

Exhibit 13–8

Trade No.	Date	Trades in December Corn	Bought	Sold	P/L ¢ per bu.	P/L Dollars
1	1/3/66	*Buy:* 15M @ 121⅜; stop-loss @ 119⅝	15M @ 121⅜		¼	37.50
2	1/12	*Move stop-loss* up to 121⅝ *Buy:* 10M @ 124⅜	10M @ 124⅜		(2¾)	(275.00)
3	1/31	Stop-loss hit @ 121⅝; total position offset		25M @ 121⅝		———
					Position Result	(237.50)
					P/L to Date	(237.50)
4	2/7	*Buy:* 15M @ 122⅜; stop-loss @ 120½	15M @ 122⅜			
5	2/18	Stop-loss hit @ 120½; total position offset		15M @ 120½	(1⅞)	(256.25)
					Position Result	(256.25)
					P/L to Date	(493.75)
6	2/25	*Sell:* 15M @ 119⅝; stop-loss @ 122⅜		15 M @ 119⅝		
7	5/23	Stop-loss hit @ 122⅜; total position offset	15M @ 122⅜		(2¾)	(412.50)
					Position Result	(412.50)
					P/L to Date	(906.25)

Exhibit 13–9

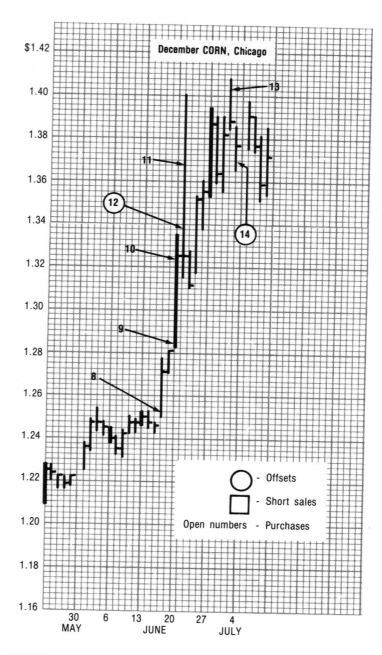

Exhibit 13–10

Trade No.	Date	Trades in December Corn	Bought	Sold	P/L ¢ per bu.	P/L Dollars
8	6/16	*Buy:* 15M @ 124⅝; stop-loss @ 121⅝	15M @ 124⅝		9	1350.00
9	6/20	*Move stop-loss* up to 124⅜				
		Buy: 10M @ 128⅜	10M @ 128⅜		5¼	525.00
10		*Move stop-loss* up to 129⅝				
		Buy: 5M @ 132⅜	5M @ 132⅜		1¼	62.50
11	6/21	*Move stop-loss* up to 133⅝				
		Buy: 5M @ 136⅝	5M @ 136⅝		(3)	(150.00)
12		Stop-loss hit @ 133⅝; total position offset		35M @ 135⅝		
				Position Result		1787.50
				P/L to Date		881.25
13	6/30	*Buy:* 15M @ 140⅜; stop-loss @ 137⅝	15M @ 140⅜			
14	7/1	Stop-loss hit @ 137⅝; total position offset		15M @ 137⅝	(2¾)	(412.50)
				Position Result		(412.50)
				P/L to Date		468.75

Exhibit 13–11

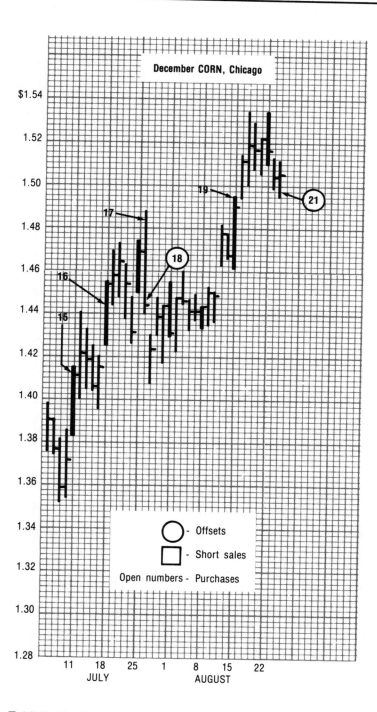

December CORN, Chicago

○ - Offsets
□ - Short sales
Open numbers - Purchases

Exhibit 13–12

Trade No.	Date	Trades in December Corn	Bought	Sold	P/L ¢ per bu.	P/L Dollars
15	7/11	*Buy:* 15M @ 141⅜; stop-loss @ 137⅝	15M @ 141⅜		3¼	487.50
16	7/18	*Move stop-loss* to 141⅝ *Buy:* 10M @ 144⅜	10M @ 144⅜		¼	25.00
17	7/26	*Move stop-loss* to 144⅝ *Buy:* 5M @ 148⅜	5M @ 148⅜		(3¾)	(187.50)
18		Stop-loss hit @ 144⅝; total position offset		30M @ 144⅝		————
					Position Result	325.00
					P/L to Date	793.75
19	8/16	*Buy:* 15M @ 149⅜; stop-loss @ 145⅝	15M @ 149⅝		¼	37.50
20	8/18	*Move stop-loss* to 149⅝				
21	8/24	Stop-loss hit @ 149⅝; total position offset		15M @ 149⅝		————
					Position Result	37.50
					P/L to Date	831.25

Exhibit 13–13

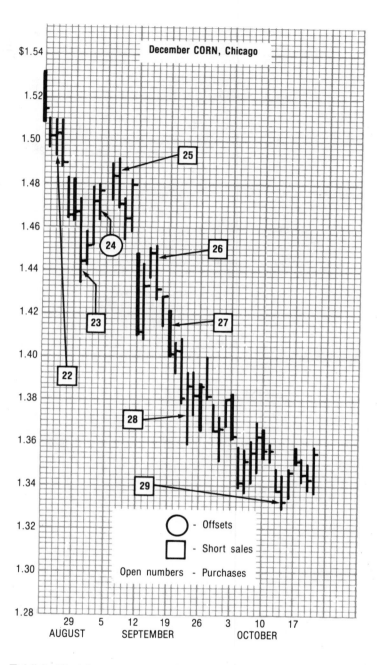

Exhibit 13-14

Trade No.	Date	Trades in December Corn	Bought	Sold	P/L ¢ per bu.	P/L Dollars
22	8/24	*Sell:* 15M @ 149⅝; stop-loss @ 153⅜		15M @ 149⅝	3	450.00
23	8/30	*Move stop-loss* down to 146⅝ *Sell:* 10M @ 144⅝		10M @ 144⅝	(2)	200.00
24	9/1	Stop-loss hit @ 146⅝; total position offset	25M @ 146⅝			
				Position Result		250.00
				P/L to Date		1081.25
25	9/7	*Sell:* 15M @ 148⅝; stop-loss @ 150⅜		15M @ 148⅝	11	1650.00
26	9/15	*Move stop-loss* to 146⅜ *Sell:* 10M @ 144⅝		10M @ 144⅝	7	700.00
27	9/19	*Move stop-loss* to 143⅜ *Sell:* 5M @ 141⅝		5M @ 141⅝	4	200.00
28	9/22	*Move stop-loss* to 141⅜ *Sell:* 5M @ 137⅝		5M @ 137⅝	even	—
29	10/13	*Move stop-loss* to 137⅝ *Sell:* 5M @ 133⅝		5M @ 133⅜	(4)	(200.00)

Exhibit 13–15

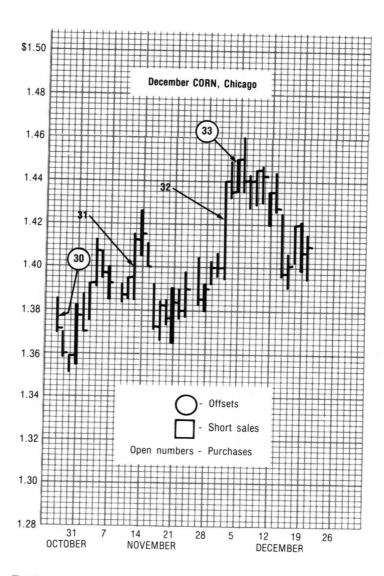

December CORN, Chicago

Exhibit 13–16

Trade No.	Date	Trades in December Corn	Bought	Sold	P/L ¢ per bu.	P/L Dollars
30	10/26	Stop-loss hit; total position offset	40M @ 137⅝			
					Position Result	2350.00
					P/L to Date	3431.25
31	11/5	*Buy:* 15M @ 139⅜; stop-loss @ 135⅝	15M @ 139⅜		5¼	787.50
32	12/1	*Move stop-loss* to 139⅝ *Buy:* 10M @ 142⅝	10M @ 142⅝		2	200.00
33	12/5	Closed out in advance of "First Notice Day" @ 144⅝		25M @ 144⅝		
					Position Result	987.50
					P/L to Date	4418.75
				Less Broker Commission on 48 Contracts @ 22.00		1056.00
					Net Proceeds	3362.75

Exhibit 13–17

The long position which was taken on January 3 was based mainly on the fact that December represented about a 5 cent discount under the September futures. However, since December represents new crop, and September represents old crop, such a differential does not—by itself—provide a sufficiently compelling reason to undertake the risks present at this early stage of contract life.

When the price dropped to 118⅜ on March 14, the stop-loss should have been moved down to the vicinity of 120½, even though no addition could be as yet made to the position. The "even dime" is a highly significant price barrier in commodity trading. If buying pressure is sufficient to penetrate the 120 level, it might be expected that, once having overcome this hurdle, it will then be sufficient to carry the price somewhat higher.

Moving the stop-loss up to 144⅝ on July 26 was an excellent decision, but adding to the position in the middle of what was clearly a short squeeze was not good judgment. It is worth pointing out that this trader bought into another short squeeze on June 21. Following a trading program too closely can sometimes lure one into such a trap.

There are times when these flurries of *short* offsetting will be subsequently sustained, as prices move higher on the crest of additional buying demand. Far more often, however, once the shorts are chased in, a downside reaction immediately follows. The reverse is equally true when the longs have largely departed in the face of falling prices: an upside correction is to be expected in the next session or two. Whether or not the anticipated reaction occurs, the trader should make plans for it, by either moving to the sidelines temporarily or placing his stop-loss in expectation of such a countermove.

In connection with stop-losses, it should also be pointed out that after the two exceedingly broad swings on June 20 and 21, a wider trading range than the 4 cents to 5 cents, which had been more or less constantly pursued, should have been contemplated and followed for the next several months. The more volatile prices are, the greater the risk on the basis of maximum swings. The only safe rule is to keep your stop close enough to adequately protect a profit or protect against a major loss. But, at the same time, keep your stop far enough away to accommodate anticipated fluctuations in the trading situation which exists. Daily limits on fluctuations offer a useful maximum guide.

As this is being prepared in October 1984, the daily price limit on corn is 10 cents per bushel. This is to say that price can move up a dime, or down a dime, from the previous session's closing (settlement) price. In view of this, it simply makes no sense to place stop-loss orders that fail to take this reality into consideration. Actually, the economic reality involved is surprisingly constant: When corn was trading around $1.40 per bushel, a 10 cent trading range (5 cents above or below the previous close) represented about 7 percent total allowable daily fluctuation. With corn currently trading around $2.90 per bushel, a 20 cent trading range (10 cents above or below the previous close) represents about the same permissible percentage of price fluctuation.

Prices do fluctuate, and in commodities they can be expected to fluctuate within the permissible trading range. People who ignore this find themselves repeatedly stopped-out of perfectly good positions, by what must be considered thoroughly predictable price behavior as it wiggles its way higher, lower, or sideways.

Soybean Trading

We have made repeated mention of price behavior in the November 1966 soybean contract. While not taking a major interest in that particular maturity, the same trader whose corn activities we have just reviewed was almost constantly involved in the May 1967 soybean contract. A review of the price chart and a recapitulation of his trading activities contains some dramatic market lessons.

Here again, the quantities involved are different from the quantities the speculator actually traded. Also, the prices designated represent the levels at which his orders were placed. Executions varied slightly, but there was only one major aberration; a stop-loss which called for offset at 334⅝ placed on September 9 was missed. He could not sell the position out on the 12th because there were no buyers in the permissible trading range. When execution was finally accomplished on Tuesday, the 13th, it was done at 322⅝.

If You Can't Stand Heat . . .

This is the sort of commodity contract that can turn a speculator gray, and move him a long step closer to the poorhouse, unless he can keep his wits about him under great stress.

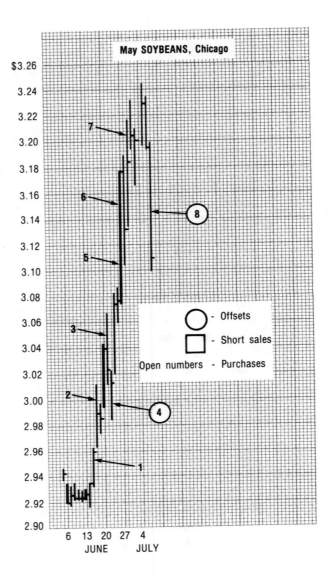

Exhibit 13–18

Trade No.	Date	Trades in May Soybeans	Bought	Sold	P/L ¢ per bu.	P/L Dollars
1	6/15/66	*Buy:* 15 M @ 295⅜; stop-loss @ 291⅝	15M @ 295⅜		4¼	637.50
2	6/16	*Move stop-loss* to 295⅜ *Buy:* 10M @ 300⅜	10M @ 300⅜		(¾)	(75.00)
3	6/21	*Move stop-loss* to 299⅝ *Buy:* 5M @ 305⅜	5M @ 305⅜		(5¾)	(287.50)
4	6/22	Stop-loss hit @ 299⅝; total position offset		30M @ 299⅝		
				Position Result		275.00
				P/L to Date		275.00
5	6/27	*Buy:* 15M @ 310⅜; stop-loss @ 304⅝	15M @ 310⅜		4¼	637.50
6	6/28	*Move stop-loss* to 309⅝ *Buy:* 10M @ 315⅜	10M @ 315⅜		(¾)	(75.00)
7	6/29	*Move stop-loss* to 314½ *Buy:* 5M @ 320⅜	5M @ 320⅜		(5¾)	(287.50)
8	7/7	Stop-loss hit @ 314½; total position offset		30M @ 314½		
				Position Result		275.00
				P/L to Date		550.00

Exhibit 13–19

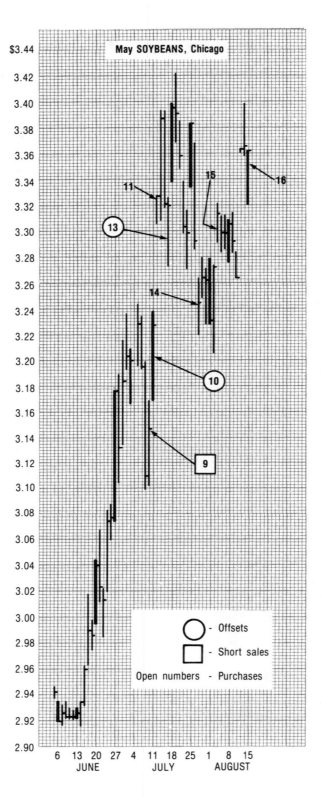

Exhibit 13–20

Trade No.	Date	Trades in May Soybeans	Bought	Sold	P/L ¢ per bu.	P/L Dollars
9	7/8	*Sell:* 15M @ 314⅝; stop-loss @ 320⅜		15M @ 314⅝		
10	7/11	Stop-loss hit @ 320⅜; total position offset	15M @ 320⅜		(5¾)	(862.50)
				Position Result		(862.50)
				P/L to Date		(312.50)
11	7/13	*Buy:* 15M @ 332⅜; stop-loss @ 327⅝	15M @ 332⅜		(2¾)	(412.50)
12		*Move stop-loss* to 329⅝				
13	7/15	Stop-loss hit @ 329⅝; total position offset		15M @ 329⅝		
				Position Result		(412.50)
				P/L to Date		(725.00)
14	7/27	*Buy:* 15M @ 324⅜; stop-loss @ 319⅝	15M @ 324⅜		12¼	1875.00
15	8/3	*Move stop-loss* to 324⅝ *Buy:* 10M @ 330⅜	10M @ 330⅜		2¼	225.00
16	8/15	*Move stop-loss* to 329⅝ *Buy:* 5M @ 335⅜	5M @ 335⅜		(2¾)	(137.50)

Exhibit 13–21

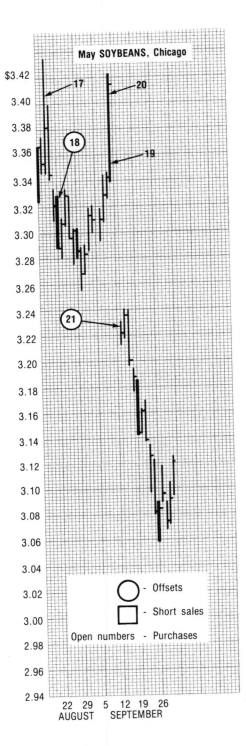

Exhibit 13-22

Trade No.	Date	Trades in May Soybeans	Bought	Sold	P/L ¢ per bu.	P/L Dollars
17	8/17	*Move stop-loss* to 332⅝ *Buy:* 5M @ 340⅜	5M @ 340⅜			
18	8/20	Stop-loss hit @ 332⅝; total position offset		35M @ 332⅝ Position Result P/L to Date	(7¾)	(387.50) 3600.00 2875.00
19	9/9	*Buy:* 15M @ 335⅜; stop-loss @ 331⅝	15M @ 335⅝		(13)	(1950.00)
20		*Move stop-loss* to 334⅝ *Buy:* 10M @ 340⅜	10M @ 340⅝		(18)	(1800.00)
21	9/12	Limit down day—(stop-loss can't be executed)				
	9/13	Stop-loss executed at 322⅝		25M @ 322⅝ Position Result P/L to Date		(3750.00) (875.00)

Exhibit 13–23

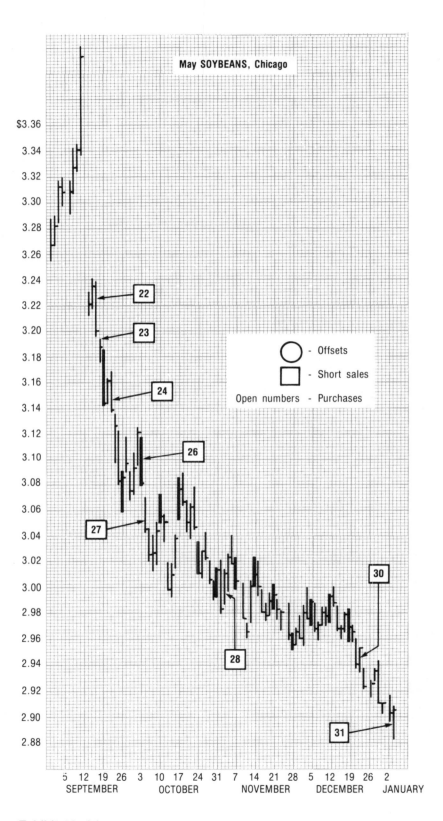

Exhibit 13–24

Trade No.	Date	Trades in May Soybeans	Bought	Sold	P/L ¢ per bu.	P/L Dollars
22	9/15	*Sell:* 15M @ 323⅝; stop-loss @ 330⅜		15M @ 323⅝	31¼	4687.50
23	9/16	*Move stop-loss* to 325⅜ *Sell:* 10M @ 319⅝		10M @ 319⅝	27¼	2725.00
24	9/21	*Move stop-loss* to 320⅜ *Sell:* 5M @ 314⅝		5M @ 314⅝	22¼	1112.50
25	9/28	*Move stop-loss* to 315⅜				
26	10/3	*Sell:* 5M @ 309⅝		5M @ 309⅝	17¼	862.50
27	10/4	*Move Stop-loss* to 310⅜ *Sell:* 5M @ 304⅜		5M @ 304⅝	12¼	612.50
28	11/2	*Move stop-loss* to 305⅜ *Sell:* 5M @ 299⅝		5M @ 299⅝	7¼	362.50
29	11/22	*Move stop-loss* to 300⅝				
30	12/22	*Sell:* 5M @ 294⅝		5M @ 294⅝	2¼	112.50
31	1/4/67	*Move stop-loss* to 295⅝ *Sell:* 5M @ 289⅝		5M @ 289⅝	(5¾)	(137.50)

Exhibit 13–25

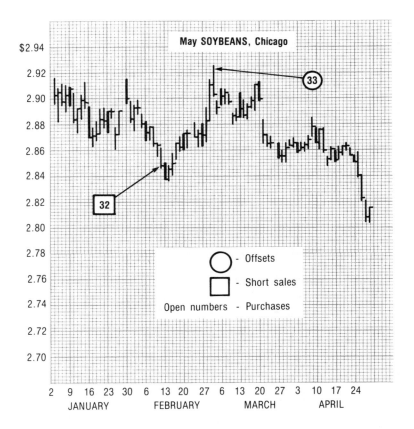

May SOYBEANS, Chicago

○ - Offsets

□ - Short sales

Open numbers - Purchases

Exhibit 13–26

Trade No.	Date	Trades in May Soybeans	Bought	Sold	P/L ¢ per bu.	P/L Dollars
32	2/10	*Move stop-loss* to 292⅜				
		Sell: 5M @ 284⅝		5M @ 284⅝	(7¾)	(387.50)
33	3/2	Stop-loss hit at 292⅜;	60M @ 292⅜			
		total position offset.				
				Position Result		9950.00
				P/L to Date		9075.00
		Less Brokerage Commission on 42 contracts @ 24.00				1008.00
				Net Proceeds		8067.00

Exhibit 13–27

The May soybean contract took off explosively almost from the start. The trader was in step from the outset, but was unfortunately stopped-out by wide daily price swings on both of his first two long positions. On July 8, he decided that the bull move had run its course. This is where his real troubles began. Two successive July positions both proved to be in the wrong direction. Then, on July 27, he reestablished a long position at 324⅜ which was right. In approximately three weeks, he had made $3,600 on it, which covered all earlier losses in the contract and produced a comfortable net profit.

There is an old saying in trading circles that "the market can give it to you in a hurry—and take it back even faster." On September 9— that fateful Friday in advance of the Government Crop Report—a run-up began in soybeans, aided in the last few minutes of trading by a short squeeze of gigantic proportions. This trader bought at 335⅜; then moved his stop-loss up and bought again at 340⅜. When the closing bell ended the session, he was long 25,000 bushels with a stop-loss at 334⅝ and, all things being equal, should have been in good shape. But appearances can be deceiving.

When the crop report figures came out, the soybean market broke dramatically. The stop-loss order which was placed at 334⅝ was meaningless. Prices fell the full 10 cents permissible on Monday, September 12, and no trading was done because there were no buyers in the permissible trading range. On Tuesday, the 13th, he was at last able to get an offset made at 322⅝. The three sessions had left him with a 13 cent loss on 15,000 bushels, and an 18 cent loss on the 10,000 bushels additional.

Now that the house had literally "fallen in," it took no particular genius for this disenchanted bull to recognize that prices were more than likely headed lower. The trader went short on September 16 and stayed short until March 2. The results were gratifying to say the least.

Always Learn the Lessons You Pay for

Several points which should be apparent in this sequence of events deserve careful underscoring. First of all, *trading into a major crop report can be brutal*. Having said this, it must also be recognized that when the market gets a big surprise, its effects are not likely to be all reflected at once. In this case, the demoralization which was contained in a higher-than-expected soybean production forecast led to progressively lower prices throughout the balance of contract life. It is also notable that from September 14 until the maturity went off the board, a 40 cent price deterioration took place without a single major upside reversal! Unfortunate longs kept reestablishing their positions (or absorbing their steady losses) at ever lower levels, but they could never win back the initiative in the market. On three different occasions during late November and early December, the market rallied precisely to the $3 per bushel level, but was unable to break above the line. From that point on, it was all downhill.

Look for the Wide Price Pattern

The key to successful program trading stands revealed in this soybean chart. The opportunities a program speculator should seek are found in those contracts which reflect a tendency to make major trend moves of a seasonal, fundamental, or a technical nature. Program trading in a situation like the one presented during the first four months of this particular contract is fraught with too much hazard to be very enticing. While major price gaps that occur in your favor are most gratifying, gaps which open in the right direction also foster other gaps that may open in the wrong direction.

The safest course to follow when the price chart begins to open up is to close out your position and wait for a more consistent pattern to develop. Failure to do so invites the possibility of your getting out of step with price movements and being subjected to the well-known "whipsaw." In such a situation, the more persistent you are in establishing new positions, the more punishment you may be forced to take.

Don't Worry about a Bad Trade

There is another lesson to be learned from this example: You can be wrong several times—and for substantial amounts of money—but if you can catch a significant long-term trend, a profitable outcome is virtually assured. The crux of the matter rests in proper management of the position. This calls for adding to the winning position at regular, predetermined intervals, and keeping your stop-loss orders close enough to hopefully avoid taking a large loss.

Finally, of course, never try to decide when the market has gone far enough. It will be its own authority on this topic, and you will know it when your stop-loss is finally activated.

14

Adding to a Profitable Position

A position which exceeds the predetermined limit on a permissible loss is always closed out. However, as we have seen, a position which justifies the speculator's profit expectation offers an opportunity for enlargement at designated price intervals, so long as it continues to perform in the proper fashion. The designation most often given to the practice of methodically adding to a profitable trade is *pyramiding*. The term implies beginning with an initial trade base and adding to it successively, as returns on the initial commitment justify. In diagramming the procedure, the pyramid will always appear to be upside down as concerns short-selling and right side up when it portrays trading from the long side.

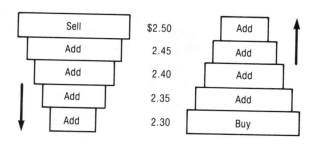

Exhibit 14—1

163

In addition to offering increased profit opportunities as the position builds, the trader's leverage situation is progressively enhanced also, since each succeeding commitment is made with a combination of his own risk funds and accrued paper profits previously realized from the trade foundation.

Picking Sell and Buy Spots

For our example, let's consider an initial short sale of 10,000 bushels of May corn at 2.94¾ executed on December 22.

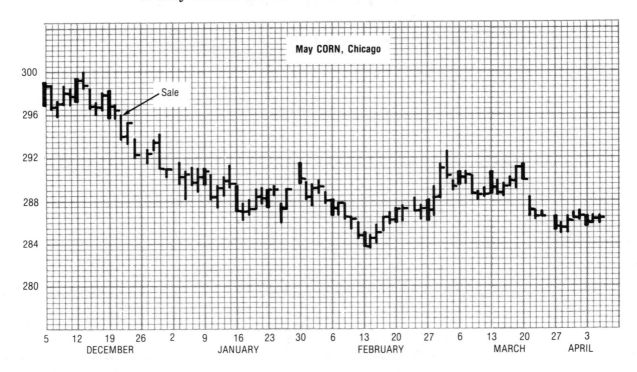

Exhibit 14—2

After fluctuating within a trading range, prices break through the $2.90 level on the downside, on January 3, while never succeeding in going over $2.99¼ on the upside. The price pattern convinces the trader that strong resistance exists in the $2.99 to $3.00 level. Once prices have fallen below the $2.90 level, the trader is likewise of the opinion that the price is even more on the defensive than it was before; and due for further downside movement. He follows the rule, "sell weakness and buy strength," but rather than just placing a resting order to sell an additional quantity of May corn at $2.89¾ the trader may attempt to obtain a better selling price. His method for doing this brings us to another fundamental rule of speculation: Sell bulges and buy dips.

Seeking to generally sell weakness and specifically sell a bulge may sound like a contradiction, but it is not. The significant development with respect to the downside price move was in breaking the $2.90

barrier. Having gone through this level, the speculator may be of the opinion that price is far more likely to penetrate the $2.90 level again— and then move lower, than to either keep dropping or work its way clear back up to the $3.00 level. Stated another way, his "selling signal" was in the penetration of the $2.90 price level. In terms of executing the sale, however, if he wants the best possible selling price, he must try to sell on a bulge in the price pattern. To do so, he will have to keep a rather close watch on the situation.

As previously noted, prices endlessly fluctuate between narrow or wide range limits. Corn, being a fairly inexpensive commodity, shows much narrower trading ranges than a higher priced commodity like beans or wheat, for example. Historically, the intrasession trading range on soybeans averages out around 10 to 12 cents. This is to say that in average markets, the lowest price recorded in soybeans in a given session may be a dime under the highest price in the same session. Corn fluctuations will be a good deal less. In active markets the greater volume of trading may reflect itself in a proportionately wider trading range, as we have seen. The speculator, in order to realize the best possible return from his position, must always consider this behaviorism in placing orders to buy and sell.

Downside penetration of the $2.90 level on May corn has convinced the speculator that prices will go lower, but in the meantime prices will continue to fluctuate. The trader has decided to sell more May corn short, but he wants to sell at the *highest possible price within the descending range*. His method for doing this might be to place an order which specifies, "Sell 5 May corn $2.91½ when the market touches $2.89¾—day order." This kind of order could be placed with a broker several days in advance of the event, or could actually have been placed with the broker at the same time the initial position was taken. If so, this additional selling order would be a "resting order," the same as the stop-loss which was placed to contemplate possible upside movement in the contract.

By checking trading ranges each day, the speculator will be able to see if the price on May corn is approaching the specified level— $2.89¾—which will automatically activate the resting sell order. The crucial day might produce a session in which prices begin working lower from the opening. The sell order is touched off and then, as is often the

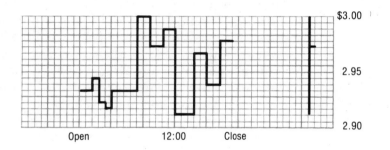

Exhibit 14–3

case, prices may turn around and move higher, reaching $2.91½ on the May corn contract. At this point, the additional 5,000 bushels of corn would be sold. After the sale is made, the price might continue to move upward to $2.92¼, then turn around once more and sell off towards the close of the session.

In the face of events set forth earlier, a lower price ($2.89¾) would activate the sell order, but its execution could not take place until prices move 1¾ cents higher on the specified contract.

The second means of accomplishing a short sale of this kind is by using a *time and price limit order*. This order might instruct the broker to "Sell 5 May corn after 11 A.M. $2.91½—stop." The thinking behind this second handling could be that the trader looks for lower prices at the opening, followed by a turnaround, and higher prices during the midsession. He only wants to make his short sale after the anticipated bulge has had a chance to have developed and passed. Moreover, while he has no real hope for picking the top of the upward fluctuation, he wants to get his short sale made near the top of the trading range which has persisted for the preceding two or three sessions. Of course, if prices do not move to the specified tick, he will not get execution. In fact his price may be hit and one or two sales executed at the level of his sell order, but his floor broker may still be unable to get a fill.

Tops and Bottoms Can Be Thin

It is worth noting that the volume of trade which takes place at the higher and lower limits of the trading range are usually quite small. A single 5,000 bushel contract may change hands to post the high for the day; the same sort of minimum trade may post the low for the day. Inexperienced traders are often disappointed to see that the price specified in a limit order was reached, but their order was still not executed. The broker's explanation invariably is that offerings or bids at the maximum level were simply not sufficient to accommodate all orders resting at the top or the bottom of the market.

So, whether through placement of the first kind of combined order, or the time and price-limit order, we will assume that the trader has succeeded in selling an additional 5,000 bushels of May corn short at $2.91½. His total position at this point is "short—15 May corn." Execution of the second order requires total margin of $1,800, since margining of each subsequent trade demands that initial margin to cover the total position be on deposit with the broker. Initial margin on corn, as previously noted, is at this writing 12 cents per bushel; hence, $1,800 initial margin is required to cover the 15,000 bushels. Of this total amount, only $1,475 represents the speculator's cash money on deposit with his commission house. The remaining $325 is represented by paper profits, made on the initial 10,000 bushel short position as it dropped from a price of $2.94¾ (the first short sale) to $2.91½ (the second short sale). At this point, the speculator has increased his position in the market by one half, but his cash margin requirement is proportionately smaller ($1,800 − $325)—thanks to the 3¼ cent paper profit generated on the first 10,000 bushels.

Whenever an opportunity for pyramiding presents itself, it materially increases the already substantial leverage situation in commodity trading. Coincidentally with selling the additional 5,000 bushels of corn, a new look must now be taken at the speculator's stop-loss. On each 5,000 bushels of grain—long or short—each price change of 1 cent results in a profit or loss of $50. By increasing the position to 15,000 bushels, each 1 cent movement in price will result in a profit or loss of $150. (Commissions are ignored in this discussion.)

At $2.91½ per bushel, the speculator has a $325 paper profit in the trade. This is to say that, commissions ignored, he can lose this amount back to the market before the position would represent a "zero profit" situation. Having added a second 5,000 bushel sale, an upward price movement of about 3¼ cents per bushel will dissipate the $325 paper profit. Hopefully, the addition will only be made if the trader feels he can safely move his topside stop-loss down from $3.00½ per bushel to about $2.95½. At the point he adds the third contract of 5,000 bushels, he will again risk the $325 paper profit, but his objective should be to get as close as possible to nothing worse than a break even on the trade.

Unless a stop-loss can be moved down, a short position should not be increased, since doing so increases risk exposure without bringing any real offsetting advantage. Moving the stop-loss insures your pyramid.

Commodity speculators usually turn in far better performances in the placement and management of initial positions than they do in making the secondary judgments which call for additions to the primary trade. This fact is often directly related to their tendency to overtrade on limited funds.

Keep Part of Your Powder Dry

It was earlier pointed out that an initial position should never require commitment of more than 50 percent of a trader's risk capital. The reason for this rule now becomes apparent: the 50 percent reserve is a guarantee that if prices move in the trader's favor, he will have the funds required to *enlarge his position* and take advantage of the greater leverage in pyramiding—"trading on profits." A modest beginning on a commodity position entails modest risks. As price movement validates a trader's judgment and paper profits accrue, larger exposures are justified—but only if safeguards can be invoked to reduce potential hazards. Maximizing profit opportunities calls for both the financial ability and willingness to enlarge a profitable position. But—to repeat for emphasis—never pyramid unless you can simultaneously move your stop-loss and cut loss potentials substantially.

Each time a position is added to, a different situation exists. Most importantly, the contract is now trading at a somewhat different price level, and the range may be wider or narrower than previously. Consequently, profit and loss expectations may be altered. The position now deserves careful reappraisal, along with increased attention on the part of its holder, since there is more at stake. This fact hardly requires emphasis, however, since there is nothing that will concentrate a speculator's attention like a large and profitable position which has been accumulated in several steps.

Don't Try to Stay Forever

The importance of getting in at the right time cannot be overemphasized. Getting out at the right time is of even greater moment with respect to profits. Inexperienced speculators have a long and undistinguished record of staying too long in losing positions. During 1966, thousands of speculators established long positions in corn futures at prices ranging from $1.35 to $1.50 per bushel. Corn prices moved sharply higher through August and September, peaked out in the $1.55 to $1.58 range and fell precipitously into the $1.30 to $1.40 range in November. Public traders who—at the contract highs—had profits of 15 or 20 cents in their corn positions, sat patiently and watched their paper gains dissipated. They consoled themselves with the forlorn thought that they still had a profit in it. A trading rationale of this kind is senseless. Regardless of paper profits remaining, every one eighth down from the contract high was a loss for the longs.

A speculator buys something to sell at a higher price; or sells it in expectation of buying it back at a lower price. In either case, profit is the sole motivation. Any time prices move sharply against a commodity position, the time has come to close it out, whether or not there is some profit left at lower price levels.

The best and surest way to guard against erosion of profits already accumulated is by careful placement of a stop-order which will automatically get offset on the positon any time prices move out of an acceptable trading range. Speculative profits must be protected as zealously in existing positions as they are sought in new positions. Failure to do so will only succeed in turning profitable trades into "breakevens"—and the losing trades will continue to deplete risk funds. The predictable result will sooner or later be disaster, of course.

Daily Price Behavior

The matter of selling on bulges and buying on dips has been referred to previously. Now we shall consider this matter from a different standpoint.

Examination of a bar chart on price movement in any commodity is convincing proof that prices rarely move up or down in a smooth and unbroken path. The *trend* may be clearly higher or lower, but the *path* followed by price in producing this trend is an unending succession of directional reversals. Depending on the commodity, and influenced to a large extent by its relative price, swings in value will be narrow or broad. Generally speaking, the more "publicly" a contract is traded, the wider its price swings may be; since a high degree of public speculator interest in a given commodity has a tendency to emphasize the short-term extremes within which its price fluctuates: The highs are rendered somewhat higher, and the lows are rendered somewhat lower than is likely to be seen in a more "commercially" traded situation. The long-range effect of speculation is to *reduce price fluctuation;* but the short-range effect of high volume speculation may be just the opposite. This is especially true where a high proportion of the trade is small public trader involvement.

Position and Day Traders

At the very hub of the market, in the pits, will be found several categories of full-time professional traders, including those who pursue a speculative program which involves taking positions in selected contracts and holding them over several weeks or several months, pending major price movements. These people are usually spoken of as *position traders*. These individuals may establish a long or short position early in the season and hold it until maturity.

Day traders, on the other hand, may be long for the first hour or so, then offset and go short for the balance of the session. In any case, the day trader intends to offset all positions and be even with the market at the closing bell; the day trader carries no positions overnight if he can help it. His speculative program is pointed exclusively to taking advantage of whatever profit opportunities exist between the opening and the close; by which time he will be evened up and out of the market.

Scalpers

The shortest of all short-term traders is the pit *scalper*. This individual performs approximately the same function in the commodity pit that the specialist performs on the securities exchanges, with one important difference: The scalper has no official designation from the commodity exchange itself. The scalper buys and sells in search of profit, with no special privileges accorded him from any quarter. He may make dozens or hundreds of trades in the course of a single session. Generally speaking, the scalper is prepared to sell at ¼ or ½ cent per bushel above the last trade; he is usually a ready buyer ¼ or ½ cent below the last trade. His success depends on exceedingly small profits on a big trade volume. He views the minimum price fluctuation in grain—¼ cent a bushel—as an acceptable transaction, and considers ½ cent per bushel an excellent return!

Commodity scalpers, like stock specialists, provide a source of supply when orders to buy exceed orders to sell. Likewise, scalpers (like stock specialists) constitute demand, when offerings exceed willingness to buy on the part of the public or commercial interests. Neither the scalper

Courtesy of the CME

Exhibit 14–4

Telephones on the trading floor, along with computer printers, are the conduits that carry orders into the market and pass confirmations back to customers. A minute is often sufficient time in which to receive an order, fill it, and relay confirmation.

nor the specialist can prevent prices from moving higher or lower in the face of altered supply/demand equilibrium, and they would not wish to do so even if they could. These somewhat similar market participants do, however, help maintain market liquidity and aid in sustaining orderly progression of prices from one level to another level. In so doing, they contribute immeasurably to the well-being of the market itself.

Like the day trader, the scalper carries no positions overnight. By the closing bell, he will have offset all of his previous trades and calculated his profits or losses on the individual session, as a trading interval which stands by itself.

All Traders Seek Profits

From the foregoing, it should be seen that the position trader, the day trader, and the scalper, all seek profits from properly anticipating price movement. Each, however, approaches the market with a different period of time in mind. The position trader looks for a situation which he may carry for weeks or months; the day trader seeks positions which he may carry for, at most, a few hours; the scalper may buy 50,000 bushels of grain and sell it 10 seconds later, or sell 50,000 bushels short and cover it in the same breath. All three classifications of traders have one thing in common. They will hold a position until profit expectations are realized, or the market moves adversely enough to require covering the loss.

It is the interaction of these buying and selling forces, along with the actions of public speculators, commercial hedgers, producers, and processors, that determine the course of price movement, minute by minute. If selling pressure gains momentary ascendancy in a pit, prices will move lower until the lower (and more attractive) price prompts new buying sentiment. When this happens, the bears may suddenly lose the initiative to the bulls; a price reversal will occur and values will move higher. The result is a constant seesaw action.

Daily trading ranges in corn rarely exceed 6 to 8 cents per bushel. In soybeans, as noted above, the trading range is more like 12 to 15 cents a bushel. These swings are approximately parallel by reason of the fact that soybeans usually trade at about twice the price of corn. A 4 cent price change in $6.00 soybeans is the same order of magnitude as a 2 cent per bushel change in $3.00 corn. It may be well to note here also that margins anticipate these differences. The initial margin on beans at this writing is 35 cents per bushel, compared to 12 cents per bushel for the corn.

Day traders strive earnestly to pick points of price reversal, since their greatest chance for a profit lies in properly forecasting price trend during the current trading session. Scalpers care little about tops and bottoms, so long as they can catch the fluctuations. Position traders tend to give major emphasis to relatively long-term price moves.

The public speculator is well advised to pursue the position trader's operational philosophy; however, selling on intrasession price bulges, and buying on price dips can easily add another cent or two to profits—and reduce loss exposure accordingly. Granting this, automatically gives rise to a question related to order placement.

Limited versus Market Orders

A *market order* to buy or sell will be immediately executed at the best level offered in the pit at the time the broker receives it. This price may or may not be advantageous in the view of the private speculator, but it is the market price when the order is called. In the face of rapidly moving prices, the trader may have no alternative but to accept whatever price the market gives him. This situation will usually apply when losses are mounting, due to a rapidly rising or falling price level. Establishing a new position, however, can ordinarily be approached somewhat more deliberately.

Experienced traders usually prefer specifying a fixed price (or better) at which they are willing to buy or sell. Obviously it will rarely make sense to place an entering order far below—or far above—the trading range, in the flimsy hope that something cataclysmic will happen to bring prices to the level of the order. Resting orders well outside the trading range are commonplace, but their execution may be deferred for days or weeks, or they may never be filled. The commodity speculator must try to find some middle ground between the price he would like and the price he can reasonably expect to get in the marketplace. There are many instances, in fact, where, for example, December corn at $2.42 per bushel represents a much more promising buy than the same contract at $2.38.

Depending on the tone of the trade, the chart pattern, and the general price trend on the futures involved, $2.42 per bushel, might be a clear indication to buy corn, while $2.38 per bushel could be an equally strong reason to sell the contract short. The speculator who is attempting to get all possible profit mileage out of his position, will put a price limitation on his orders to buy or sell, whenever he can prudently do so. In return, he will often be exposed to the unspeakable frustration of seeing prices come within a small fraction of a penny of his limit and then move away. Missing execution by $\frac{1}{4}$ or $\frac{1}{2}$ cent can be an upsetting experience; and the speculator who constantly places limit orders will know the feeling often. However, the positions he is able to acquire on the basis of his limits will ordinarily be better—more profitable—than those taken at market.

Don't Be Too Anxious to Execute

There is an old saying in speculative circles that you "can't lose a dollar on a position you don't have." Another axiom which bears on the same consideration is, "Whenever you reach, you will probably find trouble." Boiled down to their fundamentals, these two admonitions simply mean that a speculator is entitled to determine the price at which he is willing to undertake a given risk. If the market won't fill the order and do business at this level, then the speculator will either have to refuse to do business at all, or reconsider the situation and develop a second price appraisal.

The role of the speculator is that of forecasting price movement; nothing else. The only time a speculator can look forward to profits is when he catches the market quoting the wrong price on a given contract. The speculator must, in other words, catch the trade in error. Obviously if the market price is the right price, then it can only be expected to persist and there is no speculative profit to be made out of price consistency. It takes change to ring the speculative cash register. Doing this requires that the speculator's price idea be better than composite market judgment in the short-term, the medium-term, the long-term—or all of these.

It is no small assignment, which again underscores the thought that a wise speculator will be highly selective about the positions he undertakes. Additionally, and most important, unless he can find something palpably wrong with an individual price or a price relationship, he will stay on the sidelines and patiently wait for an opportunity to "catch the market with jam on its face." Anyone who insists on being constantly involved in commodity futures speculation should make a full-time business of it. Certainly there are situations every hour of every trading day which have exciting profit potentials, but finding these opportunities calls for careful study and critical analysis; in short—a full-time engagement.

The public speculator is, more often than not, an individual who has the financial wherewithal and the analytical turn of mind to make commodity speculation an interesting, exciting, and rewarding avocation. This is to say that market activities will probably not receive first priority. Granting this, the prudent public speculator will limit his market forays to those selected situations which show the best opportunities for profit. He will leave the more limited, more hazardous, short-term commitments to those who have the time, the funds, and the professional expertise with which to deal with them.

15

Special Trading Situations

The trading lives of commodity contracts are about a year, or more. Within this relatively short time span, a commodity contract comes into existence, develops some discernible personality traits, and expires. While it can be said that all wheat contracts of a given crop year, for example, demonstrate somewhat similar characteristics, it is a serious mistake to look at *all* contracts in a given commodity in the same light.

Old Crop/New Crop

Some of the most glaring idiosyncracies in futures contract characteristics relate to the point in the crop or production year in which they mature. As a case in point, the May wheat contract represents old crop wheat. The grain delivered against open long positions in May wheat will have been harvested in late summer or fall of the preceding year. The relative adequacy or scarcity of wheat stocks will exercise the most significant influence on the way May wheat goes off the board. If the harvest was ample and crop disappearance through consumption and export was not excessive, it might be expected that wheat stocks in commercial channels would be sufficient to meet ordinary demands, pending the new crop which begins to arrive in volume in late June and July.

If, on the other hand, the preceding harvest was meager, or disappearance of the crop through consumption and export has proceeded at an accelerated rate, wheat stocks may be seriously depleted. The result

174

may be that food processors and others who need the grain face some degree of crisis in fulfilling their requirements until the new crop becomes available. In the face of ample or excessive residual stocks, stable or lower May wheat prices can be confidently anticipated. Scarcity of the grain will bring higher prices for the cash product, as well as for old-crop May futures contracts which represent the commodity.

July wheat futures represent new-crop grain. Old-crop considerations are, at best, a secondary influence. The market's appraisal of the adequacy of the pending harvest in light of existing and projected new demands will be the major concern, reflected in relatively high or low prices on the July contract. If it appears that a significant imbalance is shaping up, as between expected supplies and estimated demands, wide price swings will usually document the building market consensus.

Trading in old-crop grain commodities brings the speculator to grips with the fundamental adequacy of commodity inventories remaining at the end of the crop year. New-crop contracts relate to future needs. Making these appraisals calls for careful analysis and meticulous arithmetic. Both past and projected exports must be studiously added up, along with past and projected domestic consumption figures. Appraisals require that annual data must be compared to the historical averages over not less than a five year period. Government programs which affect acreage controls, export policy, "food for freedom," etc., must also be included in any meaningful price/value equation.

Harvest Time May Vary

Reference has already been made to the fact that September contract soybeans can be either old crop or new crop, depending on how early planting was concluded and subsequent weather patterns during the growing season. A soybean is a "photoperiodic" plant. The mature beans will be ready for harvest a specified number of weeks after planting, so long as temperatures remain in an acceptable range and moisture is adequate to sustain plant development.

In view of the foregoing, the September soybean contract can be expected to reflect some volatility not present in other commodity categories. Should it appear that factors are favorable for an early harvest, proportionately lower prices on the September contract usually are seen. (The effect is one of enlarging old-crop carryover.) Should subsequent events alter this outlook, higher prices are quick to develop. This characteristic in September soybeans affords an excellent opportunity to examine the phenomenon known in commodity trading as a *weather market*. The term is descriptively accurate.

Trading in September soybeans begins in September of the year preceding harvest. Usually the new contract comes on the board at some discount to the expiring November contract. This is prompted in large measure by the continuing trend to greater soybean acreage, and increasing per-acre yields. Once trading begins in the new-crop beans, a pattern of price behavior quickly begins to develop. At the outset, disappearance of the *old crop* is the most important factor in pricing the *new crop;* since it governs the size of the carry-over which may be expected at the end of the current crop year. Government activities directed toward increased or reduced acreage are also a major factor, along with projected yields per acre. Relative prices commanded by soybean meal and oil must be given full weight, too, since these may provide an index to increasing or decreasing demand trends for the products; and which may be sustained for several months or a year later.

Ordinarily, through the winter September soybean prices will follow the leadership of the July contract. September begins to develop a personality of its own in March, when the U.S. Department of Agriculture Crop Reporting Service releases figures on soybean planting intentions. A significant increase over the past year in projected soybean acreage will usually exert a predictably bearish influence on prices. The same or reduced planting intentions will ordinarily have the opposite effect.

Once the plantings intentions report is out, weather quickly becomes the most important single influence in the contract and will remain so for some four or five months. In a year when an early spring and dry fields permit putting seed in the ground in late March or early April, the impact on the September price is substantial. By virtue of the photoperiodic nature of soybeans, early planting almost insures an early harvest—and will usually bring somewhat lower prices on both the old-crop (July) contract and the new-crop (September and November).

Should bad weather and wet fields delay planting, the opposite can be expected. If the condition persists, harvest will be delayed; and September contract now becomes old-crop. Its requirements will have to be filled out of carry-over stocks. Prices on the September maturity will, in this situation, reflect the market's appraisal of the adequacy of remaining supplies, projected to November—two months beyond the statistical end of the crop year. Understandably, the effect on price can be tremendous.

Growing Conditions Are Crucial

Early planting does not by itself lay all of the worries to rest. Ideal growing conditions for soybeans, as well as other grains, usually require temperatures between a minimum of 55° Fahrenheit and a maximum of 100° Fahrenheit. Additionally, of course, sufficient moisture must be present in the soil to sustain plant development.

Heavy early rains may threaten to wash seed out of the ground. In the face of such a possibility—provided the threat hangs over an important soybean region—prices will rise in recognition of the hazard. In the opposite weather situation, protracted periods of drought will also send prices upward in reflection of the possibility that dry weather may destroy the crop or seriously retard its growth. Each plant has its own development characteristics. The soybean is distinguished by an amazing recuperative power. While an extended period of dry weather will damage the growing plants—even to the extent of causing leaves to dry up and fall off—once the rains return, soybeans will usually put out new growth and pick up where they left off.

As summer progresses, however, soybean farmers, processors, and speculators keep a careful eye on weather forecasts. September bean prices in particular rise and fall in response to the thermometer and the soil-moisture scale. Traders repeat the market truism that "every soybean crop is lost three or four times before it is harvested." The statement merely underscores the susceptibility of *market psychology* to weather influences. When a period of dryness develops, market response tends to overemphasize its significance in the form of a price bulge. When needed rain interrupts the period of drought, prices drop in something like equal disproportion to their previous increase. In short, the market tends to overbuy bad weather and oversell good weather, offering an excellent opportunity for a speculator to buy the dips and sell the bulges through several months of the growing season.

The weather market in soybeans is especially volatile due to the already-noted fact that the September contract may be accelerated or retarded by weather patterns, to the extent of making the maturity fall into one crop year or the next. Similar considerations are also present in some other grain commodities, although to a lesser extent.

As this material is being prepared (November 1984), July 1985 wheat futures (new-crop) are trading at a 16 cent discount off the May 1985 (old-crop) maturity. Anyone who intends to trade 1985 wheat contracts had better take a hard look at what makes a bushel of wheat for Chicago delivery in May worth $3.62; and that same bushel of wheat, if held until July, worth only $3.46. In spite of the fact that the crop won't be harvested for another eight or nine months (some of it isn't even planted yet) weather is already a major factor in the inversion noted.

The southwestern wheat belt that gave us the Dust Bowl of the 1930s lives or dies on the basis of each year's weather. Farmers can prepare their fields and plant prodigious acreages to the grain, but unless rains come to instill sufficient soil-moisture levels to produce germination and growth, the seed and labor is in vain. And even if soil-moisture levels are adequate, it also takes snow to produce a good harvest. Unless a blanket of snow covers the fields, winter winds can strip topsoil and seed away, and the crop is lost.

A leathery-faced wheat farmer sat in a cafe in Hays, Kansas, and summed up the dilemma that he faces every year: "The trouble with raising wheat around here is that there's *four* ways to lose your crop—and only *one* way to bring it off!" Commodity traders recognize the hard kernel of truth in his plaint.

During the last two weeks copious amounts of rain have fallen across the Texas panhandle, Oklahoma, Kansas, and the Colorado plains, thus seeming to fulfill the first requirement for a bountiful harvest. Adequate moisture coupled with the large numbers of acres reflected in the USDA *Planting Intentions Report* seems to point to a bumper crop in our major wheat-producing area. While this is a gratifying prospect certainly, it is not an unmixed blessing.

A big harvest may outstrip market demand by some greater or lesser extent. Should this happen, export activities will have to be stepped up, or the government will have to engage in a lot of stockpile buying in order to provide a way to get the oversupply put away.

In the meantime, the traders look at this wheat situation and speculate on events to come. The discount on new-crop wheat gives us the clearest possible signal that market consensus indicates we will be seriously oversupplied when the 1985 harvest comes out of the fields. This is what results in the lower quote on the July contract.

This lower price, in turn, will be prompting a variety of activities on the part of other commodity interests. *Foreign customers* like Great Britain, Japan, and India who know they will need to augment their own stocks of wheat may wish to buy the July discount in Chicago, as a means of hedging their predictable needs. When July arrives they can then take delivery; or they can exchange the futures position for cash wheat in an "ex-pit" transaction; or they can offset the Chicago futures position through equal-and-opposite selling, and use the profits (if any) to finance the purchase of wheat in Canada, Australia, or Russia!

Grain merchants like Continental, Cargill, and Dreyfus may buy the July discount in anticipation of their needs many months or a year later, when they will be called on to supply grain to processors, or to assemble cargos for exportation to Europe, Africa, or elsewhere.

Processors like Kellogg, Ralston, and General Foods may buy the July discount as part of their forward raw materials acquisition program. If a flour miller knows he needs 5 million bushels of wheat each month of the year to keep his plants occupied and the customers supplied, he isn't going to wait until May or June to begin firming up his July requirements. Instead, he will make interim or substitute purchases of July futures. Having done so, he is assured of the wheat he needs and, of equal or even greater importance, he also knows the basis price at which it has been acquired. With this information he can assure his customers that their orders will be filled; and he can quote firm prices on his products—eight months into the future!

Speculators may buy the July discount for no better reason than that they think the 16 cent inversion between old-crop (1984) and new-crop (1985), is excessive, and that the July price will move up as open-interest in the maturity builds.

Spreaders may buy the July contract and sell the May contract, out of a conviction that the 16 cent differential is too wide and, in days or weeks to come, will narrow. Whether it narrows as a result of the July price rising, or from the May quote falling will make no difference. As long as the price differential shrinks to something less than the current 16 cents, the spreader's hope will be, to some extent, realized.

Who Will Take the Other Side?

Knowing that any open contract in commodities requires both a long-holder and a short-holder, we will now take a look at the interests and individuals who will be selling the discounted July 1985 contract.

High on the list are the producers themselves. Faced with the knowledge that a huge wheat crop is in firm prospect, a lot of wheat growers will conclude that much lower prices on new-crop wheat are in prospect as harvest time nears. Unless a farmer has adequate storage to hold his own harvest, he will be at the bleak mercies of a buyer's market in July, as the flood of wheat comes into the market looking for storage. It is at the peak of harvest activity that the lowest cash prices of the year are ordinarily posted. A producer who does not have his wheat sold or hedged before he reaps it is, indeed, likely to be in deep trouble.

In view of this bitter reality, a large proportion of new-crop hedging takes place simultaneously with the planting of the grain and the raising of it. Usually this short-hedging on the part of producers and country elevator operators is a continuing activity, with portions of the oncoming crop being systematically sold into each successively more distant contract (or the contracts that offer the most advantageous basis) throughout the planting/growing period. This early and continuing hedging pressure from country producers and handlers is probably a major element in creating the steep discount we see on new-crop wheat.

But much as a farmer or a country elevator operator hates to sell a discount, doing so is far preferable to being unhedged in the new crop year. As additional trading builds open-interest in September and December maturities, a lot of the July shorts will be moved out into the more deferred maturities, as soon as carrying-charge premiums begin to be reflected in them. In the meantime, progress of the crop and expectations predicated on a variety of inputs will continue to lead prices through great or small fluctuative aberrations as time goes on.

Weather Psychology in the Market

The impact of weather on growing crops is self-evident, of course, but the weather psychology which permeates the market during the growing season should also be recognized. No grain is raised in Chicago, but a rain storm in Chicago during the crop growing season will almost invariably reflect itself in lower commodity prices on pertinent contracts! The explanation must be that traders consider moisture bearish and lack of rain bullish and react accordingly—almost out of habit.

The foregoing should not lead the speculator to the unfounded conclusion that weather extremes are always of only transitory importance, to be later corrected by nature, and the affected crops saved. This is not the case. Extensive and persistent droughts and devastating floods have occurred in the past, and will most assuredly be seen in the future. The balance between supply and demand tends to be so sensitive that even a 2 percent or 3 percent difference in harvest yield can make a most significant difference in the adequacy of supplies; and alter the price the product commands in the marketplace out of all proportion to the percentage of crop loss or gain. It is true that weather news tends to be magnified in the short-term; but it is equally true that weather must be accorded the highest priority as concerns longer-range prices of new-crop commodities. Growing crops are absolutely dependent on benign combinations of temperature and moisture. Unless nature provides the proper climatic mix, human efforts are of no avail.

South Africa Grain Is Again Suffering from Dryness, Heat

By WENDY L. WALL
Staff Reporter of The Wall Street Journal

CHICAGO—Extreme dryness and heat are damaging South Africa's young grain crop, threatening to turn that major corn exporter into a net importer for the third consecutive year.

The troubles in South Africa, once the world's third-largest corn exporter, have helped in recent days to buoy corn prices in the U.S., the largest source of corn in world trade. Corn for March delivery rose 0.75 cent a bushel yesterday on the Chicago Board of Trade, to $2.715 a bushel, up 2.2 percent from a week earlier.

The same high-pressure weather patterns that are causing South Africa's problems are bringing about the severe famine that plagues Ethiopia and other nations. South Africa's problems bode ill for its African neighbors, not only because it shares certain weather patterns, but because it is a major source of grain for other African countries.

South Africa's "maize triangle," the major corn producing region, has received almost no rain in the past three weeks. Since severe droughts in 1983 and 1984 depleted soil moisture, plants in many areas are struggling. In addition, about 10 days ago, temperatures surged to over 90 degrees and have stayed there, putting additional stress on crops.

"It's the third consecutive year where rainfall has basically shut down during (this) crucial period," says Michael Palmerino, an agricultural meteorologist with Weather Services Corp, in Bedford, Mass.

The drought has already cut the crop at least 20 percent from the roughly 9 million metric tons originally expected, most analysts agree. Moreover, the crop is entering its critical pollination stage, when moisture is crucial.

"Their crop can disappear in just a matter of days," says Steve Nutt, grain analyst at Cargill Investor Services Inc. "If things don't improve in a hurry, they could be right back to 4.4 million metric tons," the size of last year's disastrous harvest.

A crop that small would force the South Africans to import grain once again. In 1981, the country reaped a record 14.7 million metric tons of corn, partly because of a government policy subsidizing exports. But droughts damaged or devastated the three succeeding crops. In the year ended September

30, the South Africans were forced to import 2.7 million metric tons of U.S. corn.

Another South African crop failure also would force grain-importing nations elsewhere in the world to turn to other countries for corn, probably to the U.S. or Argentina.

The South African drought could boost world prices for corn, a major livestock feed that has grown increasingly important on world markets as many nations seek to add meat to their peoples' diets.

There was evidence late yesterday that the Soviet Union, a major grain importer, may already be reacting to the South African troubles by buying U.S. corn. The U.S. Agriculture Department said private exporters had sold the Soviet Union 1.2 million metric tons of U.S. corn; rumors circulated among traders that the total purchase was more than two million metric tons, and that the rest will be reported later.

Although the Soviets don't usually buy corn from South Africa, they may nevertheless be shopping for grain now in anticipation of rising corn prices, some analysts speculated.

Although light showers are expected in South Africa's corn-growing regions today or tomorrow, the rains aren't expected to reverse the crop damage or substantially reduce the stress on the crop.

Anyone who trades in the so-called global crops must accommodate a perspective that goes far beyond national boundaries. Whether the commodity be corn, wheat, cocoa, coffee, or soybeans, weather—at some period in the growing season—will be the most important consideration the trader must grapple with. Unless weather at some point becomes manageable through technology, it will remain the major risk in agricultural activities of all kinds.

Seasonal Balance in Hedging

Of all of the special trading situations which challenge the courage and insight of the speculator, maturing contracts must be put at the head of the list. Within the contract trading life of about a year or so, open-interest grows from zero to what may be impressive proportions. For each seller of a futures contract, there must also be a buyer, and the foundation of most futures trading is provided by hedging on the part of the producers, processors, dealers, and shippers.

At the end of harvest, commercial interests are large buyers of commodities from producers. They at some point reverse their earlier position and hedge their cash grain acquisitions in the market by sale of futures. Thus, the postharvest situation usually finds commercial interests who were probably net-long throughout the spring, overwhelmingly short in the market, and speculative interests equally long. Toward the end of the crop year, this situation tends to be substantially moderated or, if a shortage of the commodity exists, it may be actually reversed.

In order to understand this development, we must review the reasons which prompt commercial hedging. By definition, a hedge is an *equal and opposite* position in futures, to the position held in cash commodities. If a grain dealer has a million bushels of corn in storage, a hedge against this cash corn position would require that he have a million bushels of corn futures sold short in the market. Obviously a commercial grain broker or processor must rely on speculators to buy his short-hedge offerings. It may also be assumed that intelligent speculators will only buy futures contracts at prices which appear to be sufficiently low as to offer a reasonable expectation for profit, in payment for assumption of the ownership risk.

It is an historic fact that prices during the harvest season tend to be lower than the yearly average. As the year progresses, the cash grain previously purchased by commercial interests is consumed and exported. As this takes place, the holders of cash grain reduce their inventories and lift their hedges by buying back (offsetting) their previously sold commodity futures contracts. Repurchase of these contracts by commercial interests takes place somewhat later in the crop year, after the initial harvest glut of the commodity has been materially reduced. One effect of this recurrent market pattern is a more or less perceptible seasonal increase in prices for most agricultural crops.

Maturing Contracts

Quite naturally, speculators who previously purchased the short-hedge offerings of the commercial interests will attempt to hold out for a price which will enable them to realize maximum profits. Note that this statement reflects a hope which may or may not be realized. The price on futures contracts at maturity is closely related to the value of the cash product. This because cash and futures prices tend to converge in the market on the last day of trading.

The holder of a short position in a maturing commodity contract has the choice of offsetting by an equal or opposite futures transaction, or he may satisfy his contract commitment by delivery of the physical commodity. The price which prevails on futures contracts at maturity will be a composite reflection of the willingness of the shorts to make delivery and the willingness of the longs to accept delivery. Excessive deliverable stocks in position will force prices down. Shortage of deliverable stocks in position will carry prices higher.

Settlement by Delivery

It should be noted at this point that only about 2 percent of the futures contracts bought and sold are actually satisfied by delivery of the cash commodity. Commercial hedgers are reticent to make delivery, since doing so entails costs and inconvenience which are acceptable in cash market trading; but they prefer offset in the futures market to any other kind of settlement, provided this can be done without economic penalty.

Speculators are ordinarily in no position to make delivery of cash commodities because they hold none; they likewise wish to avoid accepting delivery of cash commodities, since they neither own storage facilities nor have use for the physical product. Hence it will be seen that while commercial interests merely prefer offset of their futures positions, speculators usually insist on offsetting in preference to taking or making delivery.

As a contract reaches its delivery period and the last day of trading approaches, holders of both long and short positions are coming down to the moment of truth. Once trading is terminated in a given contract, all remaining shorts must make delivery and all remaining longs must accept delivery. Doing so may constitute a major catastrophe for either or both. If a shortage of the product prevails, the longs may stand firm and threaten the shorts with having to deliver. This situation is known in the trade as a *short squeeze* and may send prices skyrocketing as the shorts scramble to offset their open positions, which will remove the necessity of their delivering the cash commodity.

In the reverse situation, an excess of commodities in deliverable position may prompt the shorts to stand firm (threatening delivery) and forcing the longs to sell out their holdings at a disadvantage in order to avoid taking delivery. Sharply lower prices may result from such a *long squeeze*.

One of the best indicators of a potentially explosive situation in a maturing contract is the amount of open-interest remaining in the last few days of contract life. Ordinarily both hedgers and speculators will begin offsetting heavily during the month preceding maturity. Should open-interest remain unusually high beyond the first notice day, it can be taken as a good indication that somebody is in trouble. The problem for the speculator now is to decide whether it is the longs or the shorts who are most likely to be caught in the squeeze which may be developing.

In appraising this kind of situation, it must be remembered that only commercials are usually ready to accept delivery in large quantities; likewise, commercial interests have both the facilities and the grain stocks to make delivery to the shorts.

In light of this, it will be seen that the public is more susceptible too squeezing than commercial interests. Therefore, in order to profit from the situation, the speculator must decide whether the public is net long or net short; and whichever decision he arrives at suggests that he take precisely the opposite position.

If the public is short, the speculator may buy the contract because the public shorts will have to buy back their positions. Their doing so will likely send prices higher. If the public is long, the speculator may sell the contract short. He knows the public longs will have to sell out their positions, and doing so will probably send prices lower.

Needless to say, if the speculator takes a position in the closing days of a tight maturing contract—and improperly judges the situation—he may only succeed in joining the other position holders who are caught

CHICAGO BOARD OF TRADE
141 WEST JACKSON BLVD.
CHICAGO, ILLINOIS 60604

FUTURES TRADING AND OPEN INTEREST IN COMMODITIES TRADED ON THE CHICAGO BOARD OF TRADE, TUESDAY, SEPTEMBER 4, 1984 #171 DAILY VOLUME OF TRADING—SALES—INCLUDING EXCHANGES OF FUTURES FOR CASH, AND OPEN INTEREST—ONE SIDE ONLY—AS REPORTED BY CLEARING MEMBERS, AS OF THE CLOSE OF BUSINESS. CASH EXCHANGES ARE INCLUDED IN TRADING VOLUME. BASED UPON BEST AVAILABLE DATA OBTAINED FROM CLEARING MEMBERS. SUBJECT TO FURTHER CORRECTION.

COMMODITY	MTH	YR	TRADING VOLUME	CASH EXCHANGE	TRANSFERS	OPEN AT CLOSE	INTEREST CHANGE	DELIVERY NOTICES
WHEAT	SEP	84	14,190	7,695		26,810	8,792 −	375
	DEC	84	28,425	325		145,250	2,220 +	
	MCH	85	6,405	310	75	37,750	720 +	
	MAY	85	730			11,945	330 +	
	JLY	85	235			5,340	45 −	
	SEP	85				290		
TOTAL			49,985	8,330	75	227,385	5,567 −	375
CORN	SEP	84	48,415	11,285	640	131,540	8,365 −	
	DEC	84	117,140	3,425	11,075	424,850	17,775 +	
	MCH	85	18,325	5	5	106,445	250 −	
	MAY	85	3,465			32,570	860 +	
	JLY	85	1,350			24,175	430 +	
	SEP	85	55			1,665	30 +	
	DEC	85	265			1,520	90 +	
TOTAL			189,015	14,715	11,720	722,765	10,570 +	
OATS	SEP	84	530		205	1,530	215 −	
	DEC	84	1,860	160	35	14,570	465 −	
	MCH	85	500		250	4,920	85 +	
	MAY	85	55			910	10 +	
	JLY	85	30			560	20 +	
TOTAL			2,975	160	490	22,490	565 −	
SOY BEANS	SEP	84	13,845	185	10	24,175	4,995 −	
	NOV	84	147,760	4,715	225	165,530	3,375 −	
	JAN	85	9,250	5		40,775		
	MCH	85	4,655			19,185	410 +	
	MAY	85	1,025			6,050	55 −	
	JLY	85	3,610	810		7,405	385 +	
	AUG	85	290			1,105	150 +	
	SEP	85	5			300		
	NOV	85	975			3,155	55 +	
TOTAL			181,415	5,715	235	267,680	7,425 −	
SOY MEAL	SEP	84	5,964	444	9	3,065	773 −	906
	OCT	84	8,729	50	100	15,826	723 −	
	DEC	84	7,779	116	30	18,135	11 −	
	JAN	85	803	55		6,381	182 +	
	MCH	85	208			2,551	120 +	
	MAY	85	220			921	32 +	
	JLY	85	360		100	411	111 +	
	AUG	85	10			20	9 +	
	SEP	85				12		
	OCT	85				35		
TOTAL			24,073	665	239	47,357	1,053 −	906
SOY OIL	SEP	84	2,972	525	6	4,807	390 −	142
	OCT	84	6,077	123	200	15,828	901 +	
	DEC	84	6,106		203	18,046	428 −	
	JAN	85	571			4,715	140 −	
	MCH	85	143			2,308	48 +	
	MAY	85	62			746	35 +	
	JLY	85	163			469	111 +	
	AUG	85				39		
	OCT	85				27		
TOTAL			16,094	648	409	46,985	137 +	142

COMMODITY	MTH	YR	TRADING VOLUME	CASH EXCHANGE	TRANSFERS	OPEN AT CLOSE	INTEREST CHANGE	DELIVERY NOTICES
SILVER	SEP	84	49			70	7 −	17
	OCT	84	170			2,771	7 −	
	DEC	84	5,379		22	16,356	218 +	
	FEB	85	117		2	3,326	6 +	
	APR	85	156		12	6,059	30 +	
	JUN	85	80		2	3,942	28 +	
	AUG	85	30		1	1,135	9 −	
	OCT	85	7			199	1 −	
	DEC	85	17			135	12 +	
TOTAL			6,005		39	33,993	270 +	17
GNMAII	SEP	84	10			1,058	10 −	
	DEC	84				137		
TOTAL			10			1,195	10 −	
KILO GOLD	OCT	84	21			93	2 −	
	DEC	84	1,847			2,000	474 +	
	FEB	85	9			153	1 +	
	APR	85	2			65	2 +	
	JUN	85	2			18	1 +	
	AUG	85	3			17		
	OCT	85				2		
	DEC	85	2			7		
TOTAL			1,886			2,355	476 +	
GNMA-CDR	SEP	84	967			6,117	564 −	
	DEC	84	971			9,063	80 +	
	MCH	85	2			1,971	2 −	
	JUN	85				436		
	SEP	85				195		
	DEC	85				345		
	MCH	86				349		
	JUN	86				524		
TOTAL			1,940			19,000	486 −	
T-BONDS	SEP	84	12,694	77	76	64,366	3,287 −	1
	DEC	84	73,023	444	60	91,625	5,805 +	
	MCH	85	1,647		95	9,851	102 +	
	JUN	85	194			6,199	88 −	
	SEP	85	3			5,669	2 +	
	DEC	85	49			7,186	36 −	
	MCH	86	82			5,174	76 +	
	JUN	86	11			4,569	3 +	
	SEP	86				853		
	DEC	86				84		
	MCH	87	1			22	1 +	
TOTAL			87,704	521	231	195,598	2,578 +	1
10-YEAR TR	SEP	84	3,320	1	2	12,652	966 −	
	DEC	84	4,383			19,330	1,212 +	
	MCH	85	274			1,141	137 +	
	JUN	85				50		
TOTAL			7,977	1	2	33,173	383 +	
MAJOR MARK	SEP	84	8,417		32	4,820	230 −	
	OCT	84	18			196	11 +	
	NOV	84				16		
	DEC	84	33			625	30 +	
TOTAL			8,468		32	5,657	189 −	

Exhibit 15–1

Figures that recap all market activities are assembled by the respective exchange clearinghouses at the end of each day's session. The figures are then released to the news media, distributed to the public, and provided to the

Exhibit 15-1 (*concluded*)

Commodity Futures Trading Commission (CFTC). These data, along with information provided by commission houses and other interests that are holders of reportable positions, provide the raw information for the CFTC *Commitments Of Traders* report that is issued each month.

Cash exchanges and transfers involve "ex-pit" transactions on the part of commercial interests, wherein they exchange a futures position for the physical commodity; or use an established futures position transfer to fix a price on an anticipated cash delivery.

Of particular interest to public traders is the number of delivery notices tendered in connection with the expiring contracts. Public traders have no facilities for making or taking delivery of the actuals. Hence, if Notices of Intention To Deliver begin showing up in quantity early in the notice period, it can be a most intimidating signal to public longs that the commercials are in the driver's seat. Anyone who holds an open long position after the First-Notice-Day has to be aware of the fact that he might be tendered. Should this happen, he will either have to offset and retender the notice in the pit, or take delivery. It is for this reason that public traders should be extremely wary of staying around for the last few days in any expiring maturity.

---

in the squeeze. He may also find himself in the position of making or taking delivery, which is almost always a serious mistake. The reason should be clear:

Commercial interests control the lion's share of the cash commodity throughout most of the year, and they control practically all of the storage capacity at *all times*. They can, therefore, exercise almost complete discretion about their delivery decisions; and they do. The public speculator can rest assured that he will only get delivery, or be required to make delivery, when doing so is to his economic disadvantage; and when it is to the advantage of the commercial interest to obtain or dispose of cash goods.

There may be an occasional exception to the contrary, but it will be most rare, when becoming involved in physical delivery is less than a great mistake for the public speculator.

Government Crop Reports

Of major importance and occasionally devastating effect are the Government Crop Reports which are released at intervals throughout the agricultural crop year. This data is compiled by the Crop Reporting Board, a part of the U.S. Department of Agriculture. The figures are gathered from thousands of highly qualified observers under a cloak of the greatest secrecy. Once the individual reports are in hand, the Crop Reporting Board meets to analyze the composite situation and forecast total harvest probabilities.

These government figures always reach the trade at a time of day at which no trading in futures is underway. If the crop projections

COMMODITY FUTURES TRADING COMMISSION
233 South Wacker Drive, Suite 4600, Chicago, Illinois, 60606
(312/353–5990)
STOCKS OF DELIVERABLE GRAINS
In Warehouses Declared Regular for Delivery On
Chicago Board of Trade and MidAmerica Commodity Exchange
Futures Contracts, As of <u>FRIDAY, OCTOBER 26, 1984</u>

CLASS AND GRADE (Thousands of bushels)	CHICAGO AREA			TOLEDO/MAUMEE					
	10–26–84	Week Ago	Year Ago	10–26–84	Week Ago	Year Ago	10–26–84	Week Ago	Year Ago
Wheat									
1 Soft Red Winter	—	—	—	—	—	—			
2 Soft Red Winter	207	207	10,355	2,211	2,210	6,621			
3 Soft Red Winter	1,076	2,288	241	—	—	246			
1, 2, or 3* Hard Red Winter	—	—	—						
1, 2, or 3* Dark No. Spring	—	—	—						
1 or 2 Northern Spring	—	—	—						
Total Del. Grades	1,283	2,495	10,596	2,211	2,210	6,867			
Non-Del. Grades	0	0	0	0	0	0			
Unregist/Ungraded	3,518	2,422	1,450	3,446	4,707	2,531			
Total CCC Stocks	0	0	0	181	181	133			
TOTAL	4,801	4,917	12,046	5,838	7,098	9,531			

*Meets exchange requirements for futures delivery.

Corn	CHICAGO AREA			TOLEDO/MAUMEE			ST. LOUIS AREA		
	10–26–84	Week Ago	Year Ago	10–26–84	Week Ago	Year Ago	10–26–84	Week Ago	Year Ago
1 Yellow	—	—	—	—	—	—	—	—	25
2 Yellow	—	—	—	78	17	526	122	127	497
3 Yellow Max 15½% Moist.	75	75	430	—	—	40	30	16	3
Total Del. Grades	75	75	430	78	17	566	152	143	525
Non-Del. Grades	0	0	0	0	0	0	28	27	0
Unregist/Ungraded	1,375	354	928	2,795	1,976	5,281	208	130	290
Total CCC Stocks	10	10	264	54	54	2,475	10	10	15
TOTAL	1,460	439	1,622	2,927	2,047	8,322	398	310	830

Soybeans	CHICAGO AREA			TOLEDO/MAUMEE					
	10–26–84	Week Ago	Year Ago	10–26–84	Week Ago	Year Ago			
1 Yellow	—	—	—	21	15	—			
2 Yellow	1,413	813	18,612	10	10	6,950			
3 Yel. (No. 2 except FM)	285	285	1,740	—	—	1,065			
3 Yel. Max 14% Moist.	10	10	12	—	—	—			
Total Del. Grades	1,708	1,108	20,364	31	25	8,015			
Non-Del. Grades	0	0	0	0	0	0			
Unregist/Ungraded	1,638	2,075	1,177	3,890	1,208	12,133			
Total CCC Stocks	0	0	23	2	2	42			
TOTAL	3,346	3,183	21,564	3,923	1,235	20,190			

Oats	CHICAGO AREA			MINNEAPOLIS/ST. PAUL					
	10–26–84	Week Ago	Year Ago	10–26–84	Week Ago	Year Ago			
1 Oats	—	—	—	737	712	1,823			
2 Oats Min. Wt. 34 obs.	10	10	3,245	1,576	1,774	3,658			
1 Hvy Oats	—	—	—	316	311	403			
2 Hvy Oats	—	—	—	1,744	1,788	2,377			
1 Ex. Hvy Oats	—	—	—	3	—	31			
2 Ex. Hvy Oats	—	—	—	72	72	119			
Total Del. Grades	10	10	3,245	4,448	4,657	8,411			
Non-Del. Grades	0	0	0	702	675	1,144			
Unregist/Ungraded	99	102	1,386	1,359	1,382	3,933			
Total CCC Stocks	0	0	0	84	84	169			
TOTAL	109	112	4,631	6,593	6,798	13,657			

Regular capacity for reporting warehouses (thousands of bushels):

CHICAGO AREA	TOLEDO/MAUMEE	MINNEAPOLIS/ST. PAUL	ST. LOUIS AREA
52,416	45,663	84,697	4,725

RELEASED: TUESDAY, OCTOBER 30, 1984 This report is released each Tuesday (or Wednesday, if Monday or Tuesday is a holiday).

GUIDE

Total Del Grades: deliverable grades represented by warehouse receipts.
Non-Del Grades: non-deliverable grades represented by warehouse receipts.
Unregist/Ungraded: grain for which no warehouse receipts are outstanding.
Total CCC Stocks: all CCC-owned grain.
Nondeliverable classes or sub-classes of grain (e.g., white wheat) are not included in any of the figures.

Exhibit 15–2

Exhibit 15–2 (*concluded*)

The Commodity Futures Trading Commission releases this data each week. Its significance to the public trader can be enormous.

For example, Chicago doesn't consume a lot of wheat through milling activity. Consequently, if the Position Report begins showing a large buildup of deliverable wheat in Chicago shortly in advance of an expiring contract, the long holders in the expiring maturity might deduce that the commercials were getting ready to deliver the grain rather than offset their short-holdings in the market. A lot of cash grain overhanging the market can be a great depressant to prices, especially in the last two or three weeks of maturing-contract life. In view of this, commercials are known to sometimes move grain into Chicago, with no intention of tendering it, simply for the purpose of influencing the contract price lower, and obtaining a more attractive level at which to buy back their short-holdings.

---

contain important surprises in the form of unexpected increases or decreases in a crop, the following day's futures market openings will clearly reflect the shock.

Carrying a position, either long or short, into the teeth of a Government Crop Report can be a soul-shattering experience. The market is regularly given credit for discounting future events and adjusting prices to anticipate forthcoming news. Based on past history, futures markets have less than a flawless record in reading the minds of the government crop reporters.

In the opening days of September 1966, November soybeans were trading roughly in a range from $3.00 to $3.15 per bushel. The trade generally expected a 1966 harvest of 880 million to 900 million bushels of soybeans. The Government Crop Report was scheduled for release at 3 P.M. on Friday, September 9. The public was short a lot of soybeans when the trading session opened Friday morning. Prices on the new crop November contract began to climb perceptibly, and the farther they rose, the greater the pressure on the shorts to buy back their November soybeans. As more and more shorts were chased in, the greater the upward pressure built on November (and other) soybean futures prices. The last 30 minutes of Friday's session constituted a classical short squeeze. In about 40 minutes, the November bean price went from $3.19 per bushel to $3.28⅛—and closed near its high for the day.

At 3 P.M. Eastern time, the Government Crop Report was released, indicating a projected soybean harvest of 926 million bushels—some 36 million bushels, or 4 percent, more than the trade had anticipated. The effect was cataclysmic.

After what must have seemed like an interminable weekend to holders of open positions, November soybeans opened Monday morning, September 12, down the full 10 cent limit allowable, and with virtually no trade in the contract. Longs who wanted to sell the November contract and extricate themselves from the losing position could find no one willing to buy within the permissible trading range. The following day, Tuesday, September 13, began as a repetition of Monday. November

CORN—CHICAGO BOARD OF TRADE
COMMITMENTS OF TRADERS IN ALL FUTURES COMBINED AND INDICATED FUTURES, AUGUST 31, 1984

	TOTAL	REPORTABLE POSITIONS								NONREPORTABLE POSITIONS	
		NON-COMMERCIAL									
	OPEN INTEREST	LONG OR SHORT ONLY		LONG AND SHORT (SPREADING)		COMMERCIAL		TOTAL			
		LONG	SHORT	LONG	SHORT	LONG	SHORT	LONG	SHORT	LONG	SHORT
		(THOUSAND BUSHELS)									
ALL	712,195	16,585	34,005	34,830	34,830	452,135	266,120	503,550	334,955	208,645	377,240
OLD	139,905	15,335	9,340	60	60	92,650	49,165	108,045	58,565	31,860	81,340
OTHER	572,290	23,340	46,755	12,680	12,680	359,485	216,955	395,505	276,390	176,785	295,900
	CHANGES IN COMMITMENTS FROM JULY 31, 1984										
ALL	8,170	5,745	−20,335	13,270	13,270	890	26,440	19,905	19,375	−11,735	−11,205
	PERCENT OF OPEN INTEREST REPRESENTED BY EACH CATEGORY OF TRADERS										
ALL	100.0%	2.3	4.8	4.9	4.9	63.5	37.4	70.7	47.0	29.3	53.0
OLD	100.0%	11.0	6.7	.	.	66.2	35.1	77.2	41.9	22.8	58.1
OTHER	100.0%	4.1	8.2	2.2	2.2	62.8	37.9	69.1	48.3	30.9	51.7
	NUMBER OF TRADERS	NUMBER OF TRADERS IN EACH CATEGORY									
ALL	233	22	31	27	27	93	116	138	166		
OLD	72	11	10	1	1	24	31	36	41		
OTHER	220	28	34	10	10	81	104	115	145		

CONCENTRATION RATIOS
PERCENT OF OPEN INTEREST HELD BY THE INDICATED NUMBER OF LARGEST TRADERS

	BY GROSS POSITION				BY NET POSITION			
	4 OR LESS TRADERS		8 OR LESS TRADERS		4 OR LESS TRADERS		8 OR LESS TRADERS	
	LONG	SHORT	LONG	SHORT	LONG	SHORT	LONG	SHORT
ALL	31.5	6.5	38.4	10.7	29.9	5.3	35.9	8.3
OLD	49.2	15.3	57.9	21.8	48.7	15.3	57.4	21.7
OTHER	28.2	7.1	36.3	11.7	26.3	6.3	33.4	10.3

Exhibit 15—3

The Commodity Futures Trading Commission issues a monthly report of this kind, showing open commitments of traders in commodity futures at the end of each calendar month. The report rarely reaches the hands of its subscribers and the news media before the 12th of the month next following. In spite of this delay, it still remains the best source available for determining how the main forces in the market are deployed; and how they have been responding to the vicissitudes contained in price fluctuations.

Proceeding from this background, the astute trader can make far more reliable projections of events to be expected in reaction to future price changes.

beans again opened down the full 10 cents permissible, then a trickle of trade began which gradually increased. At the close of the second session, following the Crop Report, the price on the November bean contract stood at $3.08¾ per bushel.

In two days' time, as a direct result of a 36 million bushel surprise in soybean crop expectations, price on the commodity plummeted about 20 cents per bushel. It is salient to note that in the succeeding three weeks, prices on the November contract worked their way down to an interim low of $2.88½.

A 4 percent increase in crop size was translated into almost a 9 percent reduction in the price of the commodity in the market!

Beware the Whipsaw

This historic chain of events is recounted in some detail for two purposes: First, to demonstrate the great hazards present in carrying a commodity position into a government report; and second, because it represents a classic example of the market "whipsaw."

Holders of short positions in nearby soybean contracts were right as later events unarguably proved; the soybean harvest *was* to be larger and lower prices *were* to be the result. In the interim, however, ascending prices caught the shorts who, in their desperate efforts to buy back their positions and offset, merely added more fuel to the flames of rising prices. Thousands of shorts did offset millions of bushels at the higher prices and they took impressive losses.

Then, some of them completely reversed their position. They bought back their short contracts and then bought more, switching to a long position, after which the crop report came out and prices fell precipitously.

When events had run their course, there were some traders who had lost 7 cents or 8 cents per bushel in the upside short raid and lost another 20 cents in two succeeding days of limit-down price movement. Such may be the effect of unexpected news from a highly respected source.

Hindsight always enjoys 20/20 vision, and at 3:10 P.M. On September 9, every short who had weathered the squeeze and held his position knew that his judgment had been vindicated and that impressive profits were to be expected when the market opened next.

Every short who offset knew now that he should have stuck with his guns.

Every long could look at the crop estimate figure and know that he made one of the worst misjudgments of his trading career.

But by the time the information upon which action could be predicated was available, the time had already passed when any corrective move could be taken. Once the figure was out, there was nothing to be done except sit back and watch profits or losses mount, depending on whether one was situated on the long or short side of the soybean market.

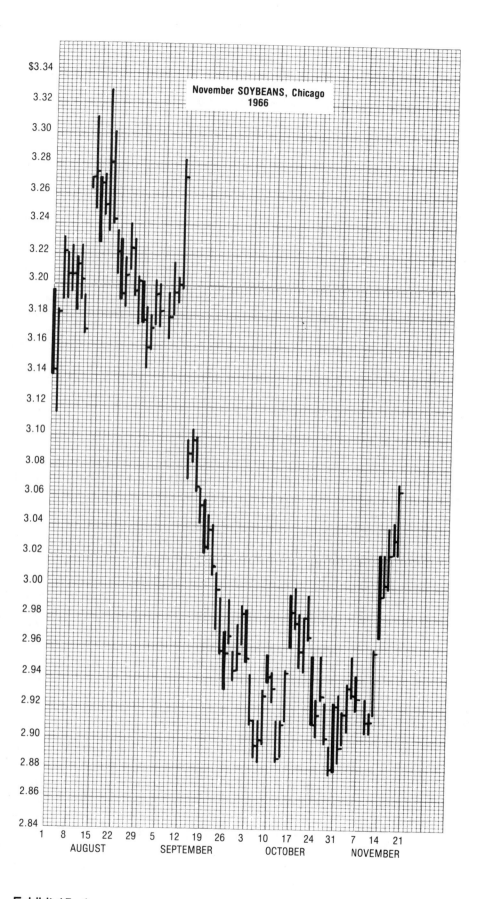

Exhibit 15—4

Exhibit 15—4 (*concluded*)

This historic price behavior could be labeled "catastrophe" for the longs, and "bonanza" for the shorts. But it was nerve-racking trading for everyone.

Suckers and Plungers

There may be some millionaire plungers who are sufficiently enamoured of high risks and supercharged economic adventure to welcome an exercise of this sort. However, it has no place in the speculative program of a prudent individual. Profitable speculation demands conservative behavior. Conservatism dictates that any open position—long or short—be closed out or otherwise protected in advance of a potentially explosive event which cannot be, to some acceptable degree, appraised. A speculator will occasionally be caught flat-footed by a declaration of war, a general strike, sudden devaluation of money, or other developments which spring from political or natural events. Their results may be written in great profits or great losses. But at least the speculator has the satisfaction of being able to say that "no one could have foreseen this thing." There is no such justification for the losses which grow, for instance, out of a crop report surprise.

These figures are released at stated intervals. The magnificent secrecy which surrounds them makes foreknowledge impossible and yet, their impact may be ruinous to the interests of the individual who is on the wrong side of the market. In brief, carrying a substantial open position into a crop report is not really speculation, unless the situation is susceptible to close preevaluation, in the light of other known factors. Doing so is a sucker's exercise.

The wise speculator—unless he holds the firmest opinion—will offset his positions, be out of the market, and able to watch events from the safety of the sidelines. Once the new information is public knowledge, ample opportunities will exist to reestablish a position in light of altered knowledge which is reflected in the new numbers.

Insuring a Position against Catastrophe

If circumstances seem to overwhelmingly urge the holding of a flat long or unprotected short position into a crop report, speculative "insurance" is available to the wary trader. In the November soybean situation discussed earlier, the squeezed shorts could have—at any time they chose—bought into the January or March bean contracts, thereby changing their flat position to a spread. What the short leg lost in the August squeeze would have been largely gained by the long leg as the price run-up unfolded. Then, once the crop report figure was known, the trader needed only to offset his long-side insurance, and ride the break down.

The reverse is equally true: A prudent long, seeing the crop report approaching, could have shorted the January or March against his long Novembers or Septembers; right up to the last second of the trading session preceding the report release. His insurance policy would have only cost the broker commission; and it would have saved him at least the 20 cents per bushel lost in the two limit-down days: A small premium to pay for the peace of mind—and the protection from loss—it would have provided!

With the opening of trade in agricultural options, still another alternative now exists for protecting profits, or minimizing opportunities for loss, as a result of crop report surprises or similar contingencies.

Instead of taking a spread posture in different futures contract months, an apprehensive long may buy a *put*—thus assuring himself of a given disposal price on his long holdings, should the news move market price against him. In the opposite frame of reference, a wary short may buy a *call* and, for a specified period of time, guarantee himself a firm minimum closeout price on his endangered futures position, regardless of what futures prices do in the interim.

These things will be dealt with in detail somewhat later in this volume.

Weekend Trading

Students of commodity price behavior know that weekends offer interesting opportunities for speculative endeavor, particularly during periods of relative commodity shortage or oversupply. Carrying a position over a weekend demands a healthy nervous system, but it can prove highly rewarding for those who are up to it.

Most public speculators and professional pit traders prefer sleeping Friday, Saturday, and Sunday nights, to contemplating possible price developments on a large open position. Proof of this is seen in the fact that commodity prices (and stock prices also) demonstrate a quite consistent selloff on Friday of each week, often followed by a discernible resurgence early the following week. Several reasons underpin the phenomenon. Major announcements from Washington are often released on the weekend in order to give the financial community an opportunity to digest the news before business is resumed in the next week. The weekend hiatus in trading is also a sufficient period of time to permit major changes in the weather pattern to take place.

Friday Selloff

While important events may not be actually concentrated in the Saturday-Sunday period, their public impact is often magnified because people spend more time listening to radios, reading newspapers, and watching television on weekends than during any other two day period. In light of all of these reasons, coupled with the fact that the public tends to be long far more often than it is short, a selloff oftentimes occurs on Friday as public speculators and pit traders close out their positions before going home Friday night even with the market. To the extent that this evening-up action introduces abnormal selling pressure into the marketplace, Friday prices may be forced lower than composite information logically would justify in a relatively undersupplied market situation.

By taking a long position on the Friday close and carrying it until the following Monday or Tuesday, a very respectable profit can often be realized in selected situations. Close examination of a vertical bar chart, which reflects daily prices, can provide a useful clue to this type of price behavior.

Weekend Arrivals

Another weekend situation which deserves speculator attention often materializes early in the harvest season. Each harvest usually begins in the face of depleted stocks in the market complex. Old-crop futures prices may be at relatively high price levels, in reflection of the current supply shortage. As harvest activities increase, crop movement into the market increases also and the largest arrivals tend to take place on weekends and be reported on Monday. Nothing disenchants the faint-hearted longs more noticeably than impressive buildups in local stocks.

Trading on this situation might attract a speculator who can carry a position over a weekend and still sleep. He may give consideration to selling a selected commodity short on Thursday or early in Friday's session (to take advantage of the higher market prices which often prevail prior to the weekend selloff) and buy back the short position at or near the opening on Monday, when lower prices are often a reflection of the heavy weekend arrivals. Again, a vertical bar chart showing daily price movements is an invaluable tool in appraising such a speculative possibility.

Better to Lose Money than Lose Sleep

One final—and general—word needs to be said with respect to all special trading situations. As the label implies, "special situations" are somewhat unique, may be unpredictable, and involve unusual opportunities for profits and perhaps commensurate opportunities for losses. Speculation necessarily involves risk, but the prudent speculator constantly evaluates the order of risk he is willing to accept in return for a given profit potential. More than money is involved in the kind of trading discussed in this section. There are those who have sufficient equanimity to carry a large open commodity commitment and never give it a thought, except at such times as the matter comes under routine scrutiny. Another type of person may find that even a small commodity

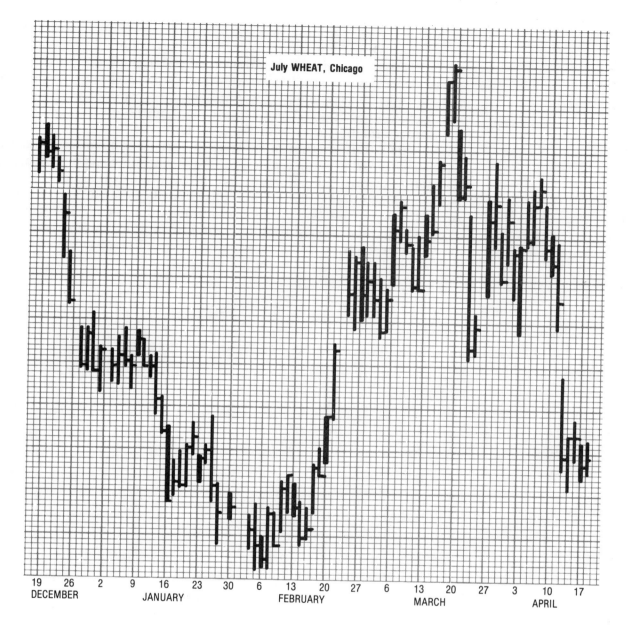

July WHEAT, Chicago

19 26	2 9 16 23 30	6 13 20 27	6 13 20 27	3 10 17
DECEMBER	JANUARY	FEBRUARY	MARCH	APRIL

Exhibit 15–5

position preempts his attention and eclipses matters of vastly greater importance.

Strangely enough, the number of dollars involved does not seem to be controlling. Human psychology varies widely. The differing capacities of people to withstand or ignore the stresses of speculation, while getting on with their other business—and obtaining a good night's sleep—is all too evident. A single 5,000 bushel contract of corn futures may suffice to keep one individual awake half of the night, while 50,000 bushels will not spoil the dreams of someone else in essentially the same economic circumstances.

The only safe rule in speculation is to "lighten up" to the point where sleep comes easily. Time, experience, and increasing success will raise the speculator's level of tolerance for carrying open positions, just as surely as repetition of any experience inevitably robs it of novelty and reduces its distractive nuisance value.

All this is but another persuasive argument in favor of protecting every new position with a stop-loss order, and perhaps a stop-buy or stop-sell to put the "second story" on the profitable pyramid. Once this has been done, most traders find it easier to play the patient game and await developments. So long as a position is unprotected, every change in price suggests reexamination of the problem. Endless rehashing of the same problem is neither conducive to good trading decisions nor good mental health.

16

Speculation in Price Relationships

Most commodity speculation on the part of public traders involves taking either a "flat" long or short position, in the expectation that prices on the selected contract will subsequently rise or fall, and in so doing will produce a profit. There is another form of commodity speculation which deserves most careful consideration by the public speculator, but which to this point in time has largely been an activity left to the professionals in the market. It is known as *spreading* in the grain market, *straddling* in certain other markets, and is synonymous with *arbitrage,* which is the term used to identify the activity in securities and financial instrument trading.

Time Differential

In a normal commodity market, we can expect to see the nearby futures selling at a price fairly close to that which prevails in the cash market for spot merchandise. Later maturities in a normal market will be priced progressively higher than the nearby contract, in reflection of the carrying charges entailed in holding the commodity until the scheduled delivery date. In corn, for example, we might find the nearby December futures quoted at $2.44 per bushel with the March contract at $2.56; May $2.64; July $2.72. In such a case, we would have a clear reflection of 4 cents per month carrying charges included in the price of each more distant contract maturity.

Geographic Differential

Likewise, in a normal market we might expect to find December corn in Chicago quoted at $2.40 and Kansas City corn at $2.35 for December delivery, in which event the 5 cents per bushel differential or spread would be reflective of the cost of transporting the commodity from the Kansas City location to the terminal market. A theoretically normal market is one which constantly reflects the economic costs of holding and/or transporting a commodity over time and/or geographical distance. Since these costs are easily calculated, it is no particular problem for the speculator to arrive at a firm notion of what constitutes a reasonable price differential or spread relationship on commodities deliverable at different points in time, or physically located at various geographical points.

Market reality is seldom so uniform, however. As a practical matter, full carrying charges are rarely reflected in commodity prices, although actual transportation costs are usually all included in the pricing structure. The reason is that competition exists between commodity warehouses, with the result that the price of storage, insurance, and interest on money—which comprise carrying charges—move up and down in response to the proportion of storage space occupied, money availability, etc. One warehousing firm may elect to take in grain at less than its full carrying cost, and in so doing the carrying charges are partially absorbed. Transportation costs, on the other hand, are more or less firmly established by interstate commerce regulations and freight schedules. Hence competition in the transport of commodities usually exists mainly between different modes of transportation; rail versus barge, or truck versus rail.

Supply/Demand Imbalance

There is a further consideration which exerts great influence on price differentials over time, as well as between geographical locations. Immediately following harvest, for example, wheat prices in Topeka, Kansas, can be expected to reflect a substantial excess of supplies over requirements in that city. Until the harvest glut is cleared out, depressed prices on the crop in such surplus areas are a natural result. Chicago, on the other hand, is a wheat deficit location for virtually 12 months out of the year, removed as it is from the great wheat producing areas of the country. As harvest supplies begin moving, the relative shortage of wheat in Chicago is relieved. On rare occasions, an oversupply of the commodity will develop in Chicago which will have the effect of making the product no more valuable in the market city than it is in the interior location.

Stated another way, the market must pay the owner of cash grain in Kansas for his transportation costs, else he will not move it. The market *may* also pay a large or a slight premium on the product for moving it out of the wheat surplus location and into the wheat deficit location, depending on relative needs. Consequently we usually expect to see Kansas City grain prices under Chicago grain prices by at least the amount of transportation and handling costs involved in shipping. We may also expect to see a slight or a substantial premium on the commodity, above and beyond transportation costs, depending on relative supply/demand balances in the two localities being compared.

With respect to price differentials between different contract months in the same commodity and in the same location, supply/demand considerations are the only influences which need be considered. It has been said that the market always "puts first things first." Presently existing shortage or oversupply reflects itself in higher or lower cash and nearby futures prices; and while an oversupply of wheat, for example, may bring lower prices to the cash and all contract maturities in the current crop year, the nearby contract will usually be affected more than the more deferred maturities. In the case of scarcity, prices on the nearby contracts will always rise more sharply than prices on deferred deliveries. Oversupply will depress nearby contracts more than prices on more distant maturities.

Price Rations Use

It is this action in the marketplace which accomplishes the rationing function so vital to matching supplies with needs. When a shortage of wheat exists, higher prices result, with the effect of reducing wheat consumption in total amount. Ordinarily, a certain amount of wheat is fed to livestock and poultry, but if the price on wheat climbs far enough, chicken and livestock producers may find it to their economic best interests to switch to some alternative food supply for their flocks and herds. In the face of high prices, only the higher priority usages are filled. Low-end usage tends to be satisfied by substitute products or, in the case of meat and poultry animals, livestock populations may be deliberately reduced in numbers until feed costs return to acceptable levels.

With the higher prices prevailing in a market that is sparsely supplied by a given commodity, additional producers are attracted to the field of endeavor. Their entry brings greater production, which tends to solve the previous shortage and forces relative values, as measured by prices, downward.

In an oversupplied market, again using the wheat simile, cheap wheat may be fed to livestock and otherwise used in low-end feeding activity. The increased consumption reduces the excessive supplies. Low prices discourage a certain proportion of the producers, resulting in a smaller harvest. As the surplus disappears through greater consumption and somewhat restricted production, prices rise once more.

Thus it is seen that *the cure for high prices is high prices; the cure for low prices is low prices*. All of this depends, of course, on sufficient market freedom for supply and demand to assert itself in trade between buyers and sellers—allowing higher prices to ration and conserve inadequate supplies, or permitting lower prices to encourage consumption and discourage excessive production.

It has been explained why, when shortage brings higher prices, the highest prices of all will be seen with respect to current or nearby considerations. When this happens, the premium which usually prevails on distant contracts may move up to the nearby contracts. The distant maturities may then show an appreciable discount.

For example, in a situation of extreme shortage, the nearby May wheat contract may be priced at $3.75 per bushel with the July contract at $3.60. The 15 cent inversion is a clear indication that concern over present shortage is taking priority over whatever problems may surround the July period. In other words, the 15 cent premium for immediate supplies is a measurement of the market's appraisal of the tight May situation as compared with the still largely unknown July situation. Both futures prices may, in the face of severe shortage, rise dramatically—along with equal, or perhaps even greater, price increases in the cash market. When this happens, usage of the product will be curtailed, out of the purest economic considerations. In thus rationing available supplies, the supply crisis may have been solved by the time the July rolls around. If it is not, further price increase in the July contract is a logical expectation in a free market.

Trading in Price Difference—Basis

Speculation in spreads involves evaluation of relative prices as between different points in time, or different geographical locations. A fundamental measurement—and all prices are merely measurements of relative values—is the price differential between cash products for immediate delivery and the nearby futures contract. This differential or price spread is identified as the *basis*. Basis, in turn, is the most reliable continuing indicator of near-term supply/demand balance. If dealers in cash commodities need more supplies, they will, of course, raise their bids sufficiently to attract a greater volume of offerings. So long as their stocks are sufficient, they will stand on lower bids, and perhaps refuse to buy at all, except at what appears to be a bargain price discount.

Bids in the cash market (in Chicago or in the "country") are quoted using the nearby futures contract as a reference point. For example, if the nearby futures (May) price on corn is $2.40 per bushel, the cash market price will be communicated at a designated premium "on" May, or discount "off" May. A cash grain merchant might be bidding for corn at "2 cents under" with the nearby contract selling at $2.40. He is therefore bidding for corn of contract quality, for immediate delivery, at $2.38 in Chicago. The bid would be proportionately less in country locations where transportation would have to be figured into the Chicago price.

As trading in the futures proceeds, the price on the May corn contract might go to $2.42; if so, the cash bid, being pegged at 2 cents under, would now automatically stand at $2.40 per bushel. Thus, cash bids and futures prices move up and down together. Should the higher price attract large offerings on the part of farmers and country elevators, a cash grain merchant might decide to lower his basis to "3 cents under" the nearby futures.

The same things which have been said concerning cash and the nearby futures also pertain to a lesser extent to price relationships between nearby and more deferred futures contracts.

Spreading a Normal Market

The speculator who wishes to trade on price relationships in a normal market should begin with a normal carrying charge as his point of departure. If he believes that the price spread between the nearby and the more deferred contract will *narrow* in days to come, he will *buy the nearby contract* and *sell the deferred contract*. (This is called a *bull spread*.) If he believes the spread will *widen* in the future, he will *sell the nearby contract* and *buy the deferred contract*. (This is called a *bear spread*.)

Spreading an Inverted Market

In an inverted market, with the nearby contract carrying a premium over the deferred, the procedure is exactly reversed: If the trader thinks the *inverse will increase,* he will *buy the nearby* and *sell the deferred.* If he expects the *inverse to narrow or disappear,* he will *sell the nearby* and *buy the deferred.*

Once such a spreading position is taken, correlative price changes can be ignored. By being long one contract and short another, a price increase of 2 cents per bushel in both leaves the speculator in the same position he was at the outset. The 2 cent price increase results in a 2 cent loss in the short position, which is exactly made up by a 2 cent profit on the long side of the spread. However, if a bear spread position was established anticipating a widening of the basis (short the nearby and long the deferred), a drop in price of ½ cent on the nearby contract and an increase of ½ cent on the deferred maturity produces a 1 cent profit for the spreader. By the same token, a 1 cent fall in the nearby, while the price on the deferred remains unchanged, also produces a 1 cent profit. The spreader will lose on his position when price differential widens or narrows in the direction not anticipated.

No Limit to Inverses

It is worthwhile repeating that the theory of carrying charges in the commodity market limits the premium that a deferred contract may carry to the amount of carrying charges involved in holding the merchandise over the period of time involved.

Theoretical Price Surface for Corn

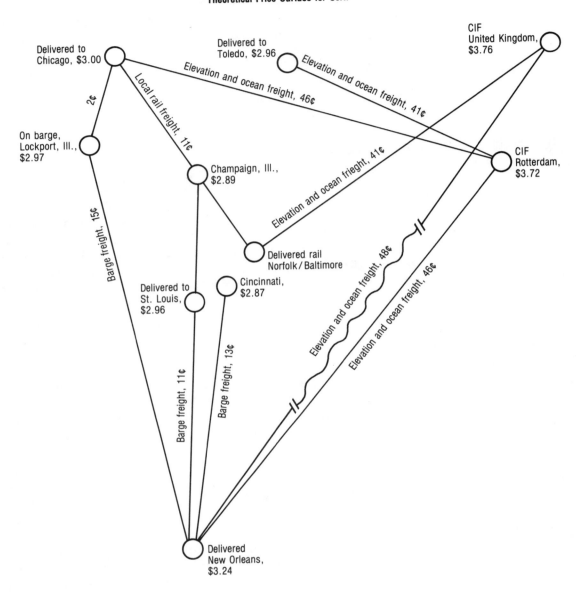

Exhibit 16-1

The price that a commodity commands in any particular location depends on a variety of things, including storage facilities, weather, and—most importantly—transportation, from its point of production or assembly. Chicago functions as a base point for grain prices purely because of its role as the primary focus for grain trading. Chicago prices are therefore a major factor in commodity prices everywhere. A strong U.S. dollar has had the effect of making U.S. commodities unusually expensive throughout much of the world, and contributing to the growing U.S. balance-of-payments deficits.

There is no theoretical limit to the extent of an *inverse,* depending on the seriousness of the shortage which produces it. Cash or nearby contracts may reflect *any amount* of price premium over more deferred maturities.

Intermarket Spreads

Most spreading takes place between contracts in the same commodity and on the same exchange. For example, Chicago May corn spread against Chicago July corn, or Kansas City September wheat against Kansas City May wheat. These positions are referred to as *intramarket* spreads. *Intermarket* spreads may also be placed. Such a position involves the purchase of Chicago May wheat against the sale of Kansas City or Minneapolis May wheat. In this situation, disparate relative scarcity and oversupply in the two selected locations would be the major consideration in evaluating the price spread opportunity, along with transportation costs on the commodity. Intermarket spreading can present some exceedingly complex problems, but on occasion offer outstanding profit opportunities with minimal risk exposure.

Intercommodity Spreads

There is still a further spreading opportunity which involves a basic commodity and its manufactured or semimanufactured products. Soybeans offer a good example for demonstration purposes. A soybean has little value in its natural state. Only through crushing and conversion to soybean meal and soybean oil does the legume become practically useful. The economic value of the soybean can be said to be the composite value of its products. Spreaders in soybean market have developed a formula which permits them to determine the normal value relationship between soybeans, and soybean meal and oil. The equation involves the following arithmetic:

Oil price per pound × 11 = oil value per bushel

Meal price per ton × .0235 = meal value per bushel

Oil value + meal value = product value per bushel

Product value per bushel − soybean price per bushel =
gross processing margin

Applying the foregoing formula, it will be seen that when soybeans are selling for $6.40, soybean meal is selling for $142 per ton, and with soybean oil at 24 cents per pound, the crusher stands to lose 21 cents per bushel for each bushel he processes; a most unrewarding endeavor!

In a situation of this kind, the spreader would be likely to buy the underpriced products and sell the apparently overpriced soybeans (known as a *reverse-crush spread*).

Oil price—24¢ per pound
        24¢ × 11 = $2.64 per bushel oil value
Meal price—$142 per ton
        $142 × .0235 = $3.34 per bushel meal value
                       $5.98 per bushel product value
                − $6.40 per bushel soybean price
        Loss   = $ .42 per bushel gross processing margin

However, in a different price situation, with soybeans selling at $4.80 per bushel, soybean meal at $142 per ton, and soybean oil at 18 cents per pound, the crusher stands to make a handsome profit—identified as gross processing margin (GPM)—and so would undoubtedly be an eager buyer of soybeans.

In this situation, the spreader would be inclined to buy the relatively underpriced soybean futures, and sell the relatively overpriced products (called a *crush spread*).

Oil price = 18¢ per pound
        18¢ × 11 = $1.98 per bushel oil value
Meal price = $142 per ton
        $142 × .0235 = $3.34 per bushel meal value
                       $5.32 per bushel product value
                − $4.80 per bushel soybean price
        Profit   = $ .52 per bushel gross processing margin

In either situation the spreader's hope for profits would depend on a return to more normal relationships between the price on the basic commodity and the component values of soybean meal and oil. About 40 cents per bushel GPM is currently considered a useful profit point, but actual margin has varied widely over the years.

Historic price behavior in these interrelated futures offers valuable guidance in detecting imbalances, nonetheless. Spreads between soybeans and the products have in the past provided one of the most attractive opportunities for multiple-position speculation in commodities.

Possibilities Are Numerous

The opportunities for spreading are limited by little except the ingenuity and imagination of the trader. For instance, there is a much discussed and broadly recognized "hog-corn ratio," which relates to the efficiency of pigs in converting corn into pork meat weight. Spreaders sometimes find situations in which high priced corn and cheap pork prices suggest selling the grain futures and buying the animal futures.

Still other spreaders take multiple positions between wheat and corn, oats and wheat, pork and beef, gold and silver, soybean oil and cotton-seed oil—the possibilities are almost unlimited.

The best spreading opportunities tend to be those in which a high degree of substitutability or convertibility exists between the commodities involved. A shortage of one and a surplus of the other will produce high prices on one hand and lower prices on the other. A spreader's profits in any case grow out of changes in price relationship over time in a single location, or at different geographical points.

It must be said that, inasmuch as price relationships tend to be more stable than flat prices, both risk exposure and profit potentials in spreads are likely to be less than those present in speculation on flat prices. This is not always the case, however, and the spreader will do well to choose his opportunities with great caution. This is especially true when considering spreads between different commodities and in different markets—where significantly different forces may operate on price/value relationships on the two sides of the open position.

Spreading Margins Are Smaller

While remembering that, except for exchange imposed *minimums,* brokerage firms may set their own margins, the generally smaller order of risk present in positions which represent spreads between multiple contracts in the same commodity, or different markets in the same (or related) commodities, gives rise to a different level of margin required to bind performance on the part of the trader. For example, with straight-position margin on wheat at 15 cents per bushel, the *spreading margin* would likely be about 10 cents per bushel—and this would apply to only one side of the position. To demonstrate, consider a trader who spreads 100 wheat between old and new crops. He might buy 100,000 bushels of May futures and sell 100,000 bushels of September futures. At 10 cents per bushel spreading margin, he would need to put up $10,000 to establish the position and, in all likelihood, would need to maintain the 10 cents per bushel "in the clear" for as long as he holds it.

Exchange Rules and Policies Pursued by Commission House

Rules vary, but it is usually true that in spreads between different commodities (e.g., wheat and corn, or corn and oats) the margin required is the margin applicable to the one side of the spread which calls for the larger margin. Thus, a spread between wheat and oats would be marginable at the wheat rate. It should also be remembered that, in order to take advantage of the lower margin requirements, amounts on each side of the position must be equivalent. One contract of May wheat would be necessarily spread against one contract of some other month—or some other grain.

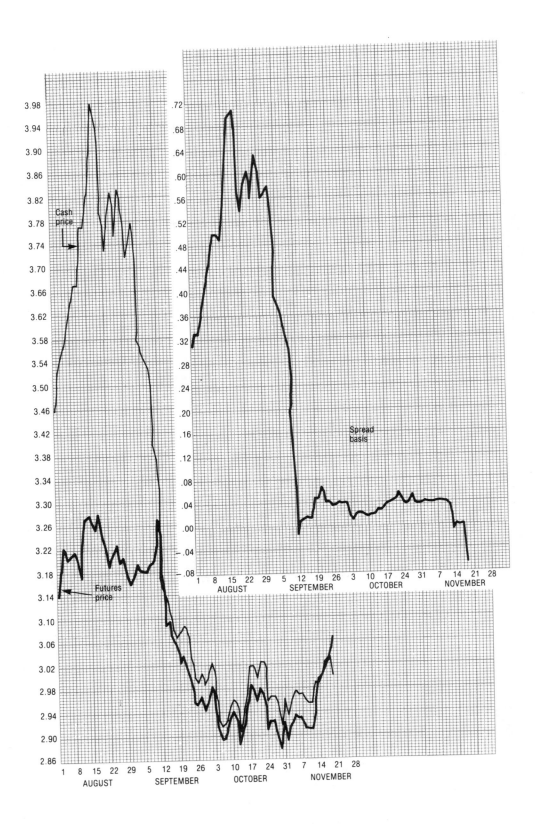

Exhibit 16–2

Both of these charts reflect the price differential between cash soybeans and the November 1966 futures. From a 71 cent inversion in mid-August, prices returned to normal in September, and the November contract expired at a 6½ cent premium.

17

Order Placement and Execution

Transaction of customer orders in the pits is the exclusive function of a highly skilled group of professional floor brokers. The greatest testimonial to their efficiency is found in the exceedingly small number of errors which they commit, even while trading in the highly charged atmosphere of fast moving, volatile markets. There are a few things, however, that even the best pit broker cannot do. Heading the list is the occasionally forgotten truth that a broker cannot read a customer's mind.

Commodity orders, like orders in the securities market, follow precise forms and are accorded specific handling depending on certain key terminology. It therefore behooves a speculator to be completely familiar with the subtle and obvious differences which exist, for example, between a *stop* order, a *limit-only* order and a *market-if-touched* order. Failure to recognize the difference in handling each of these orders will receive can produce serious disappointment on the part of the trader—and waste an infinite amount of time in futile discussions between the brokerage house solicitor, the customer, and the pit broker.

Errors in execution will occasionally occur. When they do, exchange rules ordinarily require that the broker absorb his mistakes when they operate to the disadvantage of the customer; however, when a mistake is to the advantage of the customer, market rules direct that the customer be given the windfall profit. As concerns the customer, it amounts to a sort of "heads I win, tails you lose" situation. In view of this fact, it is only reasonable that the pit broker be provided orders which are completely clear and in conformity with good order writing practice. If this is done, the public customer can almost invariably count on meticulous execution.

The first consideration in any order, of course, is the quantity involved. In the grain market, for example, orders are communicated in terms of *thousands of bushels*—"buy 5 March wheat" means to buy 5,000 bushels of March wheat futures—one contract. Oil orders are stated in *contracts*. "Buy 5 March soybean oil" directs the broker to buy five 60,000 pound soybean oil contracts. This single example should be sufficient to emphasize the importance of specifying the quantity in accordance with established practice in the market. Failure to do so can result in a fill which you don't want, but which could by no means be interpreted as a trading error on the part of the broker who handled the transaction. To repeat, don't expect the broker to read your mind!

Don't Mix Lots

On exchanges which deal in both "round lots" and "job lots," it is important that the customer specify the combination of each included in any given order. For example, if an order is placed for 8,000 bushels of soybeans on an exchange that trades job lots, it should be placed as "one round lot and three job lots." The round lot is 5,000 bushels. Each job lot is 1,000 bushels, making 8,000 bushels total. Unless this is done, the fill may be made in the form of eight 1,000 bushel jobs. The reason for this is that job-lot trading is usually handled by a separate broker who specializes in it. Often times, also, a job-lot execution may only be feasible at some slight premium to the round-lot market price.

Commodity orders are subject to a broad range of limitations as to time of execution, price, etc. The following list is by no means all-inclusive, but it will comprise a recapitulation of the more common order forms and clarify the handling accorded to each.

Price Limits

1. *Market order:* A market order is an unrestricted order as to price, which only requires that it be promptly executed upon receipt and at the best price available at the time it reaches the pit.
2. *Price-limit order:* A price-limit order is one which specifies the maximum buying price or the minimum selling price which the customer will accept. A limit order may only be executed at the limit price or better. For example, a limit order to sell at $1.40 can only be filled at $1.40 or above $1.40. A limit order to buy at $1.40 may be executed at $1.40 or any price lower than $1.40.

Time Limits

1. *Day order:* A day order is one which expires automatically at the end of the session in which it is placed. Unless otherwise noted, most houses treat all commodity orders as day orders. In order to avoid automatic expiration at the end of the session in which

it is activated, an order must usually be designated as "good-til-cancelled," "good for one week," "open," etc. It's good practice to always specify the life of an order at time of placement.

2. *Open order or good-til-cancelled order:* An open order or a good-til-cancelled order (usually referred to by the initials GTC) are orders which will remain in effect until the customer explicitly directs cancellation, until it is filled, or until the futures contract to which the order applies expires.

3. *Specific time expiration:* This order may be identified as an *off at a specific time* order, and is merely a day order with a designated time contingency. For example, "buy 5 December corn $2.35—limit, off at 12:15 P.M." This order tells the broker that he is to buy 5,000 bushels of December corn futures at $2.35 per bushel or better, at any time up to 12:15 P.M. However, if the order is not executed by 12:15 P.M., it is then to be cancelled.

4. *Time of day order:* This is an order which is to be executed at a given minute in the session. For example, "buy 10 May wheat 11:30 A.M. market." With this, the broker is instructed to buy 10,000 bushels of May wheat at 11:30 A.M. at the best price then available in the pit.

In addition to specific limitations of the sort treated above, there is another category of special orders which will be accorded standardized handling as follows:

1. *Stop order:* This is an order that is activated at a particular price level, usually above or below the current market. These orders are often referred to as *stop-loss* orders because they are most often used by customers who are interested in limiting a loss on an open long or short position. For example, a customer may have a long position involving 10,000 bushels of July corn which he purchased at $2.40. When the position is established, the customer may enter an order to "sell 10 July corn $2.35½—stop—open." This order has the effect of calling for offset of the long position at any time the price on July corn futures falls to the specified level or lower. It is designated "open," hence it will be held in force as a resting order until price movement decrees its execution, or it is specifically cancelled by the customer.

A word of warning in connection with such an order should not be amiss: Should the long position to which the stop-sell order applies be closed out at the verbal direction of the customer, the resting stop order must also be specifically cancelled. Unless cancelled, it will continue to rest until executed. Should the price move down to its limit level, it will be filled. By not cancelling the stop, the customer would suddenly find himself short 10,000 bushels of July corn, which he would have to accept.

2. *Stop-limit order:* This one gets almost the same execution as the stop order explained above. A stop-limit order goes into force as soon as there is a sale at the stop price or worse—but the stop-limit order can only be filled at the limit price. To demonstrate, an order to "sell 10 July corn at $2.35½ stop-limit—open" will

be a resting order until the specified contract sells at or below $2.35½. Once this price is reached, the stop-limit order is activated, but it cannot be executed at a price lower than $2.35½. It can, however, be filled at any price above the one designated. The danger in a stop-limit order is that in a rapidly rising or falling market, execution may prove to be an impossibility; hence the limit requirement may defeat its central purpose of extricating a customer from a losing position at the quickest and most advantageous point.

3. *Quick, or fill-or-kill:* This is an order which must be executed at once, and at a specified price, or it is to be cancelled. Obviously a market order is subject to prompt execution as soon as it reaches the floor broker, since it is not subject to either time or price limitation. A *fill-or-kill* specifies a limit price and usually takes this form: "sell 10 July wheat $3.69½—fill-or-kill." At the time the order is placed it must be presumed that the wheat contract is being traded in a range of perhaps ½ cent above or below the fill or kill limit price. In practice, when the order is received by the pit broker he will usually call the quick bid three times. Unless he finds a taker on his three calls, he marks the order cancelled and (most brokers) immediately notifies the customer "unable" or "can't quick"; and follows this advice with the current price quotation in the maturity involved. Some houses refuse to accept quick orders for execution in the first few minutes of trade or the last few minutes during each session. This is a decision which each house must make, and usually reflects their appraisal of the possibilities for execution, depending on the volume of the trade and price behavior in the selected contract.

4. *MIT or board orders: MIT (market-if-touched)* and *board* mean the same thing. Therefore, if the specified price on such an order is "touched," it becomes a market order and is filled at the best price then available. The execution price may be either higher or lower than the touched price. The MIT designation is somewhat of a misnomer in view of the fact that the specific "tick" may not be actually touched—and need not be—in order to activate the order. For example, such an order might read "MIT $2.40¼ sell 10 July corn." The price on the July corn contract may move from $2.40 to $2.40½ missing the ¼ cent tick entirely; but for purposes of an MIT order the activating price level would be considered accomplished. Execution of the MIT order would be touched off and the fill would be at the best price then available in the contract.

5. *Cancellation orders:* Next to the placement of an original order, proper cancellation of orders which are resting must be given only slightly lesser priority. In establishing a trade relationship with the broker, it is well to make certain that unless a longer time is specifically designated, all of your orders are to be considered day orders. As such, they will automatically expire unless executed during the session in which they are placed. This handling is regularly accorded commodity orders in the vast majority of commission houses, but underscoring the procedure can do no harm, and it may serve to avoid subsequent misunderstanding.

Cancellation orders may take several forms, among which are the following:

a. *Straight cancel order:* A straight cancel order simply conveys the customer's directive that a previous order is to be stricken, and will ordinarily take this form: "cancel (day) order to buy 5 July wheat at $3.69¾ stop." It is good practice to also give the solicitor your account number whenever placing orders or entering cancellations. Doing so is just one additional safeguard against error. As shown in the above example, the cancellation should recite all the pertinent elements in the previous order which is being cancelled. Do not rely on a mere request to your broker to "cancel the order I placed with you this morning." You may remember the details of the order clearly, but a solicitor is dealing with hundreds of such transactions every day. It is expecting too much that his memory will be up to the task of keeping the particulars of all of his customers' business freshly in mind.

b. *Cancel former order (CFO) with specific instructions:* A *CFO* order is one which cancels an earlier order and replaces it with a new order or new instructions, usually involving a change in price specification. For example: "CFO buy 5 July wheat $3.69¾ stop. *Enter* buy 5 July wheat $3.70¾—stop." The above advice directs that the earlier order to buy one contract of July wheat at $3.69¾—stop, is to be cancelled and replaced by a new order to purchase 5,000 bushels of July wheat at $3.70¾—stop. The only thing which has been changed is the price: the level at which the customer will accept execution has been raised 1 cent per bushel.

6. *Spread orders:* Execution of spreads always involves two separate considerations which may be:

a. Two contracts in the same commodity.

b. Two different markets in the same commodity and futures month.

c. Two separate markets involving the same commodity and different contract months.

d. A single market and two separate commodities.

e. Two separate commodities and two different contract months, and others.

The possibilities are almost endless. The prime consideration in spreading is always one of price differential between the two legs of the spread; flat price levels are only of secondary importance.

As noted elsewhere, when the spreader believes the price differential will narrow (in a normal market) he will buy the nearby and sell the more distant futures. When he believes the price difference will increase (in a normal market) he will sell the nearby contract and buy the more distant futures. In an *inverted* market (with nearby futures selling at a premium to more deferred futures) the opposite procedure applies: If the trader believes the price inversion will increase, with the nearby futures going to an even greater premium over the more deferred contract, he will buy the nearby and sell the deferred. If he believes the inversion will disappear and prices return to a more nearly normal relationship, he will sell the nearby contract and buy the later maturity.

Framing a spread order calls for careful concentration on the part of the trader, just as it requires meticulous execution by the floor broker. A typical early summertime intramarket spread order might be as follows: "buy Chicago 100 July 1985 wheat—sell Chicago 100 December 1984 wheat—10½ cents—limit—GTC." This order instructs the broker to buy the deferred contract and sell the nearby contract in equal amounts, at any time he can do so, and without regard to the specific price on either. The order is a clear indication that the trader believes that a 10½ cent inversion between the two contracts is excessive—he thinks the spread will narrow. The trader is, of course, willing to accept the spread position at anything better (wider) than the 10½ cent differential, which the order limit identifies as his minimum allowable execution. "GTC" informs the solicitor and the floor broker that the order is good until cancelled, whether this be a few hours or a few weeks. Unless the order is cancelled, it will remain a resting order until expiration of the December contract.

7. *Intermarket spreads:* The placement of an order to buy in one market and sell in another is a more complex assignment than establishing a spread position in a single market; the reasons should be obvious. In most situations, a customer will order his broker to "buy Chicago March wheat and sell Kansas City March wheat" at a specific spread difference. Depending on how closely the customer restricts his broker, the spread order may prove to be unfulfilled—or unfulfillable—by reason of its close limitations. Intermarket spreading is occasionally handled on the basis of market orders for execution at the same time of day. For instance: "buy 20 Chicago March wheat and sell 20 Kansas City March wheat—11:05 A.M.—market." By reason of constant interchange of price information over their respective ticker systems, prices in the two markets tend to maintain quite consistent relationships, influenced, of course, by the relative supply/demand considerations in the two locations. By timing execution of the two orders in the two separate markets, the customer can be sure of having close time concurrency in his trades. If he is right in his price idea about the spread, getting the fill will likely be of more importance than trying to get the last ¼ cent or ½ cent—and which could prevent execution of the order, in rapidly moving markets particularly.

8. *Intercommodity spreads:* There is a form of commodity spreading which involves separate products and which, by strict definition, are not spreads at all; for example, wheat and corn. It is true that a certain degree of substitutability exists between these two commodities. Poultry, as a case in point may be fed wheat, or their diet can be comprised largely of cracked corn. The same is true

in feeding pigs and beef. The fact has given rise to an equation which in the trade is known as the *wheat/corn ratio*. Simply stated, this premise suggests that whenever the price differential between wheat and corn narrows beyond a certain point, reflecting a price/value aberration in their respective nutritional values as livestock feed, wheat should be bought and corn sold in anticipation of a return to a more normal price spread. In the opposite situation, where the price of wheat outstrips the price of corn in light of their respective feeding values, wheat should be sold and corn bought, in anticipation of their return to a more classical price/value relationship. Although buying or selling corn against sales or purchases of wheat have on occasion proved to be extremely profitable, doing so involves two separate positions rather than a spread, as defined in the rules and regulations of some grain markets. Orders involving this kind of transaction may take any number of forms, including:

a. "Buy 50 July corn and sell 50 July wheat at 75 cents—limit—GTW." This order form instructs the floor broker to buy corn and sell wheat at a specified price differential per bushel—or better. The specific price of the corn or wheat at the time the trade is executed is only of secondary importance: flat prices on the two commodities are not even mentioned. GTW means *good this week*—until Friday.

b. "Buy 10 July corn $2.90½—limit, and sell 10 July wheat $3.65½—limit." This order accomplishes the same thing set forth in the earlier example, provided it is possible to fill it at the precise prices specified. Stated in this fashion, however, (as a two-part order) one side of the trade can only be executed if the other side of the trade can also be filled at the designated price.

A broker obviously cannot be expected to execute the corn trade in the hope that the July wheat price will come into range and permit him to get the second fill. Should he execute the corn trade, and July wheat fail to show the required limit price on his spread order, he would be left "holding the bag," with the long position involving 10,000 bushels of July corn in his own account. As a practical matter, specifying prices on two sides of a spread usually only adds to execution difficulty and often results in less advantageous fills for the customer than would be obtainable on a purely price-differential basis. Most commission houses will not accept price-specific spread orders.

9. *One-cancels-other (OCO):* This is a two-part order which covers both ends of a pair of alternatives. An OCO order might be used by a trader who has an open 20,000 bushel short position in corn, for instance, with the price hovering around $2.35. If the price goes down, he wants to add to the position; if the price goes up, he wants protection against loss. An OCO to accomplish both objectives might read: "Sell—10 May corn $2.33½—stop—*or*—buy 20 May corn $2.38¼—stop . . . OCO."

If the price hits \$2.33½ or less, the sell side will be filled and the buy side will be cancelled. If the price rises to \$2.38¼, the stop-loss will be activated; the 20,000 bushels short position will be bought in, and the sell side of the order will be cancelled.

The orders listed above are only a small representation of all the possibilities which exist. Each form, of course, has a great many variations which can be employed to meet the specific requirements of various commodities and markets. The possibilities are only limited by the imagination of the customer and the practicalities of understanding and execution on the part of the broker. In the best interests of both, orders should be kept as simple and unfettered as possible. The greater latitude you can give the pit broker, while still protecting your own interests, the better executions you will likely receive.

After all, if a pit broker can't fill an order—or can't understand it—placing it is a waste of everyone's time.

Courtesy of the CME

Exhibit 17–1

Commodity orders from all around the world are called and filled in America's huge markets. Each pit or ring in this partial view of the Chicago Mercantile Exchange trading floor deals in a different category of merchandise. Floor brokers have no way of being sure that a particular order is being handled for a government, a hedger, or a public speculator, nor do they care. All orders are accorded the same handling.

18

What a Broker Can and Can't Do for You

Public speculators must trade through brokers, and selection of a broker involves considerations which call for a careful and critical analysis of your personal needs, in light of the facilities a given commission house offers. Relationships between customers and brokers follow no consistent pattern. Some traders view their brokers as little more than functionaries, through whom they must pass orders; neither seeking nor wanting anything from them except meticulous order writing and efficient execution on the trading floor. Other public traders take every opportunity to "pick the brains" of the brokerage house representatives. They may not follow their broker's suggestions, but they want to hear his comments concerning the market in general, and about particular contracts which may be under scrutiny as presently existing or potential positions.

Discretionary Accounts

In still other situations, public traders occasionally relegate the entire decision-making function to the brokerage house and rely totally on the broker's judgment in buying and selling. An arrangement of this kind, under the rules of most commodity exchanges, requires that the customer sign a "Discretionary Trading Agreement" which, in effect, gives the broker power of attorney to buy and sell on behalf of a customer—with or without the customer's prior knowledge or approval.

215

216

Rules and regulations of CFTC as well as the exchanges require that any discretionary trading account involving commodity contracts be personally supervised by a brokerage house partner. It is also mandatory under the rules of all U.S. commodity exchanges that confirmation slips, P&S statements, and all other trading documents be supplied the discretionary customer in the same manner as if he were promulgating his own trades. Regardless of anything that might be said in its defense, giving discretion to anyone exposes the account owner to great risks. Short of outright fraud, the account owner has little recourse against either imprudence or stupidity on the broker's part.

Broker Services Differ

The essential services provided by the brokerage houses are much the same, insofar as they all receive, transmit, and execute customer orders. From this point on, however, similarities begin to diminish.

Each organized exchange establishes minimum margin rules in each commodity traded. Brokerage houses may not set customer margins below the minimums established by the exchanges—but they may, in their own discretion, require larger margins—and many of them do.

Some brokerage houses are highly selective in the kinds of orders they will accept for execution in particular circumstances. For example, some houses refuse to accept limit orders "on the open" or "on the close." Or they may refuse to accept anything but market orders in the last hour of trading in a maturing contract. Still other houses may refuse to accept spread-limit orders between two different commodities (for example, to simultaneously buy wheat futures and sell corn futures at a designated price difference).

Within the rules and regulations of the exchanges upon which a broker is transacting business, the regulations imposed by the Commodity Futures Trading Commission, and within the limitations of statutes which apply to agency relationships and contracts generally, a brokerage house enjoys a broad area of self-determination. There are rules a licensed broker must follow and which set forth things he must do to avoid running afoul of the several levels of authority under which he operates. Likewise, there are things he must not do. However, except for the specific "thou shalt—" and "thou shalt not—" a commission house is free to determine its own policies and order its relationships with customers to suit itself. The customer, in turn, has the continuing prerogative of choosing the broker who suits him best. He may elect to maintain the relationship or interrupt it at any point he sees fit to do so.

Commission houses, like other human institutions, reflect varying strengths and weaknesses. It is up to you, the customer, to determine where your interests will be best served and select your broker accordingly. Of course, honesty and efficient transmittal and execution of orders are the most important considerations. Brokerage houses are occasionally faced with the same manner of staffing problems which plague other kinds of businesses. Excessive staff turnover may fill a "wire room" with inexperienced people. Inexperience breeds mistakes and while a mistake can usually be reconciled through discussion, doing so can be time-consuming and frustrating in the extreme. Inexperience or lack of care on the part of a solicitor can result in order-writing errors; lackadaisical performance on the part of a pit broker can have disastrous results in order filling.

There seems to be no substitute for trial and error in selecting a broker who best meets your personal needs. The quality of their advertising is certainly no guide! Finding the right broker may involve two or three changes in your account; and if necessary, have no hesitancy in doing so. Commodity speculation is not a hobby; it's a business. Substantial amounts of money are at stake and the brokerage commission you will pay on every transaction should entitle you to professional treatment all the way from the customer-man's desk through the wire room, to the pit, and back again. If you settle for less than this, you are needlessly jeopardizing your funds and your speculative future. CFTC and the individual exchanges attempt to police the business, but you must also be aware of the fact that there are crooks in the commodity sector, just as there are in law and real estate.

Broker Advice

Inexperienced speculators oftentimes look hopefully to their broker for inside information that can produce guaranteed results. Obviously they rarely find it. If such authorities on market behavior exist, they aren't likely to spend their time behind a brokerage desk. People who can "read the market" are trading for their own accounts—or consulting—and making millions doing it! Brokerage house employees are rarely if ever traders. Most commission houses, as a matter of fact, specifically prohibit their employees from trading on margin in either stocks or commodities. The philosophy seems to be that a position in the market is likely to color the judgment of one who should—at all times and under all conditions—maintain an unbiased view in serving his public customers. The point is valid.

Despite the prohibition against employee trading, a great many brokerage houses produce and disseminate daily, weekly, or monthly advisory letters which briefly recap pertinent developments in selected commodities and offer some interpretation of these events, as concerns their possible impact on price behavior. Depending on the capabilities of the staff people who research and prepare these materials, a broker's letter may be exceedingly valuable; or it may be worth less than nothing. Some of them are nothing more than "tout" sheets!

In addition to recounting the news and highlights which relate to fundamental market matters, some houses offer opinions concerning chart conditions which will bear on future price patterns. Here again, depending on your own particular appraisal of charting as a speculative tool—and the technical competence of the chartist commentator—this information may be worthy of consideration or downright misleading.

A Grain of Salt Is Advisable

It all adds up to the fact that there is no consistent authority on prices except the market. While a highly skilled and well-experienced brokerage house representative may occasionally have an excellent "price idea" concerning a particular contract at a particular time, if he has the occult ability to consistently forecast prices, you might well ask yourself, "Why is he giving such valuable information away?" The market or a large client will certainly pay him more for such knowledge than any possible combination of retail customers. All he needs to do is back his judgment with some money and take the same positions for himself that he is advising others to assume.

Relying exclusively on a broker's advice—or giving him authority to exercise his own discretion in trading for your account—has one point to commend it: Since the decisions he will be making do not involve his own funds, it stands to reason that it might be easier for him to follow the trading axiom, "cut losses short and let profits run" than it would be for you. The broker is not likely to become emotionally involved with someone else's money. But, if this is the strength in the procedure, there are several weaknesses.

To begin with, a brokerage house exists to transact business. Each order placed involves a firmly established brokerage fee which usually covers the "round trip." This is to say that the present brokerage fee on 5,000 bushels of soybeans (one contract) is about $80, and covers execution of the sale or purchase which establishes the position, and the subsequent purchase or sale which will offset and close it out. This brokerage fee is the same whether a position is kept open five minutes or for the life of the contract. The brokerage fee is not affected by whether a given trade produces monumental profit or a jarring loss. It costs a predetermined amount (negotiable with each brokerage firm) to obtain execution of each order, and the success of any brokerage operation depends directly and exclusively on the number of trades they handle during each business day; not how much money they make for their customers!

Brokers Are on Both Sides of the Market

It's disquieting to many newcomers to commodity speculation to discover that the broker is both buying and selling the same contract for different customers at virtually the same time, day in and day out. Of course each purchase must, at some point, be offset by a sale. Furthermore, when hedging is involved on the part of commercial interests, a sale or a purchase may be dictated by changes in cash inventory rather than by independent appraisal of market condition or even probable price behavior. Thus, a commission house is usually on both sides of the market buying and selling simultaneously.

This should not be surprising, since the only business of a brokerage house is the execution of orders in the marketplace. It would be Machiavellian to suppose that a broker would be so unfeeling as to have no interest in whether or not his customer showed a profit; but such an interest, even when it exists, is humanitarian rather than economic. A customer does not have to succeed in his search for profit in order for a brokerage house to realize the profits it wants.

What does upset public customers from time to time is to discover that two different RRs (which stands for *registered representative*) in the same commission house, may be advising diametrically opposite actions in the same commodity contract at the same time! While most of us can accept a bullish attitude, or a bearish attitude, or no opinion whatsoever; to discover that both buy and sell advice is emanating from the same brokerage house at the same time can come as a shock to the uninitiated trader. Try to understand it.

The business of brokers is writing orders and collecting commissions for executing them. Nothing more!

Since, for every buyer there has to be a seller, and for every winner there has to be a loser, a brokerage house that mixes its business perfectly will, on any given day, have precisely the same amount of debits to report to some of its customers, as it has credits to report to the others. In fact, the ideal situation in the back room of a commission house is to be as close to balanced between long- and short- holdings as possible. This is to say that if total customer positions total 15 million bushels of short old-crop corn, that brokerage will usually be striving to have this balanced with as close to 15 million bushels of long old-crop holdings as possible. With the business spread in this fashion, losses are equalled by profits—and half of the customers are always happy. A broker can hope for nothing more!

The bad news in this situation is that every time price goes up, half of the house accounts lose. The good news is that half of them profit. But the best news of all is that the commission house is collecting its commissions and showing an operating profit on the total operation!

The speculator's business is that of making good trades.

The broker's business is that of executing all kinds of trades. This crucial difference should never be forgotten for a minute.

Discretionary Accounts Surrender Customer Control

Giving a broker informal carte blanche to make your trade decisions or formal discretion to trade in your behalf puts you at the mercy of both his judgment and his avarice. Once a discretionary trading agreement has been signed, the broker who holds it can trade you in and out of successive positions with such rapidity that your margin funds may literally disappear in commissions. Such "churning" can break you, without regard for the vicissitudes of price fluctuation. In fairness, it must be said that deliberate "churning" is a rare occurrence; however, instances of it are still sufficiently numerous as to put any prudent speculator on his guard against the possibility, however remote. CFTC is attempting to control this type of administrative fraud, but their results are not good enough to offer much reassurance to the folks who are regularly being victimized.

Listen Carefully—Decide for Yourself

There are exceptions to every rule; still the best rule in commodity speculation is to only follow the advice of a broker—or anyone else— to the extent that its validity has been proved to be reliable in practice. Then, place your own orders for execution on the basis of the best composite information obtainable, tempered in light of your own judgment of events to come. The mere fact that someone occupies a position of presumed responsibility and accepts orders for execution on commodity exchanges is no proof of either technical competence in evaluating market conditions, or skill in the management of risk capital. Automobile salesmen only rarely understand the internal workings of the machines they sell. By the same token, the average commission house employee is not likely to be an expert on price forecasting in the markets in which he deals. He need not be to perform his function efficiently and well.

It's a Lonely Business

Newcomers to commodity speculation have a deep and continuing need for reassurance, regardless of whether prices are going up, down, or nowhere. If prices on a position are moving against its holder, the broker can expect regular quizzing which asks the question (in a dozen different ways), "How far do you think prices may go?" Of course the customer is attempting to evaluate his ability to hold on and absorb the paper loss pending a price reversal.

There is nothing more distasteful or chilling to an inexperienced trader than converting any paper loss to a real loss, by closing out the position. There are situations in which the signs are so unmistakable that anyone may be able to flatly advise selling out or offsetting through purchase. More often, however, the advisor may be only slightly less confused than the customer; in which case the advice may be altogether too equivocal to have any real value. The distraught trader will often seem to listen carefully to his broker's words, but he really only hears the things which support a decision which he has already arrived at independently.

In short, the trader in such an instance is looking for companionship rather than advice; and he can usually depend on finding the companionship he seeks. Warm and reassuring as such a conversation may be, it doesn't alter the fact that if the position is a bad one, its hazards may persist and its resulting losses may grow apace. A bad trade is not to be cured by conversation. The only way to cut a loss short is by offset.

The people who most often are caught in a dilemma of this kind are those who have taken an open position in a commodity contract without a beginning plan. They have not appraised the situation from the standpoint of profit potentials and loss maximums. Therefore, they honestly have no opinion as to where they should give up, take a loss, and look for more rewarding opportunities in a different position. They hope their broker—or someone—will be able to provide some sort of miracle which will retrieve them from their own initial folly and save the day. Needless to say, they are usually disappointed, since commodity salesmen are not soothsayers; and market prices tend to pick their own directions without respect to what any of the experts might appear to believe at any given moment.

Broker Advice Can Be Valuable

The purpose of this discourse is not to downgrade the value of broker information. Some small part of it is extremely valuable. But even the best of the price forecasters and market analysts are guilty of great misappraisals which, if followed blindly, will result in certain disaster. The only safe course in commodity speculation is, as has been stated often earlier, to assume a position with a firm notion about its profit potentials and loss limits. Having done this, when prices move against the position, it must be closed; when prices move in favor of the position, it may be enlarged. "Cut losses short and let profits run" is the only formula for speculative success.

If advice from any quarter proves to be consistently profitable to you, it will more likely be a result of rigid application of this trading axiom, than a reflection of vastly superior knowledge of market fundamentals or technical considerations. By rigid application of the analysis procedure and trading program set forth earlier, a trader can develop his own position-management techniques through experience. By careful adherence to the trading rules, his results will be much better than if he relies on his own judgment part of the time and leans on the advice of others the rest of the time.

When Your Phone Rings

The telephone is an indispensable element in commodity trading. Once you have established yourself with a broker and taken a position, you are an "active account." If you are maintaining a free balance or margin funds in reserve with your broker, you can expect to receive telephone calls from him regularly. The purpose of these calls will be to inform you of any significant market information which will have come to the broker's attention and to generally impart a feel of the fundamental trading situation to you.

These calls may often contain an implication or an outright statement that a good opportunity exists in connection with one or more commodity contracts. Your brokerage representative may be personally convinced of the validity of the advice he is giving you—or it may represent an official opinion developed in the firm's "back-room" research department and passed to the solicitors for relay to their customers. Regardless of where the price idea comes from, and without respect to whether subsequent events prove the information to be right or wrong, brokers make telephone calls to customers for the purpose of *generating new business*. The mere existence of free funds in your margin account is their open invitation to urge greater activity in the market on your part. Inactive free balances do not generate commissions!

The regularity and the length of the broker calls you receive will have a direct relation to the size of the free margin balance you maintain on deposit. The information contained in such telephone calls should—at best—be viewed as only that: *Information*. Your decision as to whether action is or is not justified should still depend on your own private appraisal as to whether the opportunity is one which intrigues you as a professional risk bearer.

It should be remembered that interesting opportunities come in two forms: those producing *profits* and those producing *losses*. It's hard to imagine a more interesting situation for a speculator than being on the wrong end of a bad position. However, excitement and profits are not the same thing!

Margin Account Segregation

Even experienced securities and commodities speculators are often unaware of an important protective device which exists in connection with regulated commodity margin deposits. Under the Commodity Exchange Act and its amendments, commodity margin funds must be "segregated." This is to say that, from the time you open an account with a broker and deposit funds with him in a commodity margin account, those funds must be kept distinctly separate from all other funds in the brokerage firm. They may not be "pooled" by the broker. Neither may they be used by the broker for any purpose other than margining your regulated commodity positions, payment of your trade commissions for executions, and covering whatever trade losses you sustain.

The distinction between the segregation requirement in commodity deposits and the handling given securities deposits is most significant. Under the latitudes of governing statutes, security margin funds may be used by a brokerage house to pay its rent, light, water, salaries, etc. No problem exists so long as the firm meets the applicable requirements of solvency; customers' securities' free balances may be used by the stockbroker in virtually any fashion he sees fit. The securities customer's margin deposit appears in the records of the firm and, of course, constitutes a legal obligation. But the money itself may or may not be on hand at any particular moment. It may, indeed, be in CDs or Treasury bills, earning interest for the brokerage house!

Financial failure of brokerage houses is a comparatively rare phenomenon, due to the restrictions under which they operate and the kind of business in which they are engaged. However, some spectacular bankruptcies have occurred in the recent past and presumably some of them will take place in the future. Whenever this happens, security margin funds may be lost in the financial collapse; commodity margin funds cannot be. This, by reason of the CFTC requirement which spells out an ironclad protective procedure for holding all regulated commodity accounts separate and distinctly apart from all other funds, for as long as they are in the broker's custody.

Many traders who deal in both commodities and securities follow the practice of opening a regulated commodity account and then, as stock purchases are made, they specifically authorize transfer of the required amount of money from the commodity account to the other category. Doing so merely requires the signing of a standard transfer form. Likewise, profits realized on non-commodity activities such as securities transactions are directed to be redeposited into the segregated commodity account. In so doing, a customer can rest assured that his margin funds, although they are not earning interest, are every bit as safe as they would be if on deposit in a bank. Or, in light of recent experience, perhaps more so.

Errors Do Happen

It has already been noted that brokers, like other mortals, can make mistakes; moreover, that a broker's error may result in either an accidental profit or loss. The major commodity exchanges unanimously take the position that when an error in execution occurs, the profit, if any, belongs to the customer; and the loss, if any, must be absorbed by the broker. The existence of the rule exerts a profound influence on brokers in their striving for efficiency.

There is no reason, nor would it be possible, to outline all the various kinds of errors which might occur in the course of trading; nor to identify the individuals who could, in some train of events, be found culpable. An order may be improperly framed, resulting in an execution in the wrong contract month, in the wrong amount or at the wrong price. A pit broker may misread an order, which results in an overfill or an underfill; he may inadvertently buy, when the order directs him to sell.

Operating in the highly charged atmosphere of a busy market offers countless opportunities for mistakes. The fact that so few errors do occur is the best possible testimony to the expertise of the whole chain of function, from the solicitor's desk to pit execution, and back. When errors occur they are usually resolved immediately in the brokerage house—and in accordance with the exchange requirement cited previously; that the customer receives the profit from the error, if any, but is saved from any possible loss in the opposite situation.

Arbitration Procedure

When resolution of the difficulty cannot be worked out with the brokerage firm, each organized commodity exchange has an *arbitration committee* which sits as a referee between the interests involved. After listening to the evidence, the arbitration committee is empowered to render a decision and enforce its ruling upon a member firm. It is important to note that matters involving both members and nonmembers are eligible to be brought before this kind of exchange fact-finding body. The infinitesimal number of issues that remain unresolved following arbitration can still be taken into the civil courts for disposition.

To sum up, a broker is neither a god nor a devil. He is, in the vast majority of cases, a reasonably well-trained agent in a highly specialized and most demanding activity. His primary function is to meticulously carry out the instructions of his customer-client. Common practice regularly casts him also in the role of counselor, fortune teller, and price prognosticator. The success he may have in these latter-named fields will depend upon a great many things, none of which may be directly assessable except on the basis of demonstrated reliability—or lack of it. A speculator who believes that careful selection of a broker reduces the need for his own attention to, and study of, the market and the positions of risk he is considering, is placing an inordinate measure of faith in a second party. There are some public traders who have richly profited by pursuing this kind of program. There are a great many more who have experienced the opposite result. Most brokers are atrocious price forecasters.

Unless a person has the time, the means, and the incentive to manage his own speculative program, he should probably not speculate in commodities at all. Or he should retain an individual in whom he has unlimited confidence, turn over a designated amount of money for speculative activity, and pay no attention whatsoever to the market situation on a day-by-day basis.

The most successful public trader is one who is willing to listen to advice, evaluate all of it, discard most of it, use some of it, and then make his own judgments in light of his own willingness to assume risk exposure. Most important of all, to reiterate for emphasis, he is one who cuts his losses short and lets his profits run, knowing that if he can be right even half the time, the speculative strategy will produce a most rewarding composite result.

Appraising Advice in General

This section cannot be closed without a modest warning against placing too much confidence in the opinions of anyone who has a stake in the issue under discussion. Courts recognize that there are those who are automatically disbarred from sitting on a jury, since they have some degree of interest in the outcome. The same rule should be constantly applied in discussing the market.

From a practical point of view, how can you expect a trader to answer a question which bears on a position he holds? Ask a bear what he thinks the prospects are for sugar, and he will tell you he thinks prices will work lower. A bear almost always looks for lower prices. But ask the bear what he sees in sugar prices when he happens to hold a long position in the commodity and he will tell you that he thinks higher prices are in prospect. Any other response would be unthinkable. Moreover, the larger his position and the larger his loss—if any—in the position, the more eloquent he is likely to be in presenting the higher-prices argument. He *needs* higher prices!

The only time you can really expect to get an unbiased opinion about a trading question is when you ask it of someone who has no position in it. The statement should not be taken as a charge of dishonesty. Anyone who is long desperately wants prices to go up; anyone who is short equally wants them to go down. Economic interests are bound to cloud the objective judgment of even a veritable saint, if he holds a market position.

Before asking someone what he thinks about the price of anything, ask him if he owns any of it. If the answer is yes, go elsewhere for an unbiased opinion. He can't give you one.

Exhibit 18–1

19

Speculative Pitfalls

Several of the topics which will be treated in this chapter have already
been referred to directly or by implication in material which has come
before. But the importance of being able to identify pitfalls which exist
in commodity speculation justifies the risk of any degree of repetition.

Most of the serious losses sustained by public speculators in commodities are avoidable. They ordinarily grow out of lack of caution in
establishing a new position and/or failure to unflinchingly apply tactical
and strategic rules of prudent position management when danger signals appear. The greatest losses which speculators sustain in commodity
positions are those which are directly related to stubbornness; refusal
to recognize facts, take a small loss, and close out the proposition that
has gone sour.

As previously noted, it isn't necessary that one be right even half
of the time, in order to make handsome profits in speculation; assuming
stringent application of the trading techniques which maximize profit
opportunity and minimize the chances for loss. If *one third* of the positions taken prove to be right—and provided they are managed properly during the period of time you hold them—your speculative success
over time is virtually assured. But the market is a hard teacher and
your performance in it will be graded closely—and constantly reflected
in profits or losses. When you make a mistake, it will cost you money
every time. By the same token, good decisions always save money—or
bring cash rewards.

Overtrading

Money is the basic tool of speculation, since speculation involves dealing in valuable property held over some period of time. The property may involve a physical asset or it may be represented in a futures contract, which stands as a measurement of ownership risk. In either case, a prudent speculator will carefully determine the extent of his capital which can be earmarked for speculative activity and everything he does in his speculative program will be first checked against these risk resources. If he errs, it should always be on the side of conservatism. Undertrading can't break you; overtrading surely will.

Impressive personal fortunes have been amassed very quickly in commodity speculation. Philip D. Armour, for example, is authoritatively said to have cleared $2 million in less then 90 days by selling pork short during the last few weeks of the Civil War. The market price of pork stood around $40. Armour was convinced that the war was about to be ended and, with its end, he was confident that pork prices would fall. In pursuit of this price idea, he thought $40 pork to be unrealistically high; so he sold trainloads of the commodity for future delivery at prices ranging from $40 down to $30 per hundredweight. Suddenly the Civil War did end and the price of pork promptly fell to $25, then to $20, and finally settled around $18 per hundredweight. Armour was able to buy back his pork contracts—or buy the physical product—for about half his previous selling price. In so doing, he laid the foundation for one of the world's great companies, and one of America's greatest personal fortunes.

But every dollar Armour made on his speculation, was a dollar lost by a buyer of pork—who must have been equally convinced that demands for food to supply an army and sustain the civil population would drive prices up; and that the war would continue. Had Armour's speculative notion proved wrong, his loss might have been as monumental as his gain.

From the standpoint of professional speculation, overtrading is always a bad policy, because it can be fatal. Reversals can occur, opinions can be wrong, and what might merely be an incidental disappointment under more conservative practices, in the face of overtrading, can constitute a catastrophe from which financial recovery is impossible.

You Can Never Be Sure

A professional speculator always recognizes the fact that *any* position may prove to be untenable at some point. The rosiest outlook may, for the most unpredictable reasons, turn to one of unrelieved despair. When this happens, a loss must be taken, and the sooner it can be taken, the better. By keeping position commitments within conservative bounds,

CHAPTER 19

228

several successive losses can be sustained, but there will still be additional risk funds in reserve to enable the speculator to seek out another attractive opportunity, and back his judgment with the required capital.

Overtrading is done too often on the basis of "hunches." The overtrader is depending on luck to deliver him a windfall profit. It's a "sucker's" game. There are occasions when luck meets the hopes placed in her, but the speculator who intends to stay in the business and succeed in the business will pin his future to more solid criteria. He will never permit his open position commitments to exceed sensible bounds, regardless of how sure he feels. As a rule of thumb, the following measurements represent a useful set of maximums:

1. An *initial* position should never tie up more than 50 percent of your available risk capital.
2. An *enlarged* position should never tie up more than 90 percent of your available risk capital.

Overtrading is like Russian roulette: One loss can take you out of the game forever. A smart speculator always leaves himself some latitude for loss.

Margin Calls

There are two levels of margin which must be on deposit in connection with an open commodity futures position. *Initial margin* is usually about 6 percent of the value of the contract, and must be deposited at the time the purchase or sale is made. Once a position has been established, a minimum margin must be kept "in the clear" throughout the period of time you hold it. This is referred to as *maintenance margin* and is usually about one third less than the initial margin requirement.

As prices fluctuate on the contract positions held, the speculator's margin balance is increased when prices move favorably, and is decreased when prices move adversely. Thus, when prices fall on a contract in which a long position is held, the speculator's margin funds are said to be *impaired*; the same would be true in connection with a short position in which prices rise. A trader's *equity* in a position fluctuates almost constantly: increasing when the price of a contract held long increases, and falling when prices rise on a contract which has been sold short, and vice versa.

With respect to all kinds of futures, brokerage houses follow the practice of calling for additional variation margin as soon as price change has impaired the speculator's margin equity to less than the designated maintenance margin requirement. For example, initial Board of Trade minimum margin on wheat is currently set at 12 cents per bushel. (This is subject to change, and commission houses may require more than the exchange minimum.) In order to buy or sell a wheat futures contract, the trader must deposit 12 cents per bushel with his broker to indemnify his performance on the terms of his market obligation. One contract (5,000 bushels), therefore, requires an initial margin deposit of $600.

Maintenance margin on wheat is currently set at 8 cents per bushel, minimum. This is to say that once a position in wheat futures is taken, the price on the selected futures may move 4 cents per bushel to the disadvantage of the holder of the contract before the latitude which exists between initial and maintenance margin is wiped out. Under the practices of all brokerage houses, whenever prices have moved against the holder's wheat position to the extent of 4 cents per bushel, a call would go out for additional margin funds. In order to hold the position, more money must be deposited with the broker, to bring the margin amount back up to the initial margin level of 12 cents per bushel.

Failure to answer a call for additional margin within the period of time specified by the broker may result in the position being closed out by the broker. In the case of larger accumulations involving several contracts, the entire position will not necessarily be closed out; but a portion of it will be, in order to reduce the total risk liability present, and reduce the amount of margin funds therefore required to adequately cover the reduced position.

Never Answer a Margin Call

It is difficult to envision a situation in which answering a call for additional margin on a deteriorating position could be viewed as anything except bad speculative practice. Such a call for additional margin will not be made unless prices have already moved substantially in the wrong direction. The trader's price idea has already been proven to be invalid by the facts. Holding a losing position is bad enough; staying with a loser, when doing so requires putting up additional funds to hold on, cannot be defended on any basis. Faced with a call for additional margin as a result of price variation, two courses of action, and only two, deserve consideration:

1. *Close out part of the position* in order to free up existing margin funds and bring margin on the reduced portion of the position back up to standards.
2. Recognize the loser for what it is, and *close out the entire position.*

Traders occasionally justify answering variation margin calls with the fiction that they intended to add to their margin account deposits, anyway. If you truly intend to deposit additional risk funds with your broker, do so at any time except when price changes face you with the demand for additional margin to meet broker or exchange requirements.

To repeat for emphasis, *never answer a variation margin call!* Doing so is almost always open flirtation with speculative disaster.

Moving a Stop-Loss Order

We have previously discussed the procedure involved in evaluating the establishment of a new speculative position, and pointed out that in doing so an *initial profit objective* should be identified along with a *maximum loss limitation.*

When a contract is bought or sold, a stop-loss order should be placed above the trading range (in the case of a short sale) or below the trading range (in the case of a long purchase). The exact point at which the stop-loss is placed may be reflective of your personal appraisal of price movement within a daily or weekly trading range; or may be determined with the help of chart patterns, or otherwise. However the stop-loss level is arrived at, once fixed it should be left in force, barring the most dramatic change of circumstances.

Inexperienced speculators have an inglorious record of enlarging their losses by moving stop-losses higher or lower, thus offering the opportunity for prices to move even further to their disadvantage.

As prices move in your favor, serious consideration must be constantly given to the possibility of moving a stop-loss up in connection with a long position, and moving it down to protect profits in a short position. Failure to do so will leave your paper profits exposed to the vicissitudes of subsequent price fluctuation. And a paper profit which is yours on one day may, in the face of later price change, be taken away from you as prices rise or fall.

Move a stop to protect a profit, but a stop-loss order should never be moved upward or downward to enlarge the opportunity for loss. If a position is wrong, the closer the stop-loss, the less it will cost you to learn the bad news.

Adding to a Loss—Price Averaging

Neophytes in speculation find ingenious ways to rationalize failure. One of the recurrent means they seize on is the notion that their effective price in an overall commodity position is subject to *averaging,* up or down, through successive purchases or sales.

For example, a speculator buys 10,000 bushels of corn at $2.30. This price then falls to $2.25, which amounts to a 5 cent loss. At this point, the unskilled speculator may decide to buy another 10,000 bushels at the lower price. In so doing, he may consider that his "effective" price on 20,000 bushels of corn is $2.27½. Arithmetically the figure is correct, but in terms of speculative tactics, the procedure is absolutely and irretrievably wrong.

Each acquisition must be realistically viewed as *separate* and apart from each subsequent acquisition. The first decision to buy corn futures at $2.30 per bushel clearly stands as a mistake, since prices fell 5 cents per bushel under the purchase price. The purchase of 10,000 additional bushels at $2.25 may prove to be profitable, but this will not be known until subsequent price behavior is revealed. In any case, the first purchase is still "wrong for a nickel" until price moves above $2.30; buying more, at any price, won't change this.

Price Persistence

Price patterns, like weather patterns, have a well-recognized tendency to persistence. Prices that are moving downward tend to continue downward; prices that are moving upward tend to maintain an upward direction; prices that are moving sideways are inclined to maintain a horizontal channel. Establishing a long position in a descending market is simply the wrong thing to do. When it is done, the trader is probably attempting to "pick the bottom." Tops and bottoms are elusive things, and trading against the trend can be a fine road to bankruptcy.

Adding to a losing position, whether long or short, can only multiply negative risk exposure; it can escalate a modest loss into a debacle.

When prices are going against you, close the position out, or let your stop-loss limitation stand as protection. If the stop-loss is reached, the position will be closed out—and it *should be!*

Moving a stop-loss higher or lower to accommodate adverse price movement is mere folly; adding to a losing position in the face of a trend which is already working against you can only be considered speculative madness.

The only time an initial position should be added to is after it has produced a paper profit, which can then be recommitted, to increase your leverage situation on an additional purchase or sale. When adverse price developments identify a position as a loss, it must be considered as a candidate for closeout or, at most, something to be left alone pending improvement of its performance.

Commercial grain dealers can buy or sell up or down on scale and profit from it. Speculators should leave the practice strictly to them.

Adding to a Profit—Pyramiding

While adding to a loss position should never be done, adding to a profitable position may greatly enhance your chances for large profits.

As detailed earlier, once a position has generated a paper profit, these profits can be used to margin additional contracts in the same futures. In so doing, you will have reduced the total amount of your own cash margin required, thus increasing leverage on the money you must put up to bind your contract performance. In times of major price movement, excellent opportunities may offer themselves to accumulate substantial holdings with profits from previous acquisitions or sales.

In adding to a winning position, the possibility of price reversal converting a paper profit into a break-even or a loss must always be borne in mind. Therefore, whenever an initial position is enlarged, there should also be an opportunity to further limit loss potentials by moving the stop-loss order somewhat closer on the total position.

For example, a trader in May 1985 wheat futures in 1984 had an early opportunity to sell the contract short at $4 or above. Assuming that he did that, and kept on selling the contract at 10 cent intervals down—with protective stop-loss orders 5½ cents above his successive selling prices—let's see what the results over some five months might be. Exhibit 19–1 tells the story.

With nothing more than a decision to trade this May wheat contract from the short side, in rough accordance with the "voice from the tomb,"

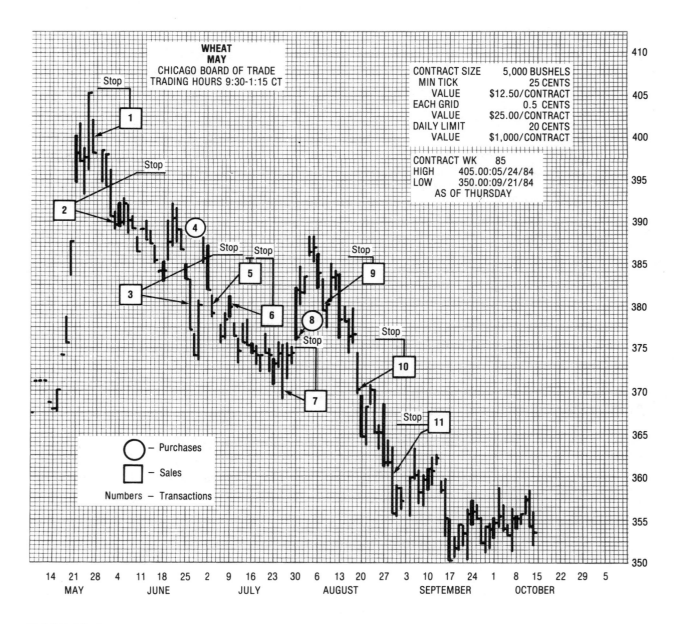

Exhibit 19–1

observe what the application of a consistent trading program accomplishes:

Transaction Number	Bought or Sold	Amount	Stop- Loss Price	Trade Result	Grand Total
1	Sold WK	5	4.05½ 4.00	$1,225	
2	Sold WK	5	3.85½ 3.80	225	
3	Sold WK	5	3.75½ 3.70	(275)	
4	Bot WK offset	15	3.75½		$1,175
5	Sold WK	5	3.85½ 3.80	225	
6	Sold WK	5	3.85½ 3.80	225	
7	Sold WK	5	3.75½ 3.70	(275)	
8	Bot WK offset	15	3.75½		175
9	Sold WK	5	3.85½ 3.80	$1,250-paper profit	
10	Sold WK	5	3.75½ 3.70	750-paper profit	
11	Sold WK	5	3.65½ 3.60	250-paper profit	

An even dime constitutes a recurrent resistance point as prices move higher or lower. Hence, the decision to trade a contract on these significant levels has some underlying logic in it: If a price goes through the even-dime level, it will likely keep going for some greater or lesser distance. But, unless there is some concerted buying or selling pressure behind it, it shouldn't carry a nickel beyond.

In pursuit of this notion, our hypothetical trader gives rein to his bearish view of this contract by selling every time price breaks through the 10 cent level *going lower*. His protective stop-loss orders rest so as to take him out every time price goes through the 5½ cent level *going higher*.

In spite of two obvious technical reversals that chased him and a lot of other short-holders into offsetting, as soon as the squeezes are out of the way price resumes its downward course. In following this downside trend, sticking to the program, and keeping his position protected at all times, the net realized profit (ignoring commissions) is $1,350, with another $2,250 in paper profits in open trades numbered 9, 10, and 11.

How Far Is Far Enough?

It is in a situation like this that the novice trader faces his greatest temptation to try reading the market's mind. Trouble begins with the question, "Hasn't the price gone far enough?" A 50 cent break per bushel is a substantial move, but nobody really knows how far is far enough. Perhaps all the good news about the 1985 crop will drive the May price to $3.00—or $2.50! Weather, export orders, growing conditions in the rest of the world, trade psychology, and government grain policies will help to spin out an answer in the form of a projected supply/demand balance that, in turn, will be translated into market price.

In the meantime, however, the trader needn't fret for his lack of a firm notion about where price is headed on this contract. *Price is its own authority*. When it has, indeed, gone down far enough it will then reverse itself and move up for a while. When this happens—along with the fireworks that usually accompanies a major price reversal—we may be able to say with some conviction that "far enough" has been attained. But as things presently stand, there is nothing to be done except wait.

Should price succeed in blowing through the $3.50 level, another sale will need to be made, along with moving the stop-loss on the entire position down to $3.55½. Conversely, if price takes another run at the $3.50 level and fails to penetrate it, a reevaluation might be in order. Three intrasession lows precisely to $3.50, without breaking through the even dime might evidence some concerted defensive buying there; on the part of commercial interests, or big speculators, or both. A reversal may be in the making. If so, evidence of it will probably be found in the behavior of trading volumes and open-interest totals on this contract.

The companion volume, *Charting Commodity Market Price Behavior,* will show you how this decision can be made.

In the meantime, however, a smart trader doesn't change a program that's working—and this one is working fine! There have to be exceedingly strong reasons to revise one's opinion about price trend. Until that overwhelming evidence surfaces, the only sensible approach to May wheat is to keep on selling it!

Regardless of price level, a smart trader doesn't argue with profitability! Neither does he summarily jump from a trading stance that's piling up profits for him.

With his stop-loss order moved into "the black," he has assured himself a profit on the remaining open position and all he needs to do is pursue his program of protected incremental pyramiding and let prices take their course. The skilled trader will realize that the persistence factor in price movement is operating for him: the longer prices fall, the more likely they are to continue falling. In the face of any unacceptable price reversal, his stop-loss order is resting to effect a quick closeout on the entire accumulated position and protect the majority of his profits.

Closing Out Too Fast

A major pitfall for inexperienced speculators is in the area of premature closing of a winning position. It takes steady nerves to resist the temptation to dump a winner after having picked up a small, quick profit on it. Such an inclination must be stoutly resisted.

As the preceding example clearly demonstrates, consistent application of the trading program allows profits to run, while cutting losses short as often as necessary. If this is done, a trader who selects right positions even 40 percent of the time is going to take some impressive profits out of the market.

Let a Stop Take You Out

A profitable position should nearly always be closed out by the activation of a stop-loss order. Rigid adherence to this rule will save you from the frustrating knowledge that you have needlessly cut profits short when a little more patience would have paid off.

Reversing Position in the Market

A major object of pity in commodity markets is the unfortunate soul who rides a price trend up, or down, for a period of time; then closes out the position with a profit—and immediately establishes a new position in the opposite direction.

For example, to use the wheat situation noted earlier, a trader of the author's acquaintance sold May wheat short at $4.02 per bushel—extremely close to the contract high for the year. The trader stayed with his short position and added to it until the contract price fell to around $3.83½. At this point he closed out his short position, having realized some 18 cents per bushel profit on the downside movement. Then on June 18, he immediately reestablished a new position by going long May wheat. He was convinced that the market had found bottom.

Instead of the price on the contract reversing its course—as the trader expected—it just paused and fluttered around for four sessions, then gapped down on the 25th and plummeted to $3.74.

My friend was "chased in" at $3.76, on June 27, along with a bunch of other weak-handed bulls; all of whom got caught in the squeeze. After having profited from an 18 cent down move on his *short* position, he then proceeded to lose nearly half of it back by his quick-change jump to the *long* side of May wheat. Every day he stayed with the losing long position he felt the price just had to go up! But it didn't go up; not until he had been blown out of his position.

A hard fact to be learned early in any successful speculative career is that prices don't have to do anything except fluctuate! There is no right price for anything except the price the market puts on it. While the 50 cent slide in May wheat prices which is being examined is a large move, there have been much larger ones—and the possibility of their recurrence can't be ignored.

The trader referred to above undertook to argue with the market. He was in step with the price move when he sold May wheat short. As price moved lower, he added to his position, which increased his opportunities for profit, and prices continued to move in his favor. Then, based on nothing more than a hunch, he decided that it was now time for a price turnup. He closed out his May wheat holdings and established a long position in the face of a dramatically deteriorating price trend!

He deserved the loss he took.

Take Time-Out between Positions

There is a great deal to be said for calling a rest period between speculative exposures in a given contract. If prices have been moving higher, at the point at which a reversal occurs a price plateau is likely to develop before a full-fledged downside correction occurs. The sideways price pattern may persist for a few hours, a few sessions, or several weeks. There is no speculative purpose served in maintaining a position in a market which is going nowhere. By remaining on the sidelines and observing price development, you will have risk capital available to step in at the point at which a new pattern does appear.

In the interim, the best position is no position. Above all else, steer clear of establishing any new position contrary to demonstrated market direction. Persistence in price movement can be a terrible enemy, and there is nothing which can prove as ruinous as being out of step with the market.

"Quick change artists" in speculation usually defeat themselves through their search for price tops and bottoms. Successful speculators look for a discernible trend and then get aboard. They don't worry about missing part of the move, so long as they can be with the parade over most of its route. The highest risk exposure in price behavior is at the reversal points (at each successive top and bottom). The prudent speculator selects the lesser risks. He leaves top- and bottom-picking to those who believe they possess second sight or have a crystal ball which is well-nigh infallible.

Trading on News

Inexperienced commodity speculators are often distressed to discover that prices sometimes fall sharply in the face of bullish news or climb suddenly on bearish news. When this kind of thing happens, the phenomenon may be viewed as a contradiction of the facts.

In order to understand the behavior of market prices in the face of news, it must be remembered that a primary function of the market is to discount the future. Stated another way, the market presumably knows everything which is known by all of the people buying and selling in it. Their orders to buy and sell are a direct reflection of each trader's personal knowledge and appraisal of events to come. The market, like a computer, accepts all of these positive and negative inputs, adds up the total and delivers an answer in the form of price stability, price increase, or price deterioration.

An inexperienced trader might consider a story in *The Journal of Commerce,* which announces the fact that a foreign government has placed an order for several million tons of U.S. grain, as being an excellent reason to buy the grain futures concerned. In checking with his broker, however, he may discover that prices on the commodity involved are actually lower as a result of the publicity. The cause and effect relationship is obvious on closer examination:

It might be assumed that the trade has been generally aware of the pending business for several weeks. As negotiations proceed, traders hear bits and trickles of information and, from these, piece together an idea concerning the size of the export order involved. Now the publicity appears; at last the story is out. It may be that the size of the order actually placed by the foreign interest is smaller than the trade had expected. Disappointment is best written in lower prices.

Wheat Prices Fall, Hurt by World Glut, Export Competition

By WENDY L. WALL
Staff Reporter of The Wall Street Journal

Most wheat futures set life-of-contract lows as the world wheat glut and fierce competition for export markets continued to weigh on prices.

Wheat for December delivery fell 4.5 cents a bushel to $3.4225, down almost 9% from 1984 highs last spring. Recent declines in wheat prices have erased the gains of October and November, which came in response to adverse weather for planting the winter wheat crop in many areas.

New indications of stepped-up competition for global markets led to some selling, analysts said. Argentina, now in the midst of its wheat harvest, cut its export tax on wheat over the weekend. Rumors circulated that the Argentines, who typically are aggressive wheat exporters, had sold two million metric tons of wheat and corn to Iran.

Many large grain-exporting nations, including Argentina, Australia, Canada and the European Community, are undercutting U.S. wheat prices, said Dale Gustafson, analyst in Chicago for Drexel Burnham Lambert Inc. Jerry Rector, world wheat analyst at the U.S. Agriculture Department, said, "The price structure of the world wheat market is very competitive right now."

The competition comes in the midst of a world wheat glut. Late Monday, the Agriculture Department raised its estimate of the 1984–85 world wheat crop slightly to 506.8 million metric tons. That's 3.6% larger than last year's bumper harvest of 489 million metric tons.

U.S. prices also have been hurt by China's evident failure to meet the terms of its long-term wheat agreement with the U.S. China, which has reaped a series of record wheat harvests, almost certainly won't renew its grain-purchasing accords with the U.S. or other trade partners.

In soybeans, prices opened higher largely because of an early easing of the dollar, but drifted lower as the dollar strengthened. A strong dollar tends to weaken overseas demand for grain priced in dollars. Also, some traders closed out positions in anticipation of an Agriculture Department report released after trading ended.

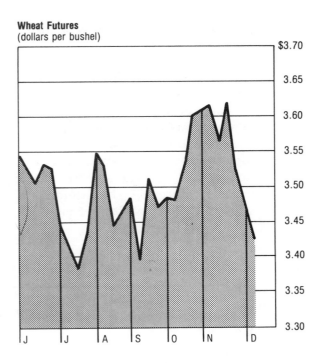

Wheat Futures
(dollars per bushel)

In that report, the department raised its prediction of U.S. soybean stock-piles as of Sept. 1, 1985, by 7.5% to 215 million bushels from the 200 million bushels it previously forecast. Next fall's pre-harvest surplus is expected to exceed this year's level by 23%.

Wheat growing and marketing is a global business. The price any farmer can expect to obtain for his crop will depend on how much of the grain is available in other regions of the world. This is the harsh fact that keeps on defeating U.S. political efforts to sustain artificial prices on agricultural products. A domestic price may be "pegged" but, unless we can consume our entire output, sooner or later the realities of the world market must be reckoned with.

The market has a tendency to overbuy good news and oversell bad news. As knowledge of the pending export business gains currency among trading interests, a flurry of excitement results and its immediate effect is seen in rising prices. As prices do ascend, holders of short positions in the affected contracts will be impelled to reduce their holdings or close out their positions entirely. In either event, the previous sellers of the grain now must become buyers as they attempt to offset. As their orders reach the market, prices are driven up even further as a result of the imbalance in sell/buy pressures which result.

The market is discounting the good news about export activity. In addition to the new buying orders which the good news triggers, a slight—or significant—short squeeze may also develop. In combination, prices may move somewhat higher than the size of the export business which started it could, by any reasonable appraisal, justify.

With public announcement of the export order which has been placed, there is no longer any room for speculation about the trade details; although the quantity involved may be sizeable, it may, nevertheless, be well under trade hopes. At the same time, many of the disadvantaged shorts may have been chased in in the face of rising prices. Thus, both the new long buying and offsetting by shorts that support higher price levels have disappeared; and without these elements, prices must fall.

There is an old saying among commodity speculators that "by the time you have heard the news, it's too late to use it." With few exceptions, the axiom will prove itself in practice. The market does not often reward a trader for being able to read a newspaper. Most people can do so. The market does reward a trader for being able to weigh unknown but forthcoming events and draw conclusions about composite effects; provided, of course, that the trader has the courage to back his judgment by taking a market position.

It Pays to Keep Informed

The foregoing should not be taken to mean that following the news is a waste of time. Most emphatically, it is not a waste of time. The value of following news developments closely, however, lies in sharpening a trader's overall perspective and feel for the supply/demand situation, and enhancing his ability to forecast probable actions on the part of governments and other official and public interests who can exert great weight in the marketplace. The events about which a trader must conjecture and from which will emanate his greatest profits or losses concerns things of which the general market is not yet aware; or about which the traders have a wrong idea. It is also worth emphasizing that, while market prices are always authoritative, the traders can be, on balance, badly wrong in their overall appraisal of a particular situation which is developing.

We will now deal with one of these examples in detail.

Trading into Major Crop Reports

There are few considerations which take precedence over supply/demand balance in the major commodities. Populations must be fed, clothed, and housed, and commodities constitute the raw materials with which these activities are made possible. The U.S. government, through the U.S. Department of Agriculture, has very properly concerned itself with making regular statistical projections of crop size and consumption at designated intervals. Through the periods which cover crop planting, growth, and harvest, estimates are made by the Crop Reporting Board which are designed to keep producers, consumers, and commercial interests apprised of the overall situation surrounding our major commodities.

Crop reports are always released at 3 P.M. Eastern Standard Time, after the commodity markets have closed throughout the country on the selected report day. Since the information is gathered from thousands of sources and maintained in the strictest confidence, the figures are available to absolutely no one before their public release to all who want them. The impact of these government reports on price can be tremendous; especially if the data contains a major surprise for the trade.

The reports always follow an established form, and the release schedule is equally firm. The first estimate is a forecast of winter wheat and rye plantings—and is made available about December 20 of the year preceding the projected harvest. The initial wheat and rye forecast is followed up by revised projections which are released at monthly intervals from April through August. Monthly forecasts of production on all spring grains are commenced in March, and comparable statistics are released at monthly intervals thereafter until the harvest is completed and the final, actual production is known.

Each crop report includes estimated production in the current crop which is either being planted, raised, or harvested; and each report compares the latest crop prospects with the estimate which was released a month earlier, and the previous year's *actual* production figure. The projection reflected in each crop forecast is the government agency's best judgment at the end of the month just passed. If weather, for example, has been disadvantageous in the meantime, the forecast figures may need to be adjusted downward, somewhat below the projection, as a result of two or three weeks of poor growing conditions, after the data was assembled.

It goes without saying that a sizeable increase or decrease in anticipated crop size, as compared with previous crop averages, can be a mighty influence on price. In 1966, as a case in point, the trade expected a soybean crop of about 890 million bushels as everyone awaited the September crop forecast. In the trading session immediately preceding release of the official figures, the price on nearby (September and November) soybean contracts climbed precipitously, posting more than 8 cents per bushel gain in the last half hour or so of trading. A surge of new buying was stimulated by people taking new long positions in the market, and shorts added to the upward pressure as they were forced to buy back their contracts. A squeeze developed against the disadvantaged earlier sellers. Higher prices ruled to the closing bell.

When the government figures were released 45 minutes after the close, the 1966 soybean crop was estimated at 926 million bushels. Soybean prices dropped the limit of 10 cents per bushel during each of the next two trading sessions and continued to steadily deteriorate for three weeks thereafter. Traders who had properly anticipated a big increase in the soybean crop, sold the commodity short, and stuck to their guns in the face of the squeeze, were richly rewarded for having done so. The market was wrong in having posted high prices on the commodity in expectation of a small crop. The longs who stayed with their long positions made large paper profits during the immediate prereport period, but sustained major losses when the crop facts were known.

Never Underestimate an Important Report

This discussion is largely repetitious of material which appears elsewhere in this volume, but its repetition is deserved for the purpose of underscoring a most valuable warning: Unless you are unquestioningly convinced that you have caught the market in error, *never carry a flat open position, either long or short, into a major crop report.* The hazards involved are far too great! The events which may follow may be ruinous!

Success in speculation does not require that a speculator plunge himself into possible financial ruin for the opportunity of realizing profits. The wise speculator will only undertake those risks which he feels offer a better opportunity for profit than for loss. A risk which is incalculable is a "sucker" risk; and a crop report may involve this order of risk. If so, it ceases to be speculation in the true sense; it comprises a gamble. And, as such, it should be studiously avoided.

Beware Trading on the Opening

Commodity markets are not continuous. Trading is conducted for only a few hours each business day. Overnight, pressures build up in the form of accumulated orders waiting for execution when the next session begins. The balance between orders to buy and orders to sell will be seen in price levels, and can produce price aberrations which are dramatic but short-lived, lasting only a few seconds or a few minutes. If buying pressure substantially exceeds offerings in a given commodity contract, it may open at a considerably higher price level than it closed on the preceding day. Overnight news which is known but has not yet had an opportunity to be introduced into the pricing equation will assert itself in the first seconds of the opening. Its influence will tend to diminish as the market has an opportunity to discount it. But, for the span of time during which it is being digested, its effect may be out of all proportion to its longer-term implications.

Placing market orders—fillable at whatever price prevails—on an opening may be an exceedingly hazardous practice, since no one really knows where prices will open. A prudent speculator should have a fairly solid notion about the price level at which he wants to buy or sell something. Opening prices are full of surprises, and surprises can be disastrous.

In view of these considerations, the better course to follow is that of waiting until the first flurry of trading has passed before drawing any solid opinions about prevailing price level. If this procedure is not desirable or feasible, then the use of price limits on an order is the next best thing; although limits will sometimes deprive the pit broker of an opportunity to obtain split-second execution.

Beware Trading on the Close

A philosophy of caution should also apply generally to trading "on the close." As previously noted, pit traders fall into several categories including day traders, position traders, and scalpers. A good deal of evening-up takes place in the last minute or two of each session, particularly in actively traded contracts. If the pit is long toward the end of the session, it can confidently be expected that before the closing bell rings there will be an appreciable amount of selling on the part of the day traders and scalpers; this, since the pit participants concerned do not want to carry any open positions overnight. When this final wave of selling hits, prices are likely to be driven down. The reverse would be equally true if the close approaches with the pit being, on balance, substantially short. As the locals buy back their short contracts, the flurry of demand which results may drive prices upward.

Many of the same hazards exist with respect to a market order on the close as was pointed out in connection with the opening of a session. However, the closing moments of trade are usually less volatile than the opening, except in the face of special circumstances which may produce extraordinary results. As a general rule, market orders at either the opening or closing of a session represent a higher order of risk, as concerns the levels at which they may be executed, than the same kind of order introduced into the market at any other time of day.

To recapitulate, then, price aberrations which represent the greatest departures from the normal trading range usually occur in the first (or the last) few minutes of the session. They grow out of pent-up overnight demand or offerings, which call for immediate execution (or may reflect position imbalance among the locals in the pit). There may be times when a public speculator will deliberately choose these situations for the accomplishment of a specific transaction, but as a general rule it should be recognized that the market's reliability in reflecting values tends to be at its lowest ebb at the beginning and the end of a session.

Beware the Last Days of Contract Life

The majority of all commodity contracts have a trading life of about one year. During this period of time, the volume of trade in the contract tends to pick up, and the open-interest usually grows proportionately. The larger the open-interest in a given contract, the more unfilled positions outstanding in it. Open-interest, as reported by clearinghouses and the Commodity Futures Trading Commission, represents only one side of open positions. For example, in a futures in which there are

1,000 contracts held long, there must also be 1,000 contracts held short; total positions, therefore, is 2,000 contracts. Open-interest would be reported as 1,000 contracts, equal to either the long or the short side of total contracts held open in the maturity.

Since less than 2 percent of all futures contracts are satisfied by actual delivery of the physical commodity, it stands to reason that most of the existing positions will be closed out by offset prior to the termination of trading in each particular futures. In the terminal phase of a maturing contract, a sort of tug-of-war develops between the longs and the shorts. Obviously, the longs want higher prices so they can sell out at a profit. The shorts want lower prices so they can buy back at a profit. The eventual outcome may rest importantly on which side is willing or able to sit tight the longest.

In order to offset, the shorts in an expiring contract must buy back the thing which they previously sold. The best place to obtain the needed futures is from the longs who likewise, in order to offset their open positions, must sell out the contracts they previously purchased.

So the economic antagonists face each other in the pit and hope prices will move in the direction of their respective advantage. The exercise is certainly thrilling and can be highly profitable if you are fortunate enough to be with the winners. Should you be a member of the vanquished camp, the results can be precisely the reverse—and great losses can be quickly sustained.

Leave the Last Days to Others

Public speculators should leave the last days of trading to the full-time professionals or to public traders who have yet to learn better. In so doing, the unpredictability of contract termination price behavior can be avoided, but this is not all. There is an additional hazard inherent in trading the tail end of a commodity contract which can hardly be overlooked: all longs who have not offset by the last bell must accept delivery of the physical commodity; all shorts who have not offset must make delivery of the physical commodity.

A public speculator is rarely ever equipped to economically fulfill delivery requirements. Taking or making delivery almost invariably represents a bad move for anyone except a producer or a dealer in cash merchandise. Holding out to the bitter end in an expiring contract is speculative brinksmanship which cannot be recommended to the public trader on any basis. This, even though the final gyrations in price which may eventuate as a volatile contract goes off the board may look most enticing.

Trading Limits Don't Apply to Cash

It has already been noted that commodity futures markets impose limitations on the maximum amount that prices may change—up or down—on each contract in a single session. In corn, for example, each futures price presently has a 10 cent maximum allowable increase or decrease in the current session, above or below the closing price of the previous session. While this provides a built-in protection for the trader in futures contracts, comparable limitations do not exist in the cash market.

A speculator who holds a short position until the expiration of futures trading must, once trading has come to an end, make arrangements to deliver the physical product. In order to do so, he must, if necessary, buy the commodity in the cash market and deliver it to a qualified long futures holder. Situations have existed where the market price on the maturing futures was at considerable variance with the effective price in the cash market. In September of 1966, for example, the shorts who were forced to deliver soybeans after the termination of trading in the expired futures had no choice except to buy them in the seriously undersupplied cash market. In order to obtain deliverable grades, many of the shorts who had failed to offset before the end of the trading had to pay as much as 25 cents per bushel over the final futures price to get the supplies they needed. Needless to say, by failing to offset, they sustained even greater losses in meeting their obligations to deliver.

The risks in last-day trading are great—and may be incalculable; and taking or making delivery involves both inconvenience and handling costs. A public speculator usually wants no part of either.

Weather Markets

Of all the imponderables which confront producers of growing crops and speculators in the commodities concerned, none is more fraught with uncertainty than weather itself.

It might be said that every crop has its own temperature/moisture combination which represents optimum growing conditions. Anything less than this ideal constitutes a greater or lesser threat to harvest prospects. From the time the new crop goes into the ground as seed until it's finally harvested, growers and traders watch weather developments eagerly—and they hardly ever like what they see! Anything which seems to threaten the well-being of the crop will send prices higher in expectation of some relative shortage. As each successive problem is relieved by moderating temperatures or the arrival of much-needed precipitation, prices which were sent higher by a weather scare return to lower levels, in recognition of the fact that the particular danger has passed.

Weather markets usually take their cues from weather averages. This is to say that the trade will view as "normal" the average temperature ranges and precipitation, as reported by the U.S. Weather Bureau in a given area over a period of 5 or 10 years.

The Crop Reporting Service and agricultural extention agencies report intentions, planting progress, and crop development at regular intervals during the planning, planting, and growing season. If excessively wet weather interferes with the normal planting pattern, a price response can be expected. With the seed in the ground, should dry weather delay germination or wind storms blow the topsoil away and expose the seed, prices will rise in direct response.

If the fields dry out and planting picks up, or should rain or snow fall in adequate amounts to germinate the seed and commence the growing cycle, the market will immediately note this in the form of reduced prices. Downturns always come in the face of conditions which seem to promise an improved or adequate harvest, and vice versa.

Weather markets offer one of the best demonstrations of the trader's tendency to overbuy bad news and oversell good news. The fluctuations in weather market prices can be sharply precipitous, and directional reversals can take place suddenly—either in response to actual weather changes, or a change in weather prospects, as reflected in overnight, 5 day and 30 day forecasts.

Nature is not really as perverse as weather market evidence, as reflected in commodity prices, would seem to indicate. Each year presents a somewhat different weather pattern in terms of the schedule of arrival followed by growing precipitation and temperatures; but when each crop year is over, the composite result usually varies only slightly from recent historic norms. Wide price aberrations, which are a distinguishing characteristic of weather markets, grow out of the fact that supply/demand relationships must stay in fairly close equilibrium in order to maintain stable price levels. Any appreciable deviation in crop size brings highly disproportionate effects in price levels. It pays to remember, "every crop is usually lost two or three times before it is finally harvested." Don't make long-term decisions on what may be only short-term conditions.

Weather markets offer excellent opportunities for short-term trading activity. The recommended procedure is always to buy dips and sell bulges. In view of the highly erratic price behavior which can be encountered during the preharvest period when weather is the major price influence, stop-loss orders must be carefully placed on every position taken, and adjusted as often as needed. Failure to do so is needlessly courting disaster. Once established, stay with a position until your stop-loss is hit. You may ride a weather move right into a long-term trend, but usually it's shorter-term.

There is no blanket rule as to whether the long or short side of the market should be preferred, except to keep in mind that the major price changes will emanate from changing weather conditions. If temperature and moisture have been marginal and prices have risen in response thereto, a continuation of the situation can be expected to gradually escalate prices further and—should bad conditions persist, threatening disaster proportions—there is no telling how far they might go. At the first hint of a rain storm in the face of unusually dry weather, however, downside price movement will come suddenly. The drop can cover the equivalent of several percentage points in product price, as the market discounts the effects contained in a changing weather pattern.

When weather conditions are good and the situation begins to deteriorate, the market will immediately read bullish implications into the change, and firmer prices will promptly result, in accordance with the market's reevaluation of the overall picture. Remember that prices usually fall faster than they rise, though.

Weather markets offer exciting and profitable speculative opportunities, but weather-market prices are always fickle. The prudent trader must constantly view the weather-market trading situation as short-term. He must be prepared to take small losses as often as necessary for the privilege of being on board for larger profits on major moves. One such larger success will more than make up for several small disappointments.

Trading Dull Markets

A quiet market, like a quiet youngster, is probably up to mischief. Several things may be involved in a market which appears in the doldrums. Whenever prices have been moving in a given direction for a period of time, and at fairly high trading volume levels, the trend usually can be expected to wear itself out eventually. A listless trade may signal the coming event.

For example, if corn begins an upward price trend at $2.20 per bushel and over a period of several weeks moves to $2.40 per bushel, it stands to reason that, in the process, the longs who bought at the lower levels will have made substantial profits; the shorts who sold in the face of the events outlined will have sustained equivalent losses.

A time will come when repeatedly disappointed shorts will move to the sidelines, unwilling to assume additional exposures. Some of the longs will provide offerings, as they elect to take their profits from the price move and drop out. But liquidation on the part of existing longs will not be sufficient, in the absence of a real price reversal, to maintain high volume activity. As the price move reaches the end of its interim cycle, trading will slow as if reflecting the market's opinion that "the price is about right." There is a trading axiom which usually can be accepted, that "A market which can't go up must go down."

This gives rise to another trading rule which can save a speculator impressive amounts of money:

> Never buy a quiet spell following a price rise.

Conversely, when prices have been consistently deteriorating over a period of time, disenchanted longs will finally despair of picking a bottom and move to the sidelines to await a clear indication of reversal. When this buying is taken out of the market, trading volume will diminish and the only real buying demand will involve shorts who have profited from the down move, and are now ready to cash all or part of their paper profits. When trading volume dries up following a major down move, extreme caution with respect to the establishment of any new short positions is clearly indicated: "A market that can't go down must go up."

> Never sell a dull market which follows a significant downside move.

The foregoing is merely a restatement of the trading principle noted elsewhere, that it makes good sense to sell bulges and buy dips. In doing so, however, the trader must always bear in mind that the dip or the bulge may be a small interval of fluctuation in a larger, and continuing, price trend. The only protection against this hazard is a well-placed stop-loss order which will close out the position, should prices resume their upward or downward channel after a "breathing spell."

Trade the Big Ones

The best trading markets are the big, active markets. In the first place, they offer the greatest liquidity. They more easily accommodate execution of buying and selling orders, with but minimal impact on price levels. Put another way, an active market has better "muscle tone." It is able to withstand greater counterforces without being deterred from its price course. A dull market is likely to be a thin market, narrowly balanced on an equilibrium point between extremely limited buying and selling pressures. It may take only a slight nudge in one direction or the other to send prices sharply higher or lower.

If a trader is enamoured of the wispy hope for finding interim tops and bottoms, market dullness is the principal symptom which should be looked for. These are the points in trading from which price reversals usually take place.

20

Equities versus Commodities: The Realities of Relative Risks

The serious student of speculation will now be well served by going back and rereading the Introduction to this volume, as a background refresher for the contents of this chapter.

The unique considerations that separate gambling, investment, and speculation from each other have already been covered in some detail there. They will only be briefly redefined here.

- *Gambling* is an attempt to predict the outcome of a contrived contest that has been given an element of economic risk by the placement of wagers. Gambling may be for entertainment or for financial gain; however the risk in gambling is a risk created by the gamblers and would not otherwise exist.
- *Investment* is the placement of money in usage where there is hope for an earned return in the form of rent, interest, and/or dividends.
- *Speculation* is the placement of money in usage where the return, if any, must be generated by a change in the price of the underlying asset. A speculative risk is a natural risk. It may be shifted from one bearer to another through the process of hedging or insurance; it can not be obviated.

The puritan work ethic has always insisted on drawing clear moral distinctions between money made via gambling and speculation, compared to investment. The moralist vote has always come down on the side of those who "make money the old-fashioned way. They *earn* it!"

Regardless of how effective the slogan may be in a television commercial, it doesn't have much economic substance.

While a $100 bet on a football game can be dismissed as sheer trivia, *investment* and *speculation* are equally crucial to the continued functioning of our business system. Neither is better, more ethical, nor more desirable than the other. In a given situation one may be more appropriate than the other, but morality has nothing to do with the judgment. This, because economics is not a moral discipline.

Speculation Is Universal and Unavoidable

A thoroughly undeserved mantle of economic virtue has long cloaked the stock markets, on the wispy fiction that stock market participants are all investors. Commodity markets, on the other hand, have by direction and innuendo been demeaned as institutions devoted to the practice of a kind of economic dark art: not illegal, perhaps, but not quite respectable either!

The actuality is that every owner of a share of common stock is a speculator by definition, unless the held equity was acquired only as a means of obtaining its dividend—and whatever price it might command in the market from time to time is of no interest. This attitude isn't held by many shareholders, regardless of how they choose to label their activities. Price appreciation is the name of the game in the stock market, whether the particular price applies to stock that the individual owns, or relates to the Dow Jones Average and is taken as the financial pulse of our economic body.

Speculation is universal and unavoidable. Speculation is the central impetus in virtually everything people undertake to do with their excess capital. Granting this—and the case seems beyond argument—the prime question to be answered is, what facet of market activity offers the best opportunity for profitable speculation? Which business arena is the most susceptible to analysis and prognostication? In which category of trading activity will the speculator find the greatest degree of even-handed treatment? These are all crucial considerations in the search for speculative success.

Speculation in Corporate Stocks

Any evaluation of equities as a speculative vehicle must begin with a clear understanding of what a corporation is and how it is managed.

When a private company issues stock and goes public, ownership is spread much more widely; but management control may be affected hardly at all. The same people who previously occupied positions of authority in the firm continue to chart the course and direct the activities of the business. Reports will be much more widely disseminated to both stockholders and the public at large, because this is required under applicable laws, rules, and regulations administered by the Securities and Exchange Commission (SEC). Internal management methods, however, may remain essentially unchanged.

The Wall Street Journal, Barron's and the financial pages of daily newspapers may carry stories that examine management effectiveness, market responses to the company's products, and profitability prospects in both the near-term and over longer periods of time. An annual stockholders meeting will be held, at which anyone who owns a share of stock in the publicly held firm is ostensibly entitled to direct praise, questions, or criticism at the management team. This done, the stockholders then vote their shares in choosing a slate of directors and officers who will preside over the corporation during the coming year. When the agenda has been completed the gavel falls; the company officers heave a great sigh of relief; and the shareholders disperse to resume their private affairs—leaving corporate management in the hands of their designees: *the insiders*.

The Who and Why of the Insiders

A stock corporation may have millions of shareholders scattered throughout the United States and around the world, the overwhelming majority of whom will never have so much as written a letter to the corporate headquarters. Their interest and involvement in the firm is limited to checking the price of its stock occasionally, and hoping that the dividend—if any—will be maintained and enlarged. Beyond these cursory attentions paid to his stock value, the public shareholder typically leaves management of the company to those who are supposed to be looking out for stockholder interests—and are being paid well to do it!

Depending on the size of the corporation and the management philosophy its principals choose to follow, the kind and amount of information about its ongoing affairs that gets out between annual stockholder meetings can vary tremendously. Most companies pursue a disclosure course that hews closely to the minimums set down by the SEC. The only time they might deliberately open up is when doing so is felt to be corporately self-serving and competitively advantageous. This is to say that, so long as informational minimums imposed by statute are met, great latitude exists for the exercise of executive judgment.

Secrecy is a well-recognized element in competitive effectiveness. It is understood that General Motors isn't going to share its new technology with Ford and Chrysler any sooner than it must. Ideally the competition will get its first glimpse of a product innovation the same time the customers do. Apple and IBM will go to almost any extremes to maintain a cloak of secrecy about the next gadget being readied in their ongoing struggle for market share of the computer business.

> We have good news—and we have bad news! We're going to give you the good news first.

Apple Says Profit Increased Sixfold in Its First Period

By a Wall Street Journal Staff Reporter

CUPERTINO, Calif.—Apple Computer Inc. expects to post earnings of more than $37 million for its fiscal first quarter, a sixfold increase from a year earlier.

At a meeting of securities analysts in San Francisco, the personal-computer maker said it anticipated per-share profit of between 60 cents and 75 cents for the quarter ended December 28. The quarterly performance has been predicted by most analysts.

Apple treasurer Charles Berger, citing particularly strong Christmas-season sales of the Apple II line of computers, said he expected revenue for the quarter will be about $700 million. That is more than double the $316.2 million the company reported in the year-earlier quarter, during which the company cut prices on several models and spent large sums to develop and market its new Macintosh computer.

In the year-ago quarter, Apple had net income of $5.8 million, or 10 cents a share. Those figures included a $1.4 million after-tax gain from the settlement of litigation.

The company expects to announce its first-quarter results within a few days. Mr. Berger said Apple had about 61 million average shares outstanding.

In national over-the- counter trading yesterday, Apple closed at $30.625 a share, up 87.5 cents.

IBM and Apple Report

By Christine Winter

INTERNATIONAL Business Machines Corp. Thursday reported higher fourth quarter and 1984 earnings that were above most analysts' projections, while Apple Computer Inc. posted dramatically higher sales and earnings.

However, price discounting and inventory problems for Apple sent its stock price down sharply Thursday.

Apple reported earnings for its fiscal first quarter, ended December 28, jumped to $46 million, or 75 cents a share, from $5.82 million, or 10 cents a share, a year earlier. Sales more than doubled, rising to $698.2 million from $316.2 million.

APPLE President John Sculley said the Cupertino, California-based company was a "big winner" over the Christmas period, selling more than 500,000 computers. A significant number of those sales were reported to have been made to educational institutions at discounts as high as 40 percent, however.

"Retail sales of the [Apple] IIe and IIc together during Christmas were double the IIe sales of the previous year, but the IBM PCjr surprised everybody and did better than either one, cutting into Apple's projected sales," said Jan Lewis of InfoCorp, a market research firm in Cupertino.

Sculley confirmed that industry sales at the retail level "fell below dealers' expectations," resulting in expanded inventory. He predicted that this would create an "extremely challenging" second fiscal quarter.

SOME ANALYSTS took this to mean that the good news is over and that hard times lie ahead. A number changed their recommendations on Apple, causing the stock to fall. Apple stock, traded over the counter, closed at $28.12, down $2.12.

Source: *Chicago Tribune*, January 18, 1985.

The tremendous increase in corporate profits during the first quarter of its fiscal year brought smiles to stockholder faces and almost a dollar surge in Apple's over-the-counter stock price. Many new buyers were attracted at the higher price also. So much for the "good news."

Three days later Sculley admitted that, while Apple had indeed sold a lot of computers, much of the sales volume had been obtained at deep discounts. The stock promptly fell $2.12. Anyone who bought stock on the basis of the January 15 publicity was neatly "trapped" for a 7½ percent loss 72 hours later.

Insiders who understood the situation and who knew the "bad news" had to come out sooner or later were in a position to make a lot of money or a lot of friends on their informational advantage.

While corporate security seeks ways to keep the competition in the dark, the same mind-set also keeps the shareholders relatively—or woefully—uninformed about things that are going on. Often these covert corporate activities have the most direct bearing on the value of the corporate shares in public hands.

Meanwhile, Back on Mahogany Row

An extremely small group of top executives make the crucial decisions in most publicly held corporations. The top-management coterie ordinarily includes most or all of the following officers:

- Chairman of the Board of Directors
- Vice Chairman of the Board of Directors
- President and Chief Executive Officer
- Executive Vice President
- Chairman of the Finance Committee
- Treasurer
- Corporate Vice President
- Secretary
- General Counsel

Beyond these individuals, the organization chart also lists a group of operating committees; usually headed up by one or more of the top officers listed above, and fleshed out by subordinate line and staff executives who are on the corporate payroll. Outside consultants and advisors chosen for their specialized credentials are often ex-officio members of the operating committees, the roster of which will include some or all of these:

- Finance Committee
- Audit Committee
- New Products Committee
- Acquisitions Committee
- Marketing Committee
- Labor/Management Committee
- Public and Stockholder Relations Committee
- Wage and Salary Steering Committee

Overarching this assortment of function and responsibility is a board of directors that, in theory at least, represents the composite judgment, philosophy, and ultimate authority of the company. Since members of the board are elected by the stockholders, it is presumed that they—out of gratitude or loyalty—will zealously protect stockholder interests against all alien forces.

Theory versus Practicality

Corporate function, as it has evolved, makes some implicit claims to virtue that fail to stand up under scrutiny. The first of these notions is that the board of directors, by reason of their being elected by the stockholders, give rank and file shareholders a powerful and continuing voice in internal corporate affairs.

In practice, the board of directors of a corporation may only meet quarterly, and one of these convocations will be the annual stockholders meeting. As a result, the time available for board business is severely limited. Corporate officers decide what items will, out of legal consideration or operational necessity, be placed on the agenda. The agenda, in turn, controls what will and what will not be discussed and voted on in any board of directors meeting.

Procedures usually exist for an individual director to raise an unscheduled concern under "other business," but it really isn't recommended. A director who persists in this kind of nonconformity risks loss of his constituency among other board members, and possible loss of his seat when the proxies are cast the next time.

In view of these considerations, day-to-day direction of a publicly held company rests firmly in the hands of its officers and its operating committees. The board of directors will rarely become involved in anything except policy matters to which their attention is invited, or issues in which executive consensus does not exist. In the interim, the officer cadre will keep the board advised of company accomplishments by a variety of means. We will now examine some of these.

Insiders Have Inside Information

The most important information in any company has to do with its profitability. In order to hold a stable price on the stock exchange, a firm must make money. In order for a stock price to improve, company performance must improve, or company prospects must improve. The influences that will send a stock price higher or lower are legion.

A wave of buying in a particular stock can result from improved sales, higher profits on sales, greater demand (cold weather) for a company's product (heating oil), restrictions (import quotas) on competitive products, merger talk, a stock-split rumor, an increased dividend, a large government contract obtained. The reverse of these bullish influences will send the price tumbling down on waves of pessimism about future prospects.

Regardless of what may be going on in or around a company at any point in time, it must be assumed that the chief executive officer will be the first to know; while the rank-and-file stockholder will be the last to know. It is this lag in communications that distinguishes the insider from the outsider in a stock corporation. Some of the communications lag is unavoidable. Much of it is deliberately engineered by corporate managers.

Most companies exist in a highly volatile atmosphere, where seasonal considerations, competitive pressures, labor/management problems, fluctuating interest rates, and like considerations keep corporate fortunes in an almost constant state of flux. Quarterly financial reports are standard in business, but the score-keeping activity never stops in the accounting department. Production data, cash flow, inventory adjustments, payroll costs, tax liabilities, and related information is being endlessly "crunched" by people and computers, and projected in the form of anticipated profit or loss.

Outsiders have to wait for the *Quarterly Report of Earnings* to find out how the company fared during the last reporting period, but insiders have virtually the same information a week—or perhaps a month earlier! It is standard practice for the company's auditors to make a preliminary report to one or more of the operating committees at least several days before the formalized information that will subsequently be released to the media is even reduced to print.

Knowing that Chrysler is going to announce an all-time earnings record, or that Apple Computer is realizing six times the amount of profit reported in the same period a year earlier, confers a tremendous trading advantage on individuals who have prior knowledge of those events taking place in the firm. The crucial question is whether or not these secrets will be kept confidential until everyone can read all about it in *The Wall Street Journal* at the same time. Before attempting to answer this, let's see who the people are who have access to inside information.

The Grapevine Never Sleeps

For all of their prepossessing facades, companies of whatever size or complexity are somewhat expanded versions of families. The production worker may not go to lunch with the executive vice president, but the production worker eats lunch with a quality control inspector; who attends aerobic exercise classes with a pool secretary; who takes a night-school class with the executive vice president's administrative assistant! Knowing this, it will come as no surprise to learn that the executive vice president and the production worker share some greater or lesser amount of their supposedly private funds of information. The conduit isn't as quick and easy as direct access, but the informal chain of interlocking relationships will still get a lot of information handled. The "trickle-down" theory has its detractors in the economic community, but that it works with amazing efficiency in transmitting company "leaks" is simply not to be denied.

Let's assume that at least one memorandum is written concerning a dramatic increase in company earnings. One is enough. Informal dissemination through secretaries, messengers, Xerox machines, and conversations in company lunch rooms—with no nefarious intentions whatsoever—can, in a matter of a day or two, make the company improvement common knowledge among at least several strata of employees. And this, well before the stockholders have any opportunity to see the story in print or hear about it on TV.

With this as a background, it should be seen that insider information is by no means limited to the ears of those usually considered to be insiders. But even if it were, the secondary dissemination potentials are still huge.

People Are Not Angels

Securities and Exchange Commission (SEC) rules governing insider trading, rumormongering, etc., are necessarily predicated on the notion that the people selected to direct the affairs of our major corporations will not—by word or deed—make personal market decisions based on their inherent informational advantage. Just how these folks are expected to leave their information in the office when they go home is never quite cleared up. However, the public is expected, perforce, to believe that their managers are of such personal probity, high ethics, and unswerving loyalty to the corporate ideal that they will uniformly shun opportunities that are sure to enrich them. Legal penalties exist to punish exceptions to the rule of presumed respectability by those awkward enough to get caught. However, the very paucity of cases brought to the bar for insider violations seems to urge a thesis that this kind of corporate sinning is, indeed, extremely rare. A more reasonable explanation is that discovering and pressing a case against someone for violation of securities laws by improperly using insider advantage is a terribly difficult case to prove beyond a reasonable doubt. In a fit of unaccustomed candor, a highly placed SEC official once assured your author, "Unless a guy is pretty stupid, we're not going to catch him! After all, they know the game as well as we do—and they've got the corporation to hide in!"

Insider Trading Charges May Put T. Boone on Grill

DAN DORFMAN
Chicago Sun Times
Corporate raider T. Boone Pickens Jr., the wily chairman of Mesa Petroleum Co. of Amarillo, Texas, may find himself embroiled in a hot new controversy: the possible use of inside information by friends to capitalize on Pickens' pursuit of big-name oil companies.

In the aftermath of its successful fight to ward off an unwanted takeover by a Pickens-led group, Phillips Petroleum scrapped its suit accusing Pickens of tipping off friends, Mesa officers, and members of the Amarillo Country Club of his impending plans to acquire stock in major oil companies.

Pickens has vehemently denied these charges, characterizing them as "completely without merit." But the entire affair may not be over.

I've learned that at least one director of Mesa, Harley Hotchkiss, and at least three members of the Amarillo Country Club—of which Pickens is a member—have traded in the securities of Pickens' corporate takeover targets. The precise timing of these trades could not be immediately determined, but it is understood that some produced huge profits.

The club members are James Besselman, an Amarillo attorney and a friend of Pickens who has represented him in personal matters; William Ware, executive vice president of the Amarillo National Bank; and Walter Watkins, an Amarillo doctor. Harold Watkins, Walter's brother and a dentist, is one of Pickens' closest friends.

The securities—said to include stocks and options—are understood to be General American Oil (later acquired by Phillips); Cities Service Co. (bought by Occidental Petroleum); Superior Oil (acquired by Mobil), and Gulf Oil (now part of Chevron).

When I asked Besselman about the trades, his response was sharp. "I'm not going to answer your question, and you and all the rest of the people like you can go to hell," he said.

Hotchkiss was at least civil. He told me he had never traded on tips or inside information, but he declined to say whether he had ever been active in any of Pickens' takeover targets.

Ware's reaction: "I have nothing to say."

Walter Watkins refused to respond to a phone inquiry.

The revelations of these securities purchases—if any are deemed illegal—could spark an expanded probe by the Securities and Exchange Commission of possible insider-trading abuses in Pickens' takeover targets.

The SEC doesn't comment on investigations, but I've learned that the commission early last year launched a probe into the trading in stocks and options of General American Oil. And in March, the SEC subpoenaed and questioned a group of current and former Mesa personnel, including present Treasurer David Batchelder and Mesa company pilot John Andrew Stone.

What, if anything, the SEC could turn up in a trading investigation into Pickens' corporate takeover targets is anybody's guess. But it's known that there have been consistent leaks of Mesa purchases of such companies' shares—characterized repeatedly by a hefty run-up in stock prices prior to public disclosure.

Pickens' reaction to all of this? The usually publicity hungry oilman refused to be interviewed.

Source: *Chicago Sun Times*, January 7, 1985.

Insider manipulation of stock prices is not limited to insiders. So-called greenmail operators set up raids against target firms and then back off for a negotiated settlement. In the meantime, those individuals who are informed of the activity can reap huge profits by trades in the threatened company's stock.

Mere fluctuations in earnings is a minor consideration in short-term stock-price behavior. Far more dramatic and more explosive are such things as merger offers, acquisitions, stock splits, secondary offerings, legal damage suits, spin-offs, and skipped or doubled dividends.

Long before any of these things can occur, extensive discussions will have taken place. A blizzard of memoranda, offers and counter-offers, stipulations, letters of intent, and cloak-and-dagger meetings will have taken place. Weeks or months before such a proposal has been brought to the attention of the full board of directors for consideration or approval, the essential details of the matter will be known to a mixed bag of officers, consultants, major stockholders, and home-office functionaries. Even though details may be lacking, the rumor effect may be only enhanced by this shortcoming. And while the leak may be subsequently deplored, a perfectly kept secret may prove to be no less devastating to those outsiders whose interests are at stake.

The Corporate Star-Chamber

Any minority stockholder must live with the harsh reality that a select group of people can go into the board room, close the door, and vote actions that will not only determine the price of his stock—but the very *existence* of the company in which he has placed his life savings. The directors may vote to acquire another company, or be bought out by a competitor. Their decision may involve merger, spin-off of a corporate division, plant closings, establishment of foreign subsidiaries, or discontinuation of product categories.

If the action promptly produces higher stock prices, compliments will abound. If results are less positive, criticism will fly—interspersed with stockholder suits—as the outsiders try to make the insiders legally answerable for what they see as a bad decision. But the record of such litigation is enough to convince most folks that minority stockholder suits are notoriously tiresome, expensive, and unavailing. If they have any value at all, it tends to be in their nuisance value. They are rarely won by the minority groups that bring them.

Whatever results the board action precipitates, a lot of people are going to be privy to the thinking that underpins it, well in advance of its being voted by the board of directors and its subsequent announcement in the public and financial media. Among those who will enjoy the informational advantage will certainly be the company officers, committee members, consultants, accountants, lawyers, real estate appraisers, underwriters, and all of their respective assistants, secretaries, and other functionaries who must share the knowledge in order for them to do their jobs. From this core group, we must proceed at least geometrically if we wish to include all of the other actual or potential sharers of the supposedly confidential information.

Searle Sale Seen Near

BY CINDY RICHARDS

Wall Street, having had three months to speculate on its future, expects Skokie-based G.D. Searle & Co. to be broken up and sold in pieces before the end of this month.

The solution may come as early as the end of this week, some analysts and industry observers believe.

While widespread theories about the fate of the pharmaceutical firm are still being labeled cautiously as speculation, Searle's stock, which closed Friday at $64, has been rising steadily on takeover rumors since members of the Searle family, who own 34 percent of the company, announced on September 27 they had asked management to "consider, in a deliberate manner, ways for the Searle family's holdings to be diversified."

Searle has consistently refused to comment beyond the September 27 statement.

Analysts who follow the company said soon after Searle made its announcement then that it would be almost impossible for the firm to find a single buyer interested in the entire company, which is comprised of a research-based pharmaceutical business, an artificial sweetener business, and a consumer products business.

Said one industry source, the firm is "making the decision to divide up the company in January," after three months of searching for a solo purchaser.

The most likely scenario is that the company will be sold in two major parts—its pharmaceutical business and its aspartame business—while its 45 percent holding in Pearle Health Services Inc. will be sold separately, analysts said.

The most oft-mentioned buyer for the pharmaceutical business is the chemical giant Monsanto Co., based in St. Louis. It was Monsanto Chairman Richard J. Mahoney's public comments in early November that his firm would be interested in buying only the pharmaceutical business that confirmed private speculation that Searle would not find a buyer willing to take the entire firm.

It is likely the over-the-counter consumer products made by Searle will be sold as part of the pharmaceutical business. Some observers believe that portion of the business—which includes Metamucil, a laxative; Dramamine, a motion sickness remedy; and Icy Hot Balm and Rub, used to relieve muscle soreness—will be resold to another buyer.

The per-share price for pharmaceuticals has been put at between $25 and $30, while the price range for the sweetener business is considered at between $30 and $45.

The potential buyer of Searle's artificial sweetener business, marketed under the brand name NutraSweet, is less clear. Most often mentioned are Dow Chemical Co., DuPont Chemical Co., and Eastman Kodak Corp.

Searle also owns a 45 percent stake in Pearle Health Services, a former subsidiary which is the world's largest retailer of prescription eye care products.
Source: Chicago Tribune, January 7, 1985.

With sale of this company expected "by the end of the month," the essential details of the transaction have certainly already been settled. The public shareholders may still be wondering what's going to happen, but the insiders aren't!

Heard on the Street

Business is not conducted in a compartmentalized vacuum.

Any comprehensive listing of top industrialists, financial people, and corporate principals will quickly dispel any notion that each corporation stands as a discrete "puddle" in the economic landscape. The same family names occur time after time in the lists of company boards of directors, clubs, and eleemosynary institutions. While interlocking boards of directors have long been outlawed in certain situations, how many official watchdogs would it take to keep people of similar interests from meeting—in a steam room, at an industry convention, or over a luncheon table—and talking about things that intrigue them?

A golf foursome comprised of executive-level players represents an impressive pooling of information, provided each of the players is well-placed in his respective firm; and provided they decide to share their funds of inside corporate knowledge. Without leveling specific charges at anyone, the countless opportunities for insider wrongdoing—with or without intent or culpability—can't be ignored by a sensible observer. With such richly promising opportunities beckoning, it must follow that our captains, lieutenants and sergeants of industry yield to their temptations far more often than instances of official retribution would seem to indicate. It could hardly be otherwise.

Almost anything can be "heard on the street" if the street in question is named Wall, LaSalle, or Montgomery. Informational incest is rampant throughout the business sector. Information is the mother's milk of the financial district, in whatever locality selected for examination. Insiders have countless ways to exchange and share the information that is always floating in the street. This is what makes them insiders.

Those who have no access to this information network are outsiders—otherwise known as the public. Their burden is a large one!

Natural Risks and Human Risks

In addition to recognizing and coping with all of the natural or inherent contingencies that can destroy stock values, and which include such things as weather excesses, war, strikes, low-priced imports, high or rising interest rates, and competitive technology, a speculator in equities has two other classifications of risk to confront and deal with. The first of these is mismanagement. All executives are not equally talented and industrious. The corporate cocoon may be thick enough to insulate incompetent management from stockholder outrage for a long time.

A classic example of this is the recent posting of the largest loss in business history, by that presumed tower of fiduciary virtue, Continental Illinois National Bank and Trust Company. While the Federal Deposit Insurance Corporation (FDIC) rides to the $4 billion rescue, book values plummet and shareholders cringe. Executives in the huge institution, meanwhile, who precipitated the debacle, are bending every effort to hang on to their six-figure salaries and munificent perquisites. Or, if turned out for their demonstrated incompetence, they strive to fashion so-called golden parachutes for themselves that add financial insult to the injuries already delivered. As these ironies are played out, the only thing a minority shareholder outsider can do is hang on, hope for the best, and take his financial beating; or sell his woefully depressed stock and take his loss.

Fact: A small stockholder is constantly at the mercy of managerial incompetence.

In the ongoing multibillion dollar fiasco, there had to be a lot of people in the back room who saw troubles mounting and the tide of red ink sweeping in. Foremost among these, of course, were the principal officers. But they were not alone. Anyone in the bank whose functions allowed him or her to see monthly profit and loss statements, cash balances and flow data, and capital asset inventories—or talk with people who did—had to know that Continental was in deep, deep trouble! Many of these same people were owners of Continental stock, obtained through option programs and purchases in the open market.

Charity might prevent suggesting that these insiders arranged for their trustworthy friends and relatives to sell Continental shares short in the market. But pragmatism forces us to believe that they did whatever had to be done in getting clear of their own bank shares before the story hit the newspapers, and the financial dam broke. For a single example, James D. Harper Jr., Continental's executive vice president and head of its real estate division, sold 69,000 shares of his own stock in the troubled institution less than 90 days before the financial house of cards began tumbling down.

To think that otherwise sensible people would sit patiently and watch their stock values melt away for months on end defies reason. The Securities and Exchange Commission to the contrary, notwithstanding, the first law of nature calls for survival. A securities regulation will never change this.

> Fact: A small stockholder is at the mercy of whatever degree of avarice or guile an internal problem may elicit on the part of its insiders. The insiders will be the first to get into the lifeboats when disaster looms.

Risk Exposures in Commodity Speculation

Now let's give our attention to the degree and type of risks that a private speculator in agricultural commodities must face in his search for profit.

First things first: The universe of risk sharing is very much larger in commodities. Unlike the relatively small and *identifiable* group of individuals and institutions who own all of the outstanding shares of United Airlines, for example, the owners of a commodity are legion and faceless. The price of wheat for December delivery in Chicago is a composite reflection of the wheat situation in the United States, Canada, South America, Australia, Europe, and Asia. Conditions in each of these wheat-growing/wheat-consuming areas will not be accorded equal weight in arriving at a Chicago price, but they will all exert some influence on the final result. Unlike the well-focused impact of a Continental Bank fiasco, the operators of the 10 largest wheat ranches on earth could take the year off from wheat raising without making a perceptible dent in world supplies. It takes some kind of natural cataclysm that affects entire wheat growing *regions* to bring identifiable alterations to the supply/demand balance.

Susceptibility to manipulation is of great and proper concern to an owner of either equities or commodities. The total supply of stock in the XYZ Corporation may be 10-million shares, with 3-million of those shares in the hands of the family that founded the firm. Thus the floating issue of XYZ Corporation is 7-million shares. A *raider* might conclude that he could gain effective control of the company by obtaining 3½ million of the shares in public hands.

Now let's consider the raiding situation in wheat. Anyone who seeks to corner and control the wheat market for even a week, has to think in terms of *billions* of bushels. Not only must the raider own or otherwise control most of the physical grain in the immediate market area, but he must also have a means of preventing outside supplies from coming in. To drive prices up and keep them there long enough to profit from his corner, the contrived shortage must be maintained. This could be accomplished by bringing a complete halt to barge, rail, and truck movements; an extremely difficult task without important assistance from subfreezing temperatures and mountainous snowdrifts. Failing this, the raider might undertake to simply buy every grain shipment that reached the market area. The amount of money involved in such an undertaking, however, would be monumental.

The huge inventories of wheat that stand in public and private storage are only the most obvious bar to any kind of effective cornering.

Grain is traded in the form of futures contracts, calling for delivery of the physical commodity at a fixed time and location in the future; unless previously offset by an equal and opposite transaction.

There is no real or theoretical limit to the number of wheat futures contracts that may be sold and bought in a day, a week, or a month. Nor any limitation on the number of outstanding contracts that may be open in the market at any time. The size of the wheat crop nationwide or worldwide has no bearing on it. All that is required is for sufficient long- and short-side holders to establish positions in the contracts and hold them for some period of time. In view of this, the raider (since he is unable to read the market's mind) has no way of knowing how much additional wheat in the form of futures contracts will also have to be taken up in order to protect his corner.

Raiding a company is not very difficult at all, as we are regularly reminded each time someone does it. The great vulnerability of companies of every size to this kind of financial assault is attested to in the emergence of so-called greenmail as a lucrative way to hold a company for ransom: The raider buys enough of the target firm's stock to give some measure of credence to his threat of takeover. Then, in order to get out of the unwelcome suitor's embrace, the company buys its stock back from him at a "negotiated" premium. The raider pockets his greenmail payoff and walks away. It's legal!

Management is so sensitive to takeover threats that any unusual accumulation of company shares in unfriendly hands raises corporate hackles and triggers a variety of defensive moves. While lawyers duel with motions and briefs, the public shareholder watches and worries— helpless to do much of anything that might protect his own interests. Usually he has just two choices: Keep his stock and hope everything turns out all right; or sell his stock rather than take his chances with new management, whose intent may be to liquidate the company rather than operate it.

One of these incidents was recently reported by *Barron's* as follows: "Occidental Petroleum and Diamond Shamrock set a modern record for the most damage done to (shareholders) in the shortest time. Having said they were talking merger on Friday, early Monday they announced a deal and then later that day said it was called off. Diamond shares, which were to be exchanged for Oxy stock on a one-to-one basis, fell 3 to 18, while Oxy rose $1\frac{1}{8}$ to $26\frac{1}{8}$."

Another highly lucrative piece of corporate greenmail was briefly acknowledged by *The Wall Street Journal,* to wit:

"A group led by Mesa Petroleum Company Chairman T. Boone Pickens, Jr. agreed to drop its hostile bid for control of Phillips Petroleum Company. The settlement would provide Pickens' group with a profit of about $90 million and involve a restructuring of Phillips. The original purchase price would have been about $9.1 billion. Phillips stock plunged on the news."

Needless to say, no place for a public stockholder to get caught!

The larger difficulties involved in raiding a commodity, as compared to raiding a corporation, are revealed in their overwhelming lack of success. Ten or twelve serious attempts to corner a commodity have been undertaken during this century. The most recent of these involved Tino DeAngelis and his salad-oil caper, and the Hunt brothers siege in the silver market. If one wants to find a winner, however, the pages of history must be turned back to Phillip D. Armour, the big Chicago meatpacker. Of all those who tried, Mr. Armour is, on the best evidence available, probably the only one who made his corner work for him. Others managed to amass huge amounts of the chosen product and/or the futures contracts that represented it. This is but the first step, requiring nothing more than money. The second step involves selling off the big stockpile for an inflated price, and thereby cashing in on the profit. In the trade this second step is referred to as "burying the body." It has rarely if ever been carried off successfully.

Barron's

Not all is well with silver and its friends, and particularly with its most ardent and richest fan, Nelson Bunker Hunt, who can hardly be doing handstands as it slowly descends into what seems a mine shaft without a bottom. Hunt, who was still buying when silver touched $50 an ounce, got the rug pulled out from under him in early 1980, wound up with some cash-flow problems, needed huge loans, but stubbornly held on to as much silver as he could—an admirable display of tenacity and conviction.

Last week silver was under $6 an ounce and many responsible people think it could see $5. Hunt, saddled with huge interest payments on a $1.1 billion bailout loan arranged for him in 1980 (payments continue through 1991) probably is shelling out more in interest payments a year than his current store of silver (thought to be around 60 million ounces) is worth.

But Hunt could have disposed of that silver at around $10 an ounce not too long ago. If he had, he'd be $4 an ounce ahead of today's price, and he could have reduced, perhaps paid off, the loan and ended the onerous interest payments. At least that's what the hangers-on in the back of the pool room are saying, and they're always right.

The Hunt family's foray into silver (they seem to be equally unlucky in sugar and oil) is only the most visible of a number of small disasters that hit precious-metals enthusiasts over the past several years. Haunted by the fear of runaway inflation, they were brought up short last year by not only a slower pace, but also talk of disinflation and deflation. The world (at least for now) isn't the same as it was a decade ago, or even five years back.

Source: Barron's, January 14, 1985.

The lure of a commodity corner can be absolutely irresistible to an occasional high-stakes player who doesn't understand the commodity territory well enough to foresee the overwhelming difficulties that stand in his way. It is debacles of this kind that give rise to the market declaration, "Small traders make small mistakes, and big traders make BIG mistakes!" Raiding stock companies is simple, by comparison.

This background is not offered with any intention of presenting commodity traders as more virtuous than their counterparts in the stock markets. Neither is it intended to show commodity exchanges as more militantly alert to trade abuses, or more protective of small-trader interests than are stock exchanges. Wherever the machinery is found, the engine of speculation is avarice: a search for profit. Traders, wherever we find them, are motivated by the same considerations; and they pursue their ends in a gamut that runs from meticulous honesty, to felonious brinksmanship, to outright banditry.

The reason commodity markets are so nearly manipulation-proof has almost nothing to do with the characters of those who trade in them. It's due to their sheer size and ponderousness. Tackling a corporation with a few million shares in circulation offers no particular problem to someone with money enough to pay the price. Going after the wheat, soybean, or silver market, with no really good idea about how much grain or metal might have to be bought in order to manipulate market prices, is a mind-boggling idea. Only an idiot would try to do it!

Specific Risks in Commodities

There are *contract-specific* risks in commodities, just as there are *stock-specific* risks in equities. This is the category of risk that grows out of the specific maturity being looked at. Heading the list of contract-specific risks is the matter of trade mix among holders of contract open interest. A heavy concentration of weak-handed public longs in a particular contract should give an astute trader a good deal of pause before deciding to join them. This, regardless of whether one is interested in trading *or* raiding!

A valuable object lesson for anyone who gets ideas about running a corner in a commodity is contained in the manner in which the CFTC picked the winners and the losers in this situation: As concentration of bullion and silver contracts continued to flow into Hunt hands, and prices soared, the Commodity Futures Trading Commission decided the thing had gone far enough. The commission halted all silver trading, except for liquidation. The order poleaxed silver prices, which began a downward spiral that took some 80 percent off the market value of the white metal in ensuing weeks.

There was no place for a holder of either ingots or contracts to dispose of his now vastly overpriced holdings. It was a market virtually devoid of bids—at any price! But while this turn of administrative events sounded the death knell for bullish hopes, the bears could hardly have been better pleased—or served. The hedgers, who had sold futures or options against inventories or commitments, made the billions that the Hunts and the rest of the long holders lost. Regardless of how the CFTC action is rationalized, the effect was a direct result of government manipulation, and palpable favoritism for the short side of the market.

This, regardless of whether one chooses to agree or disagree with the end result.

When price manipulation does occur in the commodity markets, government is regularly seen to be the biggest—and most inept—manipulator of all.

Public traders are always more susceptible to a squeeze than are commercial interests (hedgers) and large professional traders that usually operate close to the market. A large contingent of nervous longs makes for uneasy company when price begins edging downward, and should be avoided as often as possible. Such a concentration may be found in a single contract, or it may exist in varying degrees in every traded contract in the commodity. Other contract-specific considerations relate to such things as expiration date, upcoming crop reports, Notices of Intention to Deliver, and stocks on hand that are eligible for delivery. Each of these items has a specific pertinence to a particular contract maturity, and has to be viewed as part of the personality of that contract.

Systematic Risks in Commodities

We know that a speculative risk is a natural risk. It is an unavoidable risk, because it exists in the scheme of things, as part and parcel of our existence.

A useful example of a systematic risk is the open threat that fire offers to a wood structure. An arsonist is not required to send a frame building up in flames. Lightning can start the conflagration, and lightning is outside human control. It's part of the natural system and it can cause a fire.

Buying an insurance policy won't affect the flammability of the structure, but it will shift the economic effect of the contingency (fire) from the owner of the building to the insurance company. Note that the protection is specifically limited to fire. If the house is carried away in a flood or a tornado, or converted to sawdust by termites, the policy is inoperable. Moreover, the policy calls for cash settlement. If the building burns to the ground, the insurance company is not going to rebuild it. Nor will the insuror replace it with another house of similar size and appointments. In event the house burns, the company will pay its owner a certain sum of money as indemnification of the loss. Having done this, the insurance company has no further obligation or interest in the situation.

Commodity Markets Are Money Markets

The basic risks being shifted back and forth between hedgers and speculators in a commodity market focus mainly on production/consumption balances, as they are (or may be) affected by such things as bumper crops, drought, floods, insect infestations, wind, or hail damage. The relative effects of these things, and their perceived likelihood, are spelled out in dollars and cents per bushel, ounce, pound, or ton. But, like the fire policy, a futures contract is limited to a single function. A commodity futures contract cannot replace a crop lost to insects; but it will go far in protecting a particular hedger against the economic results of such an event. A commodity futures contract will not stabilize the market price for a bushel of corn for the next six months; but it offers a way to recapture part or all of the economic loss accrued over that period of time through disadvantageous price change.

Although a commodity trader is constantly looking behind price in his ongoing effort to foresee and foretell developing influences, price is the be-all and end-all of his search. And the influences he is most concerned with are well outside the control of mere mortals.

No Committee in Charge of Rain

The single most reassuring thing to a commodity trader is that there is no operating committee or board of directors calling the shots for wheat, corn, oats, soybeans, egg hatchings, hog farrowings, feed-lot activities, and cotton plantings. Regardless of political ordination, titles, election, designation, or self-annointment, there is no individual or group of individuals who can go into a conference room, close the door, and order up a surprise rain storm in western Nebraska. Nor can they double the oats crop, or blight the corn crop, or withhold snow in Kansas while sending freezing temperatures into Florida's orange groves. The things that determine the size of our cultivated crops—and a whole array of other related events concerned with food production—are the exclusive prerogatives of nature.

Bureaucrats may dabble around the edges of supply and demand, seeking to confer some kind of advantage on the political darlings of the moment; but in terms of overall effect, such tampering is no more than a short-lived nuisance rather than determinative of the true course of things. The price-support program of one year becomes the land-bank program of the next. A grain embargo under one political persuasion yields to federal alchemy and turns into most-favored-nation status in the program of the governmental inheritors. In a given year the impact of such "tinkerings" with the market machinery may be considerable. In the longer range, they are seen to be no more than distractive trivialities; born out of a chance mating between political expediency and economic ignorance.

While federal functionaries spin an every-changing skein of hypotheses and extrapolations calculated to take the "slippage" out of our economic gearbox, farmers keep on raising more and better products. Steam lard utterly disappears, replaced by a dozen superior vegetable oil substitutes. A funny-looking little yellow sphere sailed in from China, accompanied by a spate of claims that nobody really believed at the time. But some midwestern farmers planted a few acres of it out of sheer curiosity. Twenty years later our soybean harvest stands at 2 billion bushels a year, and soybean meal is competing with conventional products in usage that ranges from bakery products, to "Hamburger-Helper," to imitation bacon.

Science and agriculture join forces to produce superseeds through hybridization; and genetically remodel our old-style chickens, turkeys, cattle, and hogs into new models that convert feed more efficiently, grow faster, get bigger, produce more "white meat," and generally lose all but the most tenuous family resemblances to the species from which they were summoned a few generations ago. A commodity trader must try to outguess perverse nature, while constantly adjusting his perspectives to the fact that the producers always seem to turn out more and better. And the world's populations are never quite satisfied with the quantity, the quality, or the price!

Through all of this, a commodity trader takes comfort in the fact that Cargill, Continental, and Dreyfus all have to look at the same weather forecasts that he does. And while these great grain merchants may hire their own meteorologists, this is no guarantee that the information they get will be of any higher quality than that furnished free by the National Weather Service's satellite section. The public trader is happy to know that the CIA's Russian wheat crop estimates are made public as soon as they are compiled. The public trader is delighted that the various U.S. crop reports and projections are available to *nobody* until—at a preannounced minute and second—they are made available to *everybody!*

In sum, a commodity trader's peace of mind is tremendously enhanced by the fact that there are no insiders in his business. Or if there are, theirs is an extremely short-term advantage; of the kind that might accrue to someone who knows "the Russians are buying wheat." But it isn't the sort of continuing advantage that constantly puts him at the mercy of a management team that he doesn't know; and keeps him eternally on the tail end of the information chain.

By the same token, it must be quickly added, unique events take place in the market complex that deserve the most critical attention of both traders and market regulators. A frightening example currently is seen in the soybean complex.

A tremendous concentration of processing capabilities has taken place in this facet of the business during recent years. Instead of an assortment of soybean crushers, ranging from very large to very small, two extremely large companies presently own some 60 percent of our total U.S. soybean crush capacity. By virtue of this, Cargill and Archer-Daniels-Midland (ADM) are in a position to exert tremendous influence on the availability of soybean oil and meal in the domestic market. If the gross processing margin (dealt with earlier in this volume) becomes less than attractive, only a few days of shutdown for these facilities can bring quick adjustments in supply-demand relationships—and sharp improvement in the profitability of processing soybeans.

The question of collusive decision making can be largely ignored in acknowledging this. Processing costs are sufficiently standardized among efficient competitors that, whether or not they collude, the realities of return on investment, price elasticity in the market, etc., will lead to the same decisions on the part of each of them: When market prices make it unprofitable to convert soybeans into meal and oil, the plants that do the conversion will probably be shut down. From an economic point of view, they should be shut down. Perhaps ADM and Cargill won't shut down at the same precise moment, but, if both managements are cost-responsive, the lag will be a small one. Such a concentration of market muscle carries great danger.

The fundamental issue from the standpoint of optimal market competition, is whether CFTC, the Securities and Exchange Commission and the Federal Trade Commission are derelict in failing to see this *manipulative potential* for what it is, and then doing something to correct it. For markets to be free, competition must be as unfettered as possible. Neither monopoly, oligopoly nor government should be allowed to exercise a manipulative hand in it.

Commodity Prices Offer More Stability

Detractors of commodity markets regularly rely on terms like *explosive, violent* and *wide-swinging* to convey their feeling that the patterns of prices on commodities fall into some kind of completely irrational behavior that a prudent investor would want nothing to do with. We will now examine this idea in the light of reality, and demonstrate that—compared to rank-and-file stocks traded on the NYSE and AMEX—wheat and corn prices display a surprising lack of volatility!

Leverage, based on the much smaller margins required in futures markets, creates the illusion of great price swings; because a few cents up or down the value scale for a bushel of grain can result in an impressive relative profit, or an equally impressive relative loss. However, when commodity price movements are reduced to percentages of underlying product value, amplitudes of price change on commodities vis-à-vis common stocks take on a much different appearance. Were this not true, the respective margins required to bind performance on commodity contracts, compared to margins imposed on stock purchases, would have to be greatly increased.

To demonstrate, the current margin for a stock purchase is 50 percent of the value involved. Thus, if someone buys 100 shares of IBM at today's price of $125 per share, the purchaser will have to put up 50 percent of $12,500 in cash, or $6,250. The other $6,250 will be covered by a broker's loan (secured by the IBM stock) at an interest rate of about 12 percent per annum. The price of IBM common stock has fluctuated from a low of $99 to a high of $129 during calendar year 1984. This is a percentage change of 30 percent.

December wheat 1984, ranged from a low of $3.37, to a high of $4.18 per bushel, over the nine months of its life to date, which is a 24 percent change.

December corn 1984, has had a trading range from $2.75 to $3.30 per bushel, over the nine months it has been trading thus far. This is a trading range of only 20 percentage points!

Considering that when buying stocks it takes about $5 (plus another borrowed $5) to gain constructive control of asset values that $1 (without a broker's loan) gets in the commodity market, the better arena for speculation is clearly that of commodities. They are about five times better than stocks, as measured in leverage available on risk capital, and something like 20 percent better, as measured in price volatility!

The $125 per share IBM stock pays a $4.40 annual dividend, so little time needs to be spent on its investment attraction. Almost any kind of a savings account pays greater earnings. Ergo, when people buy this stock, they buy it for price appreciation: *for speculation.* And they pay an inordinately high price for the privilege!

The fundamental difference in function that separates stock exchanges from commodity exchanges, and stockholders from commodity traders, should now be abundantly clear:

- A stock market exists to *accumulate capital investment* with which to finance businesses that choose to share ownership publicly. A shareholder is a partial owner of the company whose stock he has purchased, for as long as he retains his shares.

- A commodity futures market exists to facilitate the shifting of the *risks of ownership* between hedgers and speculators. A commodity position holder has no proprietary interest in the underlying property (grain, metal, etc.) that only serves to *measure* the risk involved. Like an insurance company, a speculator only bears a contingent economic obligation: The insurance company takes its risk for an established premium; the speculator takes his risk for a variable opportunity for profit, based on advantageous price movement for the period of time the position is held.

In view of these facts, it is at least unfortunate that the term *margin* is used in connection with both securities and commodities. The considerations present bear no economic similarity, and we need labels for funds committed to equity markets and commodity markets that give proper recognition to the economic reality. Attempting to make direct comparisons of margin requirements in security trading, versus commodity trading, is as meaningless as attempting to correlate the downpayment on a given piece of property with the cost of an insurance policy covering its economic value. If this understanding ever permeates public consciousness, much of the confusion that continues to plague our financial arena will at last be dispelled.

21

Introduction to Financial Futures

After more than a century of watching futures markets function, it's something of a surprise to see what great misconceptions still surround them. Although most market participants have some general appreciation for the price-discovery and forward-value assignments that take place in the pits, it is unusual to find even a professional trader who can offer any coherent explanation of how these determinations arise from the market mechanism. It has always been like this. Critical insights into futures markets are improving, but a great many questions remain to be satisfactorily answered. Moreover, with the burgeoning size and complexity of these great economic arenas, it is a constant struggle to keep the mechanics of trade in step with technological capabilities and attuned to the public interest.

A major suspicion that has plagued futures markets forever—and still persists in some quarters—has to do with the "reality" of the business being transacted there. The contracts have been variously called wind wheat, paper corn and imaginary oats by such groomers of public attitudes as congressmen, newspaper editorial writers, and federal judges. With this degree of confusion in the minds of the presumed intelligentsia, small wonder that less sophisticated people continue to look at the institution of futures trading with deep suspicion, if not antipathy. The hard fact is that we are still learning about futures markets; what they do; and how they do it.

Great disagreements exist still on what types of goods deserve to bear the commodity label; what tests should be met before multiple market postures are properly designated as hedges, spreads, arbitrage, etc. When market indexes were added to the list of commodities traded in the form of futures contracts, the action revived a story attributed to Abraham Lincoln: "If we were to agree to call a dog's tail another leg, then how many legs does a dog have?" The answer, of course, is, "It makes no difference *what* we decide to call a dog's tail. A dog has four legs!"

Calling indexes commodities doesn't make them commodities. Calling an option a hedge doesn't make it a hedge. Calling opposite positions held in the same or different property (or contracts representing same) a spread, or a straddle, doesn't make it so. Disquieting shortcomings may be clearly evident that flaw entitlement to the assigned label. In broadening the scope of these terms to accommodate new concepts, we certainly bastardize their historic meanings. Economic purists cringe. But, until the language of the market fashions new labels for our new products and functions, there is little choice but to use—or *mis*use— the familiar terms, and deal with semantic inconsistencies as they arise.

Business is a dynamic art. Insights and applications evolve as our needs and economic interactions become more refined. The language of business, therefore, must remain flexible. As innovative people probe at economic problems and opportunities, we have reason to be glad that our earlier theses were not carved in granite for all time to come.

For example, the conventional wisdom surrounding commodity markets until a dozen years ago placed three firm prerequisites on anything that might be considered a candidate for futures trading:

1. It must be storable over some appreciable period of time.
2. It must be produced somewhat seasonally, and consumed more or less evenly throughout the year.
3. It must demonstrate consistent and recognizable grades.

Beyond this, market catechism held, actual deliveries of the physical product had to be contemplated in the futures contract, and needed to occur to some extent in order to impart reality to the otherwise imaginary commodity. Under this last stricture, any contract that called only for cash settlement on maturity, with no provision for delivery of the "actuals," was surely doomed to failure for its mere inability to meet one of the theoretical requirements for success!

Furthermore, the market's Moral Majority steadfastly insisted that without a delivery stipulation, a futures contract was nothing more than a gambling game. A cash-settled contract, therefore, was not only deemed to be without commercial substance, but a threat to public virtue as well. Early in the life of futures markets laws were passed prohibiting trade in cash settlements. "Cash rooms" that dealt in the outlawed contracts, and "bucket shops" that accepted customer orders to buy or sell bona fide futures contracts—but failed to place those orders on an exchange—became targets of both official and Board of Trade supported sleuths.

This game of cops-and-robbers went on for years throughout Chicago's environs, as clandestine operators used ingenious ruses to gain access to Western Union's cables and syphon off Board of Trade prices to underpin their illicit trade. Failing this, they employed fleet-footed messengers who took turns racing between the bucket shop or the cash room, and the trading floor, and returning with the latest prices which were then posted on their illegal blackboards.

Another gaggle of cash settlers met each morning in the alley behind the Board of Trade building to conduct their own open-outcry auction, augmented by hand-signaled pit prices. This was accomplished by having a "flasher" perched in the second-floor window, from which vantage point he was able to monitor trade in the pits and surreptitiously relay the privileged information to his eager beneficiaries in the alley below.

The zeal with which the Board of Trade ferreted out the cash settlers who were systematically stealing pit prices off ticker wires and otherwise may be chalked up to the exchange's desire to protect its monopoly on the business. But there were other opponents of cash settlements whose motivation couldn't be so easily challenged. Eminent jurists, including the United States Supreme Court, unswervingly held that cash settlements constituted gambling. Moreover, that it exerted a disruptive and destructive influence in the market and should be suppressed by whatever means were necessary. That is where the matter rested for about 100 years. Bucket shops and cash rooms came and went occasionally—like "moonshiners" in a more recent setting—but they were illegal in every state of the union.

Changing Ideas about Public Morality

To understand the upheaval that is presently taking place in our financial markets, we need a perspective that includes our era of moral experimentation; beginning with the end of World War I and ending about 1940.

World War I called for great sacrifices and, when won, prompted paeans of praise for the nation's warriors and self-congratulations for the populace in general. Divine assistance was hugely credited for the happy outcome in that simpler time, and the word went out from pulpits and editorial pages across the land that America's *greatness* depended on America's *goodness*. Lines of demarcation between politics and theology first dimmed and then disappeared into the fabric of a deeply reverent social structure.

Public striving to be "good" gave rise to personal, municipal, regional, and national resolutions that in retrospect seem bizarre at best. The searching after national goodness perhaps found its high-water mark in the passage of the 18th Amendment to the Constitution; and which was intended to forever free the nation from the curse of alcoholic beverages. The fumes from axed whiskey barrels had hardly cleared before other edicts circumscribing moral conduct began pouring forth from state legislatures, city councils, and self-generating civic groups pledged to the eradication of such infamous vices as card playing, skirtless bathing suits, female use of cosmetics, keeping stores open on Sunday, collection of interest on private debts, failure to salute the flag, "rough" language in print, on radio, and in motion pictures, horse racing, prizefights, prostitution, and close dancing.

Small wonder that in the eruption of a moral rash of these pandemic proportions, the clouds of suspicion overhanging futures markets grew palpably thicker. One can't be sure if Harry Truman's characterization of commodity traders as "merchants of human misery" bespoke his settled view of things, or was just a lapse into political hyperbole that he felt would square well with the composite attitude of his Missouri constituency. In either case, the commodity markets could find no comfort in it.

Under the tenets of common law, there are two broad categories of wrongdoing. The first is labeled *malum in se:* wrong because it's wrong! The definition attaches to such things as murder, rape, child abuse, etc. These activities are crimes inherently, because of the threats they carry to our individual comfort, safety, and our collective survival.

The second category of proscribed activities are lumped together and tagged *malum prohibitum:* wrong because there's a law that says they are. Within the parameters of *malum prohibitum* we find such disparate concerns as keeping pets in hotel rooms, riding bicycles on the sidewalk, and playing poker for money in Des Moines, Iowa. Protagonists of statutorily imposed "goodness" offer all sorts of abstruse arguments in support of their recurrent crusades. Usually their case boils down to some perceived threat to the rights of a group of like-minded individuals; or as presenting a current or potential threat to public morality (read: goodness).

Cash settling of futures contracts fell within the purview of *malum prohibitum.* Its opponents labeled it gambling, because the closeout procedure failed to include physical delivery as an alternative. A lot of other people who had no compunctions against gambling, opposed cash settlements in the commodity market because of their fear that acceptance of it could have the effect of disrupting and trivializing the business being conducted there. They liked the sense of reality that a few deliveries at contract expiration seemed to impart to everything that had gone on before.

The Moral Pendulum Returns

Twenty years of self-flagellation via blue laws, prohibition, and evangelistic tirades in support of institutionalized goodness proved to be about all the country could tolerate. Franklin D. Roosevelt's action to repeal the Volstead Act and put the breweries back to work during the daylight hours came as great news for the grain business, and not just because of the barley used in making beer. Repeal constituted an unmistakable signal that the moral pendulum was swinging back. Efforts to impose statutorily mandated goodness were not working out. All the evidence seemed to show that morality wasn't susceptible to legislative control—and even if it were, passing laws about personal behavior that neither inconvenienced the neighbors nor offered a threat to society was a sorry hypocritical business.

Arbiters of the public mores point to the lifting of prohibition as the beginning of our ongoing march toward public permissiveness. On the heels of that move, to be sure, came all kinds of other liberalizations in the rules that presume to order our public and private conduct. So-called blue laws were repealed, allowing stores and movie houses to do business on Sunday. Bars were licensed and liquor by the drink returned on a state-by-state basis. Horse tracks cranked up the "sport of kings" again. Casino gambling surfaced in Nevada and elsewhere. Topless bars, porno movie houses, adult bookstores, and legalized prostitution bloomed in many parts of the country.

Choice Loses Out to Necessity

A major impetus toward the more relaxed public attitudes noted above came from steadily increasing needs for more revenue dollars on the part of cities, states, and the federal government. Once a cash-strapped county has seen millions of dollars coming in from liquor licenses and cabaret taxes, the "dry" contingent had better have a sure and painless source of replacement for those dollars before they try to get the county's bars closed down. Gambling is a terrible thing in the eyes of some. But in Nevada and New Jersey, to cite just two examples, gambling has a single redeeming virtue: It provides a large share of those states operating budgets. This fact is enough to give even the most rock-ribbed antigambling taxpayer some seriously mixed feelings on the underlying moral issue.

Of all the corners turned in the trek toward public permissiveness, however, the launching of multimillion dollar state-operated lotteries stands by itself! The despicable "numbers game", under the careful grooming and promotion of the state, has been raised to a level of affluence and superrespectability that was never dreamed of by the neighborhood entrepreneurs who invented it and used to control it. Any questions of immorality that may remain are drowned in noise from the ubiquitous machines punching out numbers on the lottery cards, and mixed with the revenue collectors' happy gasps at the bonanza they have found. Tax authorities agree that halting these state lotteries would precipitate fiscal crises of the first order. With this kind of justification, it is difficult to imagine what level of opposition would have to be mustered to get them stopped. A line is thus drawn through the *malum prohibitum*—and the moral consideration, if any, falls under the guns of fiscal need.

Cash Settlements Gain Respectability

Regardless of the changing social attitudes about such things as liquor, legalized gambling, and related public laxity in the realm of personal behavior, the official watchdogs of "regulated" commodity exchanges showed little inclination to a similar liberalization of viewpoint. A thoroughly ruralized conservatism—not to say suspicion—continued to color the attitude of federal administrators toward commodity exchanges; especially as concerned the traders doing business in the teeming "pits." Clear consensus in the upper reaches of the Commodity Exchange Authority (CEA) held that commodity markets enjoyed altogether too much entrepreneurial latitude, rather than too little. Although the national conscience had learned to live with casino gambling, horse betting both off- and on-track, church-basement BINGO, and raffles, cash settling on futures contracts remained unacceptable to those empowered to render such judgments.

The 1974 dismantling of the Commodity Exchange Authority, which had been an integral part of the U.S. Department of Agriculture, and its replacement by an independently mandated Commodity Futures Trading Commission (CFTC) was crucial to subsequent developments. It is extremely doubtful that the traditional attitudes reflected in the CEA would ever have been able to accept cash settling as a sensible and legitimate means for closing out a futures contract. Hypersensitivities based on grim history left no room for entertaining proposals in favor of adopting as standard practice, the very feature that had made bucket shops and cash rooms the scourge of the commodity industry for three decades.

In addition to the new blood represented by the CFTC commissioners, their administrative prerogatives were broadened as well. Seeing this, the exchanges also saw an opportunity to get open-minded consideration of futures trading in financial instruments. They lost no time in putting their case before the fledgling CFTC. But even before this happened, one financial futures market was already in operation.

Launching the International Monetary Market

Credit for being first to open a market in financial instruments must be given to the Chicago Mercantile Exchange (CME). In 1972, a group of farsighted innovators under the spiritual leadership of Leo Melamed, then serving as chairman of the board of Chicago's second oldest and largest exchange, had made a remarkable break with tradition: They abandoned the historic mind-set that insisted on seasonality, storability, and physical consumption as prerequisites for successful futures trading. Their new vision saw the changing values of national currencies to be a kind of "ownership risk" that begged for hedge protection. The answer they devised was in the form of a unique kind of futures contract that, on maturity, would call for delivery of a specified number of British pounds, Canadian dollars, Deutsche marks, Italian lira, Japanese yen, Mexican pesos, or Swiss francs—unless "offset" was accomplished prior to contract expiration by the characteristic equal-and-opposite transaction.

Economics Nobel-laureate-to-be Milton Friedman added his considerable international weight to the undertaking in a succinctly brilliant 11-page monograph entitled *The Need For Futures Markets in Curren-*

cies. Armed with this high-level academic sanctification, Melamed and other CME officers, staff specialists, and consultants set about the thorny task of convincing government officials, Federal Reserve Board governors, and the international banking fraternity that futures trade in currencies was an idea whose time had come.

Dr. Friedman's paper appeared in December 1971. The zeal with which the selling job was pursued by Melamed, Mark J. Powers, Everette B. Harris, and other CME spokesmen and supporters proved irresistible. The new idea resulted in a new market: the International Monetary Market (IMM). The IMM was duly chartered by the State of Illinois, and began trading futures in the seven previously listed currencies on May 16, 1972.

Private trading in national currencies left some of its opponents incredulous and the rest of them aghast. Fiscal policy as a legitimate tool of political administration was (is) a major tenet of Lord Maynard Keynes's so-called New Economics, which had attracted a lot of highly placed converts. Even though it was generally recognized that the 1944 Bretton Woods Agreement, that put international treaty restraints on currency fluctuations in international trade, had utterly broken down by 1971, bureaucratic control of money values was still a prerogative that few politicians felt happy about surrendering. In retrospect, it is at least surprising that the IMM actually received permission to open trade in the world's principal currencies. That they did get the required green light was surely as much a product of official naivete as it was prompted by forward-looking attitudes. It's doubtful if anyone—including Melamed, Friedman, and the others—had any idea about the all-pervading impact that public trading in currencies would have on every facet of the money business around the world.

The real significance of the International Monetary Market was in the fact that never again would heads of state and their functionaries be able to manipulate money supplies and commensurate values with the near-impunity that had historically been possible. From the first minute currency trading began on the IMM, a heavy public hand in the determination of relative money values became a fact of economic life. The importance of this event is almost impossible to overstate.

Financials Gain Added Attention

Witnessing the almost unbelievable volume of trade being attracted to currencies, leadership groups in other exchanges raced to offer contracts in different financial categories. The Chicago Board of Trade introduced a contract involving a package of Government National Mortgage Association (GNMA) obligations in 1975. This instrument tied directly into the risks of interest rate fluctuation which in 1975 was a Damoclean sword over the heads of lending institutions and borrowers alike. The "Ginny-Mays" offered a hedging vehicle that both institutions and individuals could use for enhancement or protection of returns from current and anticipated portfolio activities.

The International Monetary Market came back into the spotlight in 1976, with a futures contract on U.S. Treasury bills. The Chicago Board of Trade followed in 1977, with a futures contract on U.S. Treasury bonds.

All of these instrument offerings had held closely to the agricultural heritage of futures contracts: They all specified *delivery of the paper, or offset,* as alternative methods of settling contractual obligations for both longs and shorts. The orthodoxy still held to its tenet that inclusion of a physical delivery procedure—whether or not it was ever used in practice—somehow imparted a reality to the activities concerned that they needed, and that could be instilled no other way.

Financial Indexes Become Commodities

While all of these single-item contracts were under industry scrutiny and preparation for trade, a group of officers and associated interests in the Kansas City Board of Trade (KCBOT) had adopted a completely different view of the future. They proposed offering a tradable contract in *composite values,* like that represented by the ever-present Dow Jones Average, for example.

Their reasoning was as simple as their case was initially startling: The standard technique for reducing fluctuative volatility in stockholdings calls for portfolio diversification in the number and kind of equities held. Granting this, what better yardstick against which to measure portfolio performance—or hedge against fluctuative risks—than a major index of actively traded equities? Moreover, for the institution or individual who wanted to participate in overall market performance, but wished to avoid the sharp price swings that often characterize individual issues, an index would offer an attractive alternative to mutual funds, etc. Finally, in view of the high liquidity that is an important feature of well-traded futures contracts, it was felt that getting in and out of a large index position should be much easier, and with far less price impact than is often encountered in the relatively "thin" stock market.

The problem with the Kansas City Board of Trade idea was that there was—and is—no practicable way in which shorts could make efficient delivery of a stock index to the waiting longs. The conferees had already settled on the Value Line Stock Index as their trading vehicle, which is made up of some 1,700 individual issues, and from which its equal-weighting arithmetic computation emanates.

There is simply no way in which such an assortment of shares can be assembled and physically transferred between sellers and buyers. Nor is there any need to do so. People trading in such a package are only using it as a yardstick with which to measure risk exposures and gains and losses, vis-à-vis composite changes in portfolio values over some finite time period. No one really wants physical possession of 1,700 different shares of stock, or fractions thereof!

Admitting this made cash settlement the only feasible settlement method, and provided ammunition to opponents of the idea, who raced to discredit it as a mere gambling game that sought to use stock market numbers instead of dice or cards. Opposition was fierce, and included people both inside and outside the commodity complex. Selling the idea required overcoming a hundred years of accumulated resistance to it. Conversations surrounding the proposal proceeded by fits and starts for nearly a decade. In addition to the cash settlement issue, there was no statutory guidance as to whether such a contract—if it were allowed to trade—should come under the supervisory eye of the Securities and Exchange Commission or the Commodity Futures Trading Commission.

Phil Johnson (CFTC) and John Shad (CEA) demonstrated a refreshing level of pragmatism by merely deciding between themselves that any kind of futures contract or options on futures contracts, involving any kind of physical or financial property, would be CFTC's responsibility. The SEC, on the other hand, would exercise jurisdiction over all options (puts and calls) on securities, CDs, treasury obligations, and assembled stock groupings to be known as indexes.

Known as the Johnson-Shad Agreement, this separation of administrative jurisdiction cleared away a lot of procedural obstacles. With an open avenue to the CFTC, the Kansas City Board of Trade folks lost no time in putting their index futures proposal before that administrative body. After recurrent negotiations that punctuated long periods in administrative limbo, CFTC approval was finally given.

Trading in the first stock index began on the Kansas City Board of Trade in February 1982. Another historic milestone in the evolution of futures trading and in financial management techniques had been passed.

Futures Contract Based on Stock Index Clears CFTC for Trading in Kansas City

By Richard L. Hudson
Staff Reporter of The Wall Street Journal

WASHINGTON—The Kansas City Board of Trade cleared a major hurdle in its push to provide a controversial new way to invest in the stock market—a futures contract based on a broad index of stock prices.

At a 3½-hour meeting, the Commodity Futures Trading Commission granted the small futures exhange permission to list the new contracts. But further regulatory snags could delay the start of trading, scheduled for next Wednesday, as other government agencies and Congress debate tax and credit rules on the new contracts.

In Kansas City, Board of Trade officials said the regulatory clearance had touched off a barrage of requests for information about the new contract. Expectations of success were running high. "This futures contract has the potential to surpass all existing contracts in terms of volume," a Board of Trade spokesman said.

The Kansas City contract is the first of several proposals by futures and stock exchanges to trade financial instruments based on broad stock-market indexes. Under the Kansas City, Mo., board's plan, the contract's value would vary with movements in Arnold Bernhard & Co.'s Value Line index of 1,700 stock prices. Supporters maintain that the contract will provide investors with a new, relatively inexpensive way to protect their stock holdings against adverse drops or rises in average stock values. Critics contend that the contract amounts to little more than gambling and could hurt the stock market.

The commission's approval came despite requests from two lawmakers to postpone action so Congress can study the issue further. The requests were from Chairman John Dingell (D., Mich.) of the House Energy and Commerce Committee, which oversees stock-market regulation, and from Chairman Benjamin Rosenthal (D., N.Y.) of a House government operations subcommittee. Both legislators plan hearings about the new contracts soon, and Rep. Dingell is pushing to get a bill passed delaying trading.

The five-member commission rejected four-to-one any further trading delays. Since the contract was proposed in 1977, it "has been studied more intensively than any other contract ever before the commission," said the agency's chairman, Philip Johnson. The financial instrument, the commission ruled, appeared to satisfy the two statutory requirements for trading new contracts: It won't be contrary to the public interest and, by providing traders with a way of protecting their holdings, it will serve an "economic purpose." The panel's ruling effectively rejected the argument that the financial instrument was tantamount to gambling.

However, the one dissenting commissioner, James Stone, argued that the new contracts might attract so many speculators that they could make stock prices more volatile and hinder capital formation. He also predicted that the contracts, because they are based on widely publicized market indexes, might lure many traders who are unfamiliar with the ways of the futures market. Mr. Stone, who was CFTC chairman during the Carter administration, argued that current regulation of futures markets isn't stringent enough to protect these new traders from fraud or unethical sales practices.

Having got through the CFTC, the contract may have other hurdles to clear. The Federal Reserve Board, for instance, has said that the proposed "margin"—or deposit—required to enter a position in the new market might be so low as to undermine the Fed's control over stock-market credit. Partly to satisfy the Fed, the Kansas City board Friday decided to boost its minimum margin to $6,500, or about 10 percent of the contract's value, from its original proposal of $4,000. The minimum margin for stock purchases is 50 percent.

The Fed met privately yesterday to discuss the new contract, but a spokesman declined to comment on whether any conclusions were reached. Last year, the Fed said it might order the margins to be raised to maintain its control over stock-market credit. Futures industry officials contend that the Fed hasn't the legal authority to set futures margins.

Furthermore, congressional aides say the Internal Revenue Service is considering how to tax profits on the new contracts. Last year's comprehensive tax bill lowered maximum rates on most futures transactions, but it isn't clear whether these new contracts qualify for the lower, 32 percent capital-gains rate. Futures lobbyists are urging lawmakers to amend the statute to ensure that the tax break applies to the new contracts.

Under the contract planned by the Kansas City board, an investor who expected average stock prices to rise during a certain period would buy an index contract. If traders in the Kansas City futures pit got bullish about stock prices, they would bid up the sales price of the index contract and the value of the investor's holding would rise. If traders got bearish, expecting stock prices to drop, the contract's value would fall.

Conversely, an investor expecting a market slump could enter a "sell" position, making a profit as stock prices declined.

As with any futures contract, trading profits and losses would be credited and charged daily to the investor's account. An investor could close out his position any time before expiration.

Opening of a futures contract in a market index marked acceptance of a completely new idea in risk dealing. Existence of the index contract provided a hedging vehicle that would revolutionize portfolio management procedures. It also offered a way for private traders to participate in general economic trends, while avoiding the stock-specific risks that always threaten small shareholders. The KCBOT's Value Line contract was a quantum leap forward in market sophistication and implementation.

Until the introduction of stock index trading, there were only a few ways to avoid the stock-specific fluctuative risks discussed earlier. First and most obvious, was through diversification of one's own portfolio, or by purchase of a mutual fund of some sort. There are problems with both of these approaches.

Even if the investor has sufficient capital to assemble a minimal group of 18 or 20 issues chosen for their composite tendency to "track" the Dow Jones or some other value-measurement index (and "small investors" by definition do not have), portfolio/index correlation is difficult to attain and may require a lot of adjustment trading to maintain. Broker commissions loom as a not insignificant damper on profits from this kind of activity carried out with actual stocks. Mutual funds, on the other hand, take time to get into and out of, and often carry heavy penalties for premature closeout.

Trading restrictions that obtain in securities markets can prove to be both bothersome and costly. The uptick requirement before making a short sale, for example, can delay or even prevent accomplishment of a crucial transaction. The more volatile and fast-moving the market is, the more likely are procedures to frustrate the trader who is in a hurry to do something.

Last, but certainly not least, the margin requirements imposed on those who wish to buy and sell stocks, as compared to the much more modest margins called for in commodity markets, can't be overlooked. To the extent that the money manager chooses to avail himself of his leverage opportunities, commodity markets offer multiples of the returns available through direct stock ownership. All of these considerations, coupled with the characteristically high liquidity, and resultant ease of getting in and out of positions, marks index futures trading as much more functionally efficient, as well as offering far greater returns on committed risk capital.

The KCBOT Value Line Index contract offered the trader—or portfolio hedger—a totally new entry into the securities arena. Now it was, indeed, possible for someone to "buy the market" or "sell the market." In doing so, the position holder was able to profit from his accurate forecast of a *general increase* or a *general decline* in composite equity values. At the same time, he was able to stand out of the way of stock-specific fluctuations that are altogether too often the nemesis of small traders; and that may grow out of management failure, shifts in competitive ascendancy, and similar spontaneous or contrived events. These are events, it should be added, that the small investor is not likely to know anything about, until the information has already been discounted into the market by those further up the information chain.

From the portfolio hedger's point of view, an index contract provides both a performance scale against which his own results can be realistically compared, and a stable value package that can be held either long or short, to enhance portfolio returns and/or provide a hedge cushion against unknown contingencies that threaten portfolio values. Certainly an index hedge is infinitely preferable to the ponderous and costly exercise of selling off vulnerable stocks in the face of some short-term threat, and then repurchasing them after the threat has passed. Likewise, an index hedge is far simpler and less expensive than the time-honored practice of going "short against the box." Finally, futures of all kinds in a normal market trade at some premium to the underlying product, in this case, the index. The convergence principle allows the short hedger to collect part or all of this premium as the futures and the index seek a common price level on the last day of trading in the particular contract.

This topic can't be closed without a firm reminder that the quality of any hedge depends on the accuracy with which the hedging vehicle reflects the characteristics of the property ostensibly being protected. The Value Line Index (VLI) is only one of several such indexes currently being traded in futures (or options) on the various exchanges. Whether one selects VLI, Standard & Poor's 500, the Major Market Index, the NYSE or AMEX offerings, the choice should be made with great care for both the nature of the particular index, and the purpose the trader intends to achieve with it. Selection of an index for purely speculative purposes is not as crucial as picking the right vehicle for a hedge. Before putting one's faith in an index hedge for a portfolio that's heavy in communications issues, for example, an acceptable degree of "tracking" between the two should be demonstrated. Unless this is done, the short index position may be nothing more than a *different* speculative posture, that increases risk exposures instead of reducing them.

Detailed explanations and examples of the speculative and hedging oportunities present in stock indexes and other types of financial instruments are beyond the scope of this book. The individual who wants to delve more deeply into these topics is referred to the Dow Jones–Irwin *Guide to Stock Index Futures and Options,* by Nix and Nix, 1984. The volume provides useful answers to basic questions, while offering an introductory-level overview of this new area of financial activity.

A more technical treatment is contained in *Stock Index Futures,* by Fabozzi and Kipnis, 1984, also published by Dow Jones–Irwin.

Whether a private investor, investment counselor, or manager of an institutional portfolio, the individual charged with day-to-day conservation and placement of risk capital cannot afford to ignore this new field of financial instruments. Prudent use of these hedging and speculative vehicles has already narrowed the chasm between so-called investment grade and go-go fund portfolios substantially. By using financial instruments to buffer risk exposures and upgrade yields, financial inventories can now enjoy the same kind of hedge protection that has been a major element in profitable commodity dealing for 125 years.

The prudent money manager has no alternative but to immediately set about schooling himself—or herself—in the use of these exciting new economic tools.

22

Introduction to Options

In order to set the stage for an exploration of the nature and function of *options* as trading entities, it will be helpful to begin by reviewing the more familiar kinds of transactions that are available to buyers and sellers.

The simplest trade to understand is a *cash sale,* which in the market is usually called a *spot sale*. In this exchange a seller with goods to dispose of presents them to a buyer who needs the merchandise. Matters of quantity and quality are resolved by examination and agreement. A price is negotiated at which the seller is willing to part with his inventory and the buyer is willing to acquire it. Money and merchandise changes hands "on the spot" and the deal is complete.

A *spot* or *cash sale* looks like this:

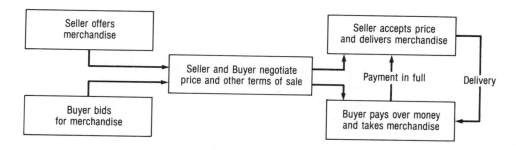

Exhibit 22–1

284

A spot sale is simple and immediate. Much of our routine business is done this way. Complications may be introduced into the buyer and seller roles, however, through such considerations as specialized delivery arrangements, large amounts of money involved, and so on. When this happens, details of the transaction may have to be altered to fit necessity or the convenience of either or both parties to the trade. Extension of time by the buyer or seller—or both—is a common occurrence throughout the business system. In the commodity sector it is often unavoidable, because crops are only harvested at specific times of the year. In view of this reality, transactions involving wheat, for example, can be made anytime, but completion of the delivery/payment steps will have to wait until the crop is harvested. In recognition of this, a *cash-forward* or *to-arrive* transaction has always been an important method for the handling of commodity business.

It is not likely that any form of goods transfer will ever totally supplant the cash-forward deal. It initially grew out of the realities of raising crops, and it persists for the same immutable reasons.

A cash-forward trade looks like this:

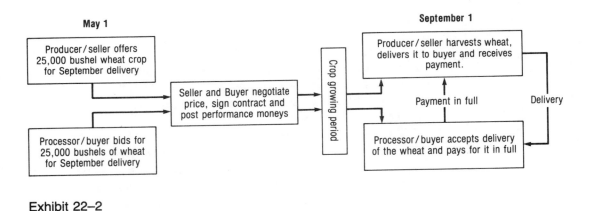

Exhibit 22–2

Again, we are looking at quite a simple transaction. In essence, this forward or to-arrive trade is nothing more than a spot trade with a *time dimension* built into it to accommodate the time element involved in growing and harvesting wheat. However, simple as the structure of the transaction is, it is not very efficient. Head-to-head negotiation between buyer and seller is time-consuming and, because of the private arrangements involved, may offer more opportunities for misunderstandings and later disagreements than either "spot" or the highly institutionalized futures trade.

Both a spot-trade and a to-arrive trade are private transactions; dependent upon the arrangements privately concurred in by the parties to the sale. Not only price, but relative quality of merchandise, when and where delivery is to be made, amount of the "performance bond" deposit required, and whether payment is to be made in dollars, yen, or kopeks, are all proper topics for negotiation in such an exchange. It is largely because of these contingencies that must be talked over and resolved, that private trading is so inefficient and generally unsatisfactory for handling the huge quantities of our commodity wealth. To efficiently manage the requirements for feeding, housing, and clothing ourselves, and maintaining an economic society, we need an established market framework to facilitate the assembly, storage, pricing, and distributive functions; and do all of these things with a minimum of time-consuming personalized involvement.

It must be a market structure that functions with complete impartiality as concerns every class of trade and trader it serves. It can show no bias in favor of buyers over sellers, nor locals over foreigners. It must give the same even-handed treatment to every order it handles, between all market participants, and at every level of transfer—from the mines and the fields, to the end users of the finished products.

When it comes to assigning root causes for recurrent waves of human starvation in places like Africa and India, inefficiencies in marketing and distribution are almost equally responsible with production shortcomings. The properly vaunted American standard of living could never be sustained without the marketing efficiency with which we handle our commodity outputs. Futures markets are the core of this mechanism, and the *futures contract* is the central idea that allows the market mechanism to function.

A futures contract is a thoroughly unique concept. In examining this trading device, neither a spot nor a forward transaction will help much in the explanations. Begin with the seeming contradiction that there is *no written contract* underlying a futures contract. Nobody signs anything. The terms of the contract are contained in the rules of the exchange upon which the trade takes place. Rule specifications standardize every element of every futures transaction *except price*.

Quantity is declared to be 5,000 bushels if it's grain; 1 kg if it's gold; or 100 tons if it's soybean meal. Quality grades are spelled out in terms of allowable moisture content, color, odor, fineness, and protein content. Premiums and discounts are specified for allowable deviations above and below "contract grade." Delivery time and place, along with method of tender and form of payment are clearly specific. In other words, the only thing that remains to be established between the buyer and the seller of a futures contract is its value. Price is the only variable, and it is subject to "negotiation" only through the required process of open-outcry auction, in the "pit" designated for such trading. Every other pertinent consideration in the trade has been institutionalized in the language that defines the contract.

A futures-contract trade looks like this:

Anatomy of a Futures Transaction

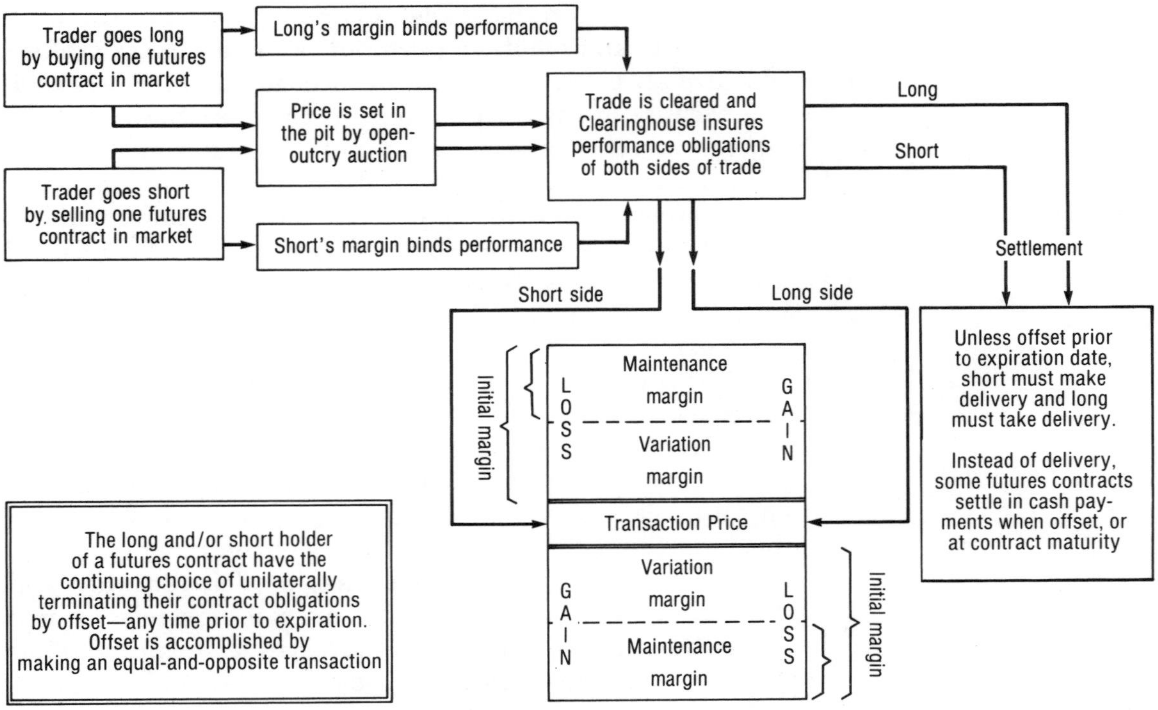

Exhibit 22–3

It takes both a long and a short to open a futures contract. However, once that trade has been cleared, the original parties to the transaction may offset and be successively replaced at any time—by any number of substitute position holders—and at any subsequent price levels that may ensue in the course of trade. This is possible because the futures contract imposes no performance requirements except *maintenance of specified margin* throughout its full trading life. So long as there are holders who are willing to keep the required margins on deposit with the clearinghouse, the position is open and secure. The holders may be one long and one short who hold their respective positions for nearly a full year. Or the holders may be a dozen or a hundred longs and shorts who successively replace their predecessors (by substitution) on one side or the other of the open contract.

A futures contract is readily transferable through repurchase or resale because, until the contract expires at maturity, all it amounts to is a blind *variable money obligation*. (The "obligation" is the margin requirement.)

One need not be an owner or a grower of wheat to be a seller of wheat futures. One need not be an exporter or a miller of wheat to be a buyer of wheat futures. Wheat futures only become wheat at contract maturity. Until maturity, a wheat futures is nothing more than an institutionalized financial risk that is variably priced through reference to a specified quantity of its underlying product. For the speculator, it constitutes a positive (long) or negative (short) economic risk of ownership, undertaken in a search for profit. For the hedger, the futures stands as a substitute purchase or a substitute sale, undertaken for the purpose of avoiding or reducing risks of ownership through value changes on cash inventory.

Firm Ties to Reality

This might lead to an improper conclusion that the ties between real products and the futures contracts that represent those products are tenuous enough to allow futures prices to lead some kind of a life of their own. Not so! When the last minute of the 21-day notice period in an expiring contract runs out, the bell rings and a 5,000 bushel contract becomes 5,000 bushels of real wheat. There are more than a few public traders around who have "accidently" become recipients of Delivery Notices who can testify to this. Throughout the life of the contract pending maturity, this ultimate reality is an ongoing restraint in determining the distance that futures prices may deviate from cash prices. Other interim effects on basis value relationships pertain to such things as supply/demand balance, storage availabilities, weather prospects, interest rates, and foreign competition.

The result is seen in futures prices that tend to track cash prices with uncanny accuracy. Immediate scarcity or oversupply may install an aberrational short-term *premium* or *discount* in the basis; but, the fact that cash and futures prices travel together is too obvious to be missed.

Differing viewpoints decree that in periods of escalating prices, buyers may have a good deal to complain about. When prices turn downward, sellers of the product may not be able to recapture their full costs of production—much less show a profit on the operation. Since the principal distinguishing characteristic of humankind is an ability to solve abstract problems, it should not be surprising to learn that some enterprising individual invented the idea of *options*—to specifically shield himself from the effect of prices that move in the wrong direction.

An Option Confers a Choice—Not an Obligation

All of the transactions reviewed to this point impose firm and reciprocally equivalent obligations on the parties to the trade.

The spot sale requires the seller to make delivery and accept the agreed-upon price. The buyer must accept delivery and pay over the specified amount of money.

The forward sale makes the same demands on buyer and seller as those seen in the spot sale, except the forward sale defers delivery and full payment to some mutually agreeable date in the future.

288

A futures position requires the long and the short to assume opposite stances with respect to an institutionalized risk in which the only contingency is price fluctuation. Both parties have the continuing prerogative of unilaterally abandoning their positions through offset and replacement by a substitute holder at any time. Unless offset prior to expiration, the short is bound to make delivery in accordance with contract terms, and the long is bound to accept delivery and make payment in full.

Once established in a futures position, the holders gain or lose in direct proportion to the full range of price fluctuations that transpire. When price goes up, money values are transferred (via the clearinghouse) from the account of the loser (short) to the account of the winner (long). When price goes down, the reverse occurs: Money values are transferred (via the clearinghouse) from the account of the loser (long) to to the account of the winner (short). Positions are "marked to market" at least daily.

Commodity markets do not create money. Commodity markets merely transfer money from the losers to the winners—after deducting commissions, fees, and related charges for transacting the business of the winners and losers. In view of this, the absolute potentials for loss in a futures contract are thus: For the long (who loses when price falls), it is the interval between his purchase price and zero. For the short (who loses when price rises), there is no theoretical limit to his loss potential since there is no way to place an absolute upper limit on any price in free trade.

The speculator in a futures trade assumes the risk of loss in return for the opportunity to profit. Loss is the direct reciprocal of profit in all futures trading.

The hedger's situation is less clear-cut. He takes a market position that is the opposite of his cash inventory (or commitments) position, in an effort to avoid the effect of disadvantageous price movement. He is willing to forego most or all of the opportunity to profit from increases in inventory values, in return for enjoying a degree of variable protection from losses in inventory value. A hedge tends to lock in a margin of profit. Once an inventory is fully hedged, subsequent profit (or loss) opportunity is effectively limited to the relatively modest changes that may occur in the *basis* between the futures price and the cash price for the underlying product. While this looms as the major difference between a *futures* contract and an *option,* it is by no means the only one.

Options Are a Different Kind of Ball Game

Unarguably, the single most enticing aspect of an option is that it ostensibly allows its holder to profit fully from price moves in the right direction, while enjoying protection from losses occasioned by price moves in the wrong direction. This by itself is enough to get the undivided attention of anyone who has ever received a margin call on a deteriorating futures position, but let's begin at the beginning.

Unlike a futures position, which requires a long and a short arrayed on opposite sides for as long as it remains open, and from which position either or both can exit via offset at any time, an *option is a right, a choice, a privilege,* which is bought and paid for at the outset. The entitlement an option conveys to its owner or holder is precise in terms and strictly limited as to the period of time during which it will remain operative. Whether an option entitles its holder to purchase a particular parcel of land for a fixed price of $1,000 per acre, for a period of one year from date of issuance; or entitles its holder to buy 100 shares of XYZ Corporation stock at a price of $50 per share, for a period of six months from date of issue, the holder—once he owns the option—is the sole judge of what, if anything, will be done with it. Thus we see that, unlike the other transactions we have examined, an option imposes *unequal* obligations on the buyer and the seller.

Should the option holder decide to exercise his privilege, the option seller (called a writer in the business) will have to deliver the land or the stock, and at the option price specified. This is true regardless of what may have happened to the values of the property in the meantime. Sounds interesting? Let's probe a little deeper.

Heads I Win, Tails You Lose!

The only thing a sharp trader is ever looking for is an uneven advantage! This is what profitable speculation is all about: Choosing those situations that, for whatever reasons, offer better probabilities for profit than they do for loss. An option, on the face of it, appears to give the buyer the edge. This, since an option holds out the opportunity for unlimited profit, while strictly limiting loss potential to the amount of the premium paid to acquire it. However, since the writers (sellers) of options overwhelmingly tend to be producers, processors, commercial merchants, large traders, and others who deserve the label of "professionals," it behooves the prudent public trader to look long and hard at the options pond before jumping into it!

Call Option Explanation

In its simplest terms, a *call* option is an agreement between the writer/seller and the buyer/holder that involves the following considerations:

The *holder,* in return for a specified premium payment, has the continuing privilege of acquiring the underlying property at a fixed price for the full life of the option. Since it is a "privilege," the call holder may choose to *exercise* his option—and "call for the optioned property at the specified price"—or he may choose to *not exercise.* His choice will depend on which action best serves his economic interests, by producing a profit or minimizing a loss.

The *writer* (seller), in return for a specific premium paid to him, has the continuing obligation to deliver the optioned property at the price specified, any time the holder "calls" for it during the life of the option. This, regardless of what it might cost him to "perform."

Note that the two parties to an option trade are a *buyer* and a *seller;* not a *long* and a *short,* as in futures trading.

Put Option Explanation

A *put* option is the opposite of a *call.*

> The *put holder,* in return for his premium payment, has the continuing privilege of selling the optioned property at a fixed price for the life of the option. The holder will be the sole judge of when and whether to exercise the option.
> The *put writer* (seller), in return for the premium paid to him, has the continuing obligation to accept the optioned property from the put holder and pay the specified price for it, at any time the holder chooses to "exercise" his privilege, during the life of the option. This, regardless of how much the then-current market price may be below the option strike price.

For emphasis, again note that the parties to this put transaction are a buyer and a seller. Unlike open-interest in futures contracts (where the number of long and short holders must be exactly the same) the quantity of put options outstanding at any given time does not limit the number of call options that might be open in the market. This is an important point to keep firmly in mind.

Building an Option Model

It has been almost 50 years since the *malum prohibitum* label was federally imposed on all trading in agricultural options. In view of this, there are hardly any traders presently active in the markets who have ever dealt in an agricultural option. There has been no legal opportunity to do so, until the ban was lifted and the Chicago Board of Trade and the Chicago Mercantile Exchange relaunched options trading in late October 1984. Like any unfamiliar activity, options will call for some careful study by anyone who wants to trade proficiently in them. The novice will help himself tremendously by drawing a picture of each option transaction being considered.

Exhibit 22–4 depicts a hypothetical 180-day call, purchased February 28, 1984, on one long contract of January 1985 soybeans. The buyer obtains this option for a premium of 50 cents per bushel, and at a strike price of $7.30 per bushel. At the indicated per-bushel premium of 50 cents, the option buyer has paid $2,500 (50 cents × 5,000 bushels) for the right to acquire one CBOT January soybean contract (long), at a fixed price of $7.30, any time during the ensuing six months.

In examining our model of this option trade, we see that in order for the buyer to show a profit on his call at expiration, the contract price will have to increase from its current $7.26 level to something over $7.80 per bushel, which is an upside move of more than 54 cents per bushel. The 54 cent total is comprised of the 50 cent premium, and an out-of-the-money sum of 4 cents per bushel, which is sometimes called an *overprice* at the point of initial purchase. The effective price of the option, which is the *strike price,* is $7.30; but the point of profitability is arrived at by adding strike price, premium, and out-of-the-money overprice. Doing this, we see that $7.80 per bushel is the point

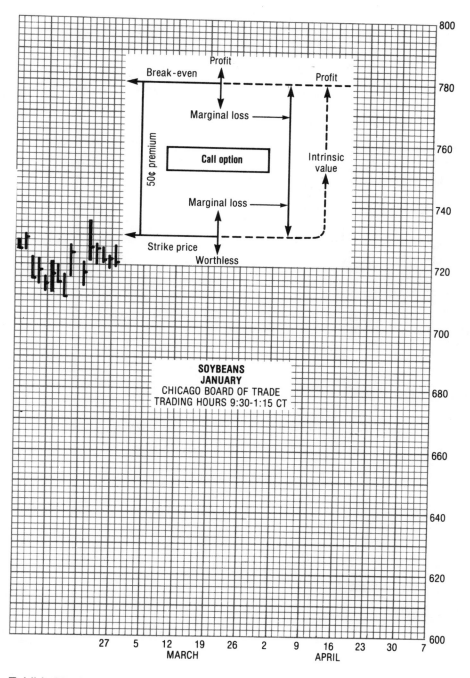

Exhibit 22–4

at which the initial outlay has been covered, and the option begins reflecting a net profit. (In all examples used herein, commissions, interest, debt-servicing costs, etc., are ignored for purposes of uncluttered clarity.)

Extending our overview of this situation to April 2, we see that during the week of March 5, the futures price climbed to a high of $7.60. At this level the call (with a strike price of $7.30) had generated intrinsic

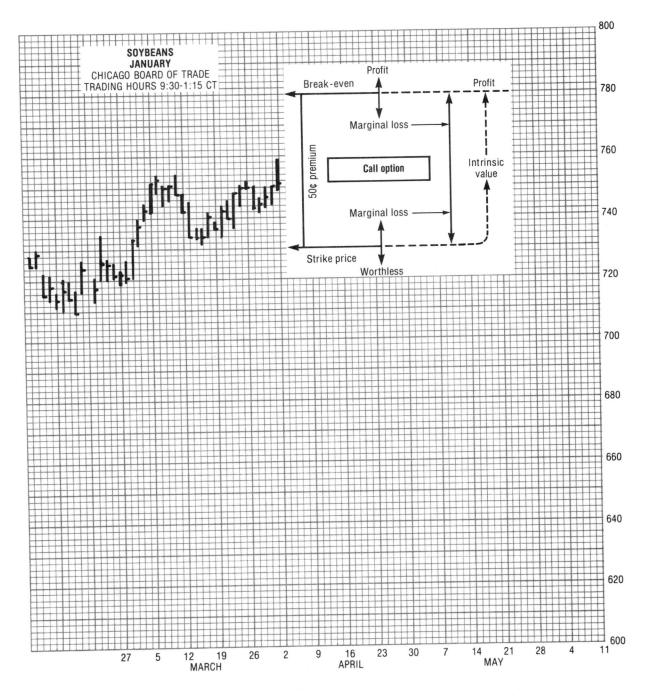

Exhibit 22–5

value of 30 cents per bushel. The paper result is still marginal, because all it has done is to reduce the initial cost of acquiring the option. There is still a long way to go before breaking into the profit area. The call holder can exercise his option here if he chooses to do so, and the writer will have to deliver one long January soybean contract position to the holder at the strike price of $7.30. However, since doing this would still leave the holder well away from even recovering all of his premium outlay, it won't happen. With nearly five months remaining in the option, there is nothing to do but wait (Exhibit 22–5).

Whatever might happen to the futures price, the option holder will never get a margin call. On purchasing the call, both the maximum price at which the privilege can be struck, and the maximum amount the option can cost its buyer (the amount of the premium), were firmly established. Should the futures price go below the strike price and stay there until expiration, the call will expire worthless. That is the worst thing that can happen to the holder of this option. Conversely, if the futures price is anywhere inside the premium range at exercise or expiration, but still below $7.80, some (marginal) portion of the premium outlay will be recovered, to stand as a deduction from the $2,500 paid out initially.

If the futures price is over $7.80 at exercise or expiration, each penny per bushel over the break-even will put $50 net profit in the holder's pocket—which, in the characteristic arithmetic of commodity markets, goes as a loss in the account of the writer/seller.

Both Futures Prices and Option Prices Fluctuate

Adding another month to our perspective, we see that on the 30th of April, a break carried the futures price back down to $7.13, a full 17 cents into the "worthless" area below the strike price. Although the holder needn't worry about a margin call, he has to live with the fact that instead of the 30 cents per bushel intrinsic value reflected on April 2, the option is now 17 cents out-of-the-money (Exhibit 22–6).

The option still has value, because there are some four months of life remaining, and "time value" is a major consideration in pricing options. With four months in which to do it, the price on this underlying soybean contract has lots of time to work higher and give the holder the profit he seeks. The time value of the option is still appreciable. By comparison, if there were only four weeks remaining until option expiration, its time value would be substantially less.

Moving on now to July 2, the June run-up, reversal, and selloff stands revealed. On June 20, the option attained break-even at the day's high price. The next week brought disaster in the form of lower quotes, however, and the July 2 close was once more well into the worthless range (Exhibit 22–7).

The Fourth of July hiatus sounded the death knell for any hoped-for profit in this call. Session after session saw prices driven lower. Except for three or four feeble "technical" rallies on the way down, the trend never changed. After some ups and downs in the $6.15 to $6.60

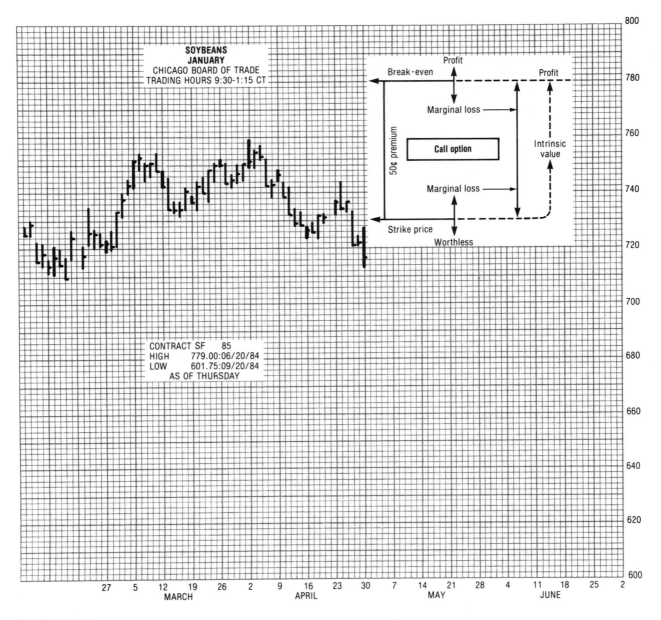

Exhibit 22–6

range, the option expires worthless at the end of August; and about 80 cents per bushel out-of-the-money (Exhibit 22–8).

The recapitulation is a simple one: The option *writer* in this situation made a $2,500 (premium) profit. The *holder* took a $2,500 (premium) loss. The buyer's loss became the seller's profit.

Option Holders May Leave Early

We have already noted that it is rare for any holder of a futures contract to maintain the position to expiration, and then take or make delivery

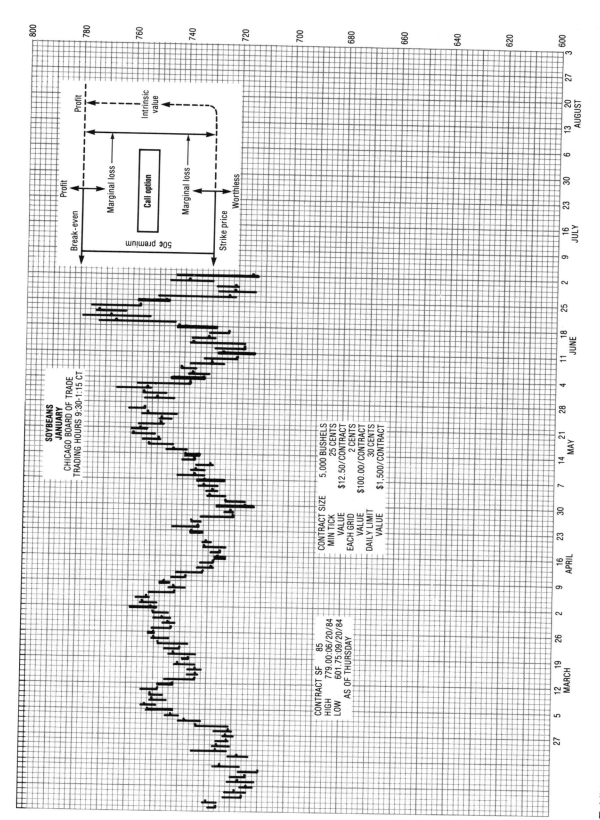

Exhibit 22-7

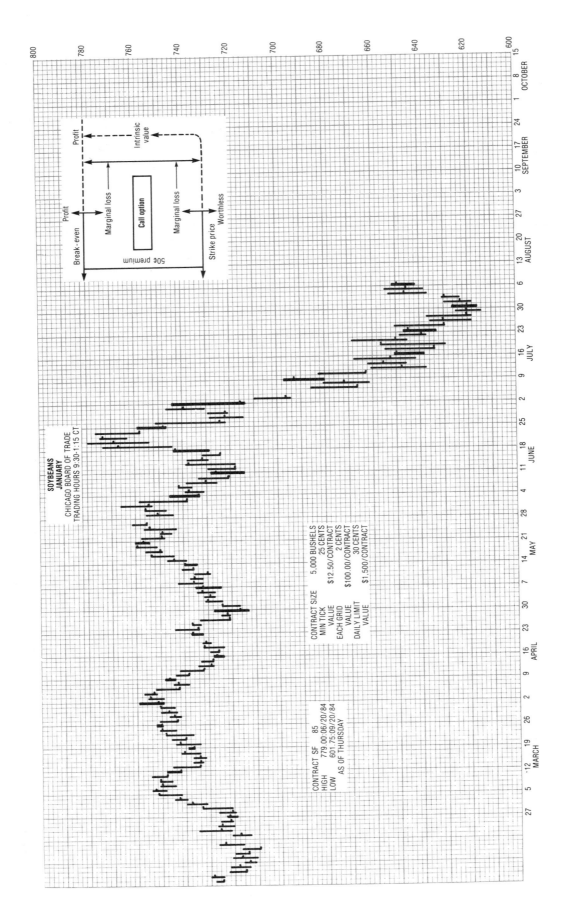

SOYBEANS
JANUARY
CHICAGO BOARD OF TRADE
TRADING HOURS 9:30-1:15 CT

CONTRACT SIZE	5,000 BUSHELS
MIN TICK	25 CENTS
VALUE	$12.50/CONTRACT
EACH GRID	2 CENTS
VALUE	$100.00/CONTRACT
DAILY LIMIT	30 CENTS
VALUE	$1,500/CONTRACT

CONTRACT SF 85
HIGH 779.00:06/20/84
LOW 601.75:09/20/84
AS OF THURSDAY

Call option
50¢ premium
Break-even
Profit
Marginal loss
Profit
Intrinsic value
Marginal loss
Worthless
Strike price

Exhibit 22-8

of the cash commodity. Commercials may occasionally do so, but private speculators almost never. The same thing can be said for exercising an option. Although an option holder may exercise at any time he chooses, and thereby obtain the long or short position that the option represents, a far simpler means for cashing the position is merely to sell the put or the call back into the market. The overwhelming majority of all profitably held options are liquidated in this fashion, rather than through exercise; and at some point prior to expiration date.

Contract Basis and Option Delta

We have already observed how futures price tends to closely follow cash price; showing premiums in normal markets, and discounts in periods of serious immediate shortage. There is a somewhat similar relationship between an option price and the price of its underlying "property"—the futures contract. The differential between cash and its corresponding futures is called *basis*. When considering the tendency of an option price to track its underlying futures price, the phenomenon is referred to as *delta*. The delta of an option will be communicated as a percentage, and measures the ability of the option to *duplicate the price fluctuations* seen in the futures contract it represents.

Since options usually expire a month or so before related contract maturities, there is no opportunity for the forces of convergence to make option and futures prices meet: Options often expire worthless. Futures contracts never do. During the life of an option, two considerations determine its value:

1. Its intrinsic value—which is the amount of money to be realized if its holder were to exercise it at any point in time (conversion benefit).
2. Its time value—which is the period remaining until expiration, and during which price change on the underlying property may generate profit for the holder (risk premium).

Intrinsic value of an option is necessarily related to the interaction of futures price fluctuations vis-à-vis the option strike price. An at-the-money call with substantial time remaining until expiration might ordinarily reflect a delta of 50, for example. This indicates that in the given situation, a 20 cent per bushel increase in the futures price would result in a 10 cent increase in the quoted option price, thus, half of the futures price change or 50 percent. Traders will dispense with the percentage, and say that the given option is reflecting a delta of 50. If the 20 cent futures price increase results in a 15 cent betterment of the option quotation, it would be a delta of 75, etc.

We thus see changing values in the option that grow out of price changes in the futures contract. There is a further determinant of option value: *time*. An option is often spoken of as a "wasting asset." This merely recognizes that option time is worth money, and the time value of an option is greatest on the day of initial acquisition. As each page is torn off the calendar, a portion of the time value of the option is gone: *wasted*. Should the option remain out-of-the- money, time is the only value it has; and this value will be totally wasted when the privilege expires worthless.

Generally speaking, the deeper in-the-money an option is, the higher its delta will be, perhaps to the extent of seeing a 5 cent increase in the futures price immediately reflected in a nickel jump in the option quotation. This would be a delta of 100. Or if an option is far out-of-the-money, it might take a contract move of a dime to tack a penny per bushel onto option value, for a delta of 10.

The foregoing information leads to two related conclusions. First, as the time value of an option erodes, its intrinsic value must increase proportionately to maintain relative worth. Second, time value in an option does not decay on a straight-line relationship. This, because as time remaining erodes, each successive day's time loss represents an ascending proportion of total time remaining (i.e., expiration-day-minus-four would lose 25 percent of remaining time value; expiration-minus-three, 33 percent of remaining time value; expiration-minus-two, 50 percent; and expiration-minus-one, 100 percent of total time value remaining in the option). Reducing these relationships to a graph gives us a curve like this:

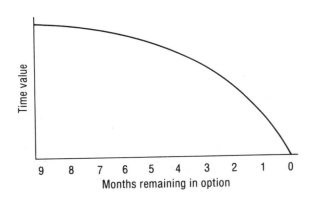

For purposes of demonstrating a put option, we will use the November 1984 soybean contract for the hypothesis. Actual examples cannot be used, inasmuch as—although options are now trading on bean futures at the Chicago Board of Trade, and on live cattle contracts at the Chicago Mercantile Exchange—the options trade hasn't been underway long enough to provide the price history we need.

In the selected demonstration, the underlying CBOT soybean contract was trading at $7.30 per bushel on March 2, when our hypothetical trader bought a 180-day put option with a strike price of $7.20. He paid a premium of 50 cents per bushel for the option. Note that when acquired, the privilege is about 10 cents out-of-the-money; with the strike price at $7.20, and the contract trading a dime higher, at about $7.30.

The model of this trade is shown in Exhibit 22–9, with the first month of price behavior following purchase revealed.

By April 2, we see that the futures price has wiggled its way up into the $7.40 range. Since it would make no sense to exercise a privilege of establishing a short position at the strike price of $7.20, when the market will let you sell 20 cents higher, the holder must wait. Until the futures price gets back below $7.20, the option is intrinsically worthless; although it does have five months of time value remaining. A lot of things can happen to a soybean price in five months!

April 30 finds the futures price backing down into the premium range. At the intraday low of $7, the put is showing an intrinsic value of 20 cents per bushel. Multiplying that 20 cents by 5,000 bushels in the contract, we see that price improvement has reduced our premium debit by an even $1,000. We still need more than 30 cents additional

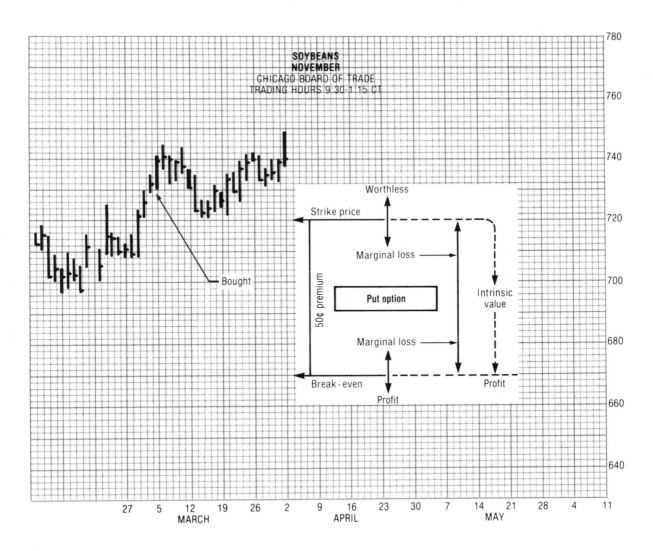

Exhibit 22–9

Exhibit 22-10

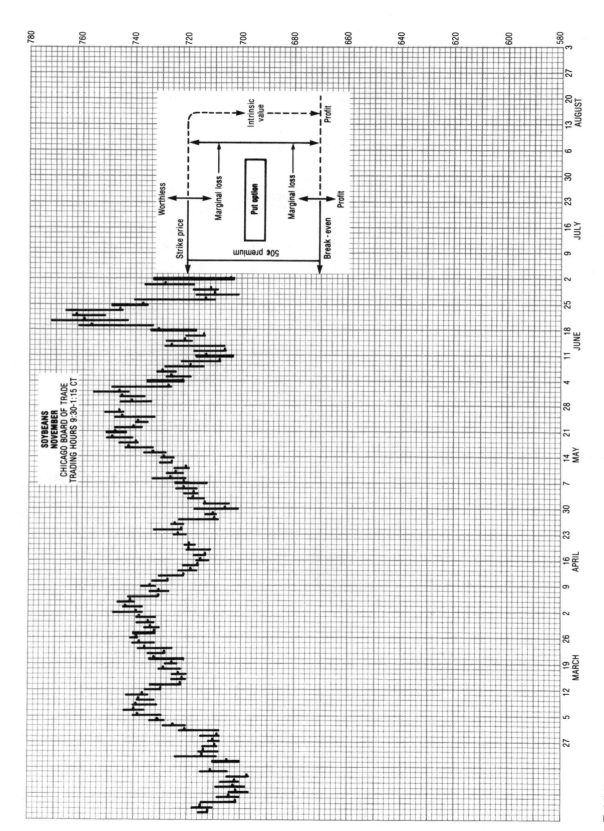

Exhibit 22–11

price deterioration before the option will begin building net profit, but the situation is looking much brighter for the holder.

Then, what April gave, May takes away. However, on June 4, after having been as much as 34 cents out-of-the-money, the futures price is back precisely at the strike level. Nothing to do but continue to wait it out. Some three months of option life remain (Exhibit 22–10).

The main feature of June trading in soybean futures proves to be a weather market psychology. Price yo-yos through a 70 cent range and, on July 2, closes at $7.02 per bushel. The put now carries a $900 intrinsic value, with only 26 cents remaining between current market price and the beginning of net-profit generation (Exhibit 22–11).

In addition to parades, picnics, and patriotic speeches, the Fourth of July holiday brought copious rains to the major soybean production area in the southcentral states. The price idea of the bulls, who had urged higher prices in expectation of a drought-damaged harvest, were dashed (Exhibit 22–12).

Eager buyers on July 2 were even more eager sellers on the following day. Then they returned from the holiday hiatus and increased the downside pressure on price. In four trading sessions the November bean contract had lost 80 cents per bushel. When the market closed on Friday, July 7, the put option we are tracing—and that had been 10 cents out-of-the-money on July 1—was in-the-money by the amount of 11 cents per bushel, for a net paper profit of $550!

Decisions! Decisions! Decisions!

Considering what the option holder has been through in some four months of sitting with this put, we might expect that when he saw the opportunity to "exercise" (take the short position at the strike price of $7.20 and immediately offset it around $6.50) and walk away with the profit, it had to look tempting. However, the option still has some seven weeks to expiration. Does it make sense to forego this time value in the interests of taking the immediate profit and running? Today's profit, we must remember, can quickly turn into tomorrow's loss.

The purpose of this discussion is to remove any notion that option trading is somehow more automatic than trading in futures contracts. It is not. Whether one holds a futures contract or an option on a futures contract, the issue is always the same: *where* to get in, and *when* to get out. Just because an option happens to be written for a maximum period of three, six, or nine months, that fact has only incidental pertinence to the issue of when to exercise—and turn paper profits into real money.

A market axiom declares that "bulls win and bears win, but hogs lose!" The obvious admonition is that a trader who stays in a position too long, trying to wring the last penny out of it, may find himself watching paper profits disappear in wrong-way price movement.

Balance this against the necessity of making *average winnings* turn out larger than *average losses*. Successful commodity speculation, whether in futures, or in options, entails lots of small losses—more than

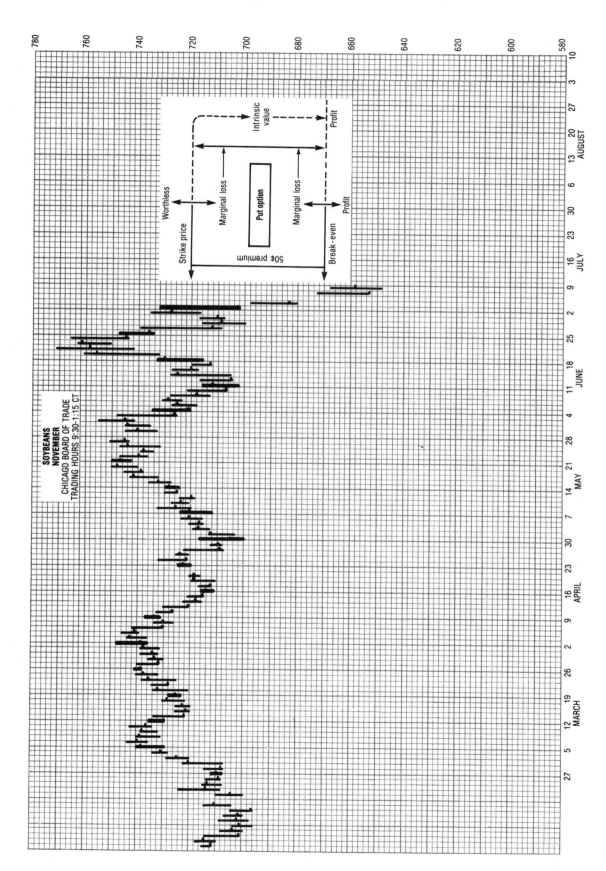

**SOYBEANS
NOVEMBER**
CHICAGO BOARD OF TRADE
TRADING HOURS 9:30-1:15 CT

Put option

50¢ premium

Strike price
Worthless
Marginal loss
Intrinsic value
Profit
Marginal loss
Break-even
Profit

Exhibit 22–12

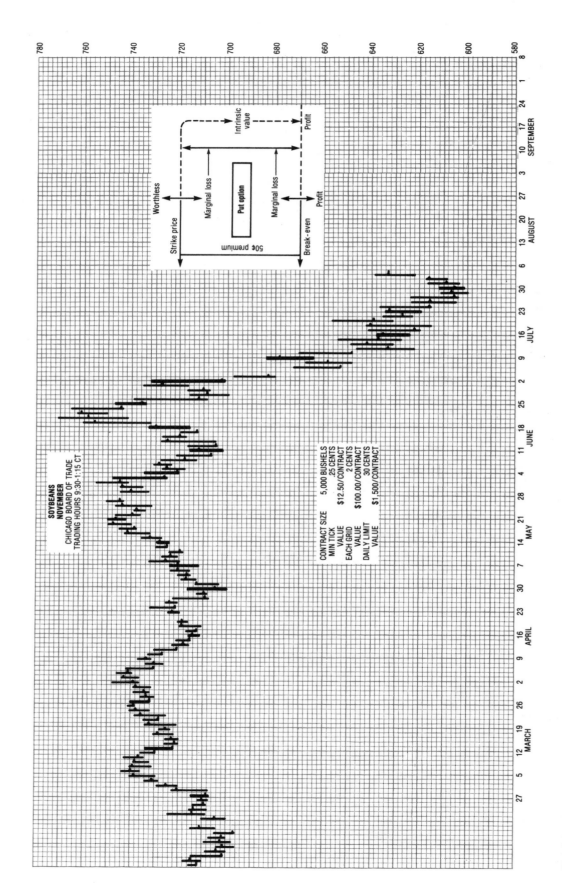

SOYBEANS
NOVEMBER
CHICAGO BOARD OF TRADE
TRADING HOURS 9:30–1:15 CT

CONTRACT SIZE	5,000 BUSHELS	
MIN TICK	.25 CENTS	
VALUE	$12.50/CONTRACT	
EACH GRID	2 CENTS	
VALUE	$100.00/CONTRACT	
DAILY LIMIT	30 CENTS	
VALUE	$1,500/CONTRACT	

Exhibit 22–13

offset by somewhat fewer, but much larger gains. Bringing this off demands that the trader have the strength of character—the sheer mental toughness—necessary to *cut losses short, and let the profits run*. This is the rule that now must govern the holder of the put we are examining.

The price reversal on July 9, is a major disappointment. The upside reversal wipes out the option profit and takes a $200 bite out of intrinsic value. Trading on the 10th again puts the price back at $6.69—and indicates a profit of $1,050. Is it a reversal, or is the price headed lower? Hold on, or take the profit and run? The trader's constant dilemma!

The session on July 11, leaves a small gap, while reaching an intrasession low of $6.22, and closing at $6.34. This is followed by three sessions that all show ranges and closes higher than those posted on the 11th. The option is now "deep in the money," with a 31 cent net profit ($1,550) ready to be taken. The Friday 21st closing posts $6.28, for an intrinsic option value of 92 cents per bushel, and a net profit to the holder (after premium deduction) of 42 cents: $2,100. He decides to hold on a little longer (Exhibit 22–13).

Patience is rewarded as, once more, we see that commodity markets tend to be creatures of momentum. Prices that are going up tend to keep going up. Prices that are going down tend to keep going down. It takes a revised and stronger composite price opinion to reverse a price trend, than it takes to continue it. The November bean price remains under pressure during the week ending July 27, carrying to $6 during the Friday session, and closing at $6.08. The put is now showing a net profit of $3,100 on paper. He decides to give the situation yet another week.

Three successively higher trading ranges and closes on July 30, 31, and August 1, shake the holder's confidence enough to prompt him to give his broker an order to *exercise* on the put as soon as possible on the morning of August 2. November beans opens 12 cents higher than the previous close, and our put holder gets execution at $6.30. Now let's look at the arithmetic on this option.

The *option writer* collected his $2,500 premium on March 2, when he sold the put. However, as the futures price moved below $7.20 on April 12, it began eroding this seller's premium. At the $7 level posted intraday on April 30, 20 cents per bushel stood "impaired;" and the seller's premium account had been reduced to only $1,500. Then, as the price rose during the following five weeks, the seller recaptured his full premium once more, as the option went well out-of-the- money in the $7.50 per bushel range. Three sessions of May 31, June 1, and June 4, once more dropped the futures price to the strike level, renewing the threat to the put writer.

If the writer of this option is a chart technician, he would have to be encouraged by the seeming impenetrability of the $7 level in this contract. As we can see in Exhibit 22–13, selloffs were turned back at precisely the even dollar on three occasions, and on June 11 the dip was reversed a cent higher. All the evidence points to some firm support at the $7 level. However, the erratic trading ranges during the last week of June might have been seen as a harbinger of lower prices to come.

Disaster arrived for the option writer in four sessions of Fourth of July week, costing him his entire premium credit on the put—and putting him at something like a 22 cent net loss on the option at Friday's low point. At this juncture he has to expect an exercise on the option, and it's likely to be an expensive one!

However, the holder seems to be in no hurry to cut profits short. He leaves the writer to watch his losses mount for three more weeks! Only when the futures bottom at $6, and then turn higher does *some seller* get a *Notice Of Exercise*. (It is as unlikely that the original option writer will still be behind the put, as it would be for the original short to still be in a given futures position some six months after its initial sale.) This, however, is not pertinent, since there is *someone* (and the clearinghouse) behind it.

Speculative Returns from Options versus Futures

The first question to be asked in appraising any speculative situation is: "What has to happen for me to make money?" Whether one buys a call option or takes a long position in January soybeans, the answer is the same: "The price on January soybeans has to go up."

The second question is: "How much must the price go up?"

There are different answers to this inquiry, depending on whether the speculative vehicle is a futures contract or an option on the futures. As has been previously demonstrated in the option model, Exhibit 22–4, the price on January beans will have to rise 54 cents per bushel to cover the 4 cent overprice and the 50 cent premium, in order to reach the break-even level. Anything above break-even is profit. Hence, as concerns the call, we can say, "In order to make a profit on this option, the futures price must rise more than 54 cents per bushel."

How about a futures contract, bought at the same time as the option? The futures will be bought 4 cents lower than the call, since all futures trading must take place within the price range for the day. There is no such thing as buying or selling a futures "out-of-the-money."

Taking a futures position involves posting margin and paying a brokerage commission on the round-trip trade. At this time at least one major commission house requires $3,500 initial margin, and $2,400 maintenance margin on a speculatively held soybean contract. Other firms handle the same business for the Board of Trade imposed minimums of $1,750 initial, and $1,250 maintenance margins. But regardless of the amount of margin required, margin remains an *account credit* to the position holder, until and unless price impairment absorbs it. Only the round-trip broker's commission of $80 or so (for making the buy and subsequent offset) is a payment for services, that is gone forever.

In consideration of these facts, the second question can be answered vis-à-vis the *futures contract* in January soybeans: "The price must go up more than 1¾ cents per bushel in order to show a profit on the long futures position."

Quite a difference!

Stated another way, the futures buyer goes into his position with an initial debit of $80, which is the amount of the broker's fee. The call option buyer goes into his position with a debit of $2,700, which is the sum of the out-of-the-money overprice ($200) and the option premium ($2,500). Until these respective amounts are covered by favorable price movement, both speculations will represent net losses.

It takes no statistical genius to recognize that the probabilities of covering an $80 position debit are much better than that of covering an initial position debit of $2,700. Two cents per bushel will handle the former, while it takes 54 cents to wipe out the larger figure. The 54 cent move that only brings the option holder to his break-even point, will give the futures holder a $2,700 gross profit. In order for the option holder to profit equally with the futures trader, his gross will have to total $5,400.

In these comparisons, it is assumed that both the futures contract and the option are held "flat"—with no spread "leg" to mitigate direct price-change impact.

Why Trade Options?

The foregoing demonstrations should go far in underscoring the hazards of using flat options (no spread or straddle posture) as speculative vehicles. The surface enticement of unlimited opportunity for profit, and a limited opportunity for loss quickly fades in the realization that a difficult and perhaps insurmountable obstacle to profits exists in the form of the option premium. Until the initial outlay is recaptured, nothing can happen to swell the buyer's bank account. *Unless* that initial outlay is recaptured the trade must be written down as a loss. An option trader must constantly weigh the perceived opportunity for profit against the size of the handicap he is required to take on as a precondition of buying the put or the call. Writers of options earnestly endeavor to set premiums on their offerings that will prove insurmountable over the period of time involved. They will succeed more often than not.

The public inclination to take the bullish side of the market has already been covered in detail in the portion of this book dealing with futures. Even in the short period of time soybean options have been trading on the CBOT, the public preference for the long side of things continues unabated: On November 26, after about one month of trading, there were 1,654 calls held open in the market, compared to 861 puts. During this time period, soybean futures have lost about 25 cents per bushel across the board. Result: There will be few flat calls on soybean futures showing any profits whatsoever. Most of them will be well down the premium range or languishing "worthless" except for some remaining time value.

For Every Loser There's a Winner

The meticulous arithmetic of a commodity market assures us that every dollar lost on one side of a trade will be gained by the other—less brokerage fees and other market costs, of course. This being true, we will now direct our attention to some of the major beneficiaries of commodity options-on-futures. The situation for an option seller, who is writing against a cash inventory (actual or potential) is vastly different than the one facing the public speculator.

For our first exercise, consider a farmer who has 5,000 bushels of soybeans in storage on the farm at the end of February. He isn't ready to sell the inventory yet, but he need not sell his beans to make some money on them while he waits. To do this he sells a "covered" call against his stored soybeans.

With all of the details conforming to those previously set forth in Exhibit 22–4, the call is written at $7.30, which is an out-of-the-money overprice of 4 cents on the January 1985 contract. The option term is 180 days. The strike price of $7.30 represents the level at which he may have to "perform" on his sold call. However, with the characteristic spring releases of stored beans pressing the market, the farmer foresees no great probability of the price improving dramatically for at least several months. The call is sold at a 50 cent premium and the $2,500 goes into the farmer's brokerage margin account.

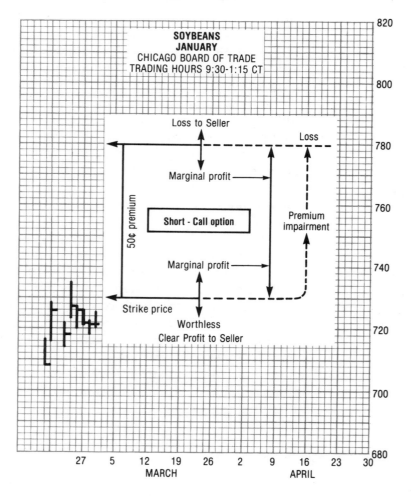

Exhibit 22–14

Although this is a hedging (covered) sale, the farmer must still post margin to secure the underlying long futures contract he may be required to deliver to the option buyer if the option is exercised. However, hedging margins are less than speculative margins. In this situation, for example, the farmer's margin requirement would be about one third less than if he were not hedging.

With the option sale at $7.30, the 50 cent premium covers the seller's marginal impairments all the way to $7.80 per bushel. Unless the futures price goes over $7.80, the farmer is going to realize some profit on the deal. Thus we see that when prices move up through the premium range, the *seller's* premium account is being reduced, while the *holder* gains intrinsic value (Exhibit 22–15).

The June run-up again bites into the seller/writer's option premium. But as he loses option premium dollars to the price rise, he gains value

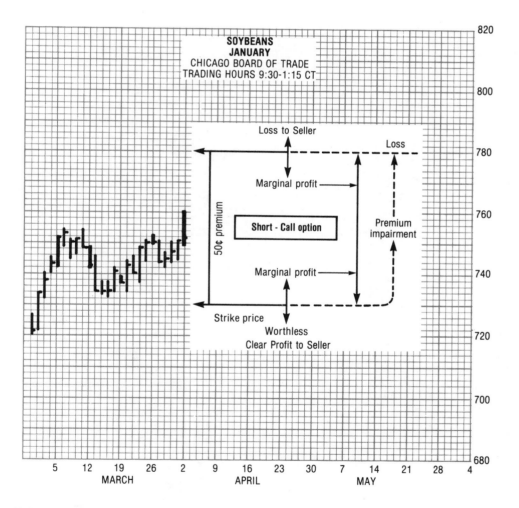

Exhibit 22–15

On April 2, the futures price has risen to a high of $7.60. But even at that level the seller still has a 20 cent per bushel profit in the position. May 7 shows the price back down around the strike price, and the entire $2,500 premium once more in the clear (Exhibit 22–16).

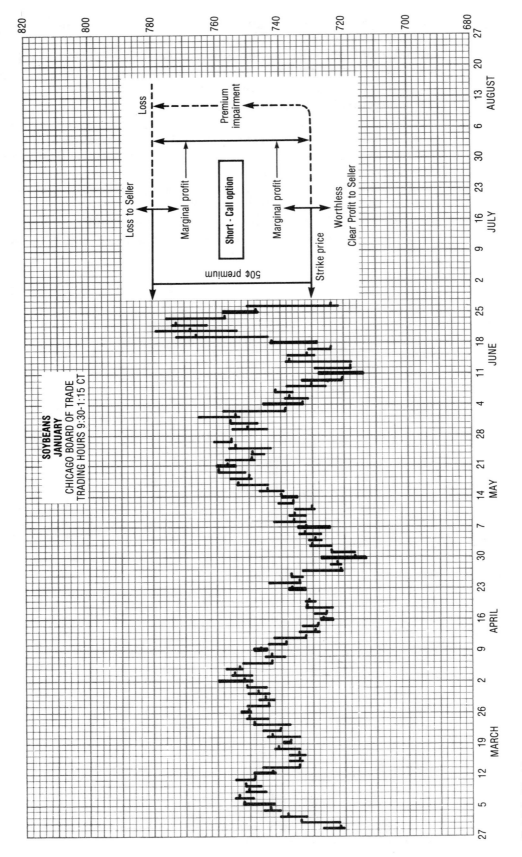

Exhibit 22–16

on his stored soybeans. This is what hedging is all about. He decides this is a good time to sell his bean inventory and free up the storage space for other crops. Consequently, he sells the cash soybeans and buys back one short-call at $7.30, on June 26 (Exhibit 22–16).

By selling a call option as a hedge against his cash, the farmer has had interest-free use of the premium funds for four months. But this is not all.

A major consideration in pricing options is time: The longer the life of an option, the greater the opportunity for price to move into the profit area for the buyer—and the loss area for the writer. The call we are examining here was written for a period of six months, for a premium of 50 cents per bushel. When it is offset by repurchase of a call in the options market, only two months remain to expiration. Two thirds of the option life has "wasted"—and with the offset price at the same level as the market price, time value is the only value the option has. Hence, the buy-back is made for a per-bushel premium of 20 cents, for a profit of 30 cents per bushel—or $1,500—to the seller.

Even had the futures price gone to $8, and the call been exercised, the seller's gross loss of 70 cents per bushel (from $7.30 to $8.00) would have been reduced to a net loss of only 20 cents per bushel, by virtue of the 50 cent option premium collected at the outset.

Futures Hedge Locks in Profit

If, instead of selling the call option, the farmer-hedger had chosen to go *short* one soybean contract, the result would have been much different. With the futures hedge placed on February 28, at an in-range $7.26, cash price and the futures price would have tracked together for the four-month interval. Basis changes between cash and the futures are the extent of potential profits on a cash/futures hedge, and rarely exceed a few cents per bushel within the relatively short time period we are dealing with here.

The unique virtue of using options for hedging purposes is that they generate their maximum profit—the amount of the premium—if price remains unchanged. Moreover, any adverse futures price movement against the writer will be cushioned to the extent of the option premium collected. The single shortcoming of an option hedge—from the standpoint of the hedger—is that adverse price movement is only covered to the extent of the premium. Once price has gone through the break-even level (higher, in the case of a call, lower in the case of a put) the seller has no further protection against market realities. His performance obligation may require acquiring a short position well below the option premium range, or taking a long position far above the premium range.

Futures prices, on the other hand, can be counted on to keep in quite close step with cash prices—almost always. The only notable exceptions are encountered in *inverted* markets, when immediate shortage may drive cash prices to large premiums over futures prices in nearby maturities. If the shortage that prompts the inversion is sufficiently severe, there is no theoretical limit to the extent of inversion which may result.

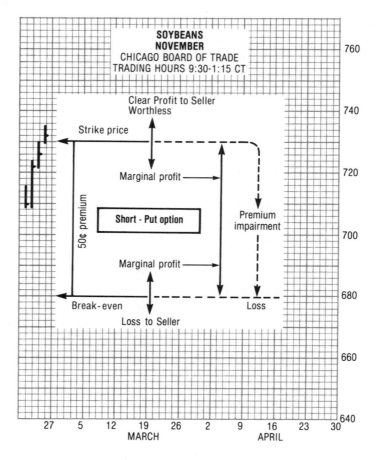

Exhibit 22–17

Selling Puts to Protect Purchase Price

This exercise assumes a situation in which a processor, fearing there might be some modest increase in soybean prices, wishes to protect himself from having to pay up for supplies. On March 2, he sells puts at a strike price of $7.30, 180 days, for a premium of 50 cents. The premium per contract is $2,500, which the processor-*writer* collects.

With the put hedge in place, the processor—although not completely protected—has helped himself appreciably. Should bean prices move clear up to $8 per bushel, his effective purchase price will be $7.50; which would be "market" less the premium he collected on the sold puts. But what happens to him if price falls? (Exhibit 22–17.)

Assuming the bean price goes to $6.50 per bushel, and the put is exercised, our processor would be faced with a gross loss of 80 cents per bushel in performing on his short-put obligation. However, this gross loss is reduced by the amount of the premium previously collected, thereby reducing the net loss to 30 cents a bushel. In any case, as an experienced hedger, the processor isn't likely to stay around for anything approaching that amount of position impairment.

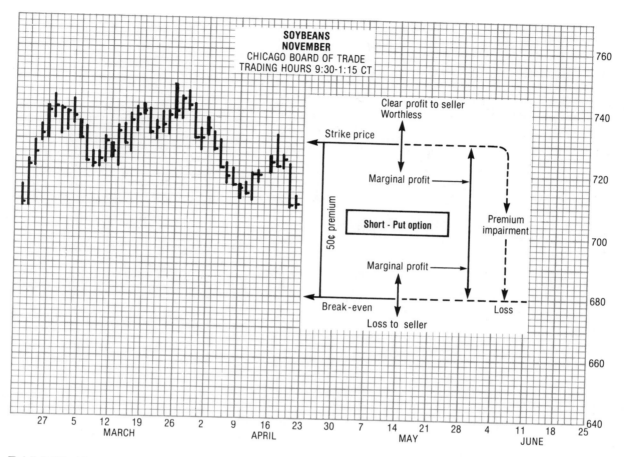

Exhibit 22–18

After a modest price dip the November futures contract gathers strength, closing back at $7.34 on April 2. It then falls to $7.12 at month's end, which leaves it nearly in the middle of the premium range. The option hedge appears to be working well (Exhibit 22–18).

The entire month of May brings successively higher prices. At the end of the month the futures price stands at $7.46, and is showing signs (in volume and open interest data) of being "toppy." The short-put is now out-of-the-money, with the full premium amount completely unencumbered. In other words, the hedger's short-put is now reflecting the maximum amount of profit it can ever generate—regardless of how high the futures price may climb. Consequently, the hedger decides to buy back his put (or one just like it) to offset his short option position. This done, he will then look for another opportunity to hedge his forward purchasing requirements, or protect the forward prices of his manufactured products. Which course he chooses, and whether he will pursue it by selling or buying puts or calls, by writing puts or calls, or by going long or short futures contracts will depend on his current appraisal of the market (Exhibit 22–19).

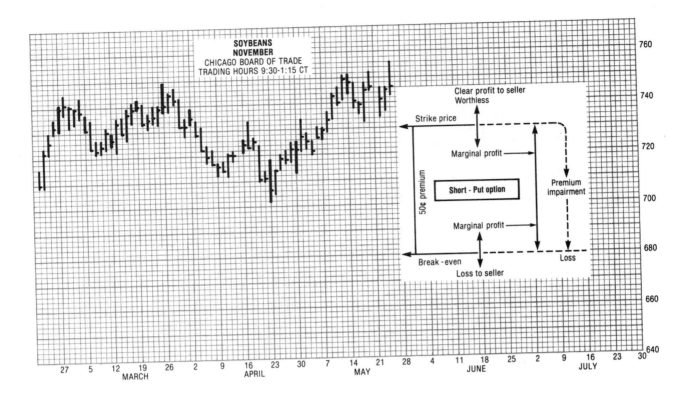

Exhibit 22-19

Matching Options to Market Attitudes

Whether a speculator or hedger buys or writes puts or calls, or chooses futures as the market vehicle best suited to his needs, will always depend in large measure on how he views the market at any given time. There is no practicable way to reduce this selection process to exactitudes, but there are some useful guidelines that should be kept in mind.

Buying Calls Is Inherently Bullish

The speculator buys a call on the expectation that price on the underlying futures will move *substantially* higher, thus allowing him to exercise or offset his lower-priced right, and then dispose of it in the higher-priced current market. A grain merchant may have qualms about writing a fixed-price order calling for the delivery of soybeans to a customer several months hence, when he knows that in the interim the price of the product may rise, costing him the profit on the sale. To protect himself against this contingency, the merchant may buy calls. Being long the calls hedges him against the price risks in the short cash-forward commitment.

Buying Puts Is Inherently Bearish

A speculator buys puts when he thinks the underlying futures price is headed *much* lower. If his judgment is vindicated, he will be able to close out his higher-priced right in the then-current lower-priced market and profit from the interim decline in price. A hedger buys puts to protect against value losses on inventory or purchase commitments at fixed prices. A farmer who in May would like to assure himself of today's quotation of $7 for November soybeans as a floor price for his crop, might buy puts to get the price protection he seeks. At the same time, he will be able to benefit from any interim price improvement during the period he holds the privileges.

Selling Calls Is Inherently Bearish or Neutral

Writing calls against cash inventory is a relatively low-risk means of enhancing income for owners, commercial dealers, producers, etc. Maximum return (the amount of the premium) is realized even if no price change occurs during the period the position is held. Marginal return is generated on a diminishing scale as price on the underlying futures moves up through the premium range. A short-call provides a fixed (premium) cushion against loss in inventory values.

Selling Puts Is Inherently Bullish or Neutral

Writing puts against forward purchase requirements that will have to be made at market prices offers protection against interim price increases. Maximum return on the put (the amount of the premium) is realized even if no price change occurs during the period the position is held. Marginal return is generated on a diminishing scale as price on the underlying futures moves down through the premium range. Although the option premium will help offset any loss sustained by reason of the seller's higher acquisition prices in the market, should prices move lower (below break-even at the bottom of the premium range) the writer would be required—on exercise by the holder—to purchase soybean futures at the strike price reflected in the option. His loss in thus performing would be calculable by deducting the amount of the premium previously collected, from the gross difference between strike price and exercise price.

While the foregoing explanations and examples only represent a minuscule sampling of the full range of applications options offer both speculators and hedgers, the modest recountment should be sufficient to convince both camps that there are few if any easy answers in the options market. Time and experience will surely develop some more or less stylized approaches to options that tend to optimize profit opportunities and minimize loss exposures for both hedgers and speculators.

For now, however, everyone who makes bold to discourse on the topic is necessarily speaking theoretically. This is true because as previously noted there have been no agricultural options markets for almost half a century! Even when traded before then, they rarely carried time periods of more than one week. Hence, there has been no opportunity for acquiring the skills and insights needed to underpin a settled professionalism in option trading. Only time will correct this. In the interim learning period, a cautious respect for the unfamiliarities of this new trading entity is the first component of prudence.

Spreads and Straddles

On paper, some of the best opportunities for public, nonhedging, speculation in options appears to be through *spreads and straddles,* in which a call option is held against a short futures position. Or conversely, where a put is arrayed against a long futures position. However, the seeming relative safety of such an approach is flawed by the absence of the *convergence principle* that operates between cash commodities and futures contracts.

Options Prices and Futures Prices Do Not Converge

It will be remembered that the theory of carrying costs provides us with the firm assurance that, "The cash price of the commodity and the price of the expiring futures contract must converge on the last day of trading in said contract." This because, on expiration, the matured contract *becomes* the cash commodity: All remaining shorts must make delivery of the physical merchandise, and all remaining longs in the contract must take delivery and pay for it in full. For every short there must be a long; and unlike options, there is no such thing as a "worthless" traded commodity.

In further contrast to futures, there is no pairing between puts and calls that may be outstanding in the options market at any given time, nor at exercise or expiration. And because there is no such thing as a worthless commodity, neither is there such a thing as a worthless futures contract that represents it. But *options* that expire "worthless" are far from unusual!

The reality that in theory keeps options prices in line with the market is there, but it is a much longer and more elastic tether than the one that keeps cash commodities and their futures contracts on the same track: The three-tiered relationship in a normal market may be viewed as follows:

1. Base price = cash price for the physical merchandise.
2. Futures price = cash price + carrying costs ± perceived supply/ demand imbalance.

3. Options price = futures price + market-determined premium charge.

4. Premium charge = consensual value of limited variable protection from fluctuative losses on the underlying merchandise for a fixed maximum time interval.

Pricing Options

The potential buyer or writer of an option, like his counterpart in the futures sector, begins by checking current comparative quotations on puts and calls before taking a position for himself. But how reliable are market bids and offers likely to be as guides to the inherent speculative opportunity in an option? The futures trader considering a position in soybeans can find some derivative guidance in the corresponding prices of soybean oil and soybean meal. His perspective might also be enhanced by making some relative comparisons with marginally substitutive products like corn, oats, and rapeseed.

Whether buying or selling a futures contract, a single price at market will likely apply.

Writers of options price their offerings to maximize whatever disparities differing levels of market demand allow. Calls usually carry higher prices than puts, regardless of the illogic therein, because more

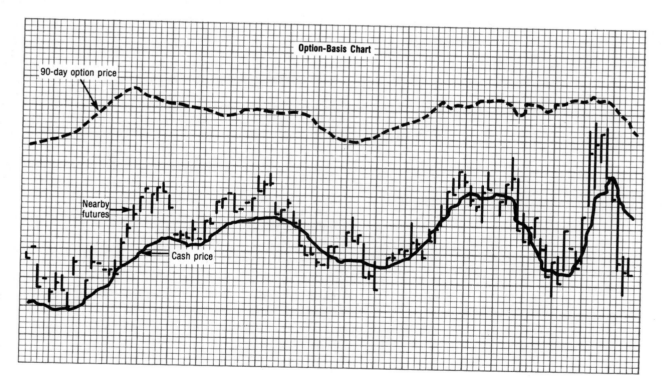

Exhibit 22–20

people want to be long than want to be short the underlying futures. It takes no more than this trade preference to maintain the price skewing; which has almost nothing to do with such considerations as trend, bias, etc.

Mathematical Modeling

In consideration of the need to be able to put an economic yardstick on options prices, a variety of formulas have been set forth by mathematical analysts that purport to assay the components giving rise to a particular premium on a selected put or call. Only limited experience background exists to help one choose between the proffered equations. Perhaps it makes little difference which formula one settles on, as long as it is applied consistently. The most such an appraisal exercise will offer in any case is a relative gauge of under or overpricing; as compared to other option alternatives, involving different out-of-the-moneys and longer or shorter time periods.

Accepting this notion *arguendo,* the *Black Pricing Model* offers what might be seen as a useful analytic middle ground. Professor Black's methodology is much less complex than that of more technically exacting investigators. It is more inclusive than the simplistic approaches of those who give small import to much beyond time value and volatility indexing. The Black model has a further virtue of being easily programmable in any of the current crop of personal computers.

Black's Option Pricing Model

Call: $C \quad = \quad e^{-rt}[UN(d_1) - EN(d_2)]$

Where:

$d_1 \quad = \quad [In(U/E) + (sd^2t)/2]/sd\sqrt{t}$

$d_2 \quad = \quad [In(U/E) - (sd^2t)/2]/sd\sqrt{t}$

C	=	call premium
U	=	underlying futures price
E	=	exercise price
r	=	short-term interest rate
t	=	life of option expressed in years
sd	=	market volatility (standard deviation of market returns on an annualized basis)
N	=	symbol denoting normal cumulative probability distribution
e	=	2.1783: base of the natural logarithm
In	=	the natural log of the term

Put: $P \quad = \quad -e^{-rt}[UN(-d_1) - EN(-d_2)]$

In application, consider a call option in which the following inputs are present:

Soybean futures market price is at $7.25 $(U = \$7.25)$
Exercise price on the option is $7.00 $(E = \$7.00)$
Short-term interest rate stands at 9 percent $(r = .09)$
Market volatility is established at 20 percent $(sd = .20)$
About 90-days ($\pm\frac{1}{4}$ year) until expiration $(t = .25)$

$$
\begin{aligned}
C \;&=\; e^{-(.09)\,(.25)}[7.25N(.40) - 7.00N(.30)] \\
&=\; .98[7.25(.6554) - 7.00(.6179)] \\
&=\; \$.42 \text{ per bushel, or } \$2,100.00 \text{ per 5,000 bushel} \\
&\quad\ \text{contract.}
\end{aligned}
$$

Where

$$
\begin{aligned}
d_1 \;&=\; [In(7.25/7.00) + (.2^2 \times .25)/2]/2\sqrt{.25} \\
&=\; .40 \\
N(d_1) \;&=\; .6554 \\
d_2 \;&=\; [In(7.25/7.00) - (.2^2 \times .25)/.2]\sqrt{.25} \\
&=\; .30 \\
N(d_2) \;&=\; .6179
\end{aligned}
$$

By using this price model (or an alternative) the option trader can develop a far more valid notion about pricing aberrations than is to be had from merely perusing price/premium quotations. The economic components of an option premium are much more complex and less directly relative to the underlying futures/cash prices, than are futures prices-to-cash prices. By adding an opportunity to trade options to the historic duo of cash merchandise and futures contracts, the menu of speculative choices—both directly and in combinations—has been increased in geometric proportions.

By taking an option position against a different option *class* or *type,* one level of risk/reward potential is created. By holding options against the underlying futures and/or the physical commodity, or other optioned property, an entirely different risk/profit potential can be established.

In order to participate fully—and profitably—in this exciting new financial sector, the serious trader has no choice but to develop the skills required to make prudent decisions based on careful evaluations. When it comes to picking optimal speculative opportunities from within the full scope of available choices in the cash/futures/options trinity, more than luck, hunches, and gut feelings are required. Until this kind of preparatory information has been acquired, the public trader will best serve both his solvency and his peace of mind by confining his speculative forays to more familiar terrain.

In order to do justice to the wide-ranging ramifications of option trading, a new category of business literature must be created. In addition to theoretical enlightenment, we need the benefit of experience as well. The greatest problem facing the newcomer to options trading now is the dearth of materials available to guide his or her initiation into the area. It's a situation quite similar to the one that surrounded futures markets until some 20 years ago, when the first serious efforts to make commodity trading understandable to the public were undertaken—by this writer and others. The same kind of information "explosion" around options markets can now be confidently predicted.

In the meantime, caution in this new financial sector should be the watchword. Playing any money game one doesn't fully understand is something other than sound business—and speculation, it can't be too often repeated, IS A BUSINESS!

23

Futures Markets and the Markets of the Future

Should anyone ever ask when the revolution began, the correct answer is May 16, 1972. That is the date upon which the first trade in international currencies was transacted on the floor of the International Monetary Market in Chicago. With that single cataclysmic event to build on, nothing would ever again be the same in the business of economic risk management; regardless of whether those risks related to growing crops, money values, interest rates, or stock prices.

Once having broken with the time-honored misconception that in order to be successfully traded in a futures contract, the underlying property had to be seasonal, storable, and consumable, the list of things to which the convenience label "commodity" might be applied was suddenly much longer!

The second date that stands out in the market revolution is April 26, 1973. On this day the fledgling Chicago Board Options Exchange opened call-option trading on 16 listed stocks. The action moved privilege trading out of the back rooms of a handful of brokerage firms and into the public arena. What had been an esoteric activity of a miniscule segment of the financial community, quickly blossomed into a major facet of the speculative and financial hedging market.

Whatever ties remained to risk-management orthodoxy were sundered on February 24, 1982, when the Kansas City Board of Trade opened trading in a cash-settled composite stock index; in which the underlying financial commodity was an arithmetically determined *value*, extrapolated from a list of 1,700 Value Line equities. With all contract obligations—both interim and at expiration—geared exclusively to payment of cash values between longs and shorts, an historic milepost of economic sophistication had been reached: *Risk* stood revealed as the essential consideration in all trading that is not directly undertaken for the purpose of supplying an *immediate need.* The fundamental verity stands, regardless of whether the particular risk is measured against a value yardstick that is calibrated in bushels of grain, barrels of oil, quantities of currency, ounces of metal, shares of stock, or instruments of obligation drawn against a trusted source. Beyond the full range of specific commercial goods, another totally different order of values could now be created by the use of composites assembled from among appropriate "classes" of economic goods.

Acceptance and official approval of a stock-index futures contract that settled in cash only, offered irrefutable evidence that the stigma of *malum prohibitum,* that had been applied to the concept for half a century, was without justification on any sensible basis. Public opinion had come full circle and, in doing so, had decided that even such an august body as the U.S. Supreme Court could be temporarily blinded by bias and misconception. The high court decision that had—for half a century—proscribed cash settlements of futures contracts as gambling was, in effect, set aside in the legislation establishing the Commodity Futures Trading Commission. By empowering the CFTC to determine the definition of a futures contract, Congress had also given the commission authority to decide what classifications of economic goods might be considered "commodities." Everything that followed must be tied into that single legislative change of heart.

The opening salvo in the battle for cash-settled financial instruments attracted little attention. Perhaps it was planned that way. In any case, while the conflict surrounding the acceptance of a market index as a trading entity raged on, the International Monetary Market leadership took another step into the future. Almost unnoticed in the public press, Melamed and the others had approached the Commodity Futures Trading Commission with a proposal for a cash-settled (no delivery procedure) futures contract on Eurodollar Time Deposits (EDs). A tremendous amount of American dollars had been exported to Europe via the Marshall Plan and similar postwar reconstruction and aid programs. A strong case could be made that, by offering a hedge vehicle, the foreign funds would be less of a threat to our domestic money values and therefore to the securities markets. By being able to hedge Eurodollars "in place" there would be less attraction to repatriate them in large volumes, thus further contributing to highly worrisome inflationary pressures.

For whatever reasons or rationale, the CFTC did succumb to IMM blandishments, and the Eurodollar futures contracts began trading in December 1981. This stood as the first cash-settled contract, but it would soon be joined by many more.

For purposes of clarification it should be noted that although contracts in foreign currencies on the IMM were settled by the passage of the money between longs and shorts (or offset), this did not constitute "cash settlement" per se. It was a delivery procedure only. Cash settlement involves payment of *differences* made and lost by the respective holders in money. The contract package only serves as an economic yardstick for the calculation of those debits and credits.

New Futures Validated by Growth

It's easy to identify a bad idea in the commodity market: A contract that isn't needed, isn't traded. Any number of considerations may render a given contract unnecessary, ranging from lack of volume in the particular item (pistachio nuts), lack of fluctuative price risk (a government "loan" program that guarantees a fixed price), or lack of uniformity that prevents grade consistency (textiles). Or a contract may be eclipsed by changing technology or new consumption patterns. Steam lard was an actively traded commodity on the Chicago Board of Trade until vegetable oils came along to displace it as the shortening of choice in America's kitchens.

But regardless of the underlying reason, if a contract doesn't fill a substantial economic need for a significant market segment, it will never be able to attract enough participation to become—or remain—viable. Speculation by itself is hardly ever sufficient. To survive, a contract must have a solid foundation of commercial hedging, represented in positions taken and held by interests or individuals who are seeking to shift risks of ownership of the underlying property—or its near-equivalent.

From the outset, the need for financial-instrument hedging devices was documented in huge introductory volume figures. The first seven months of currency trading on the IMM saw 144,928 contracts bought and sold. In 1973, its first full year of existence, volume almost tripled—to 417,310 contracts traded.

During May 1973, the first full month of operation of the Chicago Board Options Exchange, total volume was 34,599. In January 1976, the monthly volume figure had swelled to 2,500,000 contracts, representing 250 million shares of stock. The Chicago Board Options Exchange grew from the smallest securities exchange in the U.S., to the second largest—in less than three years!

In the first nine months of trading in the KCBOT Value Line Index, 352,248 contracts moved. During the first full year of index trading, the volume more than doubled to 738,497.

With broad-scale industry usage documented in figures like these, the die-hard critics had little room in which to charge that the newly launched financial-instruments markets were a mere contrivance of the participants; in a search for alternatives to Las Vegas and Atlantic City. After a decent period of "hiding and watching," a veritable parade of banks, insurance companies, pension funds, mutual funds, and other fiduciary organizations began lining up for the specialized kinds of protection that contracts predicated on value changes in currencies, stocks, and stock-index averages now offered—for the first time in the history of the world!

In addition to the institutional users, private individuals quickly saw instruments as a ready and cost-efficient means for both cushioning portfolio holdings against sharply swinging price quotations, and a way to "buy (or sell) the market" via an index position. No longer was a private investor/speculator limited to specific-stock ownership, with its attendant volatility exposures, or to "funds," with their checkered performance records. Now it was possible for an individual to literally own symbolic shares in the *American business system*. A position in a stock index is precisely that. Truly, a mind-boggling concept!

More Instruments Offered

Having been loosed from the straight-jacket definition of "what is a commodity?" and "how must a futures contract be settled?" the exchanges vied with each other to rush into the marketplace with an assortment of financial instruments. All were intended—and tailored—to provide hedge correlation with interest rates, industry-category risks, and a spate of other more or less specialized economic risk exposures. By the end of 1983, international currencies and financial "paper" constituted the largest single category in the futures/options industry, and far outstripped the total of equity values traded on all of the U.S. stock exchanges combined. An abbreviated roster of traded "commodities" will demonstrate the situation better than words.

Trading Category	Number of Items	
Currencies	10	} Currencies and instruments—37
Financial instruments	27	
Foodstuffs	14	
Grains	9	
Industrial materials	14	} All other traded commodities, including precious and monetary metals—58
Livestock products	9	
Metals	7	
Oilseed products	5	

Not all of the contracts approved for trading are active, but salient figures leave little doubt about where current market interest is being focused:

Year	Category	Total contracts traded
1977	Grains	7,928,127
1983	Grains	17,793,846
1977	Metals	8,864,229
1983	Metals	26,316,268
1977	Financial instruments	604,622
1983	Financial instruments	40,154,894

New-Contract Proposals from U.S. Commodities and Securities Exchanges

EXCHANGE	CONTRACT	PROJECTED TIME OF OPENING (Where Available)
Approved by Regulators		
Philadelphia Stock Exchange	Value Line Stock Index Options	Jan. 11
Pending Approval by U.S. Regulators		
Chicago Board of Trade	Municipal Bond Futures	First quarter
	Treasury Note Futures Options	Second quarter
	Silver Futures Options	N/A
	Corn Futures Options	N/A
Chicago Board Options Exchange	Options on Individual OTC Stocks	N/A
	Options on the West German Mark, British Pound, Swiss Franc, Japanese Yen, Canadian Dollar	N/A
Philadelphia Board of Trade*	Eurodollar Futures Options	First quarter
	OTC Stock-Index Futures and Futures Options	Second quarter
Chicago Mercantile Exchange	Futures Options on the Swiss Franc, the British Pound, Eurodollars	N/A
	Live Hog Futures Options	N/A
New York Mercantile Exchange	Heating Oil Futures Options	N/A
	Crude Oil Futures Options	First half 1985
	Natural Gas Futures	N/A
New York Coffee, Sugar and Cocoa Exchange	Futures on Auto Sales, the Consumer Price Index, A Corporate Earnings Index and Housing Starts	N/A
New York Futures Exchanges	Futures on the Commodity Research Bureau Index	First quarter
London International Financial Futures Exchange	Eurodollar Options, Long Gilt Options, Sterling Options, Short Gilt Futures	N/A
New York Stock Exchange	Options on Individual Stocks	N/A
Amex Commodities Corp.	Gold Options	First quarter
Mid America Commodity Exchange	Soybean Futures Options	N/A
Baltic Exchange	Ocean Freight Futures	Mid–1985

*A proposed new exchange seeking regulatory approval to open.

Exhibit 23–1

Anyone who believes the financial instruments list is approaching completion should be dissuaded by this roster of new products already scheduled for trade, or in some stage of preparation or approval in the final month of 1984.

The presently available list of financial instruments that can be traded in either futures contracts, options, or options *on* futures contracts may appear quite adequate to the casual observer. However, there is no reason to think that we have seen the end of such offerings, by any means. Someone has said that "The business of America is business!" Ours is at once the most productive, most efficient, and most specialized economic complex on earth. We operate the world's finest businesses, and turn out the world's finest business managers. Given some statutory latitude within which to innovate, the end of our money-management refinements is nowhere in sight! (Exhibit 23–1.)

Competition Sets the Pace

It is at least remarkable that it remained for a group of commodity traders to establish the first organized exchange devoted to the trading of options on common stocks. Any one of the four active stock exchanges (located in New York City, Chicago, and San Francisco) would appear to have been far better situated for such an undertaking. That none of those institutions saw fit to do so can only be charged up to contentment with what constituted their own status quo in an activity that hadn't changed much since Jay Gould and Hetty Green were names to contend with. It was only after the Chicago Board Options Exchange had turned an unimpressive beginning into a soaring accomplishment that the Big Board and Amex began to take the options business seriously.

When the IMM began posting volume figures that could no longer be ignored by either private or public money-watchers, the guiding lights in the New York Stock Exchange had to concede that there might be a place for currency trading in the market complex.

When the Value Line, Standard & Poor's 500, and Standard & Poor's 100 Indexes simply kept on posting volume record after volume record, the stock exchanges did make an effort to get into the parade. But it's too late for them! New concepts, coupled with new technology, in the hands of their aggressive, innovative competition has too large a head start in the business to ever be overtaken now.

Where Is the Business Headed?

There is an ironic parallel to be drawn from the grain business, as a means for explaining present developments in the financial complex.

When Mr. Haines agreed to rent the second floor of his feed store out to a bunch of "speculators" who wanted to meet there every day and trade "to-arrives" on corn and wheat, he would never have guessed that it wouldn't be long before his "real" business would be almost totally controlled by the "wind-wheat" and "paper-corn" business going on upstairs! How could a serious-minded businessman who merchandised actual grain be expected to pay that surging yelling mob up on the second floor any real attention? Expecially, when everybody knew that most of the speculators never held a bushel of grain in their lives—and didn't want to!

Mr. Haines's attitude was given a modern echo when, in response to the IMM decision to begin trading currencies, a distinguished international money expert declared for publication, "I'm amazed that a bunch of crapshooters in pork bellies have the temerity to think that they can beat some of the world's most sophisticated (money) traders at their own game!" Amazement, in this case, proved to be the first step along the road to wisdom. What the gentleman failed to realize is that markets are the very *incubators* of competition. Regardless of how one might find the mousetrap business, the world does indeed beat a path to the better market. And the better money market turned out to be just a few blocks up the same Chicago River that had run behind Haines's Feed Store, 125 years earlier!

It didn't take long for the cash-grain business to become an almost incidental appurtenance to the burgeoning futures trade. Mr. Haines and his merchant peers knew it had happened when, in order to buy *real* grain, they had to enter bids that were pennies per bushel *on* or *off* the nearest *futures* price. Once established, the same method for pricing the "actuals" has proceeded uninterruptedly for more than 100 years. Cash tables used to be an integral part of the noisy, roistering trading floor in the Chicago Board of Trade. No more! Cash trading isn't relatively important enough to justify giving it trade-floor space.

The Realities of Stock Trading

Our economic society has, from time to time, made some really serious efforts to cloak stock ownership in the raiment of patriotism. The notion is not without historical justification. Stockholdings on the part of rank-and-file Americans played an indispensable part in accumulating the capital with which to bankroll our industrial revolution. Public faith in the system never wavered until the "crash" in 1930–31; but, having experienced that unequalled economic debacle, full public confidence in corporations and the people who manage them was never quite restored.

Holding two or three stocks is a hazardous thing to do, by reason of the fluctuative exposures involved. The notion of portfolio diversification, although it has been a universal faith among market authorities almost forever (it's a statistical concept, actually), didn't begin catching on with the public until after World War II. While small investors by definition are unable to acquire and hold the minimum 15 to 25 assorted equities that most experts insist upon, a new investment entity came along in the post-war period that accomplished the same result with a monthly-payment plan. It was called "mutual funds," and represented the first significant break with traditional stock-ownership patterns.

By holding a widely diversified assortment of stocks, the *stock-specific* risks related to such things as mismanagement, price manip-

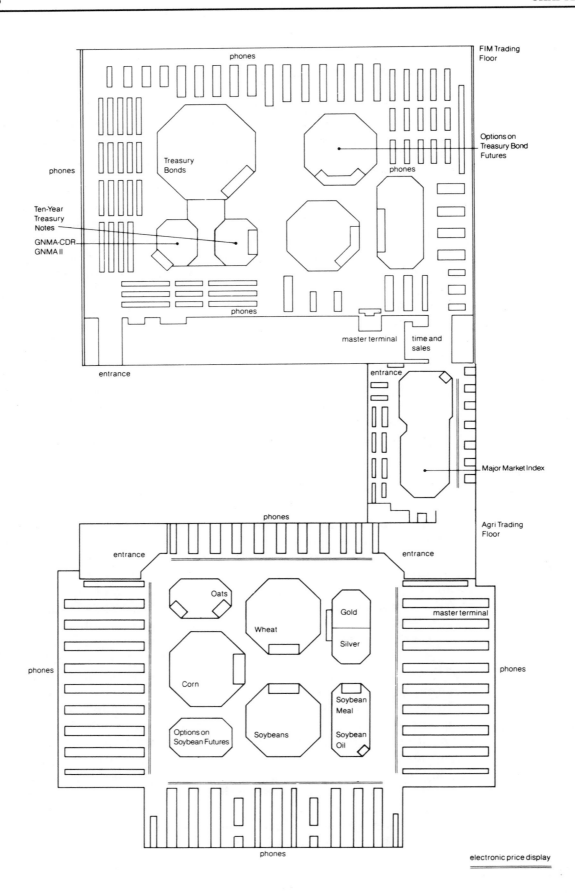

electronic price display

Exhibit 23–2

Cash tables were a prominent feature of the CBOT trading floor until 1970, occupying a significant place in the market—both physically and economically. Now there is no longer a trade in cash grains in the exchange. The connection between cash and futures is understood, but the marketing of actuals takes place elsewhere.

---

ulation via rumors, raids, etc., and the handicap of poor information channels were substantially overcome. Price volatility in the fund's holdings was mitigated by averaging it out to some greater or lesser extent. More importantly, by having large amounts of money to put into whatever companies engendered their confidence, fund managers quickly found themselves being wooed by corporate executives. Fund managers, therefore, began sharing the same information network as the insiders.

Performance Competition

As competition between the funds increased, *performance* entered the Wall Street vocabulary. The conservatism that had marked the first mutual funds' approach to portfolio management no longer satisfied a large and growing segment of potential fund investors. Thus, the *performance fund* came into being. This was soon followed by the *growth fund*—and then the *go-go fund*.

With no exact tool to classify these several kinds of money-management attitudes, suffice it to say that the first mutual funds were content to "duplicate the Dow." That is to say that if at the end of the year the fund managers could point to a growth and earnings result that was equal to the 30 companies comprising the Dow Jones Industrials, they felt their management efforts were vindicated.

The performance funds looked to the Dow Jones Average also; but their success was calculated on "outperforming the Dow." They hoped to accomplish this result by exercising more selectivity in choosing issues to hold for earnings and price appreciation.

The growth funds built their identities on what has been called the technological revolution. The 1960s and 70s were heady times in our business system, with companies like Hewlett-Packard, Hunt-Wesson Foods, Syntex, Xerox, Polaroid, Texas Instruments, and IBM bringing off balance-sheet miracles that left their stockholders mesmerized. Conglomerates were put together like children assemble Tinkertoys. Raiders like Lytton and Wolfson made headlines; and the headlines made millions for shareholders who happened to be in the right place at the right time. The growth fund managers sought to pick their winners out of this seething cauldron of corporate upheaval. Some times they succeeded.

Standing alone at the very apex of risk exposure were the go-go funds. Managed by a group of gimlet-eyed financial gunfighters who bore the label of "young Turks" on the street, they wanted nothing to do with either modest risks or modest returns. Their quest was for new technology, new companies, new corporate combinations, and new management teams that, although unknown and untried, carried that magical spark that lights up a potential miracle in the marketplace. Some of the go-gos specialized in firms involved with inorganic chemistry innovation. Others focused their attention into electronics, communications, information handling, or genetics. The only inflexible requirement for the young Turks seemed to be that a company chosen for investment have no track record whatsoever; and that it be headed by someone no more than two years away from his or her most recent graduation.

Rarely if ever has speculation been approached with such a sense of utter abandon. In response to a question on how his selections were made, one such manager replied, "It's just a gut feeling, and statistical probabilities. If I can get into *enough* of these hot new ideas, one of 'em is bound to pay off—and one's enough to make us all rich!" Flimsy as such an approach may sound, it worked for this fund manager. He happened to own a piece of a microchip business when the personal computer "explosion" occurred. Both he and his fund participants just couldn't be happier with the results.

Your Money Matters

By Scott McMurray
Staff Reporter of The Wall Street Journal

As though small investors didn't already have enough problems, Wall Street professionals have given them something else to worry about: program trading.

That's the name of a popular institutional-investment technique in which a brokerage firm guarantees to buy or sell stocks for an institution at an agreed price. For institutions, which often have hundreds of millions of dollars to invest annually, program trading eliminates the fear the market will move against them as they switch huge sums into or out of stocks. It is also supposed to reduce the effect the institutions' mammoth trades have on market prices.

But some institutional investors and brokers charge that program trading has increased the volatility of stock prices and led to instances of market manipulation. The New York Stock Exchange says it is ready to recommend enforcement action against one of the technique's practitioners as part of a broader investigation. And the Securities and Exchange Commission is watching the Big Board study.

Those who use program trading deny wrongdoing and say allegations of manipulation are greatly exaggerated. But John J. Phelan Jr., chairman of the New York exchange, says, "Clearly the potential is there for manipulation." He says the exchange's "concern is that Aunt Minnie in Kansas City is getting as good a price for her stock" as the professionals are getting.

By analyzing share-price movements and staying abreast of market rumors about program trades, professional traders can sometimes divine when a stock has been affected. Small investors can read about such guesses in the stock market columns of this and other newspapers.

There is little or nothing, however, that investors can do if they suspect their stocks have been affected by manipulation associated with program trading. With institutional investors accounting for nearly three fourths of the trading on the New York exchange, the effects of program trading—and any market manipulation it spawns—are likely to grow even more widespread, industry officials say, unless it can be effectively deterred by regulators.

Program trading developed in the mid-1970s as banks using index funds, which aim to match the performance of broad stock market averages, sought to minimize the effect on the market of their trades. But the technique gained widespread use in the past 18 months, when the market became less liquid as small investors, stung by falling prices, fled to the sidelines. The increased volatility that resulted from the declining stream of small orders led to greater use of program trading by institutions.

Bankers Trust Co. and Wells Fargo Bank, extensive users of index funds, are among the leaders in using program trading. The leading brokers handling such trades, Wall Streeters say, are Goldman, Sachs & Co. and Salomon Brothers Inc. All say they conduct their business honestly.

One of the major problems confronting a private trader in the stock markets is the very size of his or her competitors. Funds and institutions that have millions of dollars to place every day can, by their sheer economic muscle, exert tremendous influence on the companies they invest in, as well as the market itself.

Investment Funds as Syndicated Speculation

What these various kinds of funds represent, of course, is syndicated speculation on an ascending scale of economic risk. There is a vast difference in exposures between "blue-chip" conservatism and go-go adventuring. One is no more commendable than the other, nor more vital, or moral. Indeed, the go-go fund manager is perhaps the most patriotic of all, because putting money in a new enterprise calls for a high order of faith as well as daring. Unless there are people who are willing to undertake such high risk exposures, economic and technological stagnation is inescapable. But everyone is not equally equipped for financial derring-do. In order for people to optimally participate in the overall market's essential role of accumulating venture capital, every kind and level of investment/speculative risk needs to be available and understood.

Grading Risks in the Financial Market

In view of everything that has gone before in these pages, a good deal of guidance has been set down from which to empirically assign levels of risk exposure to specific classes of property that may be acquired and held over some flexible time period. The following roster is not intended to be all-inclusive. It is intended to provide some perspective on the matter of risk-capital placement, and the commensurate hazards present in doing so. Proceeding from the highest risk to the lowest risk, the rankings—in your author's considered opinion—look like this:

1. New business formation   Greatest order of risk.
2. Common stock holdings
3. Preferred stock holdings
4. Commodity contract flat-price holdings
5. Commodity contract spreads
6. Corporate bonds
7. Institutional certificates of deposit
8. Federally insured deposits
9. Government obligations   Lowest order of risk.

The diminishing levels of risk in each of these major financial categories relate to such considerations as institutional dependability, quality of information available to the public participant, liquidity of the market concerned, and susceptibility to inflationary deterioration. Grant also, these are "categorical" risks: A share of stock in ABC Corporation may be a vastly different order of risk than a share of common in the XYZ Corporation. However, the holding of shares in a stock company (without sufficient diversification to offer portfolio protection) is a risky proposition, per se!

Risk and Leverage Relationship

It should not be necessary to belabor the point that, while leverage has *everything* to do with potential returns from a finite amount of risk capital, it has *nothing* to do with the element of *risk* present in any particular situation. Whether a $10,000 loss represents utter failure of a small business, a 20 percent deterioration in the price of 100 shares of stock, or 10-cent per bushel impairment in a wheat futures position, the only real difference is in the amount of money initially required to hold the position that sustained the $10,000 loss:

• The $10,000 small business loss requires that the full $10,000 be invested.

- The $10,000 stock loss requires a $50,000 initial investment (or $25,000 in cash and an equivalent brokers' loan).
- The $10,000 loss on the wheat futures position represents a dime a bushel on 20 contracts of 5,000 bushels each—and a margin deposit of $12,000.

We may postulate that the small business had an inherent value of $10,000, so the loss was 100 percent of product value. The stock value was $50,000, so the loss in product value was 20 percent. If the wheat futures was trading at $4 per bushel, the 20 contracts had an intrinsic value of $400,000, and the $10,000 loss represents a .02½ percent reduction in underlying product value.

As will be seen, however, the only effect of *relative leverage* in these situations was to determine how much money had to be put down to participate in each economic activity. The *relative risk* in each undertaking depended on its susceptibility to analysis and forecasting of an outcome. The *relative attraction* of each proposition depended on potentials for monetary return; which, in turn, depends on accurate *forecasting of outcome,* and the *leverage the situation offers.*

Capital Accumulation for Economic Growth

A hornbook principle in an economic society is that *economic growth* will be limited to the difference between the totals of economic *production* and economic *consumption.* It may be less. It cannot be more. In other words, economic growth depends on savings in the first instance, and on economic participation (including stock ownership) in the second. Mere saving (nonspending) is economically counterproductive until the accumulated savings are put to work building stores, factories, and infrastructure. This is the function that stock markets have historically performed: Standing as interlocutor between cash-hungry industry on one hand, and cash-surplus holders on the other, the stock market makes a business of exchanging shares for money. Historically, it has been a "retail" kind of business.

Individuals were the only buyers and sellers of stock when the NYSE was little more than a gentleman's club, and the American Exchange conducted its trade on the streetside curb down below. As the trading of shares matured, however, the participants in the activity evolved rapidly. Infamous "trusts" bought and sold huge blocks of corporate equities for no other purpose except to manipulate prices and enrich themselves at the expense of their defenseless corporate victims—and the hapless public shareholders. Only after repeated panics, precipitated by the baldest sorts of public fraud, did government see fit to enact some regulatory statutes calculated to bring order into stock trading. Try as they might, however, the federal regulators discovered that not even the most Draconian penalties were sufficient to suppress all of the market banditry—if a particular game appeared to be worth the candle.

The same rule still applies as often as a loophole of some kind attracts a securities crook to a scam that looks too good to pass up.

It was in large measure an effort to escape these recurrent market manipulations in individual stocks, that increasing numbers of public shareholders opted for mutuals and other kinds of funds, rather than continue to rely on the questionable mercies of individuals and forces that they neither knew nor could find much historical reason to trust. The effect of this public falling-away worked great changes in the personality of the securities business—and in the exchanges themselves.

Some on SEC Seeking Harsher Penalties for Flagrant Violators of Securities Law

BY BRUCE INGERSOLL
Staff Reporter of The Wall Street Journal
WASHINGTON—Sentiment is growing at the Securities and Exchange Commission for barring flagrant violators of securities laws from serving as officers or directors of publicly held companies.

Several SEC commissioners and senior officials say they are fed up with corporate officials who repeatedly violate securities laws. And in speeches, some of them have begun venting their exasperation, contending that the SEC should do more than simply ask the courts to enjoin corporate miscreants from breaking the law again.

Nobody is more vociferous than James Treadway, the first commissioner to advocate invoking the seldom-used enforcement option of asking the courts to bar blatant repeat offenders. Mr. Treadway also favors asking Congress to give the SEC explicit statutory authority to issue debarment orders. "Here's a tool we need to deal with a certain class of egregious violators," he asserts. "You can enjoin them 15 times and it still isn't going to mean anything to them."

Mr. Treadway, however, cautions that debarment isn't "a kind of power you invoke at the drop of a hat."

At a recent American Bar Association meeting, Daniel Goelzer, the SEC's general counsel, served notice that the agency is likely to take more drastic action. "The problem of repeat violators and of the enforcement resources needed to hunt them down as they move from scheme to scheme is a real one," he says. "I believe the commission will seek to utilize that tool (debarment) more frequently."

High-Level Thievery

Commissioners Aulana Peters and Charles Marinaccio share Mr. Treadway's views. Debarment is the way to deal with those who "are basically practicing very sophisticated high-level thievery," Mrs. Peters says. Mr. Marinaccio adds that piling injunction upon injunction is ineffective because bringing contempt-of-court charges against a person who defies an injunction is such a "ponderous" process. Debarment, he says, "has the virtue of clarity."

Chairman John Shad says that he would resort to debarment only in cases of "outrageous rip-offs where individuals are pocketing money at the expense of shareholders." Such a remedy would be far too harsh for repeat offenders caught in technical violations, he says.

Mr. Shad says that it is impossible to predict how he and other commissioners would vote on debarment before they take up any cases.

But it appears that Commissioner Charles Cox, a free-market advocate, would be the least inclined to vote for debarment. "If the shareholders want to put a recidivist in a top management position, I believe that's their decision," Mr. Cox says. In certain circumstances, however, he says he might go along with debarment.

Since 1975, the SEC has gone to court about twice a year and, under consent decrees, forced corporate directors and executives to acquiesce to debarment, either permanently or for a certain period.

Florafax Chairman

In a recent settlement with the SEC, Joseph H. Hale, chairman and chief executive officer of Florafax International Inc., a flowers-by-wire service based in Tulsa, Okla., agreed to step down for three years. He was charged with participating in accounting and corporate-disclosure violations. A federal judge had enjoined him in 1983 from violating the securities laws. In both cases, Mr. Hale neither admitted nor denied any wrongdoing.

So far, no defendant has fought debarment as an alternative to settling with the SEC. The next step for the commission, says Mr. Marinaccio, is to seek a decision in a contested case. Mr. Treadway believes the SEC should seek explicit debarment authority from Congress. The commission, he points out, already has statutory power to bar law-violators from associating with brokerage firms, investment companies and investment advisers. "If that's logical, why doesn't the same remedy exist for other companies?" he asks.

The New Face of the Securities Industry

In the 25 years between 1950 and 1975, the securities industry went through a transformation the like of which had never been seen before. The root cause may be laid to all kinds of ancillary developments, including new technology, inflation, internationalization of trade, or competition between industry and the tax collectors for all available surplus funds. Apologists for what happened may do so, but at the heart of the transformation was a huge public exodus from brokerage offices all over the land. The unending sequence of corporate raids, takeovers, spin-offs, liquidations, logo changes, etc., had turned disenchantment loose in the streets where resided Mr. and Mrs. American Investor, erstwhile stockholders, once-proud owners of "shares in American business."

They didn't stop saving something from each month's paycheck just because they had sold their stock. But they looked for new places to put their savings; where, hopefully, they wouldn't have a lump in the throat every time they opened a newspaper to the business section, or sat down to watch the evening news. The repositories they found were savings and loan associations, insurance programs, retirement trusts, insured savings accounts, certificates of deposit, government bonds, and funds of every imaginable type and risk inclination.

Money came out of the market and went into these mushrooming fiduciary organizations at a rate that almost proved unmanageable. Billions of dollars went looking for a new home and, in it's wake, left a securities business in shambles. Some commission houses simply closed their doors. Others cut staffs to the barest bones and managed to hold on. Many of them sought out mergers and acquisitions, which allowed them to avoid the stigma of outright failure. When the fire storm had ended—if it has—the list of stockbrokers in the Yellow Pages had been reduced to a small fraction of its former length and opulence.

The brokerage business had fallen on hard times, and the reason was too plain to be missed: The private investor crowd had departed and, in their place, a hard-bitten bunch of fund and portfolio managers were the only folks left who had business to place. The new crowd was looking to place big-block orders, but they wanted wholesale brokerage fees that would have been considered ludicrous two years earlier. The choice was between extending discount commissions, or not getting the business. Predictably, some of the remaining firms took this trade, those that didn't had reason to regret their intransigence later. This, because the entire industry went "negotiable" within a matter of two years. Since May 1975, any commission in the industry, whether for transacting trades in stocks, bonds, warrants, rights, commodities, options, or the cash articles, is determinable on the part of each commission firm—and is renegotiable as often as someone walks through the door with a piece of business that's big enough to justify the discussion. The brokerage business has, indeed, fallen far from its former state of unquestioned grace and regulation-protected affluence.

Funds Make the Market

The trouble with having a relatively few huge operators make up most of any market, is that their orders to buy and sell are also huge. And unless there is a large component of public (read: random) buying and selling present to dilute and diffuse the impact of the huge orders when they hit, market response as measured in price changes can be disconcertingly wide. This is the situation presently existent in U.S. stock markets—especially in the two largest ones.

"The funds and the institutions *own* this place on any day they want to!" complained a wizened old NYSE "specialist" who has been making a market in several popular stocks for almost 30 years. "It's getting harder and harder to make a dollar at it!" If he and his contemporaries are paying any attention to the handwriting on the wall, they have to realize that their lot can only get still harder with the passage of time.

Money-Fund Assets Surge Again, Reach $213.31 Billion

By a Wall Street Journal Staff Reporter

NEW YORK—Assets of the nation's 332 money market funds surged $1.82 billion, to $213.31 billion, in the week ended Wednesday, according to the Investment Company Institute.

The Washington-based trade group said it was the 15th consecutive weekly increase and also the highest level of assets in two years. The assets reached $217.77 billion Dec. 22, 1982.

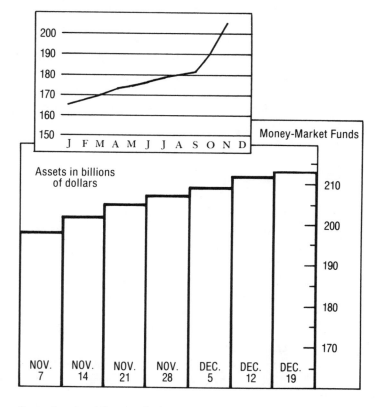

Source: Investment Company Institute.

The assets of 182 general-purpose funds rose $69.5 million, to $64.72 billion. The assets of 85 broker-dealer funds increased $334.3 million, to $92.03 billion. Assets of 65 institutional funds jumped $1.42 billion, to $56.55 billion.

The average seven-day yield for funds, in the week ended Tuesday, dropped to 8.60 percent from 8.69 percent a week earlier, according to Donoghue's Money Fund Report. The Holliston, Mass., newsletter reported the average 30-day yield for funds slipped to 8.84 percent from 9.01 percent, and the average maturity of funds rose to 46 days from 43 days.

Nowhere is the public flight from the stock markets better documented than in the phenomenal growth of funds. As a result, stock trading is being increasingly concentrated in the hands of fewer individuals. Professional money managers, instead of buying and selling a few hundred shares at a time, place orders that move thousands of shares in blocks and involve millions of dollars in a single trade. Better fund performance can only further deplete the ranks of small public traders.

This is not to say that trading in stocks is doomed to extinction. The activity is crucial to our ongoing need to accumulate venture capital and funnel it into selected areas of economic opportunity. The stock markets perform this function better and more efficiently than any other known or imaginable mechanism. Stock markets will persist, just as the cash grain market lives on cheek by jowl with the vastly larger futures market; and the stock exchanges will come to occupy about the same relative place as the cash market does, vis-à-vis their much larger and more active inheritors. Enough evidence is already in hand to underpin some confident speculative forecasting.

The Small Stock Trader Is Gone

In spite of wistful predictions that "the public is just waiting for a good place to get back in," each time the public decides to get back into stocks, they return in ever-decreasing numbers. Each individual holder's portfolio is larger, hence his or her aggregate business is larger; but the total number of people who are active in the stock markets is declining dramatically, and has been doing so for four decades.

The trend will continue for several excellent reasons.

An ever-increasing amount of personal wealth is going into such things as real estate, insurance, retirement programs, and "timed" or "open" savings accounts. This leaves the individual—especially the individual identified as the small investor—with fewer dollars to discretionarily put to work. He prefers the implied safety of ongoing asset-creating *programs,* to the constant worry about something happening to his nest egg in an unbuffered collision with unimaginable contingencies. Moreover, the small investor is getting *smarter* all the time. The role of diversification of holdings is being increasingly understood. Without the necessary surplus capital to do this, funds offer the only sensible alternative.

This all adds up to the fact that the small investor is gone for good, insofar as stock ownership is concerned. His funds will still find their way into the equity market, but they will get there via a fund manager or some sort of fiduciary conduit. The securities business, therefore, has changed from "retail" to "wholesale."

S&P Index of Stocks Again Outperforms over Two Thirds of Money Managers

By RANDALL SMITH
Staff Reporter of The Wall Street Journal

For the second consecutive year, the Standard & Poor's Corp. index of 500 stocks outperformed more than two thirds of the nation's money managers, the institutional investors who get paid to beat the market.

From January 1, 1984, to December 21, the S&P 500 beat 69 percent of portfolio managers monitored by Indata, a Southport, Connecticut, investment-analysis firm. In 1983, the index beat 73 percent of the managers. And for the 23½ months from January 1, 1983, to last December 21, 73 percent of the managers fell short of the index.

As a result, Barton Biggs, managing director of Morgan Stanley & Co., whose stocks trailed the S&P index by 2½ percentage points through November, forecasts "disappearances, consolidation and declining compensation in the investment management business. . . . We have been like rock stars, but the fun is over for a while now that the customers think we can't sing."

He added, "We were all overpaid anyway."

The managers offer their customers performance, and for the five years or so until mid–1983, that performance was mostly to be found in thousands of smaller growth stocks outside the S&P 500. But last year, growth stocks got slaughtered, while large-capitalization stocks—which tend to pay higher dividends, fluctuate less, and fare better in weak markets—more than held their own.

Such companies as General Motors Corp., which have hundreds of millions of shares outstanding, are considered to be large- capitalization stocks. Smaller companies may have only 10 million to 20 million shares outstanding.

The biggest 50 stocks in the S&P 500 returned 7.8 percent through November, while the index itself returned 3.5 percent and the broader Wilshire 5000 index of all publicly traded stocks returned a negative 2 percent. The returns include dividends as well as price changes.

Dimensional Fund Advisers, a hot new manager that attracted $1.4 billion in 2½ years by systematically buying only small stocks, returned a minus 8.1 percent. Some growth-stock managers were down 10 percent to 25 percent, and a few hyperaggressive funds plunged 30 percent or more.

"Most institutional portfolios are going to have a small-stock bias in their portfolios relative to the S&P. They're typically looking for the new rising stars," says James Martin, chief of equities at College Retirement Equities Fund, whose $3 billion in active stocks trailed the S&P index slightly in 1984. "They have to be selling something different," says Don Korytowski of SEI Corp., an investment- performance measurer.

Some managers were unrepentant. Stocks that outperformed in 1984 were "a lot of the dull old companies," says Joel Leff of Forstman-Leff Associates, which trailed the S&P index by seven points in late December. "This has not been a stellar year for anyone that I know of, because I don't know any of the old-timers."

While active money managers may face the kind of shakeout envisioned by Morgan Stanley's Mr. Biggs, passively managed index funds only aiming to match the S&P index stand to gain. The nation's two biggest indexers both mushroomed in 1984. At Bankers Trust New York Corp. indexed stocks grew to $14 billion from $12.5 billion. And at Wells Fargo & Co., they grew to $13 billion from $8 billion.

Funds Will Continue to Grow

Because of the newly available financial tools at hand with which to hedge portfolio risks and enhance yields, overall fund performance can be confidently expected to improve dramatically in the next few years. How soon this happens depends only on how quickly fund managers learn to use financial instruments, indexes, etc., to minimize risk exposures, while enhancing yields. Money managers will have to travel the same road that commercial grain dealers did, in discovering that the "hedging department" is just another—and often the *best*—profit center in the company.

As managerial expertise improves, "outperforming the Dow" will be the least of the fund manager's expectations. With the menu of instrument choices available, and accessible immediately, and at unheard-of cost-efficiencies, financial management techniques will vastly upgrade the returns on venture funds and commitments. Conservative, growth and go-go may still be used to describe money-management inclinations, but by being able to fine-tune portfolio risks exposures, better results can be expected all along the line; and bottom-line comparisons will narrow.

Corporate Management Efficiency Will Improve

The comfort level on Mahogany Row is in inverse proportion to the number of large stockholders in the company. This just means that anyone who has impressive amounts of money sunk in any enterprise is going to keep a close eye on his investment. Nothing can exert a more signal influence on company management intensity than to have a well-respected fund buy up a chunk of the stock.

When the purchase takes place, good publicity abounds. Having won the approval of the "Inter-Galactic Fund," other less celebrated interests race to follow the example. But consider the opposite situation: When Inter-Galactic *sells,* a shudder goes through the company, and everybody again follows the example.

Suffice it to say that a chief executive officer is far more comfortable with 1,000 shareholders holding 1,000 shares each, than he is with an Inter-Galactic Fund sitting on a million shares! A small stockholder can be largely ignored between annual meetings—unless he hires a lawyer. But a letter of pointed inquiry from a large fund, almost without regard for the number of shares the fund actually owns, will get prompt and careful attention. This is the reason that *more* large shareholdings and *fewer* small shareholdings will surely improve corporate management performances. It has to do with the comfort level on Mahogany Row—purely.

Market Attention Is Shifting

When someone buys 100 shares of stock, he next subscribes to *The Wall Street Journal* and *Barron's,* and begins checking the *Tribune* business section before turning to sports. As fewer people are personally involved in stock ownership, the usefulness of daily listings of some 1,500 NYSE-traded securities, for example, will diminish accordingly. Or they diminish in terms of the proportion of subscribers who use the information, in any case.

Conversely, as more public and institutional involvement is shifted to futures and options markets, the need for prompt, accurate, and complete reportage in the full gamut of commodities, instruments, currencies, and traded obligations will grow apace. Financial editors, wherever found, have long shared a common lack of understanding apropos futures and options markets, and something like equal lack of interest in them. Stocks have been the first priority in any newspaper, radio, or television program that gives any space at all to business topics.

This is now changing. The biggest business in the world today is what *used* to be known as the commodity business. A whole new coterie of reporters will have to be trained to cover and report on this exploding facet of trade. The transition will be agonizing at best, and will prove impossible for some. Abbreviated market reporting will no longer suffice in this multibillion dollar complex. If newspapers can't do it, computer service organizations will.

The first obligation rests with the exchanges, to upgrade both the quality and the quantity of information made publicly available. For a single example: It is inexcusable that volume and open-interest figures from a given trading session that ends at 1:15 P.M. *today,* will not be available until midmorning *tomorrow!* And then, only in the form of a Xeroxed *trading-floor handout.* The public will not have the information until, at soonest, the following morning's newspaper. Floor traders, therefore, have this vital trading data some 24 hours in advance of the public.

Both the Commodity Futures Trading Commission and the exchanges themselves should not rest until this patent inequity is corrected. This is the age of computers and instantaneous communications. To perpetuate such a bald public disadvantage is neither defensible nor necessary.

Bad News for OPEC

NEW YORK TIMES NEWS SERVICE
NEW YORK—Michael Milano is in the oil business. He is enough of a presence there that—if pressed—he would acknowledge he can be just as important as Saudi Arabia.

Here he was working the other day. His arms were flying over his head, as if he had temporarily lost motor control. He was yelling as loudly as he could at a crowd of other hand-waving people. Among the things he was shouting: "March 79! March 79!"

Mike Milano doesn't work in the executive suite of a big oil company but in a "ring" in the World Trade Center, home of the New York Mercantile Exchange, now the front line of the oil pricing game.

Milano—38, gray-haired, trim—trades oil futures. He is a speculator who trades only for himself and is gambling on where oil prices will go months from now.

As one of the heaviest traders—a "big shooter," as they are known—he plays a key role in what companies and consumers will eventually pay for their gasoline and heating oil.

There's significant oil news almost every day and demand has been shrinking.

Against this backdrop, what has happened is that pricing is being determined more by the bellowing on the floor of the New York Merc than by the Arab sheiks' frame of mind. The Organization of Petroleum Exporting Countries, whose 13 members hold most of the world's oil reserves, still sets a basic "official" price of oil, currently $29 a barrel, but increasingly that price is being ignored.

Earlier this month, for example, plunging prices for oil at the New York Merc were taken as a sign of market doubts that OPEC members could defend their price. The spot market, where traders and brokers haggle over shiploads of oil and arrive at prices in private transactions, had been the pivotal bazaar.

More and more, the oil world studies the results from the madcap Mercantile rings, where everything is out in the open.

Although less than 2 percent of the oil traded on the New York Merc is ever actually delivered, oil dealers around the world watch the prices that "lots" are going for at the exchange and employ them as a framework for their dealings on the spot or open market.

"Just the thought that you have this sort of control over as great a commodity as oil is tremendous," Milano said.

Source: *Chicago Tribune*, January 13, 1985.

Should the Organization of Petroleum Exporting Countries (OPEC) ever wonder why they were unable to continue to hold up the rest of the world with extortionate crude prices, they might begin their search for truth at the New York Mercantile Exchange. With the first public trade in a crude oil futures contract, OPEC's monopoly was broken.

A monopoly cannot exist alongside a free market. In view of our worldwide and almost instantaneous communications, the entire global market is constantly aware of the market price for crude in New York. This price is more significant than anything the "oil sheiks" may be saying on the subject.

Need for a Data Bank

Hopefully it is just a matter of time before one of the great informational sources in the industry launches an all-inclusive subscriber-accessible data bank. The service should include various levels of information, ranging from news reports, to minute-by-minute prices from all exchanges and for all traded equities, instruments, options, and contracts, to complete charting graphics for those who are willing to pay for it. This is the first time since markets were invented that the technology exists to literally accomplish the theoretical ideal of an "equally and perfectly informed universe of traders." It's hard to imagine anything that could make a larger contribution to marketing efficiency and reliability in the discovery of prices.

The Endless Trading Day

While all of these things will present their own problems for some and opportunities for others, the most challenging hurdle of all will be found in adapting to a 24-hour trading day.

Wherever markets presently exist, they are open some six hours a day—while the sun is hovering somewhere over that particular geographic location. This arrangement couldn't be improved upon until such time as technology existed to link up Chicago, New York, Antwerp, Calcutta, Osaka, and San Francisco in a single, articulated, commercial "loop." That technology is now available, and the next market configuration will bear little similarity to the ones we now know.

SEC Begins Securities Industry Talks on Global Trading within Two Years

By Bruce Ingersoll
Staff Reporter of The Wall Street Journal

WASHINGTON—The Securities and Exchange Commission has begun discussing with stock-exchange officials and securities-industry leaders the prospects and pitfalls of global, 24-hour securities trading within two years.

SEC Chairman John Shad described the discussions as informal and emphasized, "It's just in the gestation stage." He added that he and other top SEC officials have been talking with representatives of the New York Stock Exchange, the American Stock Exchange, the National Association of Securities Dealers and the Securities Industry Association in a series of meetings and telephone calls.

The agency's division of market regulation already is drafting an issue paper that will be released to evoke public comment on the implications of the securities markets becoming increasingly international, Mr. Shad said.

The purpose of the informal discussions, the chairman said, is to identify the potential problems of around-the-clock, global trading and come up with possible solutions. "I'd like to facilitate the increasing internationalization of securities markets while at the same time providing the same kind of investor protection and orderly markets," Mr. Shad said.

Proxmire Urges Action

Sen. William Proxmire (D., Wis.) already has urged the SEC to begin planning for "the world trading system of the future" and for the U.S. to take a leadership role in that system.

In an Oct. 23 letter to Mr. Shad that the Senate Banking Committee just released, Mr. Proxmire said that some securities professionals foresee "a fight for control of the benefits that will flow from this international market as British, Japanese, American, and other nations' securities firms wrestle to become the dominant market- makers."

Sen. Proxmire urged the SEC to establish an advisory committee on global trading similar to the panel that prepared a lengthy report last year on tender-offer regulation. He also recommended eventually creating an international planning committee under U.S. leadership.

The SEC's advisory committee, Mr. Proxmire suggested, should consider the effects of technological developments on off-the-floor trading, the need for greater international cooperation in market surveillance and enforcement, the design of a worldwide clearing system for securities transactions and the SEC's future role.

Public Comment Cited

Mr. Shad didn't rule out the possibility of such an advisory panel. But he said the SEC could obtain more quickly a wide variety of views on the matter by issuing a so-called concept release for public comment.

Richard Ketchum, SEC director of market regulation, said that he doesn't think the entire issue is sufficiently "ripe" to warrant the immediate creation of an advisory committee.

Commissioner Aulana Peters already has suggested that the Securities Industry Association consider forming a committee to study the trend toward international trading. In a recent speech, she predicted that securities firms will face a growing challenge to "provide excellence in customer service while adapting to kaleidoscopic market-structure conditions" throughout the world.

Edward I. O'Brien, president of the SIA, said that the group "might very well' consider setting up such a committee. Among SIA members, however, there isn't any discernible consensus on 24-hour, global trading, he said. As for extended trading hours, he added, members who favor it slightly outnumber those who are opposed.

John J. Phelan Jr., Big Board chairman, noting that the exchange has a committee studying the implications of 24-hour trading, said that greatly extended trading hours are strictly a "question of when, not if."

Tied together by a satellite-supported computer network, trade in foodstuffs and other vital commodities will proceed without regard to geographic or time limitations. A cargo of corn bound from Chicago to Europe may be hedged in-transit in Chicago, or London, or on the Paris

Bourse. A cargo of Chinese soybeans enroute to Argentina may be hedged in Osaka, Japan, New York, or Chicago.

The price of a bushel of wheat in Hong Kong will be priced "basis-Chicago" or "basis-Melbourne" or "basis-Odessa"—because once global trading begins, it won't take long for everyone to join the game. And everyone will eat better because of it.

Traders will "spread" between countries half a world apart. Regional surpluses will follow the lure of prices—and the shortages that continue to exist will be less punishing because of it. Producers will have the world's full 6 *billion* customers in their potential market, needing only equivalent systems for transportation and distribution to transform "potential" to "actual."

It is said that unless commerce crosses a border, armies will. Perhaps the opposite is also true: When commerce crosses borders, armies won't. If so, a worldwide marketing complex with universal participation in it may yet produce the kind of international amity and pragmatic co-operation that sensible people everywhere pray for—and that continues to elude our grasp. And even if the effort fails to fully meet such a lofty challenge, it can't be less than a long step along the road to a better provisioned and a more secure human family because of it.

Comex, Australians Agree to a Linkup for Gold Contracts

By a Wall Street Journal Staff Reporter

NEW YORK—The Commodity Exchange in New York said it reached an agreement to set up a computerized gold futures trading link with the Sydney Futures Exchange in Australia.

Pending approval by the federal Commodity Futures Trading Commission, the Sydney linkage agreement would make the Comex the second U.S. exchange with an overseas trading link. The Chicago Mercantile Exchange opened linked financial futures trading with the Singapore International Monetary Exchange last September.

The proposed Comex-Sydney arrangement would enable traders to initiate trades on one exchange and close them out on the other; it would provide more than 19 hours of trading for participants in both markets. Under the agreement, the trading day would begin at 7 P.M. EST in Sydney and end the following day at 2:30 P.M. EST, when the Comex ends trading.

The Sydney Futures Exchange, which approved the agreement with the Comex several weeks ago, has markets in agricultural commodities, financial instruments and precious metals. Under the agreement, Sydney will offer a 100-troy ounce gold futures contract identical to the one traded at the Comex.

All gold contracts traded at Sydney will be cleared through the Comex, making the trading subject to U.S. trading regulations.

Big Board Mulls Link to Pacific Stock Exchange

By Scott McMurray
Staff Reporter of The Wall Street Journal
NEW YORK—The New York Stock Exchange is holding "serious discussions" with the Pacific Stock Exchange on potential joint ventures that could lead to the merger of the exchanges, a Big Board spokesman said.

The spokesman said no agreement has been reached, but that talks are continuing among senior officials of both exchanges.

The talks are part of the movement within the securities industry toward a 24-hour, global market for stock trading.

The Big Board spokesman also said the two exchanges recently informed John S.R. Shad, chairman of the Securities and Exchange Commission, of their discussions. No formal presentation has been made to the SEC, which oversees stock-exchange activies.

There is no longer any serious argument with the idea that a 24-hour global market structure is on its way. The only questions remaining relate to technological linkage, and adapting individual market practices to a single common market usage.

24

Conclusion

Hopefully, both the methods and the usefulness of professional commodity speculation have been clarified in these pages. It should be seen that in selling short the speculator is contributing to *demonstrated supply;* in buying long he is adding to *demonstrated demand.* Price stands as a measurement of these opposing forces, and the role of the market is to discover prices.

The role of the speculator is to forecast prices. Thus it must be said that in a given situation, the speculator can only fulfill his economic obligation by selling short. In the opposite frame of reference, he can only meet his economic responsibility by going long.

The question of morality will likely continue to be raised in connection with commodity speculation. Morality, it should now be clear, has little to do with either the form or the practice. Economics is not a moral discipline: High prices are only preferable to low prices when viewed through the eyes of the seller. Milk is worth more than water, because the market is usually willing to pay more for the white liquid. Whiskey is worth more than milk, proven by the fact that it commands a higher price in trade.

All manner of judgments can be made with respect to what is "good for the people," or "good for society," or "constructive," or "destructive." We may do so, but the market has no way to appraise side issues. The market accepts things offered by sellers, presents them to buyers, and discovers the price at which merchandise will change hands.

The buyer of wheat may represent a starving nation and the seller of wheat may hold millions of excess bushels in storage. The price at which the transaction takes place only measures supply and demand. Conditions under which each trader enters the market are only important insofar as respective urgency may influence the level of their bids and offers. To put it most bluntly, the market can't "feel" hunger, which is merely propensity to consume, unless it is also coupled with willingness to buy and ability to pay.

Drawing qualitative distinctions between investment and speculation is about as reasonable as attempting to present outright purchase of an asset as being somehow preferable to renting or leasing the same facility. Each handling contains elements of both utilitarian strength and weakness, and the approach which is selected should be the one which best suits the needs and the inclinations of the individuals concerned.

One last thing can be said, however, and without fear of successful contradiction from any source whatever: Free markets have written a record of accomplishment which is unequaled by any other form of administered prices, managed production, or controlled exchange. Modern commodity markets have made a contribution to national and world well-being which will probably never be fully appreciated unless, on some unfortunate day in the future, commerce becomes the captive of official planners and the search for profit is outlawed in favor of some politically expedient brand of enforced sharing.

It should never be forgotten that the greatest crimes of the 20th century have been perpetrated under the sweet-sounding economic dogma of Marxist socialism that swears fealty to "the greatest good for the greatest number." Free markets, on the other hand, enable each buyer and each seller to pursue his own interests, with a decent regard for ethics and legalities.

There can be little room for argument as to which has performed best in the past. Or which offers more for the future of individuals, nations, and the world at large.

Glossary

Accumulate   Buying by traders who expect to hold the contracts for a period of time. Building up a position over time.

Acreage Allotment   The limitation on planted acreage established by the government for each farmer for basic crops.

Acreage Reserve   A part of the farm program which applies to basic commodities, under which the farmer receives payment from the government for not planting part or all of his acreage allotment.

Actuals   The physical commodities, as distinguished especially from futures contracts.

Afloat   Grain which is loaded in vessels, in harbor, or in transit, but which has not reached its destination and been unloaded.

Arbitrage   Simultaneous purchase of cash commodities or futures in one market against the sale of cash commodities or futures in the same or a different market to profit from a discrepancy in price. Also includes some aspects of hedging. *See* **Spread.**

At-the-Money   An option whose strike price is at, or nearly at, the same level as the underlying optioned property.

Basis   The spread or difference between the spot or cash price and the price of the near future. Basis may also be used to designate price differentials between cash and more distant futures, as well as different locations as specified.

Bear   One who believes prices are too high and will decline.

Bear Market   One where large supplies and/or poor demand cause a decline in price.

Bearish and **Bullish**   When conditions suggest lower prices, a bearish situation is said to exist. If higher prices appear warranted, the situation is said to be bullish.

Bid   A price offered subject, unless otherwise stated, to immediate acceptance for a specific amount of commodity.

Board Order or **Market-if-Touched (MIT) Order**   An order to buy or sell when the market reaches a specific price. A board order to buy becomes a market order when the commodity sells (or is offered) at or below the order price. A board order to sell becomes a market order when the commodity sells (or is bid) at or above the order price.

Board of Trade (Chicago)   Licensed contract commodity exchange located in Chicago, Illinois; affords facilities for trading both futures and options on futures.

Bot   Abbreviation for bought.

Break   A sharp price decline.

Broad Tape   A teletype reporting system which automatically prints out news, weather, markets, etc., as furnished from professional and government reporting services.

Broker   An agent entrusted with the execution of an order. He may be employed in the office of the commission house that carries the account or a floor broker or pit broker who actually executes the order on the trading floor. *See* **Customers' Man.**

Brokerage   The fee charged by a floor broker for execution of a transaction. The fee may be a flat amount or a percentage.

Brokerage House   *See* **Commission House.**

Bucket, Bucketing   The illegal practice of some brokers in accepting orders to buy or sell without executing such orders. Such a broker hopes to profit by pocketing the loss which a customer may experience when closing out the transaction. If the customer closes out at a profit, the broker pays the profit. The illegality lies in an agent's direct dealing with his principal without disclosing the fact.

Bulge   A sharp price advance.

Bull   One who believes prices are too low and will advance.

Bull Market   One where small supplies and/or strong demand cause prices to rise.

Buy in   To cover or liquidate a sale.

Buy on Close or Opening   To buy at the end or beginning of a session at a price within the closing or opening range.

Buyer   In options, the purchaser of either a put or a call. Also referred to as a holder. An option purchase may be made to either open or close an option position.

Buyer's Market   A condition of the market in which there is an abundance of goods available and hence buyers can afford to be selective and may be able to buy at less than the price that had previously prevailed. *See* **Seller's Market.**

Buying Hedge   Buying futures to hedge cash sales in present or future. *See also* **Hedging.**

Call A period in which trading is conducted to establish the price for each futures month at a particular time, i.e., an opening or closing call.

Buyer's Call Purchase of a specified quantity of a specific grade of a commodity at a fixed number of points above or below a specified delivery month in futures, with the buyer being allowed a certain period of time within which to fix the price by either purchasing a futures for the account of the seller, or indicating to the seller when he wishes to price-fix.

Seller's Call The same as buyer's call with the difference that the seller has the right of determining the time to fix price.

Call An option permitting its holder (who has paid a fee for the option) to call for a certain commodity or security at a fixed price in a stated quantity within a stated period. The broker is paid to bring the buyer and seller together. The buyer of this right to call expects the price of the commodity or security to rise so that he can call for it at a profit. If the price falls the option will not be exercised. The reverse transaction is a put. *See* **Privilege.**

Call Level The price level at which additional margin money must be put up by the holder of an impaired open position.

Carload For grains, may range from 1,400 to 2,500 bushels.

Carrying Costs Those charges incurred in warehousing the actual commodity, generally including interest, insurance, and storage.

Cash Commodity Physical merchandise; goods available for delivery immediately or within a designated period following sale; includes a commodity bought or sold to-arrive.

Cash Forward Sale of a cash commodity for delivery at a later date.

Cash Price The current bid or offering price for a cash commodity of designated grade and for immediate delivery.

Cash Transaction Purchase or sale of physical merchandise; can be in futures.

CCC The Commodity Credit Corporation.

CEA The Commodity Exchange Authority. Superseded by Commodity Futures Trading Commission.

Certified Stock Stocks of a commodity that have been graded, have passed various tests and been found to be of deliverable quality against futures contracts, which are stored at the delivery points and in warehouses designated regular for delivery by the exchange.

C&F Cost and freight paid to port of destination.

CFTC Commodity Futures Trading Commission. The federal authority that supervises all commodity exchanges and futures/option trading on specified commodities trading.

Chart Any of a variety of systems by which prices, output, consumption, or related considerations may be plotted on paper for ease of visual reference.

Charter An engagement of a vessel to a given destination at a fixed rate.

Chicago Board of Trade An organized commodity exchange which houses most of the world's agricultural futures trading. Also trades options.

Chicago Board Options Exchange World's largest market for trading options on securities. Also trades options on financial instruments and debt obligations.

Chicago Mercantile Exchange Second largest futures market in the world, and parent organization that launched the International Monetary Market, and futures trading in national currencies of many countries.

Churning Excessive trading in and out of commodity positions. When done, has the main objective of generating commissions to the broker.

CIF Cost, insurance, and freight paid (or included) to a port of destination.

Class of Options All puts or all calls written against the same underlying property, and that carry the same expiration date.

Clearances Total marine shipments from domestic and foreign ports.

Clearing Contracts The process of substituting principals to transactions through the operation of clearing associations, in order to simplify the settlement of accounts.

Clearinghouse The (separate) agency associated with a futures exchange through which futures contracts are offset or fulfilled and through which financial settlement is made. Also clearing association.

Clearing Member A member of the clearinghouse or association. Each clearing member must also be a member of the exchange. Each member of the exchange, however, need not be a member of the clearing association; if not, his trades must be registered and settled through a clearing member.

Clearing Price *See* **Settlement Price.**

Close The period at the end of the trading session during which all trades are officially declared as having been executed "at or on the close." The closing range is the range of prices on trades made during this designated period.

Closing Transaction An offset. A purchase or sale that is equal and opposite the opening transaction. It liquidates an open position in futures or options.

COFO Commercially objectionable foreign odor.

Commission Fee charged by a broker for performance of specified market functions.

Commission House A concern that buys or sells for the accounts of customers. Also called brokerage house, sometimes wire house.

Commodity An economic good of broad use and value, as distinguished from a service.

Commodity Credit Corporation (CCC) A wing of the U.S. Department of Agriculture which functions as the holding and marketing agency in connection with administered farm commodities.

Conservation Reserve The section of the Soil Bank Program calling for long-term contracts for the conversion of crop land into grasses, trees, and water conservation uses.

Consignment An unsold shipment of grain placed with a commission man who will offer it for sale.

Contract (1) A formal multilateral agreement between two (or more) parties in interest, which binds each to certain stipulated performances. In commodity trading, is usually synonymous with futures contract. (2) A unit of the commodity being traded. Orders must specify the number of bushels to be bought and sold. *See also* **Round Lot; Job Lot.**

Contract Grades The grades of a commodity listed in the rules of an exchange as those that can be used to deliver against a futures contract.

Contract Market An organized commodity futures market which qualifies under the Commodity Exchange Act, as amended.

Contract Maturity   Relates to a given month: July, September, March, etc. Options on futures expire in the month preceding the underlying contract expiration.

Controlled Commodity   Commodities subject to CFTC regulation; listed in the Commodity Exchange Act, as amended.

Core Sample   *See* **Sample.**

Corner   (1) To corner is to secure such relative control of a commodity or security that its price can be manipulated. (2) In the extreme situation, obtaining more contracts requiring the delivery of commodities or securities than the quantity of such commodities or securities actually in existence.

Cost of Storage   Rate charged for physical warehousing of a commodity; (may include in or out elevation charges). *See* **Carrying Charge.**

Country Elevator   A grain elevator located in the immediate farming community to which farmers bring their grain for sale or storage, as distinct from a terminal elevator which is located at a major marketing center.

Country Price   The price which prevails in an area removed from the central market (usually quoted as being "on" or "off" a designated futures price).

Cover   The purchase of futures to offset a previously established short position.

Crop Report   Any of several forecasts made by both private and official sources. The major ones emanate from the Crop Reporting Board of the U.S.D.A. and equivalent bodies in Canada and elsewhere.

Crop Year   Period used for statistical purposes, from the harvest of a crop to the corresponding period in following year. U.S. wheat crop year begins July 1 and ends June 30; cotton, August 1–July 31; varying dates for other commodities.

Crude Oil   Oil which has undergone the first stage(s) of refinement.

Crush (Soybeans)   The process which converts soybeans into meal and oil. Also, a term used to describe a particular spreading posture between soybeans and products.

Crush Spread   In soybeans, the purchase of bean futures and simultaneous sale of an equivalent amount of meal and oil futures.

Current Delivery   Means delivery during the present month.

Current Quotation   The last price, bid, or offer on a designated futures, cash, etc.

Customers' Man   An employee of a commission house, also called a broker, account executive, solicitor, or registered representative, who engages in soliciting or accepting and handling orders for the purchase or sale or any commodity for futures delivery on or subject to the rules of any contract market and who, in or in connection with such solicitations or acceptance of orders, accepts any money, securities, or property (or extends credit in lieu thereof) to margin any trades or contracts that result or may result therefrom. Must be licensed by CFTC when handling business in commodities covered thereby.

Daily Fluctuation Limits   *See* **Trading Limits.**

Day Orders   Those limited orders that are to be executed the day for which they are effective, or are automatically cancelled at the close of that day.

Day Trader   One who carries no open positions overnight.

Deferred Any contract which matures later than the nearby.

Deliverable Grades *See* **Contract Grades.**

Delivery Month The calendar month during which a futures contract matures.

Delivery Notice The notification of delivery of the actual commodity on the contract, issued by the seller of the futures to the clearinghouse.

Delivery Points Those locations designated by commodity exchanges at which a commodity covered by a futures contract may be delivered in fulfillment of the contract.

Delivery Price The price fixed by the clearinghouse at which deliveries on futures are invoiced and also the price at which the futures contract is settled when deliveries are made.

Designated Markets (By CFTC) *See* **Contract Markets.**

Differentials The price difference between classes, grades, and locations of a given commodity or commodities.

Discount Applied to cash prices that are below the future, or to deliveries at a lesser price than others (May at a discount under July) or to lesser prices caused by quality differences.

Discretionary Account An account for which buying and selling orders can be placed by a broker or other person without the prior consent of the account owner for each such individual order, specific authorization having been previously granted by the account owner.

Distant or **Deferred Delivery** Usually means one of the more distant months in which futures trading is taking place. *See also* **Cash Forward.**

Dockage *See* **Foreign Material.**

Ensilage Chopped animal feed which is stored in bulk, usually in a moist condition.

Evening Up Buying or selling to adjust or close out an open market position, also called offset.

Exchange of Spot or **Cash Commodity for Futures** The simultaneous exchange of a specified quantity of a cash commodity for the equivalent quantities in futures, usually instituted between parties carrying opposite hedges in the same delivery month. Also known as "exchange for physical" or "against actuals," or as "giving up futures for cash." In grain, the exchange is made outside the pit.

Exercise The action taken by an option holder when he wishes to exchange his privilege for the underlying property—or its cash value to him.

Exercise Price Means the same thing as strike price.

Expeller Press A machine used in soybean oil extraction.

Expiration The date before which an option must be exercised, or it expires. Options on futures contracts, for example, expire on a specific date in the month preceding the named futures month. Hence, an option on a May futures would carry an April expiration date.

Ex-pit Transaction A trade made outside the exchange trading ring or pit which is legal in certain instances. It is primarily used in price-fixing transactions involving the purchase of cash commodities at a specified basis.

Ex-store Selling term for commodities in warehouse.

Family Farm   In common usage, a non-specializing farm of modest size which is presumed adequate to support a rural family.

FAQ   Fair average quality.

Farm Prices   The prices received by farmers for their products, as published by the U.S. Department of Agriculture; determined as of the 15th of each month.

Fibers   Raw materials, either natural or synthetic, from which a wide range of cloth and other products are fabricated.

Fill-or-Kill Order   A commodity order which demands immediate execution or cancellation.

First Notice Day   The first day on which notices of intentions to deliver actual commodities against futures market positions can be made or received. First notice day will vary with each commodity and exchange. It usually precedes the beginning of the delivery period.

Fixing the Price   The determination of the exact price at which a cash commodity will be invoiced after a call sale has previously been made based on a specified number of points on or off a specified futures month.

Flake   A soybean morsel from which the oil has been extracted.

Flash   Hand signals used by pit brokers.

Flat Price   Price on a single position; differing from spread price, which relates to a dual position.

Floor Broker   Any person who, in or surrounding any pit, ring, post, or other place provided by a contract market for the meeting of persons similarly engaged, executes for others any order for the purchase or sale of any commodity for future delivery on or subject to the rules of any contract market, and who for such services receives or accepts a prescribed fee or brokerage.

Floor Phone Man   An employee of a brokerage house who serves as the communication link between his firm's office and the brokers in the pits.

Floor Trader   An exchange member who executes his own trades by being personally present in the place provided for futures trading.

FOB   Free on board. Usually covers all delivery, inspection, and elevation costs involved in putting commodities on board whatever shipment conveyance is being used.

Forage   Natural pasture for livestock.

Foreign Material   Anything other than the designated commodity which is present in a lot.

Forward Shipment   A contract covering cash commodities to be shipped at some future specified date.

Free Balance   Margin funds on deposit with a broker, and which are not committed against existing open positions.

Free Market   A theoretical trade situation in which buying and selling decisions, production, and use judgments, etc., are unfettered by any uneconomic considerations such as price controls, export quotas, etc.

Free Supply   The quantity of a commodity available for commercial sale; does not include government held stocks.

Frost-Drop   Planned destruction of a designated portion of a growing crop for the purpose of restricting unwanted production.

Full Carrying Charge   (1) In market parlance, the cost involved in owning cash commodities over a period of time; including storage, insurance, and interest charges on borrowed working capital. (2) In futures, the cost, including all charges, of taking actual delivery in a given month, storing the commodity, and redelivering against the next delivery month.

Fundamentalist   A market participant who relies principally on supply/demand considerations in his price forecasting activities; especially one who tends to give technical considerations small weight in his decisions.

Futures Commission Broker   *See* **Customer's Man.**

Futures Contract   Agreement to buy and receive or sell and deliver a commodity at a future date, with these distinguishing characteristics:
1. All trades in the same contract, such as a 5,000 bushel round lot of grain, have the same unit of trading.
2. The terms of all trades are standardized.
3. A position may be offset later by an opposite trade in the same contract.
4. Prices are determined by trades made by open-outcry in the pit within the hours prescribed, or visually posted.
5. The contract has a basic grade, but more than one grade may be deliverable.
6. Delivery is required during designated periods.
7. The trades are cleared through a clearinghouse daily. (Traders in cash or spot goods usually refer to sales for shipment or delivery in the futures as deferred or forward sales. Such sales, however, are not standardized as are futures contracts just described above).

Futures Price   The price bid or offered for contract grade commodities, for delivery at a specified period in the future.

Futures Transaction   Purchase or sale of a futures contract; exchange of a futures position for the cash commodity.

Give-Up   This is a contract executed by one broker for the client of another broker, which the client orders turned over to the latter broker. Generally speaking, the order is sent over the leased wires of the first broker who collects a wire toll from the other broker for the use of his facilities.

Good-Till-Cancelled (GTC)   An order which will remain open for execution at any time in the future until the customer cancels it. For example: Sell one May soybean meal at $166.00 GTC.

Grain Futures Act   A federal statute which regulates trading in grain futures. Administered by the U.S.D.A.

Grains   For purposes of the Chicago Board of Trade: wheat, oats, rye, corn, and soybeans.

Gross Processing Margin (GPM)   In the case of soybeans, GPM refers to the difference between the price paid for soybeans and the sum of prices received from the sale of oil and meal products after processing.

Growths   Description of commodity according to area of origin; either refer to country, district, or place of semimanufacture.

GTC   Good-till-cancelled. Usually refers to open orders to buy or sell at a fixed price.

Hard Spot   An interval of strength in the market, usually resulting from considerable buying.

Harden A term indicating a slowly advancing market.

Heavy This is applied to a market where there is an apparent number of selling orders overhanging the market without a corresponding amount of buying orders.

Hedge A market posture that involves opposing long and short holdings of cash commodities and futures or options. The objective of a hedge is to minimize value impairment through adverse price movement, while retaining a variable opportunity for hedging profit through beneficial basis changes.

Hedgers Usually a dealer in physical commodities who holds positions in futures or options which are opposite his cash positions (e.g., long cash corn; short corn futures or options on futures).

Hedging Briefly stated, hedging is the sale of futures or options against the physical commodity or its equivalent as protection against a price decline; or the purchase of futures or options against forward sales or anticipated requirements of the physical commodity as protection against a price advance.

Hedging on futures markets consists of buying (or selling) futures contracts or options in the amount to which one is long (or short) the actual commodity. Usually the hedge transaction is nearly simultaneous with the spot transaction. Hedgers thereby fix or protect a carrying charge, a processing margin, etc. A futures hedge is a temporary substitute for an ordinary transaction which will occur later. Hedging also provides opportunities for added profit.

High The highest price posted within the designated period: day, contract, etc.

Holder Same as buyer, in futures and options.

ICC Interstate Commerce Commission.

In Bond An inspected, sealed, and cleared shipment, actually in transit or scheduled for export.

In-the-Money An option that is reflecting intrinsic value at the current underlying property price quotation. A call is in-the-money if its strike price is below the current market price. A put is in-the-money if its strike price is above the current market price.

Incentive Payment Plan The type of support program used for domestic clip wool in which a cash subsidy is paid to the wool grower based upon his selling price.

Initial Margin The amount of money required to bind performance on a newly established futures position. *See* **Variation Margin.**

Inspection In commodity marketing, an official evaluation procedure which results in a grade or class designation being assigned.

Intercommodity Spread A multiple position between two substitutive or related commodities (e.g., corn and oats).

Intermarket Spread A multiple position between two exchanges (e.g., Minneapolis wheat/Kansas City wheat).

International Monetary Market (IMM) (Chicago) World's first and largest market for the trading of futures contracts in currencies and financial instruments.

International Wheat Agreement   A multigovernment treaty arrangement which fixes the price of this commodity in international trade between the participating nations.

Intramarket Spread   A multiple position between commodities traded on a single exchange (e.g., Chicago soybeans/Chicago soybean oil).

Intrinsic Value   The amount of money that could be realized by immediate exercise. Intrinsic value may cover part or all of the previous premium outlay, as well as reflecting any amount of net profit on the transaction. *See* **In-the-Money.**

Inverted Market   A futures market in which the nearer months are selling at premiums to the more distant months; hence, a market displaying inverse carrying charges. These price relationships are characteristic of situations in which supplies are currently in shortage.

Investor   One who commits capital to a given business proposition, with his hopes for return tied exclusively to interest, dividends, rent, etc.

Invisible Supply   Uncounted stocks in the hands of wholesalers, manufacturers, and producers that cannot be identified accurately; stocks outside commercial channels, but available for commerce.

Job Lot   A unit of trading smaller than the regular round lot, usually, in grains, 1,000 or 2,000 bushels.

Jumped Stop   *See* **Stop-Loss Order.**

Kansas City Board of Trade   An agricultural futures market, and the first organization to introduce futures trading in assembled-value products. The KCBOT launched trading in the Value Line Index, which was the first of such indexes.

Land-Bank Program   A government program that seeks to manage agricultural production by taking land out of use or returning it to use, depending on projected needs.

Last Trading Day   The day on which trading ceases for a particular delivery month. All contracts that have not been offset by the end of trading on that day must thereafter be settled by delivery of the actual physical commodity, or by agreement. *See* **Wash Sales.**

Leverage   In speculation, the increased power of money committed in a situation involving margin (which is less than the total value of the property covered in the commitment).

Life of Delivery or **Contract**   The period between the beginning of trading in a particular future to the expiration of that future.

Limit-Only   In trading, the definite price stated by a customer to a broker restricting the execution of an order to buy for not more than, or to sell for not less than, the stated price.

Limit (up or down)   The maximum price advance or decline from the previous day's settlement price permitted in one trading session by the rules of the exchange.

Limited Order   One in which the client sets a limit on the price, as contrasted with a market order.

Liquidating Market   One in which the predominant feature is longs selling their holdings.

Liquidation   The closing out of a long position. It is also sometimes used to denote closing out a short position, but this is more often referred to as covering.

Loan Price   The statutory price at which growers may obtain crop loans from the government.

Loan Program   The primary means of government price support in which the government lends money to the farmer at a preannounced price schedule with the farmer's crop as collateral. The primary method by which the government acquires stocks of agricultural commodities. *See* **Non-Recourse Loans.**

Long   A position held in either futures or options, and against which there is no opposing short holding. A holder may be long either puts or calls.

Long the Basis   This is said of one who has bought cash or spot goods and has hedged them with sales of the futures. He has therefore bought at a certain basis on or off futures and hopes to sell at a better basis with the futures for a profit. *See* **Hedging.**

Long Hedge   The purchase of futures or options against sales of cash (usually for deferred delivery).

Long Squeeze   A market situation in which longs are forced to liquidate in the face of falling prices.

Long-Term   A period of time adequate to permit unfolding of major trends in production, consumption, utility patterns, etc.

Low   The lowest price posted within the designated period: day, contract, etc.

Maintenance Margin   *See* **Variation Margin.**

Margin   The amount deposited by buyers and sellers of futures to insure performance on contract commitments; serves as a performance bond rather than a down payment.

Margin Call   A request to deposit either the original margin at the time of the transaction, or to restore the guarantee to maintenance margin levels required for the duration of the time the contract is held.

Margin Funds   Moneys on deposit with a broker (or the clearinghouse) to bind performance on commodity futures positions.

Margin of Cultivation, Extensive   The situation in which unit doses of labor and capital applied to less and less productive land finally reach land of such poor quality that the product just pays for the labor and capital.

Market Order or **Board Order**   An order to buy or sell when the market reaches a specified point. A board order to buy becomes a market order when the commodity sells (or is offered) at or below the order price. A board order to sell becomes a market order when the commodity sells (or is bid) at or above the order price.

Market Price   The price which prevails in the central market, as compared to country price.

Market Psychology   The composite attitude of bulls and bears, especially as it relates to prospects for price behavior.

Market Technician An individual who attempts to forecast prices through evaluation of supply/demand balances, and/or quality and volume of trade, etc.

Market Trend General direction of prices without regard to short-term fluctuations.

Marketing Quota A federally enforced restriction on the amount of a commodity that a producer is permitted to sell. Usually conforms to the quantity of wheat, corn, etc., the farmer can grow on his acreage allotment.

Marketplace Broadly, the area in which buyers and sellers deal in selected goods and in which transportation, exchange of information, common currency, and methods of trade are sufficiently uniform to create a more or less distinct economic arena.

Maturity The period within which a futures contract can be settled by delivery of the actual commodity; the period between first notice day and last trading day. Often used as a synonym for contract (e.g., July corn maturity, December wheat maturity, etc.).

Medium-Range A period of time sufficient to accommodate fundamental changes in supply/demand balance. Usually one crop year or less.

Members' Rate The commission charge for the execution of an order for a person who is a member of and thereby has a seat on the exchange. It is less than the commission charged to a customer who does not have a seat on the exchange.

Moving Average Price A composite of individual prices over a given period of time. Often employed by chartists to define a price trend, as compared to short-term price fluctuations.

Naked or **Naked Writing** Writing (selling) a put or a call without holding an offsetting market position in either futures, other options, or in the cash product. Also called an uncovered sale.

Nearby The futures contract which is nearest to maturity.

Nearby Delivery The nearest traded contract month.

Negative Carrying Charge *See* **Inverted Market.**

Negotiable Warehouse Receipt Document issued by a regular warehouse that guarantees existence and grade of commodity held in store. Transfer of ownership can be accomplished by endorsement of the warehouse receipt.

Net Position The difference between the open contracts long and the open contracts short, held in any one commodity.

New Crop The projected harvest.

Nominal Price A declared price for a futures month. Used at times to designate a closing price when no trading has taken place in that particular contract during the final few minutes of the trading session. It is usually the average between the bid and the asked prices.

Non-Recourse Loans A loan under the U.S. agricultural program to farmers on the security of surplus crops that are delivered to the government and held off the market. The loan must be liquidated as provided by the government's program but the government has no recourse against the farmer for a deficiency if the security fails to bring the amount of the loan.

Notice Day   Any day on which notices of intent to deliver on futures contracts may be issued.

Notice of Intention to Deliver   A document furnished by a short-seller indicating his intention to fulfill his contract obligation by delivering cash merchandise.

OCO   One cancels other, in which filling of one order cancels customer's alternative order.

Off   In quoting the basis, the number of points the cash price will be under a specified futures price. Example: 20 points off December.

Off the Board   Close of trading in a maturing contract.

Offer   An indication of willingness to sell at a given price. (Opposite of **Bid**.)

Official Inspection   *See* **Inspection**.

Offset   Usually the liquidation of a long or short futures position by an equal and opposite futures transaction.

Oils   In commodity trading, usually includes soybean oil, cottonseed oil, olive oil, and other edible fats that are broadly substitutive.

Old Crop   The past harvest.

Omnibus Account   An account carried by one futures commission merchant with another, in which the transactions of two or more persons are combined rather than designated separately and the identity of individual accounts is not disclosed.

On   In quoting the basis, the number of points the cash commodity is above a specified futures month. Example: 20 points on December.

On-Consignment Grain   Usually refers to grain conveyed to a broker for sale in the cash market.

On the Close   The last few (two or three) minutes of each trading session (varies).

On the Open   The initial two or three minutes of trading session (varies).

Open Contract   Contracts which have been bought or sold, without the transactions having been completed by subsequent sale or repurchase or actual delivery or receipt of the commodity.

Open-Interest   The total of unfilled or unsatisfied contracts on one side of the market. (In any one futures delivery month, the short interest always equals the long interest, since the total number of contracts sold must equal the total number bought.)

Open-Order   *See* **Good-Till-Cancelled**.

Open-Outcry   Required method of registering all bids and offers in the pits.

Opening Bell, Closing Bell   The signal which begins and ends each trading session on each exchange.

Opening Range, Closing Range   In open auction with many buyers and sellers, commodities are often traded at several prices at the opening or close of the market. Buying or selling orders at the opening might be filled at any point within such a price range.

Opening Transaction   A sale or purchase of an option or a futures that establishes a new position.

Option   A term sometimes erroneously applied to a futures contract. It may refer to a specific delivery month, as "the July option." Puts and calls or privileges which are now legal in regulated commodity exchanges are true options, entailing no delivery obligation. Futures contracts are not options.

Original Margin   The margin needed to cover a specific new position.

Out-of-the-Money   An option holding without any intrinsic value. This would be true of a call whose strike price is *above* the underlying product's current market quotation; or a put whose strike price is *below* the current market price quotation.

Overfill   A trading error in which an excessive purchase or sale is made.

Overprice   The amount by which a call strike price exceeds then-current market-price at the time of an initial transaction: Out-of-the-money.

Oversold or **Overbought Markets**   When the speculative long interest has been drastically reduced and the speculative short interest increases, actually or relatively, a market is said to be oversold. At such times, sharp rallies often materialize. On the other hand, when the speculative long interest has increased rapidly and the speculative short interest decreases sharply, a market is said to be overbought. At such times, the market is often in a position to decline sharply.

Oversupply   A market situation in which available commodities exceed demonstrated demand. Result is usually seen in lowering prices. *See* **Undersupply.**

Paper Losses   The total extent of impairment in the margin deposited against an open position.

Paper Profit   The profit that might be realized if the open contracts were liquidated as of a certain time or at a certain price. Margin requirements are adjusted according to paper profits, hence they are to some extent real.

Paper Trading   A method by which market trading can be simulated for purposes of gaining experience and background information in the activities concerned.

Parity   A theoretically equal relationship between commodity prices and all other prices; equality of relationship. Specifically, in farm program legislation, parity is defined in such a manner that the purchasing power of a unit of the commodity is maintained at the level prevailing during some earlier historical base period.

Pits   Designated locations on the trading floor where futures trading takes place in particular commodities.

Point   The minimum price fluctuation in futures. It is equal to 1/100 of 1 cent in most futures traded in decimal units. In grains it is ⅛ of 1 cent.

Position   To be either long or short in the market.

Position Limit   The maximum number of contracts one can hold open under the rules of the CFTC.

Position Trader   One who holds a long or short position open overnight or longer; as contrasted to the day trader and the scalper.

Posted, on the Board   The point at which a given price, bid, or offer is made known to the trade.

Premium (1) The excess in price at which one delivery or quality of goods is selling over the value of another delivery, or quality, or the price relationship between cash and future. (2) Option price. The premium is the amount of money a buyer pays for the option privilege and the amount the writer/seller receives for the rights he confers on the option holder.

Price Averaging The practice of adding to losing positions on the theory of averaging selling price upward, or buying price downward.

Price Dip A sharp price drop.

Price Fix *See* **Fixing the Price.**

Price Plateau An area of congestion in trade where buying and selling forces remain in close balance and create a sideways pattern in a bar chart.

Price Rationing The action of higher prices in discouraging consumption and encouraging production, and lower prices in encouraging consumption and discouraging production.

Price Spread Price difference between commodities, maturities, or geographical locations.

Primary Market The centers to which the producers bring their goods for sale, such as country grain elevators.

Private Wire A leased or owned communication link for the exclusive use of a single individual or brokerage house.

Privilege In the stock market, the term for an option contract. *See* **Call; Put; Spread.**

Professional Speculator Anyone who voluntarily owns valuable property over time or assumes the risks of such ownership in the hope of earning a profit through price change.

Program Trading Pursuit of a speculative program that calls for successive steps at designated price intervals, especially as the practice relates to pyramiding.

Public Elevators Grain storage facilities in which space is rented out to whoever wishes to pay for it; where grain is stored in bulk. These are licensed and regulated by the state and/or federal government, and may also be approved as regular for delivery on an organized commodity exchange.

Public Speculator A private person who trades in futures contracts or options through a brokerage house.

Purchase Agreement A form of government price support in which the government agrees to buy commodities from a farmer at a specified time at a designated loan price.

Purchase and Sales Statement (abbreviated P&S) A statement sent by a commission merchant to a customer when his futures position has changed. It shows the amount involved, the prices at which the position was acquired and closed out, the gross profit or loss, the commission charges, and the net profit or loss on the transaction.

Put Option An option that gives the holder the right to sell (or acquire a short position) the underlying property or futures contract, at the specified strike price, at any time prior to the expiration date.

Put An option permitting its holder to sell a certain commodity at a fixed price for a stated quantity, and within a stated period. Such a right is purchased for a fee paid the one who agrees to accept the goods if they are offered. The buyer of this right to sell expects the price of the commodity to fall so that he can deliver the commodity (the put) at a profit. If the price rises, the option will not be exercised. The reverse transaction is a call. *See* **Privilege.**

Pyramiding Using the profits on a previously established position as margin for adding to that position.

Quick Order *See* **Fill-or-Kill Order.**

Quotations The changing prices on cash and futures.

Range The difference between the highest and lowest prices recorded during a specified trading period.

Reaction Downward tendency in prices following an advance.

Realizing Taking profits.

Recovery Advance after a decline.

Registered Representative *See* **Customers' Man.**

Regulated Commodities Those commodities over which the Commodity Futures Trading Commission has supervision are known as regulated. This does not mean that the prices are controlled. The C.F.T.C. simply concerns itself with the orderly operation of the futures market and at times investigates abnormal price movements. Under the Commodities Exchange Act, approved June 15, 1936, as amended, definite regulations were established providing for the safeguarding of customers' money deposited as margin. Commodities currently supervised by the C.F.T.C. include wheat, cotton, corn, rice, oats, barley, rye, flaxseed, grain sorghums, bran, shorts, middlings, butter, eggs, potatoes, onions, wool tops, grease wool, lard, tallow, soybean oil, cottonseed meal, cottonseed oil, cottonseed, peanuts, soybeans, soybean meal, livestock, livestock products, peanut oil, frozen concentrated orange juice, heating oil, lumber, financial instruments, currencies, and precious metals.

Resting Order Instructions to buy at a figure below the present market price or sell at a figure above it.

Restricted Stocks Loan stocks, etc. A separate segregation which, during recent years of control, has been applied to supplies officially off the market for a definite or indefinite period.

Reversal Point The point on a price chart at which prices have reversed themselves in the past, and/or in the future are expected to do so.

Ring *See* **Pits.**

Round Lot A full contract as opposed to the smaller job lot. Round lots of grain are 5,000 bushels.

Round Turn The completion of both a purchase and an offsetting sale or vice versa.

Rules The regulations governing trading established by each exchange.

Sample In marketing, one or more units of a product given free (or sold at a price far below market) in order to induce prospective buyers to give it a trial, or to enable them to determine its characteristics by inspection or analysis.

Sample Grade In commodities (except grains), usually the lowest quality acceptable for delivery in settlement of a futures contract.

Sampling In statistics and research, a sampling is an approximation of the nature or magnitude of some characteristics of a universe, arrived at through actual measurement of some of the individual units or elements of that universe called a sample, which may be chosen at random or by other criteria.

Scalper A speculator operating on the trading floor who provides market liquidity by buying and selling rapidly, with small profits or losses, and who holds his position for a short time. Typically, a scalper stands ready to buy at a fraction below the last transaction price and to sell at a fraction above.

Securities The various classes of stocks which are issued by corporations and which represent equity ownership in the issuing firms.

Seller The writer of an option, whether a put or a call. May also be a holder who becomes a seller in accomplishing offset of a previously purchased put, call, or long futures position.

Seller's Market A condition of the market in which there is a scarcity of goods available and hence sellers can obtain better conditions of sale or higher prices.

Seller's Option The right of a seller to select, within the limits prescribed by a contract, the quality of the commodity delivered and the time and place of delivery.

Selling Hedge *See* **Hedge; Hedging.**

Series All options of a given class, carrying the same strike price.

Settlement Price The daily price at which the clearinghouse clears all the day's trades; also a price which may be established by the exchange to settle contracts unliquidated because of acts of God, such as floods, market congestion, or other causes.

Short The selling side of an open futures contract; also describes the position of a trader who has sold futures or options into the market, but who holds no offsetting position in either futures, options, or the underlying cash merchandise.

Short of the Basis This is said of a person or firm who has sold cash or spot goods and has hedged them with purchases of options or futures. He has therefore sold at a certain basis and expects to buy back at a better basis for a profit.

Short Hedge Sale of futures against the purchase of cash.

Short Squeeze A sharp run-up of futures prices which forces shorts to offset (buy back open positions) in order to avoid larger losses.

Soften A slowly declining market price.

Soil Bank A government program designated to take farmland out of productive use. The government pays the farmer to not plant crops; instead, to plant the land in grass or trees.

Sold Out Market A market in which liquidation of weakly held contracts has largely been completed and such offerings have become scarce.

Solicitor A member or nonmember who solicits business for a member.

Speculation The owning of valuable property over time (or assumption of the risks of such ownership) in the hope of profiting from a change in market value.

Speculative Capital The portion of a speculator's assets that have been earmarked for use in the risk market.

Speculative Interval The period of time left in the life of an option or a futures contract during which it can be traded; or the period of time which largely governs speculative activities of public speculators, position traders, day traders, and scalpers.

Speculator (Professional) One who voluntarily deals in physical property (or risks) and relies on price change to produce a profit (risk premium) for him.

Spot Commodity Goods available for immediate delivery following sale; improperly used to include a commodity bought or sold "to-arrive." Also called actuals. *See* **Cash Commodity.**

Spot Price The price at which a physical commodity is selling at a given time and place.

Spread Simultaneous holding of both long and short positions in the same type of futures or options. In futures, usually involves a single commodity, with different contract maturities. In options, may involve a long-call with one strike price and expiration date, held against a short-put with a different strike price and expiration date. *See also* **Straddle.**

Stipulation of Compliance In commodity usage, formal assurance on the part of an individual or firm that an administrative request or order from CFTC or other regulative body will be followed.

Stock Specialist Securities market principal who is required to buy or sell whenever public offerings to buy or sell are inadequate to maintain an orderly market.

Stockpile Commodities Commodities which are accumulated and held under government programs: gold, wheat, butter, etc.

Stop Order or **Stop-Loss Order** An order entered to buy or sell when the market reaches a specified point. A stop order to buy becomes a market order when the commodity sells (or is bid) at or above the stop price. A stop order to sell becomes a market order when the commodity sells (or is offered) at or below the stop price. The purpose of a stop-loss order is to limit losses or protect a profit.

Straddle Simultaneous holding of a short position in a put and a call, or a long position in both a put and a call. Straddling seeks profit as a result of changes in price differentials between the two opposed holdings. *See also* **Spread.**

Strike Price The price at which the option holder may acquire (call) or sell (put) the underlying property for the term of the option.

Strong Hands Usually refers to commercial hedgers and well-financed professional speculators who are hard to shake loose from an established market posture.

Subsidy A sum of money offered by government to assist in the establishment or support of an enterprise or program which is considered to be in the public interest.

Supply/Demand Balance   The known or estimated adequacy of supplies in light of known or projected needs. Also called supply/demand equilibrium.

Switch   The liquidation of a position in one future of a commodity and the simultaneous reinstatement of such positions in another future of the same commodity. It may be done at market or at a specified difference.

Tape Trader   A speculator who follows current market prices somewhat constantly on a ticker or some other quotation device.

Technical Rally (or Decline)   A price movement resulting from conditions developing within the futures market itself and not dependent on outside supply and demand factors. These conditions would include changes in the open interest, volume, degree of recent price movement, and approach of first notice day.

Tender   Delivery against a futures position.

Terminal Elevator   A grain storage facility at one of the major centers of agricultural product marketing.

Ticker Tape   A stock or commodity quotation system. *See* **Broad Tape.**

Time-Limit Order   An order to buy or sell when time of day is the controlling consideration.

Time Value   The amount by which an option premium exceeds its intrinsic value. If an option is written at the strike price or worse, it has no intrinsic value. Hence its total premium represents time value.

Track-Country-Station   Usually involves a price designation; indicates the cost of a given commodity loaded in rail car and ready for shipment from an interior location.

Trading Limit   In virtually all North American commodity contracts, there is a maximum price change permitted for a single session. These limits vary in the different markets. After prices have advanced or declined to the permissible daily limits, trading automatically ceases unless, of course, offers appear at the permissible upper trading limit or bids appear at the permissible lower limit.

Trading Range   The interval between the highest and lowest price on a given contract or classification of goods in a designated period: daily, weekly, life-of-contract, etc.

Trading Rules   Usually refers to the rules and regulations of an organized exchange, which govern activities of both members and nonmembers who trade in the particular market.

Trading Session   The period from the opening to the close on a single day.

Transfer Notice or **Delivery Notice**   A written announcement issued by a seller signifying his intention of making delivery in fulfillment of a futures contract. The recipient of the notice may make a sale of the future and transfer the notice within a specified time to another party on some exchanges directly, and on others through the clearing association. The last recipient takes delivery of the commodity tendered. Notices on some exchanges are not transferable.

Trend   The direction in which prices are moving.

Trier   *See* **Sample.**

Types of Options   There are only two: puts and calls.

Underfill   A trading error in which a smaller than intended purchase or sale is made.

Underlying Property   In a futures contract, may be the cash commodity or other designated merchandise. In options, may be a futures contract (either long or short) or other real or paper asset.

Underprice   The amount by which a put strike-price falls short of then-current market price at the time of an initial transaction: Out-of-the-money.

Undersupply   A situation in which demand for a commodity exceeds physical stocks offered for sale in the market. Result is usually seen in rising prices. *See* **Oversupply.**

USDA   United States Department of Agriculture.

Variation Margin   The amount of money required to be kept constantly on deposit throughout the period a futures position remains open, as a binder of performance on the contract.

Variation Margin Call   A request for additional margin funds as collateral, occasioned by negative price movement against the held position.

Visible Supply   The amount of a particular commodity in store at loading centers. In the grain markets, the total stock of grain in store in public and some private elevators in the principal primary markets, plus certain stock afloat.

Volume of Trading   The purchases and sales of a commodity futures during a specified period. Inasmuch as purchases equal sales, only one side is shown in published reports.

Warehouse Receipt   A document evidencing possession by a warehouseman (licensed under the U.S. Warehouse Act, or under the laws of a state) of the commodity named in the receipt. Warehouse receipts, to be tenderable on future contracts, must be negotiable receipts covering commodities in warehouses recognized for delivery purposes by the exchange on which such futures contracts are traded.

Wash Sales   Fictitious transactions contrived by two or more brokers in order to create a market price for a security or for tax evasion. It may also consist of two or more outside operators who match their orders for purchase and sale so that a seeming market activity is given to stock. Illegal and prohibited by law and by the exchanges. Tax law usually considers a repurchase within 30 days at a loss to be a wash sale. In commodity futures, contracts left open after the last day of trading may be settled by wash sales in lieu of delivery.

Weak Hands   Usually refers to poorly capitalized public traders who cannot be expected to stick to their guns in the face of adverse price movement.

Weather Market   A market characterized by erratic price behavior based largely on weather developments or weather prospects, vis-à-vis particular growing crops, delivery conditions, etc.

Wire House   Refers to a commission house with branch offices connected by telephone, teletype, telegraph, or cable.

World Market   Total global supply and demand, subject to such trading barriers as are erected by governments from time to time.

Writing   Selling a put or a call in an opening transaction.

Appendix

United States Crop
Reporting Dates

1985 Crop Reporting Board CALENDAR

JULY

Monday	Tuesday	Wednesday	Thursday	Friday
1 Egg Products; Poultry Slaughter	2 Dairy Products	3	4 Holiday	5 Celery
8 Noncitrus Fruits & Nuts— Midyear Supplement	9	10 Crop Production; Grain Stocks ●	11 Mink	12 Turkey Hatchery
15	16 Milk Production	17	18	19 Vegetables; Catfish
22 Cold Storage; Cattle; Cattle on Feed; Livestock Slaughter ○	23 Farm Prod. Expenditures, 1984; Eggs, Chickens, & Turkeys	24	25 Peanut Stocks & Processing	26
29	30 Egg Products	31 Agricultural Prices		

AUGUST

Monday	Tuesday	Wednesday	Thursday	Friday
			1 Poultry Slaughter	2 Dairy Products
5	6 Celery	7	8	9 Vegetables
12 Crop Production ●	13 Mushrooms; Turkey Hatchery	14	15 Sugar Market Statistics, Milk Production	16
19	20 Cranberries; Farm Labor	21 Catfish	22 Eggs, Chickens, & Turkeys	23 Livestock Slaughter; Cattle on Feed; Cold Storage ○
26	27	28	29 Peanut Stocks & Processing	30 Egg Products; Agricultural Prices

SEPTEMBER

Monday	Tuesday	Wednesday	Thursday	Friday
2 Holiday	3 Poultry Slaughter	4 Dairy Products	5	6 Celery
9	10 Vegetables	11 Crop Production; Rice Stocks ●	12 Turkey Hatchery	13 Milk Production
16	17	18 Hop Stocks	19	20 Citrus Fruits; Catfish
23 Hogs & Pigs; Cattle on Feed; Cold Storage; Livestock Slaughter ○	24 Eggs, Chickens, & Turkeys	25 Peanut Stocks & Processing	26	27 Potatoes & Sweetpotatoes
30 Egg Products; Agricultural Prices				

JANUARY

Monday	Tuesday	Wednesday	Thursday	Friday
	1 Holiday	2	3	4 Celery; Poultry Slaughter
7 Dairy Products	8	9	10 Vegetables	11 Crop Production; Turkey Hatchery ●
14 Noncitrus Fruits & Nuts- Annual; Turkeys	15 Potato Stocks ○	16	17 Milk Production	18
21	22 Catfish	23	24	25 Livestock Slaughter; Crop Production Annual; Cattle on Feed; Cold Storage
28 Eggs, Chickens, & Turkeys; Layers & Egg Prod.- Annual	29 Sheep & Goats	30 Crop Values	31 Agricultural Prices	

FEBRUARY

Monday	Tuesday	Wednesday	Thursday	Friday
				1 Egg Products; Poultry Slaughter
4 Dairy Products	5	6 Celery	7	8
11 Crop Production; Cattle; Grain Stocks; Rice Stocks	12	13 Turkey Hatchery	14 Potato Stocks; Milk Production ○	15 Prospective Plantings; Sugar Market Statistics ●
18 Holiday	19 Farm Labor	20	21 Catfish	22 Livestock Slaughter; Cold Storage; Cattle on Feed ○
25 Eggs, Chickens, & Turkeys	26	27	28 Agricultural Prices	

MARCH

Monday	Tuesday	Wednesday	Thursday	Friday
				1 Egg Products; Peanut Stocks & Processing
4 Dairy Products; Poultry Slaughter	5	6 Celery	7	8 Vegetables
11 Crop Production ●	12 Turkey Hatchery	13	14 Potato Stocks ○	15 Livestock Slaughter- Annual; Milk Production; Floriculture Crops
18 Hatchery Prod.- Annual	19	20 Hop Stocks; Catfish; Cold Storage- Annual	21 Eggs, Chickens, & Turkeys	22 Livestock Slaughter; Hogs & Pigs; Cold Storage; Cattle on Feed ○
25 Wool & Mohair; Vegetables	26	27	28 Peanut Stocks & Processing	29 Agricultural Prices

OCTOBER

- 1 Poultry Slaughter
- 2
- 3 Dairy Products
- 4 Cherry Utilization; Celery
- 7
- 8
- 9 Vegetables
- 10 Crop Production; Soybean Stocks ●
- 11 Turkey Hatchery
- 14 Holiday
- 15
- 16 Milk Production
- 17
- 18
- 21 Catfish
- 22 Eggs, Chickens, & Turkeys
- 23
- 24 Peanut Stocks & Processing
- 25 Livestock Slaughter; Cattle on Feed; Cold Storage ○
- 28
- 29
- 30 Egg Products
- 31 Agricultural Prices

NOVEMBER

- 1 Poultry Slaughter
- 4 Dairy Products
- 5 Celery
- 6
- 7
- 8
- 11 Holiday
- 12 Crop Production; Grain Stocks; Rice Stocks ●
- 13 Turkey Hatchery
- 14
- 15 Sugar Market Statistics, Milk Production
- 18
- 19 Farm Labor
- 20 Catfish
- 21 Eggs, Chickens, & Turkeys
- 22 Livestock Slaughter; Cattle on Feed; Cold Storage ○
- 25
- 26 Peanut Stocks & Processing
- 27 Commercial Fertilizers- Consumption
- 28 Holiday
- 29 Agricultural Prices

DECEMBER

- 2 Egg Products; Poultry Slaughter
- 3 Dairy Products
- 4
- 5 Celery
- 6
- 9
- 10 Crop Production ●
- 11
- 12 Turkey Hatchery
- 13 Potato Stocks; Milk Production ○
- 16
- 17
- 18
- 19 Catfish
- 20
- 23 Eggs, Chickens, & Turkeys; Hogs & Pigs; Cattle on Feed; Cold Storage; Livestock Slaughter ○
- 24
- 25 Holiday
- 26
- 27 Peanut Stocks & Processing
- 30 Vegetables Preliminary
- 31 Agricultural Prices

APRIL

- 1 Egg Products, Poultry Slaughter
- 2
- 3 Meat Animals- Prod., Disp., & Income
- 4 Dairy Products
- 5 Celery
- 8
- 9
- 10 Vegetables, Crop Production ●
- 11
- 12 Potato Stocks; Turkey Hatchery ○
- 15 Poultry- Prod., Disp., & Income
- 16 Milk Production
- 17
- 18
- 19 Catfish
- 22 Cattle on Feed; Cold Storage; Livestock Slaughter ○
- 23 Eggs, Chickens, & Turkeys
- 24
- 25 Peanut Stocks & Processing
- 26
- 29
- 30 Egg Products; Agricultural Prices

MAY

- 1 Poultry Slaughter
- 2
- 3 Dairy Products; Dairy Products- Annual
- 6
- 7 Celery; Milk Prod., Disp., & Income
- 8 Vegetables
- 9 Crop Production; Grain Stocks; Rice Stocks ●
- 13 Potato Stocks; Turkey Hatchery ○
- 14 Sugar Market Statistics, Milk Production
- 15
- 16
- 17
- 20
- 21 Catfish; Farm Labor
- 22
- 23 Eggs, Chickens, & Turkeys; Peanut Stocks & Processing
- 24 Livestock Slaughter; Cattle on Feed; Cold Storage ○
- 27 Holiday
- 28
- 29
- 30 Egg Products
- 31 Agricultural Prices

JUNE

- 3 Minn.-Wis. Mfg. Milk Final- 1982-84; Poultry Slaughter
- 4 Dairy Products
- 5 Celery
- 6
- 7 Vegetables, Vegetables, Annual
- 10 Crop Production ●
- 11
- 12
- 13 Turkey Hatchery
- 14 Milk Production
- 17
- 18
- 19 Catfish
- 20 Vegetables
- 21 Livestock Slaughter; Cold Storage; Hogs & Pigs; Cattle on Feed ○
- 24 Eggs, Chickens, & Turkeys
- 25 Farm Prod. Expenditures Summary Report
- 26 Cherry Production (Tent.); Peanut Stocks & Processing
- 27
- 28 Agricultural Prices- Monthly; Agricultural Prices- Annual

CROP REPORTING BOARD ● STATISTICAL REPORTING SERVICE ● U.S. DEPARTMENT OF AGRICULTURE ● WASHINGTON, DC 20250

Lockup: ○1:15 - 3:00 p.m. ● 8:30 - 3:00 p.m.

Exhibit A-1

Release dates vary slightly from year to year.
(Released at 3 P.M., EST, or 2 P.M., CST)

January 11 Crop production. Turkey hatchery output.

January 25 Livestock slaughter. Annual crop production totals. Cattle on feed. Cold storage inventories.

February 11 Crop production; cattle. Grain stocks on hand. Rice stocks.

February 15 Prospective plantings for year, as indicated by reported intentions for corn, durum wheat, other spring wheat, oats, barley, flaxseed, cotton, all sorghums, and soybeans; acreage for harvest of hay. Sugar market statistics.

April 10 Indicated production of winter wheat; indicated percentage of winter wheat seedings harvested for grain, United States; condition of rye and pasture; stocks of corn, wheat (all and durum), oats, barley, rye, flaxseed, soybeans, and sorghum grain on farms as of April 1.

May 10 Acreage remaining for harvest as of May 1, yield per acre and indicated production of winter wheat; percentage of winter wheat seedings harvested for grain for United States; condition of rye, hay, and pasture; stocks of hay on farms.

June 9 Indicated yield per acre as of June 1 for winter wheat; indicated production of winter wheat, spring wheat, condition of rye, hay, and pasture.

July 11 Stocks of corn, wheat (all and durum), oats, barley, rye, flaxseed, soybeans, and sorghum grain on farms as of July 1; planted acreage of corn, winter wheat, durum wheat, other spring wheat, oats, barley, flaxseed, soybeans, peanuts, and sorghums; acreage for harvest, indicated yield per acre as of July 1, and indicated production of corn for grain, winter wheat, durum and other spring wheat, oats, barley, rye, flaxseed, and hay; acreage for harvest of soybeans for beans, and sorghums; indicated production of wheat by classes; condition of pasture.

August 10 Indicated yield per acre as of August 1 and indicated production of corn for grain, winter wheat, durum and other spring wheat, oats, barley, rye, flaxseed, soybeans for beans, and hay; indicated production of wheat by classes; condition of pasture.

September 11 Stocks of soybeans on farms as of September 1; indicated yield per acre as of September 1 and indicated production of corn for grain, winter wheat, durum and other spring wheat, oats, barley, flaxseed, sorghums for grain, hay, and soybeans for beans; acreage for harvest of sorghums for grain; indicated production of wheat by classes (U.S.); condition of pasture.

October 10 Stocks of corn, wheat (all and durum), oats, barley, sorghum grain, rye, and flaxseed on farms as of October 1; indicated yield per acre and indicated production of corn for grain, all wheat, durum and other spring wheat, flaxseed, sorghums for grain, hay, and soybeans for beans; indicated production of wheat by classes (U.S.); condition of pasture.

November 9 Indicated yield per acre as of November 1 and indicated production of corn for grain, sorghums for grain, soybeans for beans; condition of pasture.

December 19 Annual summary of acreage, yield per acre, production of all crops for current year, with comparisons.

December 20 Seeded acreage and indicated production of winter wheat; and seeded acreage and condition of rye for next year's crop.

(Note) On or about January 11, stocks of corn for grain, wheat, oats, barley, rye, soybeans, and hay on farms as of January 1, will be reported.

Oilseeds Reports

January 10 Soybeans for beans and flaxseed stocks on farms January 1, with comparisons.

January 24 Soybean and flaxseed stocks in all positions. Reports as of January 1.

March 20 Prospective plantings for current year—flaxseed, soybeans, and peanuts.

April 10 Farm stocks soybeans. Report as of April 1.

April 24 Soybean and flaxseed stocks in all positions. Report as of April 1.

July 11 Farm stocks soybeans. Report as of July 1.

July 11 Acreage for harvest. Report as of July 1.

July 11 Indicated production flaxseed; planted acreage. Report as of July 1.

July 11 Acreage peanuts; condition. Report as of July 1.

July 11 Revised estimates of the current year peanut crop. Report as of July 1.

July 24 Soybean and flaxseed stocks in all positions. Report as of July 1.

August 10 Indicated production flaxseed, peanuts picked and threshed; indicated production of soybeans. Report as of August 1.

September 11 Indicated production flaxseed, soybeans, peanuts. Report as of September 1.

September 11 Stocks of soybeans on farms.

September 25 Stocks of soybeans in all positions.

October 10 Farm stock flaxseed; indicated production flaxseed, soybeans for beans and peanuts picked and threshed. Report as of October 1.

October 24 Flaxseed stocks in all positions.

November 9 Indicated production soybeans, peanuts picked and threshed. Report as of November 1.

December 19 Annual production soybeans, peanuts, and flaxseed, final. Current year, with comparisons.

Soybean and Soybean Products

Monthly reports are issued which include soybean receipts at mills, crushed or used, and oil mill stocks of soybeans on end of month. Exact publication dates for these reports are not available, but they are released approximately 23 days after the close of the reporting period.

This report also shows soybean oil factory production, factory consumption, factory and warehouse stocks on end of month. Soybean meal production, shipments and transfers, end of month stocks.

Other Reports Concerning U.S. Crop Production

Wheat stocks on farms and off farms in all positions; rye stocks in all positions: 3 P.M., EST January 24, April 24, July 24, and October 24.

Corn, oats, barley, and sorghum grain stocks in all positions with comparisons, January 24, April 24, July 24 and October 24.

Soybean and flaxseed stocks in all positions: January 24, April 24, July 24, and soybeans September 25. Flaxseed October 24.

Reports on Cotton

Release dates vary slightly from year to year.
(Released at 11 A.M., EST or 10 A.M., CST)

May 8 Acreage, yield per acre, production of cotton lint and seed, value of production of lint, disposition and value of cottonseed, monthly marketing by farmers.

July 10 Acreage of cotton in cultivation on July 1.

August 8 August 1, indicated yield per acre, indicated production and acreage for harvest.

September 8 September 1, indicated yield per acre, indicated production.

December 8 Yield per acre as of December 1, probable production, acreage for harvest, planted acreage, production of cottonseed.

Ginning Reports

Date of Report		Report as of Close of Business	
August 1985	8	July 1985	31
August	23	August	15
September	8	August	31
September	25	September	15
October	9	September	30
October	25	October	17
November	8	October	31
November	21	November	13
December	8	November	30
December	20	December	12
January 1986	23	January 1986	15
March 1986	20	End of season	

Cotton Production in the United States. Annual bulletins containing statistics on cotton production and ginnings, and active and idle gins, by states and counties, issued in July or August, of the year following the crop.

Cotton Production and Distribution, Season. Annual bulletin, containing statistics on U.S. production, consumption, and stocks; imports and exports of cotton, cottonseed, and cottonseed products; issued in the summer following.

Cottonseed and Cottonseed Products. Monthly reports are issued on fats and oils which include receipts, crushings, and stocks of cottonseed; and on production, shipments, and stocks of cottonseed products at mills. Exact publication dates for these reports are not available, but they are released in approximately 23 days after the close of the reporting period.

Poultry and Egg Production, Monthly. Numbers of layers on hand during month, eggs per 100 layers, total eggs produced by states, issued with monthly Crop Production report, also numbers of layers and rate of egg production per 100 layers as of first of month by geographic divisions and United States.

Butter

Weekly creamery butter production—Tuesday of each week. Monthly creamery butter production by states: January 26, February 24, March 24, April 26, May 26, June 27, July 26, August 25, September 27, October 26, November 28 and December 27.

Agricultural Prices

Prices received by farmers for principal crops and livestock products, index numbers of prices received by farmers, prices paid for feed, seed, and other items bought by farmers, indexes of prices paid by farmers for articles bought and parity prices: January 30, February 28, March 30, April 28, May 31, June 29, July 31, August 30, September 29, October 30, November 30, and December 29.

Annual Summary—May or June.

Canadian Crop Reporting Calendar

Release dates vary slightly from year to year.

March 17 Intended acreage of principal field crops.

April 14 Stocks of grain on March 31.

May 10 Telegraphic crop report—Canada.

May 17 Telegraphic crop report—Prairie provinces.

May 24 Telegraphic crop report—Prairie provinces.

June 7 Telegraphic crop report—Canada.

June 14 Progress of seeding: winter-killing and spring condition of winter wheat, fall rye, tame hay and pasture; rates of seeding.

June 21 Telegraphic crop report—Prairie provinces.

July 5 Telegraphic crop report—Canada.

July 12 Telegraphic crop report—Prairie provinces. (Including preliminary acreage report Prairie provinces.)

July 19 Telegraphic crop report—Canada.

August 4 Preliminary estimate of crop and summer fallow acreages.

August 9 Telegraphic crop report—Prairie provinces.

August 18 Stocks of grain at July 31.

August 23 Telegraphic crop report—Canada.

September 1 August forecast of production of principal field crops.

September 13 Telegraphic crop report—Canada.

October 4 September forecast of production of principal field crops.

November (date uncertain) November estimates of production of principal field crops, area and condition of fall sown crops. Progress of harvesting in the Prairie provinces.

Reports on Livestock

(All Washington, D.C., reports released at 12 noon except slaughter reports, which are released at 3 P.M.)

Release dates vary slightly from year to year.

January 13 Sheep and lambs on feed January 1. Number on feed, by states.

February 13 Livestock and poultry inventory, January 1. Number, value, and classes by states.

February 21 Calf crop. Number of calves born during the preceding year, by states.

February 23 Lamb crop. Number of lambs saved during the preceding year, by states.

March 14 Sheep and lambs on feed and early lamb crop.

April 24 Revisions (previous year) commercial slaughter by states and by months and total livestock slaughter, meat, and lard production by quarters.

April 27 Meat animals—farm production, disposition, and income. Data by states.

June 21 Pig crop report: Current year December–May pig crop; and June–December farrowings indicated by breeding intentions, by states.

July 21 Lamb crop. Number of lambs saved during the year, by states.

July 24 Calf crop. Expected number of calves born and to be born during the year, by states.

November 14 Sheep and lambs on feed November 1. Seven states.

December 22 Pig crop report: June–November pig crop of current year, and December–May farrowings in coming year indicated by breeding intentions, by states. Pig report: (quarterly). Sows farrowing and inventory numbers, 10 states. March 21, June 21, September 21, December 22.

Commercial Livestock Slaughter and Meat Production. Number of head and live weight of cattle, calves, hogs, sheep, and lambs slaughtered in commercial plants by states, meat production by species and lard production for the United States: January 30, February 28, March 31, April 28, May 31, June 30, July 28, August 31, September 28, October 30, November 30, December 29.

Cattle and Calves on Feed as of First of the Quarter. Total number on feed by states; number on feed by classes, by weight groups, and by length of time on feed, leading states. Cattle sold for slaughter at selected markets: January 17, April 18, July 18, and October 17.

Cattle and Calves on Feed as of First of the Month. Total number on feed in selected states. Cattle sold for slaughter at selected markets: January 17, February 10, March 10, April 17, May 12, June 13, July 17, August 11, September 13, October 17, November 14, and December 12.

Shipments of Stocker and Feeder Cattle and Sheep. Number received in several corn belt states from public stockyards and directs during the preceding month by states. Monthly shipments from public stockyards by market origin and state of destination: January 26, February 24, March 24, April 25, May 25, June 26, July 25, August 25, September 25, October 26, November 24, December 26. Annual report of monthly data for 1986 in monthly issue of January 26.

Western Range and Livestock Report. Condition of ranges, cattle, and sheep, first of month by states, Western states: January 11, February 9, March 9, April 12, May 12, June 13, July 13, August 9, September 13, October 12, November 8, December 13.

Special Wheat Pasture Report: September 22, October 25, November 27, December 27.

Index